Perspectives of EU Pension Law to Facilitate Worker Mobility and Sustainability

Perspectives of EU Pension Law to Facilitate Worker Mobility and Sustainability

Elmar S. Schmidt

international publishing

Published, sold and distributed by Eleven International Publishing
P.O. Box 85576
2508 CG The Hague
The Netherlands
Tel.: +31 70 33 070 33
Fax: +31 70 33 070 30
e-mail: sales@elevenpub.nl
www.elevenpub.com

Sold and distributed in USA and Canada
Independent Publishers Group
814 N. Franklin Street
Chicago, IL 60610
USA
Order Placement: (800) 888-4741
Fax: (312) 337-5985
orders@ipgbook.com
www.ipgbook.com

Eleven International Publishing is an imprint of Boom uitgevers Den Haag.

ISBN 978-94-6236-160-7
ISBN 978-90-5931-568-6 (E-book)

© 2020 Elmar S. Schmidt | Eleven International Publishing

Printed in the Netherlands

TABLE OF CONTENTS

Chapter 1: Introduction

1   Introduction

As labour markets shift from secure employment to flexible labour and economies undulate between booms and busts, workers in the EU appear to find themselves in ever more uncertain conditions. The economic crisis is reported to have rendered job markets more competitive and to have caused rising job insecurity, wage freezes and cuts, increasing stress at work and a host of other concerning developments.[1] Studies conducted by the European Parliament and Eurofound, the EU agency for the improvement of living and working conditions, report that all employment relationships – full-time or part-time, marginal and involuntary part-time or fixed term work, self-employment etc. – are under some risk of precariousness[2] and that social insecurity is a persisting problem.[3]

A dignified retirement – a basic human right as guaranteed by the EU Charter of Fundamental Rights[4] – seems all the more well-deserved under these conditions. But to add insult to this seemingly already injurious situation, pension systems in the EU are groaning under the weight of demographic change. In fact, demographic – and economic – developments are placing pressure on pension systems in many EU Member States.

Eurostat, the EU's statistical office, reports[5] that the composition of the EU's population will change significantly over the next decades. Of special relevance to pension systems is the dependency ratio: the ratio of the number of elderly people compared to the number of people of working age, a ratio which is projected to nearly double by 2080.[6] Whereas there were nearly four working-age persons to support every retiree in 2014,

---

1   Eurofound, *Impact of the crisis on working conditions in Europe* (2013), available at www.eurofound.europa. eu/publications/reports/2013/impact-of-the-crisis-on-working-conditions-in-europe accessed 18 September 2019.

2   European Parliament, *Precarious Employment in Europe – Part 1: Patterns, Trends and Policy Strategy*, Study for the EMPL Committee (Publications Office of the European Union 2016); See also Eurofound, *New types of casualisation still put workers at a disadvantage* (2015), available at www.eurofound.europa.eu/sl/news/news-articles/working-conditions-labour-market/new-types-of-casualisation-still-put-workers-at-a-disadvantage accessed 18 September 2019.

3   Eurofound, *Living and working in Europe 2015-2018* (Publications Office of the European Union 2019) 8; Eurofound, *Quality of life: Social insecurities and resilience* (Publications Office of the European Union 2018).

4   Articles 25 and 34 of the Charter of Fundamental Rights of the European Union guarantee respectively "rights of the elderly to lead a life of dignity and independence and to participate in social and cultural life" and "the entitlement to social security benefits and social services providing protection in cases such as maternity, illness, industrial accidents, dependency or old age, and in the case of loss of employment, in accordance with the rules laid down by Community law and national laws and practices."

5   Eurostat, *People in the EU: who are we and how do we live?* (Publications Office of the European Union 2015) 158 et seq.

6   ibid 163.

that number will halve by 2080, with the sharpest increase occurring before 2045 caused by the retirement of the baby-boom generation.

The aforementioned demographic problems are exacerbated by the aftermath of the financial crisis, in which budgetary austerity measures and low interest rates are placing pension systems under additional strain.[7]

Finally, the EU's increasingly mobile workforce is still facing pension-related obstacles in potential losses of pension rights when moving from one Member State to another, which conflicts with the right to free movement enshrined in the Treaty on the Functioning of the European Union (TFEU).

In response to these challenges, both the Member States themselves[8] and the EU legislator have acted on several fronts. Although regulating pension systems is still for the most part a national prerogative,[9] EU action can help deepen the internal market for pensions, creating "a richer set of building blocks" to help the retirement security of European citizens.[10] For instance, the Single Market can allow for more opportunities for specialisation, more international risk-sharing, a more efficient allocation of capital, as well as greater labour mobility by removing obstacles caused by pension systems[11] and greater opportunities for economies of scale.[12]

The EU's measures have – broadly speaking – focused on two major themes: the use of the EU's Single Market to achieve adequate, safe and sustainable pensions and the promotion of worker mobility. These two themes are discussed in more detail in section 4. This study is an assessment of the measures taken by the EU from the perspective of pension scheme members. The research focus and questions are explained in sections 8 and 9.

This introductory chapter begins with an overview of the diversity of European pension systems before discussing the challenges these systems face in more detail. It then introduces the policy responses of the EU, after which it introduces the research focus and questions as well as the structure of this study.

---

7   European Central Bank, 'The Impact of Regulating Occupational Pensions in Europe on Investment and Financial Stability' (2014) No. 154 Occasional Paper Series 10-11, available at www.ecb.europa.eu/pub/pdf/scpops/ecbop154.pdf accessed 18 September 2019.

8   G Carone and others, 'Pension Reforms in the EU since the Early 2000's: Achievements and Challenges Ahead' (2016) European Commission Discussion Paper 042, available at ec.europa.eu/info/sites/info/files/dp042_en.pdf accessed 27 November 2019.

9   D Natali, 'Reforming Pensions in the EU: National Policy Changes and EU Coordination' (2011) European Social Observatory 13, available at www.ose.be/files/publication/dnatali/Natali_2011_-FLCaballero_251011.pdf accessed 27 November 2019.

10 L Bovenberg, 'European pension reform: A way forward' (2010) Vol 16 (2) Pensions 76.

11 ibid.

12 European Commission, 'Impact Assessment Accompanying the document Proposal for a Directive of the European Parliament and of the Council on the activities and supervision of institutions for occupational retirement provision' SWD(2014) 103 final.

2   THE EUROPEAN LANDSCAPE OF OCCUPATIONAL PENSIONS

The European occupational pensions landscape is diverse.[13] Studying European measures in occupational pensions should not be undertaken without being mindful of the great diversity of national pension systems that exists across EU Member States, as this heterogeneity seems to prevent the application of a one-size-fits-all solution and is also the ground of fierce debate during EU legislative procedures.

The organisation of pension systems remains in principle (as long the organisation is in conformity with EU law) for the most part a national affair: the Member States have through the years built their own systems in response to national needs. Although this book does not concern itself with a close study of national pension systems, the great divergence between these systems plays an important role in the EU's ability of responding adequately to occupational pension-related challenges that lie within the remit of its prerogatives. The major relevant powers of the EU legislature to legislate in this field include, for instance, the free movement of capital,[14] services[15] and workers.[16] On the basis of those prerogatives, the EU can and has influenced Member States' pension systems in order to advance its objectives, as are discussed in this chapter.

To become familiar with the different types of national systems, the following section first introduces the terminology used to characterise national pension systems. In addition, it aims to paint a picture of the European landscape of pension systems in all their diversity. This diverse landscape is attributable to the history and traditions of each Member State.[17]

---

13   EIOPA, '2017 Market development report on occupational pensions and cross-border IORPs' (2018) EIOPA-BOS-18/013, 8, available at eiopa.europa.eu/publications/reports accessed 18 September 2019.

14   Artt. 63-66 Treaty on the Functioning of the European Union (TFEU).

15   Artt. 56-62 TFEU.

16   Artt. 45-48 TFEU.

17   See, on this, Commission of the European Communities, 'Supplementary social security schemes: the role of occupational pension schemes in the social protection of workers and their implications for freedom of movement' (Communication from the Commission to the Council) SEC (91) 1332 final, 1-2; European Parliament, Directorate-General for Internal Policies, *Pension Schemes*, Study for the EMPL Committee (Publications Office of the European Union 2014) 14 et seq.

2.1   Beveridge and Bismarck

There are several techniques used to characterise national pension systems. A common distinction used to classify pension systems is based on their original purpose.[18] This distinction yields two types of systems: Beveridgean and Bismarckian systems.[19]

In a Beveridgean system, named after Sir William Henry Beveridge,[20] statutory schemes regulate flat-rate benefits covering all residents, which are paid either from their contributions plus tax-subsidies or completely from tax revenues.[21] The Dutch *Algemene Ouderdomswet* (AOW), covering all residents and providing a flat-rate benefit, dependent on the type of household, for instance, qualifies as an example of a Beveridge-type system. In a country with this type of pension system, supplementary retirement systems in the form of occupational and private pension systems play a relatively important role in topping up the statutory pension in order to maintain acquired living standards. The lower the benefits from the statutory system, the greater the need for a supplementation of income from occupational and private pension provision.[22] The UK and Ireland also feature Beveridge-type pension systems in which occupational pensions can play an important role.[23]

The Bismarckian system, named after the German Chancellor Otto von Bismarck, under whose government parliament adopted, in 1883, statutory pension systems financed through social security contributions paid by employers and employees which provide wage-related pensions, i.e. pensions whose level depends on the average level of wage during the working career. Consequently, in view of the relatively high pension

---

18 European Parliament, Directorate-General for Internal Policies, *Pension Schemes*, Study for the EMPL Committee (Publications Office of the European Union 2014) 15.

19 For a description of such systems, see, *inter alia*, D Natali, *Pensions after the financial and economic crisis: a comparative analysis of recent reforms in Europe* (2011) Etui Working Paper 2011.07, 7 and the literature cited there; K Hinrichs, 'Active Citizens and Retirement Planning: Enlarging Freedom of Choice in the Course of Pension Reforms in Nordic Countries and Germany' (2004) ZeS-Arbeitspapiere/Universität Bremen No. 11/2004; K Hinrichs, 'Elephants on the move. Patterns of public pension reform in OECD countries' (2000) European Review 353, 356 et seq; A Rohwer, 'Bismarck versus Beveridge: Ein Vergleich von Sozialversicherungssystemen in Europa' (2008) Vol 61 (21) ifo Schnelldienst, ifo Institut für Wirtschaftsforschung an der Universität München 26; B Ebbinghaus & M Gronwald, 'The Changing Public-Private Pension Mix in Europe: From Path Dependence to Path Departure' in B Ebbinghaus (ed), *The Varieties of Pension Governance: Pension Privatization in Europe* (Oxford University Press 2011).

20 In 1942, a commission, installed by the government, presided by Sir Beveridge published a report in which he made proposals for the UK's post-war social security system. See W Beveridge, *Social Insurance and Allied Social Services* (The Beveridge Report, London, HMSO 1942). See also A Dijkhoff, *International social security standards in the European Union: The Cases of the Czech Republic and Estonia* (Intersentia 2011).

21 K Anderson, 'Pension Reform in Europe: Context Drivers, Impact' in S Scherger (ed), *Paid Work Beyond Pension Age. Comparative Perspectives* (Palgrave Macmillan 2015) 179.

22 C Bittner, *Europäisches und internationales Betriebsrentenrecht* (Mohr Siebeck 2000) 2.

23 European Commission, *Pension Adequacy Report 2018*, Vol 1(Publications Office of the European Union 2018) 82.

(compared to the previously earned income) , in Bismarck-type systems, the role of occupational pensions and private pension savings is comparatively modest.[24]

"A large majority" of EU Member States set up Bismarckian pension systems in the first half of the 20th century.[25] This majority still exists today, although it must be noted that none of the countries utilise a pure form of either system, and elements from one system have been introduced in the other.[26]

2.2   Three Pillars

Another common classification of pension systems – and apparently the more common one used since this classification has been introduced[27] – is the three-pillar taxonomy. This classification divides pension systems, as the name suggests, into three pillars. It is used throughout this book, and is explained below.

General

The three-pillar taxonomy has been used by various institutions, each applying their own nuances. However the World Bank[28] is said to have popularised the three-pillar classification.[29] The ILO and the OECD have also devised their own interpretations of the three-pillar model.[30]

According to this model, the first pillar consists of statutory social security schemes, the second of occupational pension schemes and the third of personal pension plans. In practice, the line between the pillars cannot always be drawn clearly.

The first pillar is characterised by strong government involvement.[31] Some Member States provide exclusively flat-rate benefits as a safety net against poverty (Beveridge), while other Member States' first-pillar systems offer wage-related benefits (Bismarck).

---

24   K Anderson, 'Pension Reform in Europe: Context Drivers, Impact' in S Scherger (ed), *Paid Work Beyond Pension Age. Comparative Perspectives* (Palgrave Macmillan 2015) 179.

25   K Hinrichs & J Lynch, 'Old-Age Pensions' in F Castles and others (eds), *The Oxford Handbook of the Welfare State* (Oxford University Press 2010) 355-356.

26   CESifo, 'Bismarck versus Beveridge: A Comparison of Social Insurance Systems in Europe' (2008) 4/2008 DICE Report available at www.ifo.de/DocDL/dicereport408-db6.pdf accessed 18 September 2019.

27   European Parliament, Directorate-General for Internal Policies, *Pension Schemes*, Study for the EMPL Committee (Publications Office of the European Union 2014) 15. It certainly appears that this is the more common taxonomy used in EU legislative and policy documents and (academic) pension law literature.

28   World Bank, *Averting the Old Age Crisis* (Oxford University Press 1994).

29   See, for instance, European Parliament, Directorate-General for Internal Policies, *Pension Schemes*, Study for the EMPL Committee (Publications Office of the European Union 2014) 15.

30   ibid.

31   European Parliament, Directorate-General for Internal Policies, *Pension systems in the EU – contingent liabilities and assets in the public and private sector* (2011) 26.

This pillar is commonly financed on a pay-as-you-go (PAYG) basis through taxes or contributions, meaning that members of the workforce finance the retirement benefits of current retirees. It can also "coinsure against long spells of low investment returns, recession, inflation and private market failures."[32] These so-called pillar 1bis-arrangements add a funded element to the statutory pension system. This element is managed by private institutions. In other words, these "are funded pillar 1 pensions where the participant chooses the pension provider."[33] Pillar 1bis schemes are a common phenomenon in Eastern Europe.[34]

The second pillar is the occupational pension pillar, in which the pension in principle is based on an employment relationship that provides for the building-up of a pension for the employee. It can be fully funded, meaning that funds are accumulated and invested and are – ideally – equal or greater than the liabilities. That is the case in, for example, the Netherlands and the UK. The second pillar in France, however, is financed by a PAYG mechanism, whereas in Germany occupational pensions are overwhelmingly[35] financed by book reserves. Book reserves are pension obligations reserved on the employer's balance sheet, and the financing methods are unrestricted and therefore need not necessarily be backed by cash or other assets.[36]

Pension plans in this pillar are provided by the employer to the benefit of the employee. The World Bank model advises this pillar should be made mandatory. However, that is not the case in most EU Member States. In the World Bank's model, this pillar carries out income smoothing – meaning that part of a worker's current wages are deferred into retirement – and saving for all employees within the population and therefore does more than merely avoiding old-age poverty. In this pillar there has to be a link between the benefits received by participants and the costs of running the scheme, and the system should therefore be immune to political and economic distortions. Not all EU Member States dispose of such a pension pillar. There are nine countries in the EU that either do not possess occupational pension plans or where such plans are practically irrelevant: the

---

32 World Bank, *Averting the Old Age Crisis* (Oxford University Press 1994) 16.
33 Towers Watson Perspectives, "The scope of a revised Directive", 2013.
34 EIOPA, 'EIOPA's advice on the development of an EU Single Market for personal pension products (PPP)' (EIOPA-16/457, 2016) 88, available at eiopa.europa.eu/Publications/Consultations/EIOPA's%20advice% 20on%20the%20development%20of%20an%20EU%20single%20market%20for%20personal%20pension% 20products.pdf accessed 25 September 2019.
35 The German Association for Occupational Pensions *aba* reports that as of late 2017, book reserves – known as *Direktzusagen* in German – are still the dominant form of occupational retirement provision in Germany at 49,5% of total occupational pension assets. See www.aba-online.de/news/28/a-prozentuale-aufteilung-de r-deckungsmittel-in-der.html accessed 25 September 2019.
36 S Hopfner & K U Erdmann, *Praxishandbuch Arbeitsrecht: Beginn, Durchführung und Beendigung des Arbeitsverhältnisses* (VVW 2017) 684.

Czech Republic, Estonia, Greece, Latvia, Lithuania, Hungary, Malta, Romania and Slova-kia.[37]

The third pillar covers provisions for people who want to supplement their income from their first- and/or second-pillar pensions – or have no access to these pillars alto-gether. These are personal pension savings that can take many forms, and contributions to these arrangements are often tax-incentivised. These are a person's personal savings for old age, and examples include bank savings, annuity policies or life or other insurance products.

What differentiates second and third-pillar pension savings from 'ordinary' savings is that they are both incentivised by government measures, such as tax deduction or con-tribution-matching by the government, and they also feature limitations regarding with-drawal options, such as the timeframe within which withdrawals are possible and the profile of withdrawal.[38] Withdrawal can often take place only from a certain age, with early withdrawal being impossible or made less attractive by financial penalties. There can also be restrictions or conditions on how the money can be withdrawn, such as lump sums, life annuities or annuities for a certain period. Savings in these schemes are gen-erally not very significant for most EU Member States.

Even though all three pillars are present in many EU Member States, the relative importance ascribed to each differs widely,[39] as discussed below.

---

37 R Davies, 'Occupational Pensions: 'Second pillar' provision in the EU policy context', Briefing Library of the
    European Parliament (Library of the European Parliament 2013) 3, available at www.europarl.europa.eu/
    RegData/bibliotheque/briefing/2013/130589/LDM_BRI(2013)130589_REV1_EN.pdf accessed 25 Septem-
    ber 2019.

38 European Parliament, Directorate-General for Internal Policies, *Pension systems in the EU – contingent
    liabilities and assets in the public and private sector* (2011) 38.

39 European Central Bank, 'The Impact of Regulating Occupational Pensions in Europe on Investment and
    Financial Stability' (2014) No. 154 Occasional Paper Series, 9, available at www.ecb.europa.eu/pub/pdf/
    scpops/ecbop154.pdf accessed 18 September 2019. See also European Commission, *Pension Adequacy Re-
    port 2018* (Publications Office of the European Union 2018) for more detailed information.

Figure 1

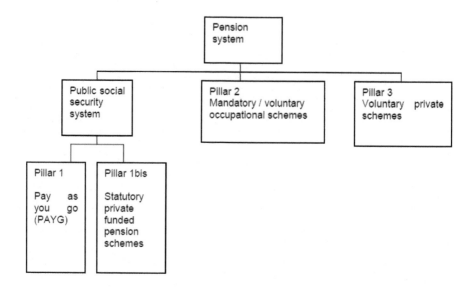

Source: European Parliament, Directorate-General for Internal Policies, Pension systems in the EU – contingent liabilities and assets in the public and private sector (2011) *26.*

2.3   The Three Pillars in the EU

In EU Member States that feature all three pension pillars, the emphasis on each pillar varies widely per country with different relative sizes and features. This, along with very different traditions and legal approaches, makes the occupational pensions landscape in the EU a diverse one. Regarding occupational pensions, the sector is characterised by "a huge heterogeneity across counties."[40] Accordingly, the coverage of supplementary pension schemes varies significantly throughout the EU. The differences are both in terms of the shares of the respective pension pillars and regarding regulatory frameworks.[41] In some Member States, occupational pensions play a marginal role due to the generosity of the first pillar.

---

40   EIOPA, 'IORPs Stress Test Report 2015', 4, available at https://eiopa.europa.eu/Publications/Surveys/EIO-PA%20IORPs%20Stress%20Test%20Report%202015%20bookmarks.pdf accessed 25 September 2019.

41   See European Commission, *Pension Adequacy Report 2018* (Publications Office of the European Union 2018) for more detailed information.

Coverage of supplementary pensions by type, 2016, % of population aged 15-64

	Occupational pensions (pillar 2)	Personal pensions (pillar 3)
Austria	15	23.8
Belgium	59.6	38
Bulgaria	0.2	12.9
Croatia	1.1	9.3
Cyprus	39.1	Not available
Czech Republic	Not applicable	52.6
Denmark	63.4	18
Estonia	Not applicable	12.3
Finland	6.6	19
France	24.5	5.7
Germany	57	33.8
Greece	1.3	Not available
Hungary	Not available	18.4
Ireland	35	12
Italy	9.2	11.5
Latvia	1	17.1
Lithuania	Not available	2.8
Luxembourg	5.1	Not available
Malta	Not available	Not available
Netherlands	88.0	28.3
Poland	1.6	~10
Portugal	3.7	4.5
Romania	Not applicable	3.3
Slovakia	Not applicable	26.3
Slovenia	36.5	1.4
Spain	3.3	15.7
Sweden	~70	24
UK	43 (total)	

Source: EU pension adequacy report 2018 Volume 1, pp. 79-80.

For example, in the Netherlands the benefits from the first pillar, the AOW, are relatively modest. The AOW's primary goal is to provide a minimum income floor[42] and is a flat-rate scheme, in the sense that all persons having been resident or subject to the Dutch legislation for the requisite number of years receive the same amount, the level depending on whether they are married or single. In addition, an important role is given in the Netherlands to fully-funded second-pillar occupational pensions. In principle, there is no general obligation either for employers or employees to be involved in a second-pillar scheme, however over 90% of employees in the Netherlands are covered by an occupational pension scheme, since collective labour agreements can make pension affiliation compulsory.[43] There is a close connection between the AOW and occupational pensions. Occupational pensions in the Netherlands are important, as – according to the OECD – income from the statutory AOW corresponds to only 30% of the average wage in the Netherlands.[44]

Just as in the Netherlands, Denmark and Sweden also offer an extensive coverage of the population via occupational pensions. However, Sweden's second-pillar arrangements are much less significant in terms of the income they provide to retirees.[45] Sweden's first-pillar, public pension system consists of three elements:[46] the income-related *inkomstpension* and the funded premium pension, as well as the guaranteed flat-rate pension. The first two elements are earnings-related[47] while the third is for poverty relief for individuals whose income is below a certain threshold. Sweden's second pillar plays a much smaller role in terms of the pension income it provides to pensioners, is quasi-mandatory in addition to the first pillar, and is effectuated through collective agreements, which is also the case in the Netherlands. While coverage of second-pillar pensions is nearly universal due to sectoral agreements, the share of income derived from such pensions makes that Swedes rely mainly on the public pension system, with the second-pillar system being mostly relevant for high-income earners.[48]

---

42 N Draper, A Nibbelink & J Uhde, 'An Assessment of Alternatives for the Dutch First Pension Pillar the Design of Pension Schemes' (2013), CPB Discussion Paper 259, 7.

43 D Chen & R Beetsma, 'Mandatory Participation in Occupational Pension Schemes in the Netherlands and Other Countries: An Update' (2015) No 10/2015-032 Netspar Academic Series, 10, available at ssrn.com/abstract=2670476 accessed 25 September 2019.

44 OECD, *Ageing and Employment Policies: The Netherlands 2014: Working Better with Age* (OECD Publishing 2014) 52.

45 Centraal Planbureau, 'Internationale vergelijking van pensioenstelsels: Denemarken, Zweden, Chili en Australië' (2015) 2, available at www.cpb.nl/publicatie/internationale-vergelijking-van-pensioenstelsels-denemarken-zweden-chili-en-australie accessed 25 September 2019.

46 N Barr, *The pension system in Sweden*, Report to the Expert Group on Public Economics of the Swedish Ministry of Finance 2013:7 (Elanders Sverige 2013) 27 et seq.

47 Ministry of Finance of Sweden, *The Swedish pension system and pension projections until 2070* (2017) 2, available at ec.europa.eu/info/sites/info/files/economy-finance/final_country_fiche_se.pdf accessed 25 September 2019.

48 ibid 7.

Similar to the Netherlands, Denmark's second-pillar pension is a significant addition to the income derived from the statutory system.[49] Like both in the Netherlands and Sweden, coverage of such pensions is high, with collective agreements providing supplementary pensions to 93% of employed Danish in the age range of 30-60 years old.[50]

France's occupational pension schemes are mandatory by law, but play a less important role in comparison with the country's first-pillar scheme. The same goes for Austria and Finland, where second-pillar pensions have a relatively small presence due to the generosity of the first pillar. Austria's small occupational pension sector results from the inclusion of virtually all labour market participants in the country's pay-as-you-go (PAYG) public pension system.[51] Although the volume of both second and third pillar pensions has increased rapidly during the decade spanning 2008-2018,[52] just 5% of all pension benefits paid out originated from private (both occupational and private) pensions in 2007,[53] and 95% percent of retirees draw from their public pension as their primary source of retirement income.[54] The replacement rate of the public pension in Austria can be as high as 80% if an individual has contributed to the system for 45 years and retires at 65, making additional retirement provisions largely superfluous.[55]

Finland has a pension system that fulfils the functions of the first and second pillar within the same scheme, combining a "compulsory legislative basis, similar benefits for all, partial funding and private organisation of the pension provision."[56] The system can be described as consisting of three elements, with (1) mandatory, partially-funded earnings-related pensions and (2) a non-contributory national pension and a pension guarantee for poverty relief. In addition there are (3) voluntary employer-level and individual pensions. The mandatory earnings-related and non-contributory national systems qualify as first-pillar systems.[57] Supplementary and voluntary pensions play a relatively small

---

49 OECD, 'Pension Country Profile: Denmark' in: *OECD Private Pensions Outlook 2008* (OECD Publishing 2009) 180.

50 I Guardiancich, 'Denmark: Current pension system: first assessment of reform outcomes and output'(2010) European Social Observatory, available at http://www.ose.be/files/publication/2010/country_reports_pension/OSE_2010_CRpension_Denmark.pdf accessed 27 November 2019.

51 T Url, 'Occupational Pension Schemes in Austria' (2003) 2/2003 Austrian Economic Quarterly 64.

52 Austrian Federal Ministry of Finance, *Austrian Country Fiche on Public Pensions* (2018) 8, available at ec.europa.eu/info/sites/info/files/economy-finance/final_country_fiche_at.pdf accessed 25 September 2019.

53 Austrian Federal Ministry of Finance, *Austrian Country Fiche on Public Pensions* (2012) 4.

54 ibid 1.

55 At the same time, sustainability concerns about the Austrian systems exist, as Austria's public pension expenditure is among the highest in the EU and is set to increase slightly through 2070. See European Commission, *The 2018 Ageing Report: Economic & Budgetary Projections for the 28 EU Member States (2016-2070)* (Publications Office of the European Union 2018) 66; European Commission, *Country Report Austria 2019*, SWD(2019) 1019 final, 4-5, 17 et seq.

56 N Barr, *The pension system in Finland: Adequacy, sustainability and system design* (Finnish Centre for Pensions 2013).

57 ibid 23.

role, since there is no contribution or benefit limit in the mandatory system and opting-out is impossible.[58]

Several Central and Eastern (CEE) countries have undertaken to weaken or close their second-pillar schemes, largely due to economic woes brought on by the 2008 financial crisis.[59] In Poland and Hungary, this economic downturn led to severely strained budgets, prompting the governments of those countries to close their funded second-pillar pension systems. These systems were already weakened by problems built into their architecture, with incomplete designs and a funding strategy that partly diverted funds from the first-pillar to the second pillar, leaving gaps in public pension financing.[60] Hungarian authorities nationalised the assets collected in the second pillar when they ordered the pension management companies to transfer their funds to a fund that aimed at filling holes in the national budget.[61] The funds were nationalised in 2011. In Poland, a similar chain of events took place that substantially weakened the Polish second pillar.[62] Finally, the Czech Republic closed its voluntary second pillar in late 2015 after a short life of under three years.[63] It has not re-introduced a second pillar since.[64]

---

58 Finnish Pension Alliance TELA, 'The Finnish earnings-related pension system is one of a kind in the EU', available at www.tela.fi/en/pension_sector/legislation/the_eu_and_the_pension_system accessed 25 September 2019.

59 H van Meerten & P Borsjé, 'Pension Rights and Entitlement Conversion ('invaren'): Lessons from a Dutch Perspective with Regard to the Implications of the EU Charter'(2016) 18 (1) European Journal of Social Security 46, 52 et seq.

60 E Fultz, 'The retrenchment of second-tier pensions in Hungary and Poland: A precautionary tale' (2012) Vol 65 (3) International Social Security Review, 3.

61 ibid.

62 Both in Hungary and in Poland, the second pillar was financed by diverting finds from the first to the second pillar. Because the Polish government wished to avoid budget cuts and to remain under the 3% Maastricht limit for its planned entry into the Eurozone, it planned on implementing pension cuts. The options were an increase in retirement age, slashing subsidies to the farmers' pension fund or reducing diversion form the first pillar to the second. It opted for the latter option, and contributions diverted to the second pillar to the first were reduced substantially. See E Fultz, 'The retrenchment of second-tier pensions in Hungary and Poland: A precautionary tale' (2012), Vol 65 International Social Security Review, 14 et seq.

63 European Commission, *Pension Adequacy Report 2018* (Publications Office of the European Union 2018) 26. See also K Krzyzak, 'Czech second-pillar pension system to close by January 2016' (Investment and Pensions Europe, 13 November 2014) available at www.ipe.com/news/regulation/czech-second-pillar-pensi on-system-to-close-by-january-2016/10004774.fullarticle accessed 25 September 2019; K Krzyzak, 'Czech second-pillar pension closure moves ahead' (Investment and Pensions Europe, 23 June 2015) available at www.ipe.com/countries/cee/czech-second-pillar-pension-closure-moves-ahead/10008615.fullarticle accessed 25 September 2019. For a history of reform efforts of the Czech pension system, see D Adascalitei & S Domonkos, 'Reforming against all odds: Multi-pillar pension systems in the Czech Republic and Romania' (2015) Vol 68 (2) International Social Security Review 85.

64 Ministry of Finance of the Czech Republic, *Pension Projections of the Czech Republic* (2017) 1, available at ec.europa.eu/info/sites/info/files/economy-finance/final_country_fiche_cz.pdf accessed 25 September 2019.

3   CONTEXT

3.1   Introduction

This section provides the reader with some context within which this research is to be placed. Government-provided, statutory pension systems (1st pillar) have been under pressure over the last decades, as an aging population is causing a reduction in the ratio of working people compared to those in retirement. Across much of the EU, measures taken to ensure the future financial sustainability of public pension systems – which are funded in a pay-as-you-go (PAYG) fashion in most EU Member States[65] – result in lower income replacement rates by public systems. Future pensioners will likely have to contend with a lower income from their public pension system than current retirees.[66] PAYG systems fund the retirement benefits for current retirees with the contributions of workers. These systems are not pre-funded, hence the pay-as-you-go (PAYG) moniker. Because the balance between the working population and retirees is skewing ever more towards retirees, costs of such systems are ballooning while cash inflow is decreasing. The replacement rate of public systems is expected to drop by 8 percentage points (pps.) on average among the EU Member States between 2016-2070 and is projected to plummet by as much as 29.4 pps. in Poland and 31.1 pps. in Spain during that period.[67]

Because of those developments, the European Commission foresees a greater role for *supplementary pension provision* (i.e. the second, occupational pillar and the third, private pillar) and has aimed at accommodating and encouraging growth in the second and third pillars to ratchet up retirement provisions for European workers.[68] The possible adverse effects of population ageing on national pension systems have been identified by the Commission since at least 1991, when it published a Communication on occupational pension schemes.[69] Supplementary pension systems, however, are experiencing problems

---

65   The European Parliament notes that most public pension schemes are PAYG, see European Parliament, 'Prospects for occupational pensions in the European Union' (Briefing of September 2015) available at www.europarl.europa.eu/EPRS/EPRS-Briefing-568328-Prospects-for-occupational-pensions-EU-FINAL. pdf accessed 25 September 2019.

66   European Commission, *The 2018 Ageing Report: Economic & Budgetary Projections for the 28 EU Member States (2016-2070)* (Publications Office of the European Union 2018). See, in particular ibid Table II.1.18 on page 84. For more detailed information on each Member State, see European Commission, *Pension Adequacy Report 2018* (Publications Office of the European Union 2018).

67   ibid.

68   European Commission, 'Impact Assessment Accompanying the document Proposal for a Directive of the European Parliament and of the Council on the activities and supervision of institutions for occupational retirement provision' SWD(2014) 103 final, part 1/2, 24; European Parliament, 'Prospects for occupational pensions in the European Union' Briefing of September 2015, available at www.europarl.europa.eu/EPRS/ EPRS-Briefing-568328-Prospects-for-occupational-pensions-EU-FINAL.pdf accessed 25 September 2019.

69   Commission of the European Communities, 'Supplementary social security schemes: the role of occupational pension schemes in the social protection of workers and their implications for freedom of movement' (Communication from the Commission to the Council) SEC (91) 1332 final.

of their own. Since these are typically funded and their assets invested – i.e. they accumulate large sums of cash in the form of pension premiums collected from scheme members – they are sensitive to fluctuations in interest rates, conditions on stock markets and the general economic climate. The effects of the financial crisis and the subsequent low-interest environment in which pension funds are finding themselves and their investments leave them in a vulnerable position.[70]

The Commission believes that the EU's internal market could offer the advantages required to make pension funds more efficient. These advantages could help to alleviate the pressures caused by changing demographics and future economic slumps. The Commission contends that cross-border activity by pension funds could create more efficiency by harnessing the potential of the EU's internal market to create economies of scale.[71] For instance, small pension funds struggling to cope in a low-interest environment could consolidate to save costs on the administration of pensions. The EU's policy goals in this respect are discussed in the next section, Section 4.

The following subsections give more attention to the relevant socioeconomic developments, the backdrop against which the EU has formulated its policy goals.

3.2   *A Problem of Demographics*

An Aging Continent

The European Continent faces inauspicious demographic prospects over the coming decades. The description of the problem ranges from "a demographic challenge"[72] to a veritable "demographic time-bomb."[73] Pension systems are placed at risk by these developments. Whatever term one chooses to describe these demographic developments, it is

---

70   EIOPA, *Financial Stability Report December 2018,* available at eiopa.europa.eu/Publications/Reports/EIO-PA%20FSR%20December%202018.pdf accessed 25 September 2019.

71   European Commission, 'Impact Assessment Accompanying the document Proposal for a Directive of the European Parliament and of the Council on the activities and supervision of institutions for occupational retirement provision' SWD(2014) 103 final, part 1/2, 22.

72   European Parliament, 'On the demographic challenge and solidarity between generations' (Report of the Committee on Employment and Social Affairs, 6 October 2010) available at www.europarl.europa.eu/sides/getDoc.do?type=REPORT&reference=A7-2010-0268&language=EN accessed 25 September 2019; European Central Bank, 'The 2015 Ageing report: How costly will Ageing in Europe be?' Economic Bulletin 2015 (4) 52, available at www.ecb.europa.eu/pub/pdf/other/eb201504_focus07.en.pdf accessed 25 September 2019; European Commission, 'Green Paper towards adequate, sustainable and safe European pension systems' COM(2010) 365 final, 3.

73   European Commission, 'Five ways to defuse the demographic time bomb' Press Release 12 October 2006, available at europa.eu/rapid/press-release_IP-06-1359_en.htm accessed 25 September 2019; The Economist, 'The demographic time-bomb', *The Economist* 27 August 2008, available at www.economist.com/certain-ideas-of-europe/2008/08/27/the-demographic-time-bomb accessed 25 September; European Parliament, Directorate-General for Internal Affairs, *Demography and family policies from a gender perspective*, Study for the FEMM Committee (2016) 12.

abundantly clear that action must be taken to adapt government policies to adequately face future scenarios.

Consider these projections by Eurostat.[74] While the population of the 28 Member States of the EU is expected to increase by a modest 2.6% overall between 2014 and 2080 – peaking at 526 million in 2050 – its composition will change significantly due to the combined effects of migration flows, a low fertility rate and increasing life expectancy.[75] For instance, increases in life expectancy mean that people will draw pensions for an increasing number of years if the Member States do not adapt their statutory retirement age. The median age of Europe's populace will increase by 4.2 years by 2080, making the median age for men 45.2 years and that of women 47.6. Over the next 35 years, the working-age population will shrink from 333.8 million people to 292.3 million: a loss of 41.5 million working-age persons, or a decrease of 12.4%. Meanwhile, the share of the elderly will increase from 18.5% to 28.7%.

All these numbers add up to the following scenario: the old-age dependency ratio will exhibit explosive growth over the next six-and-a-half decades. This ratio is the ratio of the number of elderly people compared to the number of people of working age. It is projected to nearly double by 2080.[76] Whereas there were nearly four working-age persons to support every retiree, that number will halve to just two, caused by the retirement of the baby-boom generation.

In order to face the challenges caused by changing demographics, the EU legislator acted on several fronts. One of those action points was a first step towards the creation of a European market for occupational pensions by the first IORP Directive.[77] Although the regulation of pension systems is in principle still for the most part a national prerogative,[78] EU action can help deepen the internal market for pensions, creating "a richer set of building blocks" to help the retirement security of European citizens.[79] For instance, the Single Market can allow for more opportunities for specialisation, more international risk-sharing, a more efficient allocation of capital, greater labour mobility by removing

74 Eurostat, *People in the EU: who are we and how do we live?* (Publications Office of the European Union 2015) 158 et seq.

75 European Commission, *The 2015 Ageing Report: Economic and budgetary projections for the 28 EU Member States (2013-2060)* (Publications Office of the European Union 2015).

76 ibid 163.

77 Directive 2003/41/EC of the European Parliament and of the Council of 3 June 2003 on the activities and supervision of institutions for occupational retirement provision [2003] OJ L 235/10 (IORP I Directive).

78 D Natali, 'Reforming Pensions in the EU: National Policy Changes and EU Coordination' (2011) European Social Observatory, 13, available at www.ose.be/files/publication/dnatali/Natali_2011_-FLCaballero_251011.pdf accessed 27 November 2019.

79 L Bovenberg, 'European pension reform: A way forward' (2011) Vol 16 (2) *Pensions*, 76.

obstacles caused by pension systems[80] and greater opportunities for economies of scale.[81] This is one concept behind cross-border IORPs.

3.3   An Increasingly Mobile Continent

The number of EU nationals moving across borders in the EU is on the rise. Although as a percentage of the total population of the EU[82] the number of movers may not seem that great at being 'just' 4.1%, the tally of "EU-28 movers" – EU citizens (all ages) living in an EU Member State other than their country of citizenship – stood at 17 million in 2017, of which around 12 million were of working age.[83]

With respect to pension provision for mobile citizens, there are still several hurdles that have, despite decades of EU commitment, not yet been overcome. As explained in Chapter 3, persons moving from one Member State to another can face a (partial) loss of their occupational pension rights owing to a lack of coordination of their acquired pension rights. This loss of pension rights stems from long waiting and vesting periods – the periods that prevent workers from either entering a pension scheme or acquiring pension rights, respectively[84] – as well as minimum age requirements. EU provisions currently in place dealing with worker mobility and occupational pensions have fallen short of their initial goals, as will be explained in Chapter 3.

At the same time, the free movement of workers is one of the cornerstones of the internal market.[85] The possible loss of occupational pension rights for workers has been

---

80 ibid.
81 European Commission, 'Impact Assessment Accompanying the document Proposal for a Directive of the European Parliament and of the Council on the activities and supervision of institutions for occupational retirement provisions' SWD(2014) 103 final.
82 The total population of the entire EU stood at nearly 513 million people, according to Eurostat. See Eurostat, 'EU population up to nearly 513 million on 1 January 2018' News Release 115/2018 of 10 July 2018, available at ec.europa.eu/eurostat/documents/2995521/9063738/3-10072018-BP-EN.pdf/ccdfc838-d909-4fd8-b3f9-db0d65ea457f accessed 25 September 2019.
83 European Commission, *2018 Annual Report on intra-EU Labour Mobility* (Publications Office of the European Union 2019) 18.
84 A vesting period is a period during which benefits are being accrued, but not yet vested, i.e. scheme members are not entitled to their benefits before the vesting period has elapsed. A waiting period is the period of time an employee must work for an employer before they become eligible to participate in the pension scheme. Although both periods are important tools to foster employee loyalty, they can become an obstacle to take up employment in another Member State or to leave ones current employer, as non-completion of the waiting and vesting periods could lead to a loss of pension rights. This would occur if the waiting and vesting periods exceed the term of employment.
85 See, for instance, Article 3 TEU, which states that the EU "is to offer its citizens an area of freedom, security and justice without internal frontier, in which the free movement of persons is ensured" and Article 45 TFEU, which proclaims that the right to free movement of workers entails the right to accept offers of employment and to move freely with the territory of Member States for this purpose. For a more extensive discussion, see W Baugniet, *The protection of occupational pensions under European Union law on the freedom of movement for workers*, dissertation European University Institute Florence (2014) 128 et seq.

recognised by the European Court of Justice as an obstacle to the freedom of movement of workers that may prevent them from exercising this right.[86] From the early 1990s until the present day, the adverse effects of relocating to another Member State on occupational pension rights has remained a priority for the EU. The Commission is especially concerned that the absence of portability of acquired occupational pension rights significantly affects employment decisions, "thus limiting the freedom of movement of workers, one of Europe's fundamental freedoms."[87] Actual EU legislation adopted to deal with this problem seems to fall short of initial aims, as explained in Chapter 3.

3.4   Economic Challenges

The aforementioned demographic problems are compounded by the aftermath of the financial crisis and current low interest rates. Whether or not one speaks of first-pillar statutory pensions, second-pillar occupational pensions or third-pillar personal pension arrangements, all three of these pillars face challenges of an economic nature.[88] These problems manifest themselves both on the liabilities side and on the asset side. On the liabilities side, low bond yields have caused the obligations of pension providers to their members to grow disproportionately to their assets, resulting in plummeting funding ratios.[89] The value of assets has been under pressure, owing to poor asset returns on volatile markets, low yields and uncertainty. In addition, low interest rates wreak havoc on the coverage ratios of pension funds.

4   EUROPEAN PENSION POLICY

4.1   Introduction

In response to the abovementioned challenges, the EU has launched several policy initiatives. Two main themes appear to be dominant in EU pension policy: 1) the mobility of European workers and 2) the use of the Single Market with a view to achieve safe, adequate and sustainable pensions. The latter topic is broad, within which various policy

---

86 Case C-379/09 *Casteels* [2011] ECLI:EU:C:2011:131.

87 I Guardiancich & D Natali, 'The cross-border portability of supplementary pensions: Lessons from the European Union' (2012) Vol 12 (3) Global Social Policy, 302.

88 European Central Bank, 'The Impact of Regulating Occupational Pensions in Europe on Investment and Financial Stability' (2014) No. 154 Occasional Paper Series, 10-11, available at www.ecb.europa.eu/pub/pdf/scpops/ecbop154.pdf accessed 25 September 2019.

89 ibid.

goals and objectives were debated by the Commission, ranging from investment freedom to better pension returns to scale economies.[90]

4.2 Worker Mobility

The issue of worker mobility has remained a constant topic from the beginning of European Union policies dealing with supplementary pensions until present. Although the EU made an early start with the coordination of statutory pensions, it would take until the late 1980s before the first efforts in the field of supplementary pensions were made. Legislation on statutory pensions covers the coordination of social security schemes, i.e. providing for aggregation rules to satisfy waiting periods, rules on determining the applicable legislation, payment of benefit across borders and the prohibition discrimination on ground of nationality.[91] Such coordination was deemed essential to promote the free movement of workers by preventing the loss of their statutory pension rights. The exercise of the right to free movement is not only a fundamental right in EU law, but also necessary for the Single Market to function efficiently by promoting the allocation of labour to where it is needed most.[92]

The lack of coordination provisions for supplementary pension rights was a cause for concern for the Commission. Starting in 1989, the Action Programme Relating to the Implementation of the Community Charter of Basic Social Rights for Workers[93] identified the coordination of "supplementary social security" as an important prerequisite for freedom of movement of workers. According to the Commission, the problems related to losing pension rights when moving to another Member State represented a problem for an increasingly mobile workforce. Workers could be discouraged from moving to another Member State because there were no provisions protecting workers against losing their occupational pension rights. Subsequent Commission documents[94] retained this focus,

---

90 See section 4.3.
91 Initially Regulations 3 and 4, succeeded by Regulations EEC No 1408/71 and 574/72, now replaced by Regulation (EC) No 883/2004 of the European Parliament and the Council of 29 April 2004 on the coordination of social security systems [2004] OJ L 166/1; see also F Pennings, *European Social Security Law* (Intersentia 2015).
92 International Labour Organization, *Coordination of Social Security Systems in the European Union: An explanatory report on EC Regulation No. 883/2004 and its Implementing Regulation No. 987/2009* (ILO 2010).
93 Commission of the European Communities, 'Communication from the Commission concerning its action programme relating to the implementation of the Community Charter of Basic Social Rights for Workers' COM(89) 568 final.
94 See Commission of the European Communities, 'Supplementary Social Security Schemes: the role of occupational pension schemes in the social protection of workers and their implications for freedom of movement' (Communication from the Commission to the Council) SEC(91) 1332 final; Commission of the European Communities, 'Report from the Commission concerning social protection in Europe 1993' COM(93) 531 final; European Commission, *Report of the High Level Panel on the free movement of persons chaired by Simone Veil* (Publications Office of the European Union 1998).

and undertaking action to provide protection against these losses remains a policy goal of the Commission to this day.[95]

Over the years, the EU appears to have succeeded in introducing legislation regulating the *retention* of supplementary pension rights. However, the *individual transferability* (i.e. "moving" accrued pension rights from a provider in one Member State to another in individual cases) and *portability* (i.e. remaining with a particular pension provider irrespective of movement between Member States) remain problematic.

Two directives deal with worker mobility and occupational pensions directly and a third, the IORP II Directive,[96] facilitates such mobility indirectly. None deal with individual transferability of pension pots to other providers upon changing employer,[97] nor do they enable cross-border membership.

The first is the so-called Safeguard Directive,[98] which is based on Articles 48 and 352 TFEU and provides for equal treatment regarding the preservation of acquired occupational pension rights when leaving a scheme to join another scheme in another Member State. This equal treatment entails non-discrimination between scheme members who leave a pension scheme and join a new scheme within the same Member State and those who leave a scheme to join another scheme in another EU Member State.[99] The Directive also ensures that benefits can be paid on a cross-border basis.[100] Cross-border membership (also referred to as portability), meaning that employees can remain with their occupational pension scheme even if they work for a different employer in a different Member State, is possible only for posted workers.[101] Nor does the Directive regulate matters such as vesting and waiting periods.[102] In that regard, the Safeguard Directive

---

95 See, inter alia, EIOPA, *Seventh Consumer Trends Report* (Publications Office of the European Union 2018) 49; EIOPA, 'Final Report on Good Practices on individual transfers of occupational pension rights' (2015) BoS-15/104, available at eiopa.europa.eu/Publications/Reports/EIOPA-BoS-15-104_Final_Report_on_Pensions_Transferabity.pdf accessed 1 October 2019.

96 Directive 2016/2341/EU of the European Parliament and of the Council of 14 December 2016 on the activities and supervision of institutions for occupational retirement provision (IORPs) [2016], OJ L 354/37 (IORP II Directive).

97 L van der Vaart & H van Meerten, 'De pensioen opPEPPer?' (2018) 1 Tijdschrift voor Pensioenvraagstukken 38.

98 Council Directive 98/49/EC of 29 June 1998 on safeguarding the supplementary pension rights of employed and self-employed persons moving within the Community [1998] OJ L 209/46.

99 ibid Article 4.

100 ibid Article 5.

101 The goal of cross-border membership to an occupational pension scheme was articulated by the Commission as early as 1991, but was ultimately abandoned because it would be too difficult in practice. See Chapter 3.

102 A vesting period is a period during which benefits are being accrued, but not yet vested, i.e. scheme members are not entitled to their benefits before the vesting period has elapsed. A waiting period is the period of time an employee must work for an employer before they become eligible to participate in the pension scheme. Although both periods are important tools to foster employee loyalty, they can become an obstacle to take up employment in another Member State or to leave ones current employer, as non-completion of the waiting and vesting periods could lead to a loss of pension rights. This would occur if the waiting and vesting periods exceed the term of employment.

can be described as only a "modest attempt at dealing with the freedom of movement" of workers and self-employed persons.[103]

The second directive dealing with worker mobility and supplementary pensions is the Supplementary Pension Rights Directive, based on Article 46 TFEU.[104] That directive harmonizes waiting and vesting periods,[105] the minimum age for vesting pension rights as well as the preservation of dormant pension rights.[106] The initial proposal[107] for the Directive was far more ambitious, with strict requirements on waiting and vesting periods, and originally aimed to make occupational pensions truly transferable throughout the EU in the sense that accrued pension rights could be transferred to another scheme.[108] Debate on the directive was "lively and even acrimonious throughout the legislative process" in the European Parliament,[109] and even caused a "proper outcry"[110] on the part of particularly vocal Member States and the pensions industry.[111] The first 2005 proposal was "overambitious and untimely",[112] exhibited by the fierce resistance from the pensions lobby and the Member States. A subsequent proposal marked the "shift from portability to minimum requirements",[113] and a final proposal continued along the path of "diminishing ambitions."[114] The considerations of the final directive specifically note that the directive does not provide for the transfer of vested pension rights.[115]

Although a lack of an EU framework regulating individual cross-border transfers of pension rights does not make an individual transfer an impossibility, individuals will face

---

103 C Bittner, 'Occupational Pensions: a Matter of European Concern' (2001) Vol 2 (2) European Business Organization Law Review 401, 408. See also M. Wienk, 'Europese coördinatie van aanvullende pensioenen' (Doctoral dissertation, Koninklijke Universiteit Brabant 1999) 146.

104 Directive 2014/50/EU of the European Parliament and of the Council of 16 April 2014 on minimum requirements for enhancing worker mobility between Member States by improving the acquisition and preservation of supplementary pension rights [2014] OJ L 128/1.

105 ibid Article 4(1)(a).

106 ibid Article 5.

107 Commission of the European Communities, 'Proposal for a Directive on improving the portability of supplementary pension rights' COM(2005) 507 final.

108 ibid Article 6.

109 W Baugniet, *The protection of occupational pensions under European Union law on the freedom of movement for workers*, dissertation European University Institute Florence (2014) 186.

110 I Guardiancich, 'Portability of Supplementary Pension Rights in Europe: A Lowest Common Denominator Solution' (2015), Vol 1 (1) European Policy Analysis 74, 85.

111 W Baugniet, *The protection of occupational pensions under European Union law on the freedom of movement for workers*, dissertation European University Institute Florence (2014).

112 I Guardiancich, 'Portability of Supplementary Pension Rights in Europe: A Lowest Common Denominator Solution' (2015) Vol 1 (1) European Policy Analysis 74, 84.

113 M Del Sol & M Rocca, 'Free movement of workers in the EU and occupational pensions: conflicting priorities? Between case law and legislative interventions' (2017) Vol 19 (2) European Journal of Social Security 141.

114 ibid.

115 Directive 2014/50/EU of the European Parliament and of the Council of 16 April 2014 on minimum requirements for enhancing worker mobility between Member States by improving the acquisition and preservation of supplementary pension rights [2014] OJ L 128/1, recital 24.

a number of hurdles should they wish to transfer their rights.[116] Cross-border membership is also impossible under this directive.

Although one of the stated goals of the IORP II Directive (see Section 5 of this chapter) is to increase worker mobility, it deals primarily with the conditions under which pension providers (i.e. IORPs) can function in the internal market and its provisions do not seem to deal with worker mobility directly. However, its recitals mention worker mobility in several places and in different contexts. For instance, its provisions on governance, the provision of information and its aims of transparent and safe occupational retirement provision is touted by the Directive's fourth recital as facilitating worker mobility. In addition, the possibility of cross-border service provision for IORPs should help to achieve that goal as well.[117]

Specifically, cross-border IORPs aim to aid cross-border mobility for groups of employees belonging to the same (corporate) group of employers.[118] When changing employer, the employee need not change pension provider and can forego potentially cumbersome and costly transfers of accrued pension rights: the RESAVER pan-European pension fund for researchers relies on this concept,[119] as do the cross-border pension funds of multiple multinational corporations.

RESAVER was set up in the context of the European Partnership for Researchers, and the Commission pledged to help set up this fund by providing technical support to the Consortium of the Retirement Savings Vehicle for European Research Institutions. That Consortium was set up in October 2014 to create a single pension arrangement for research institutions with a view to stop pension issues "being a barrier to researchers' mobility" and facilitate their mobility across the EU. It has been in place since 2015, accepting contributions since late 2016 and has an 'Organisme de Financement des Pensions' (OFP), a Belgian IORP, as its pension vehicle. It is a multi-employer, pan-European pension fund to which various European universities are members.[120]

All three directives have in common that they fall (well) short of the EU's initial intentions, and it appears that the Union's lack of (direct) competences on occupational pensions is at least partly to blame. As explained in Chapter 3, the EU outlined several goals – such as cross-border membership of occupational pension schemes and a single

---

116 See EIOPA, 'Final Report on Good Practices on individual transfers of occupational pension rights' (2015) BoS-15/104, available at eiopa.europa.eu/Publications/Reports/EIOPA-BoS-15-104_Final_Report_on_Pensions_Transferabity.pdf accessed 1 October 2019. On page 15, it notes that: "It is generally not allowed to transfer occupational pension rights upon ending active membership to any pension scheme the member wishes to, as almost all Member States provide for conditions/restrictions regarding the receiving scheme where a member has the statutory right to transfer. As a consequence of the requirements for transferring and receiving schemes, many transfers cannot be carried out."
117 Recital 35 of the IORP II Directive.
118 M Reiner, 'Entwicklung und Probleme des europäischen Betriebspensionsrechts am Beispiel der Mobilitäts-richtlinie' (2017) Vol 1 (2) Journal für Arbeitsrecht und Sozialrecht 168, 180.
119 ibid.
120 For current member universities, see www.resaver.eu/resaver/consortium/ accessed 1 October 2019.

market for occupational pensions – that have only been partially achieved. The Safeguard Directive gave effect to the Commission's initial objective of guaranteeing cross-border membership only for posted workers.[121] Regarding the Supplementary Pension Rights Directive, Baugniet opines that institutional constraints, in particular the principle of subsidiarity, have been responsible for "watering down" the ambitions of the directive.[122] The same could be said about the IORP II Directive. Chapter 3 extensively discusses the history of the IORP II Directive, as well as the challenges that influenced its final form.

4.3 Using the Internal Market to Achieve Safe, Adequate and Sustainable Pensions

From an early stage in its efforts to regulate supplementary occupational pensions, the Commission has sought to harness what it saw as the benefits of the EU's internal market to bring benefits to pension scheme members, pension providers and employers.[123] The need for pension reform by the Member States – with assistance from the EU – was of special importance given the adverse demographic developments many Member States are facing.

In 1991, the first proposed directive[124] in supplementary occupational pensions appeared to have as its primary goal the free movement of capital: it was to ensure freedom of investment for pension funds throughout the EU. It sought to do away with restrictions on investments imposed by Member States. That Directive failed on account of disagreement among Member States – more on that in Chapter 3 – but it would not be long before the Commission would again launch new efforts[125] seeking to make use of the

---

121 C Bittner, 'Occupational Pensions: a Matter of European Concern' (2001) Vol 2 (2) European Business Organization Law Review 401, 408.

122 W Baugniet, *The protection of occupational pensions under European Union law on the freedom of movement for workers*, dissertation European University Institute Florence (2014) 218 et seq.

123 See, for example, Commission of the European Communities, 'Report from the Commission concerning social protection in Europe 1993' COM(93) 531 final; Commission of the European Communities, 'Supplementary Pensions in the Single Market: A Green Paper' COM(97) 283 final; 'Implementing the framework for financial markets: action plan' COM(1999) 232 final; Commission of the European Communities, 'Towards a Single Market for supplementary pensions' COM(1999) 134 final.

124 Commission of the European Communities, 'Proposal for a Council Directive relating to the freedom of management and investment of funds held by institutions for retirement provisions' COM(91) 301 final.

125 Beginning in 1997 with the Green Paper on Pensions (Commission of the European Communities, 'Supplementary Pensions in the Single Market: A Green Paper' COM(97) 283 final).

internal market to achieve what it calls "safe, adequate and sustainable"[126] pensions. Among other things, pension systems living up to that description ought to be governed by appropriate prudential rules (safe), make use of investment freedoms and scale economies to bring better pension results for pension scheme members (adequate) and be prepared for demographic change with fewer workers and more retirees (sustainable).

One of the efforts meant to aid in achieving safe, adequate and sustainable pensions was the 2003 IORP Directive. That directive was to "allow private funded pension schemes to make the best use of investment opportunities, set high standards for the protection of beneficiaries and pave the way towards the cross-border management of occupational pension schemes. Enhancing the security and efficiency of these institutions and allowing them to fully benefit from the Single Market should contribute to the safety and sustainability of pension systems".[127]

The Directive was recast in 2016[128] with a view to further facilitating the "internal market for occupational pensions" that the first IORP Directive envisaged. However, the proliferation of cross-border IORPs, which – according to the Commission – should be able to achieve better pension results for scheme members – to date has fallen short of expectations. What is to be made of the concept of cross-border IORPs? How are they to be seen from the perspective of pension scheme members? The next section briefly introduces the IORP II Directive and the cross-border IORP as a concept. Chapters 4 and 5 assess the cross-border IORP from the perspective of a pension scheme member.

---

126 For instance, Commission of the European Communities, 'The Future Evolution of Social Protections from a Long-Term Point of view: Safe and Sustainable Pensions' (White Paper) COM(2000) 622 final; Commission of the European Communities, 'Supporting national strategies for safe and sustainable pensions through an integrated approach' COM(2001) 362 final; Commission of the European Communities, 'Joint report by the Commission and the Council on Adequate and sustainable pensions' (Draft) COM(2002) 737 final; Commission of the European Communities, 'Working together, working better: A new framework for the open coordination of social protection and inclusion policies in the European Union' COM(2005) 706 final; Commission of the European Communities, 'Dealing with the impact of an ageing population in the EU (2009 Ageing Report)' (Communication from the Commission to the European Parliament, the Council, the European Economic and Social Committee and the Committee of the Regions) COM(2009) 180 final; European Commission, 'The final implementation report of the EU Internal Security Strategy 2010-2014' (Communication from the Commission to the European Parliament and the Council) COM(2010) 365 final; European Commission, 'An Agenda for Adequate, Safe and Sustainable Pensions' (White Paper) COM(2012) 55 final.

127 Commission of the European Communities, 'The Future Evolution of Social Protections from a Long-Term Point of view: Safe and Sustainable Pensions' (White Paper) COM(2000) 622 final.

128 IORP II Directive (see footnote 96).

5 THE IORP II DIRECTIVE AND IORPs: AN INTRODUCTION

5.1 Introduction

One measure borne out of the EU's pursuit of its supplementary pension ambitions was the Institutions for Occupational Retirement Provision (IORP) Directive of 2003.[129] That directive has since been repealed and superseded by the IORP II Directive – itself a recast version of the first IORP Directive.[130] Moving forward, this book will refer to the IORP II Directive unless explicitly stated otherwise. One of the Directive's goals is to create a so-called single market for occupational pensions, in which pension providers – Institutions for Occupational Retirement Provision (IORPs) in EU parlance – can pursue business throughout the EU's territory without obstacles. The theory, as expressed by the EU legislator, is that cross-border activity would lead *inter alia* to greater efficiency and risk diversification.[131] This would help achieve the EU's goal of adequate, safe and sustainable pensions by securing, inter alia, benefits for pension scheme members in the form of a better pension result, supporting the goal of pension adequacy. Mobility should be aided by enabling workers to remain with the same IORP as they move across the EU,[132] avoiding cumbersome and costly pension transfers and the risk of losing pension rights.[133] As explained in more detail in Chapters 3 and 4, worker mobility is only indirectly addressed by the IORP II Directive, and is the primary concern of the Safeguard Directive and the Supplementary Pension Rights Directive.

5.2 What is an IORP?

In non-technical terms, an IORP is a pension provider such as a pension fund. Article 6 (1) of the IORP II Directive describes what an IORP is: it is "an institution, irrespective of its legal form, operating on a funded basis, established separately from any sponsoring undertaking or trade for the purpose of providing retirement benefits in the context of an occupational activity on the basis of an agreement or a contract agreed [individually or collectively] and which carries out activities directly arising therefrom."[134] It is, in short, and according to the Explanatory Memorandum of the Directive's proposal, any institu-

---

129 IORP I Directive (see footnote 77).
130 IORP II Directive (see footnote 96).
131 See the Explanatory Memorandum to the IORP I Directive, COM(2000) 507 final; Explanatory Memorandum to the IORP II Directive, COM(2014) 167 final.
132 Explanatory Memorandum to the IORP I Directive, COM(2000) 507 final.
133 See Chapter 3.
134 This definition remained in place in the IORP II Directive (see footnote 96).

tion that receives and invests retirement contributions with the "sole purpose" of paying out retirement benefits.[135]

Put simply, occupational pension providers typically provide occupational pension services (i.e., "operate" a pension scheme) on the basis of a contract concluded with employers.[136] That contract may have resulted from collective bargaining between the employer and employees or their representatives, or may have been concluded by the employer on his employees' behalf.

To more clearly differentiate an IORP from other types of financial institutions, the Memorandum notes that it is important that an IORP cannot pay out the retirement benefits until the retirement age has been reached; "In other words, the rights acquired cannot be 'surrendered' before the age of retirement, otherwise the scheme does not constitute a pension scheme but a savings product."[137] Article 2 of IORP II excludes a number of institutions from the definition. It is not a (first-pillar) social security institution, nor – in principle[138] – is it an institution already covered by the Life Assurance Directive or any other type of financial institution identified in Article 2(2)(b), nor an institution that operates on a pay-as-you-go (PAYG) basis, nor is it an institution where the employees of a company have no legal rights to benefits (such as a German 'Unterstützungskasse'[139]) nor is it a company using a book-reserve scheme.

An IORP is, therefore, defined by what it is, as much as by what it is not.[140] In light of this rather broad definition, it appears that the Member States are left with considerable discretion in specifying under their national legislation which domestic institutions will be considered IORPs and which ones will not.[141] The definition is "generic enough" to accommodate the large diversity of institutions found in the EU.[142] This manner of describing what constitutes an "IORP" has been retained in the IORP II Directive.[143]

---

135 Explanatory Memorandum to the IORP II Directive, COM(2014) 167 final.

136 M Reiner, 'Strukturfragen zum Zusammenspiel von Aufsichts- und Arbeitsrecht im europäischen Pensionsfondsgeschäft gemäß IORP II' in D Krömer and others (eds), *Arbeitsrecht und Arbeitswelt im Europäischen Wandel* (Nomos 2016) 193.

137 Explanatory Memorandum IORP II Directive, COM(2014) 167 final.

138 In principle, because Member States may voluntarily apply certain provisions of the IORP Directive to the occupational pensions business of life assurance undertakings (LADs) in accordance with article 4 of the Directive. This clause has been included in order to prevent the distortion of competition between IORPs and LADs by applying the same prudential requirements to the occupational pension business of LADs.

139 European Federation for Retirement Provision, *European institutions for occupational retirement provision: the EFRP model for Pan-European pensions* (European Federation for Retirement Provision 2003).

140 ibid.

141 ibid 6.

142 C Bittner, 'Occupational Pensions: a Matter of European Concern' (2001) Vol 2 (2) European Business Organization Law Review 401, 417-418.

143 Compare the Article 6(a) of IORP I Directive (see footnote 77) and Article 6(1) of IORP II Directive (see footnote 96).

5.3   Why Cross-Border IORPs?

This section will consider the theory surrounding cross-border IORPs. Several European
multinationals are enjoying the benefits of pan-European consolidation of their pension
schemes.[144] There are also commercial, multi-employer pension providers entering the
market seeking to attract business from employers across the EU.[145]

Efficiency

Cross-border IORPs are intended to benefit the sustainability of European pension systems by offering lower costs and better investment returns.[146] The European Insurance
and Occupational Pensions Authority (EIOPA), one of the three EU supervisory authorities for the financial market, touts scale economies as "one of the main advantages" of a
cross-border IORP.[147] It also notes that before the adoption of the IORP Directive, IORPs
would operate mainly within their own Member State and that cross-border activity existed only between the UK and Ireland due to the similarity of their legal systems. It notes
that, because of this, "a company operating in 15 Member States would have called on the
services of 15 different IORPs incurring a cost of up to €40 million a year."[148] The lower
costs are achieved through economies of scale by cross-border consolidation of multiple
funds, bundling the administration of multiple funds resulting in lowering administration costs. Efficiencies are also achieved by saving money on investment and custody fees;
the Commission notes that "[a]n estimate suggests that a multinational company combining five pension schemes from different countries with assets totalling € 1 billion could
expect to save around € 1-2 million per year."[149] The possibility of cross-border consolidation therefore appears to have attractive benefits for multinational corporations. But it

---

144 See, for example, B Nürk & J Macco, 'Cross-Border – von Frankfurt nach Wien: Nicht so einfach nach
   Österreich' (LEITERbAV.de, 08 December 2015) www.lbav.de/nicht-einfach-so-nach-oesterreich/ accessed
   13 November 2019; N Trappenburg, 'Pensioenverhuizing naar België bijna een feit' *Financieel Dagblad*
   (2 June 2016); B Ottawa, 'HINTERGRUND: Erster deutsch-österreichischer pensionfonds am Start" *IPE
   Institutional Investment* (23 November 2015); L Kok & H Geboers, *Grensoverschrijdende Pensioenuitvoering*
   (SEO Economisch Onderzoek 2016); Ernst & Young, *Pan-European pension funds in a future world* (Ernst &
   Young 2009) 17; For the reasons motivating Dutch employers to accommodate their pension schemes with a
   provider from another Member State, see L Kok, F van der Lecq, E Lutjens, *Verplichtgestelde bedrijfstakpensioenfondsen en het algemeen pensioenfonds* (SEO Economisch Onderzoek 2015) 15 et seq.
145 Such as Aon Hewitt's United Pensions, www.unitedpensions.nl/ accessed 13 November 2019.
146 I Guardiancich, 'Pan-European pension funds: Current situation and future prospects' (2011) Vol 64 (1)
   International Social Security Review 15, 22 et seq.
147 EIOPA, '2017 Market development report on occupational pensions and cross-border IORPs' (2018) EIO-
   PA-BOS-18/013, 18, available at eiopa.europa.eu/publications/reports accessed 18 September 2019.
148 ibid, p. 18.
149 European Commission, 'Impact Assessment Accompanying the document Proposal for a Directive of the
   European Parliament and of the Council on the activities and supervision of institutions for occupational
   retirement provision' SWD(2014) 103 final.

can also be attractive for smaller pension funds struggling with low efficiency and high cost. Regarding the benefits for smaller funds, several Dutch studies have concluded that especially smaller funds could benefit from consolidation to save on administrative and investment costs.[150] The costs of small funds in the Netherlands are higher than those of larger ones.[151] The ongoing trend of fund consolidation is not unique to the Netherlands, and is perceptible across the EU.[152]

The idea of national consolidation should hold true also in an international context: if national funds consolidate on an international level, the economies to be achieved could potentially be even higher than in a national context. "For European pension funds, it seems that bigger is better."[153]

Governance and Operational Risk

For a multinational corporation with pension obligations in a number of different EU Member States, operating pension schemes from one entity can provide a better overview of risks and weaknesses. In particular, it would allow for improved coordination of and control over benefit design, funding, investment, administration and communication.[154]

Simplification: Benefits for Employer and Employee

The fact that pension schemes can be administered from one country offers not only efficiency gains but also avoids time-consuming, costly and complex asset transfers involved in changing pension scheme and provider in case of (cross border) job changes. It also offers the advantage of having one contact point: "Being insured in one pan-European fund means dealing with a single payout institution."[155] This benefits the mobility of an employee who can keep paying into the same scheme with the same company and helps employers – often a multinational corporation – save costs by not needing an administrative office in every country in which they are present, avoiding costs of "duplication."[156] This can be achieved by centralisation and standardisation of several as-

---

150 J Bikker, 'De kostenefficiëntie van pensioenfondsen' (2013) Vol 4 Tijdschrift voor pensioenvraagstukken 15.

151 J Bikker, 'De optimale schaal van pensioenfondsen' (2013) 98(4662) Economisch Statistische Berichten 378.

152 L Blows, 'Better together', European Pensions February/March 2014, available at www.europeanpensions. net/ep/feb-mar-better-together accessed 9 September 2016.

153 ibid.

154 Ernst & Young, *Pan-European pension funds in a future world* (Ernst & Young 2009) 17; J Lommen, 'De API is een no-brainer' (2009) No 25 Netspar NEA Papers 27 et seq, available at www.netspar.nl/assets/uploads/ NEA_25_WEB.pdf accessed 20 November 2019; European Federation for Retirement Provision, *European institutions for occupational retirement provision: the EFRP model for Pan-European pensions* (European Federation for Retirement Provision 2003) 21-22.

155 I Guardiancich & D Natali, 'The EU and Supplementary Pensions: Instruments for Integration and the Market for Occupational Pensions in Europe' (2009) 2009.11 ETUI Working Paper 19.

156 Ernst & Young, *Pan-European pension funds in a future world* (Ernst & Young 2009) 17.

pects relating to the pension plan, such as asset management, administration, risk management and communication.

As noted previously, the mobility for workers can also be enhanced by their benefits within a single European fund, which means dealing with one payout institution. Additionally, workers would have the benefit of consistent and comparable benefit structures, as the pension schemes for the several Member States in which the employer is active can mimic these.[157] This should allow for a well-informed choice when taking up work in another Member State.

Cost savings cannot be achieved only by multinational corporations: businesses operating on a small or local-scale could, according to the Commission also save costs by joining an existing IORP.[158] These companies could benefit from institutions with great experience offering their services in Member States where the market for occupational pensions is underdeveloped.

5.4   What is the IORP II Directive?

First and foremost, the IORP II Directive is a financial services directive that regulates the activity of IORPs. It does in principle not regulate the products or schemes that these institutions offer:[159] according to the Directive, the Member States remain responsible for the organisation of their own pension systems.[160] The IORP II Directive does, however, directly influence national legislation determining the basic operation of national pension systems. It regulates, *inter alia*, the cross-border activity of IORPs,[161] as well as funding requirements,[162] governance requirements,[163] requirements for the information to be given by the IORPs to their scheme members,[164] supervision of IORPs and enforcement rules for their home state supervisory authorities,[165] enshrines the so-called 'prudent person principle' (to be discussed in chapter 3),[166] etc. It does not affect how Member States tax pension contributions and benefits.

The Directive has paved the way for an internal market for occupational pensions. By prescribing the mutual recognition of pension providers and the supervisory regimes

---

157 European Federation for Retirement Provision, *European institutions for occupational retirement provision: the EFRP model for Pan-European pensions* (European Federation for Retirement Provision 2003) 19.
158 European Commission, 'Impact Assessment Accompanying the document Proposal for a Directive of the European Parliament and of the Council on the activities and supervision of institutions for occupational retirement provision' SWD(2014) 103 final.
159 See, to this effect, Explanatory Memorandum to the IORP I Directive, COM(2000) 507 final.
160 Although, as discussed in Chapter 2, that is a debatable contention.
161 See Article 11 IORP II Directive.
162 Title II IORP II Directive.
163 Title III IORP II Directive.
164 Title IV IORP II Directive.
165 Title V IORP II Directive.
166 Article 19 IORP II Directive.

between Member States, the IORP (II) Directive makes cross-border activity of pension providers possible, "thereby opening up a potentially massive space for the Europeanization of second pillar old- age protection."[167]

Yet the total number of cross-border IORPs has remained fairly low. At the end of 2016, just 73 IORPs out of 155,481 were active on a cross-border basis.[168] Pension stakeholders offer a variety of explanations for this low pan-European activity, such as a lack of awareness of the existence of a cross-border framework and the duration, cost and complexity of setting up a cross-border IORP caused largely by diversity in national legislation (see Chapter 5).[169]

Consequently, critical authors opine that the Directive "did not lead to full liberalisation as member states with more restrictions on investments largely succeeded in defending their domestic rules (especially for occupational schemes with solidarity aims)"[170] and that it moreover did not solve all cross-border-related difficulties: the Directive does not aim to bring about a harmonisation of national pension systems and does not touch upon fiscal barriers between the Member States.

Nevertheless, the fact that the IORP (II) Directive has made a first step towards a single market for occupational pensions and that cross-border IORPs have been set up successfully make this directive an important achievement of EU legislation. In addition, the possible advantages a cross-border IORP could have for pension scheme members makes it an interesting research subject, however so far academic literature on it has been fairly limited.

5.5   How Do Cross-Border IORPs Operate?

When engaging in cross-border activity, IORPs are under the prudential supervision of their home Member State, while the pension schemes they offer in another Member State are to comply with the applicable local legislation to occupational pension schemes, called social and labour law. Prudential legislation comprises matters such as the funding re-

---

167 I Guardiancich & D Natali, 'The Changing EU 'Pension Programme': Policy Tools and Ideas in the Shadow of the Crisis' in D Natali (ed), *The New Pension Mix in Europe: Recent Reforms, Their Distributional Effects and Political Dynamics* (PIE Peter Lang 2017).

168 EIOPA, '2017 Market development report on cross-border occupational pensions and cross-border IORPs' (2018) EIOPA-BOS-18/013, 19, available at eiopa.europa.eu/publications/reports accessed 18 September 2019.

169 ibid 22-24.

170 I Guardiancich & D Natali, 'The EU and Supplementary Pensions: Instruments for Integration and the Market for Occupational Pensions in Europe' (2009) 2009.11 ETUI Working Paper 11. See also A Hennessy, *The Europeanization of Workplace Pensions: Economic Interests, Social Protection, and Credible Signaling* (Cambridge University Press 2013) 73; M Haverland, 'When the welfare state meets the regulatory state: EU occupational pension policy' (2007) Vol 14 (6) Journal of European Public Policy 886, 899..

quirements of an IORP, investment rules and the governance of IORPs.[171] The scope of these rules differs between the Member States.

There is no generally agreed-upon definition of what social and labour law is and what it encompasses, and the definition of what comprises social and labour law is left to the Member States.[172] Despite the lack of a definition, it becomes apparent from the registry of national social and labour law that EIOPA keeps – with information pamphlets submitted by the Member States themselves – that social and labour law comprises matters such as vesting and waiting periods, provisions regarding pension contributions and benefits, contract law, legislation on guarantees and risk sharing and pension transfers.[173]

Figure 2

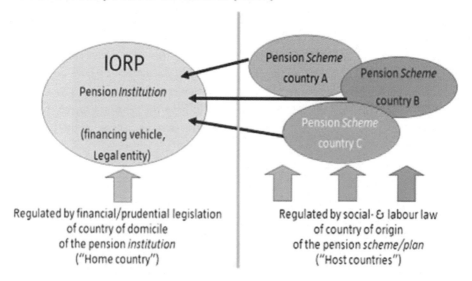

Cross-border pension institution (IORP)

Source: J. Lommen 'De API is een no-brainer', Netspar NEA Papers 2009, No 25, p. 15.

According to Article 11(2) IORP II, an IORP proposing to carry out cross-border activity and to accept sponsorship from a sponsoring undertaking must receive prior authorisation of the relevant competent authority of its home Member State. The IORP is to notify its supervisory authority of its plans regarding cross-border activity and supply it with information.[174] That authority then grants its authorisation, "unless it has issued a rea-

---

171 Article 46 IORP II Directive.
172 See Chapter 5.
173 See the EIOPA webpage on Social and Labor Law at eiopa.europa.eu/regulation-supervision/pensions/occupational-pensions/social-and-labour-law accessed 20 November 2019.
174 Article 11(3) IORP II IORP II Directive.

soned decision that the administrative structure or the financial situation of the IORP or the good repute or professional qualifications or experience of the persons running the IORP are not compatible with the proposed cross-border activity."[175]

The home state authority then forwards the information it has received from the IORP to the competent authorities in the planned host state. The authorities in the host state inform the home state authority of the applicable social and labour law under which the pension scheme sponsored by an undertaking in the host Member State must be operated and of the information requirements of the host Member State which applies to the cross-border activity. The home state authority subsequently provides that information to the IORP.[176]

6 TAKING EU-LEVEL ACTION: THE POLITICAL CONTEXT

As discussed in the previous paragraphs, to a greater or lesser extent, all Member States' pension systems are facing largely the same challenges of demographic change, economic challenges and pension-related obstacles to mobility for their citizens. In a bid to respond to these challenges, the EU has formulated a number of policy goals and launched various legislative initiatives, to be discussed in-depth in Chapter 3.

However, at the same time, the European landscape for occupational pensions is complex and diverse, with different philosophies, architectures and traditions in all Member States. The social security systems of the Member States "are primarily the result of circumstances individual to each Member State."[177] They were borne out of circumstances such as "national economic and demographic changes, national ideological and political traditions and of the balance of power between government, workers, employers and the self-employed."[178]

Consequently, a policy area as sensitive as pensions is bound to come accompanied by some reservation and opposition from the Member States. Indeed, Member States regard pensions as a national prerogative that is to be fiercely defended. Haverland posits two reasons for the reluctance on the part of Member States to accept EU involvement.[179] First, the provision of welfare systems is an important factor in legitimising the nation state, and welfare state policies yield "allegiance to political parties." Second is a practical reason, namely that the different architectures of welfare systems in the EU "complicate

---

175 Article 11(4) IORP II IORP II Directive.
176 Article 11(7) IORP II IORP II Directive.
177 D Pieters & S Vansteenkiste, *The Thirteenth State: Towards a European Community Social Insurance Scheme for Intra-Community Migrants* (Acco Uitgeverij 1993) 10.
178 ibid.
179 M Haverland, 'When the welfare state meets the regulatory state: EU occupational pension policy' (2007) Vol 14 (6) Journal of European Public Policy 886.

common European policies". Member States seem reluctant to cede social policy competencies to the EU.[180]

Certainly when adopting harmonising legislation, attention must be paid so as not to disturb the often delicate relationships between various components of national social security systems. Pieters and Vansteenkiste note that any attempt at harmonisation of national social security systems "would be in danger of artificially breaking [...] socio-economic balances."[181] This logic seems to apply to occupational pensions as well. Harmonisation of the occupational pension systems of every Member State could also upset the balance between the pillars, potentially destabilising the social security systems of the Member States extending beyond pillar 2 pension systems.

Despite the EU Treaty provisions that (indirectly) allow for regulating occupational pensions, to be discussed in Chapter 2, the political challenges that present themselves when legislating in this field can be observed in the legislative processes surrounding secondary pension law. For instance, the Netherlands[182] and the United Kingdom[183] governments initially forwarded subsidiarity concerns to the Commission over the recast of the IORP Directive.[184] While national governments showed a generally positive attitude towards the reshaping of the IORP directive, political parties voiced concern over too much meddling by the EU in their national pension policies.[185] Such concerns led the Dutch Parliament to issue a yellow card in the recast procedure of the IORP Directive,[186] and prompted the Prime Minister to announce that he would resist the reform.[187] National exigencies also made it challenging to shepherd the original IORP Directive through the legislative process; countries with large book reserve schemes, such as Germany, opposed application of the directive to such schemes and succeeded,[188] consequently the IORP Directive does not apply to such schemes and therefore these IORPs

---

180 ibid.
181 D Pieters & S Vansteenkiste, *The Thirteenth State: Towards a European Community Social Insurance Scheme for Intra-Community Migrants* (Acco Uitgeverij 1993) 12.
182 Parliament of the Netherlands, Letter from Dutch Parliament to the European Commission, 15 May 2014, www.eerstekamer.nl/eu/overig/20140514/brief_tweede_kamer_aan_de/f=/vjjsijdsxjzt.pdf accessed 29 August 2016.
183 House of Lords, Letter from the House of Lords to the President of the European Commission of 9 July 2014 on the Proposal for a Directive of the European Parliament and of the Council on the activities and supervision of institutions for occupational retirement provision (recast).
184 The IORP Directive and its history will be discussed in Chapters 3 to 5.
185 Kamerstukken II 2015/16, 33 931, nr. 18; Party electoral program VVD 2012-2017, 17 https://www.vvd.nl/verkiezingsprogramma_s/ accessed 29 December 2019.
186 Pensioenfederatie, "Tweede Kamer trekt gele kaart over IORP-richtlijn", http://www.pensioenfederatie.nl/actueel/nieuws/Pages/Tweede_Kamer_trekt_gele_kaart_over_IORPrichtlijn_775.aspx, accessed on 9 September 2016.
187 Transcript of the Parliamentary hearing on 14 May 2014 on "Steering by Europe in the social and economic arenas", where the Prime Minister was quoted as having said: "Daar zullen wij ons als Nederland tegen verzetten. Ik beloof me daarvoor in te zetten", available at www.eerstekamer.nl/behandeling/20140514/aansturing_vanuit_europa_op/document3/f=/vjkdh48wnbzb.pdf, accessed 20 November 2019 .
188 A Hennessy, *The Europeanization of Workplace Pensions: Economic Interests, Social Protection and Credible Signaling* (Cambridge University Press 2013) 90.

need not be fully funded – as opposed to occupational pension schemes in the Netherlands and the UK.[189]

Another example is the failed "portability directive"[190] – initially intended to allow in particular for the portability of pension rights with an intent to remove obstacles to the free movement of workers between Member States.[191] That directive eventually became the Supplementary Pension Rights Directive.[192] Owing largely to the Netherlands' "unprecedented veto in the Council"[193] and Germany's "vociferous" opposition,[194] as well as a failure of social partners to reach an agreement,[195] the end result was a "lowest common denominator solution" that avoided the most salient issues, such as the transferability of pensions.[196]

The Safeguard Directive, too, exhibited a successive watering-down of initial proposal, reducing it to a directive of little practical import in the mobility of workers.[197]

These responses reflect the difficulty with which the EU is sometimes faced when it comes to legislating on pensions. However, EU-level action in this field could add value in certain areas if action by the Member States alone is not sufficient to attain the desired objective. Examples of such cases are the aforementioned issue of pension portability or the access of pension funds to the EU's Single Market. In the Impact Assessment accompanying the revised IORP Directive, the Commission noted that action by the Member States alone will not "(i) remove obstacles to cross-border activities of IORPs; (ii) ensure a higher EU-wide minimum level of consumer protection; (iii) lead to scale economies, risk diversification and innovation inherent to cross-border activity; (iv) avoid regulatory

---

189 T van den Brink, H van Meerten & S de Vries, 'Regulating Pensions: Why the European Union Matters' (2011) Netspar Discussion Paper, 39, available at ssrn.com/abstract=1950765 accessed 20 November 2019.

190 Commission of the European Communities, 'Proposal for a Directive on improving the portability of supplementary pension rights' COM(2005) 507 final.

191 The main goals of the proposed portability directive were to harmonize conditions on the acquisition, preservation and transferability of occupational pension rights. See the 2005 proposal (COM(2005) 507 final).

192 Directive 2014/50/EU of the European Parliament and of the Council of 16 April 2014 on minimum requirements for enhancing worker mobility between Member States by improving the acquisition and preservation of supplementary pension rights (Supplementary Pension Rights Directive). See, on this process, W Baugniet, *The protection of occupational pensions under European Union law on the freedom of movement for workers*, dissertation European University Institute Florence (2014)..

193 I Guardiancich, 'Portability of Supplementary Pension Rights in Europe: A Lowest Common Denominator Solution' (2015) Vol 1 (1) European Policy Analysis 74, 85.

194 A Hennessy, *The Europeanization of Workplace Pensions: Economic Interests, Social Protection, and Credible Signaling* (Cambridge University Press 2013) 96.

195 W Baugniet, *The protection of occupational pensions under European Union law on the freedom of movement for workers*, dissertation European University Institute Florence (2014) 183 et seq.

196 I Guardiancich, 'Portability of Supplementary Pension Rights in Europe: A Lowest Common Denominator Solution' (2015) Vol 1 (1) European Policy Analysis 74.

197 W Baugniet, *The protection of occupational pensions under European Union law on the freedom of movement for workers*, dissertation European University Institute Florence (2014).

arbitrage between financial services sectors; (v) avoid regulatory arbitrage between Member States; and (vi) take into account the interests of cross-border workers."[198] All six identified reasons are reasons that can justify EU intervention, especially considering that legislative action will not strike at the heart of Member States competences: the organisation of their pension systems is still primarily in their hands.

7   RESEARCH FOCUS

The main focus of this research is on the legislative measures taken as a consequence of the challenges discussed in Section 3 and how those efforts are to be perceived from the perspective of European pension scheme members. I will discuss in detail the (second) Directive on the activities and supervision of institutions for occupational retirement provision[199] (IORP II Directive[200]), as well as the so-called PEPP Regulation[201] – introduced in Chapter 6 – and what consequences these legislative acts bring for European pension scheme members. This research focuses on European pension law, it does not cover matters pertaining to taxation.

Given the diversity of the EU's pensions landscape, it may seem somewhat strange to speak of European pension law – there are many pension laws within the EU. But although the pension systems of the EU Member States are primarily regulated at the national level, the EU has concerned itself with the pension systems of the Member States for several decades. It has adopted directives and regulations that coordinate and/or harmonize certain aspects of occupational pensions. For the purposes of this book, European pension law includes all EU primary and secondary legislation applicable to pensions, as well soft law instruments, European Court of Justice (ECJ) case law and legal principles consequential to pensions. The EU's concrete powers in the area of pensions are discussed in Chapter 2.

8   THE MAIN RESEARCH QUESTION

Europe's population is ageing. This development seems to drive up the cost of public systems of retirement provision in the Member States. In addition, workers still face occupational pension-related hurdles when moving to other Member States. Over the years, the EU has spelled out policy goals and, based on these, has taken several initiatives

---

198 European Commission, 'Impact Assessment Accompanying the document Proposal for a Directive of the European Parliament and of the Council on the activities and supervision of institutions for occupational retirement provision' SWD(2014) 103 final.
199 In non-EU law terms, Institutions for Occupational Retirement Provision (IORPs) are pension funds.
200 IORP II Directive 2016/2341/EU (see footnote 96).
201 European Commission, 'Proposal for a Regulation of the European Parliament and pf the Council on a pan-European Personal Pension Product (PEPP)' COM(2017) 343 final.

to address these problems. The EU has also adopted two directives aimed directly at facilitating worker mobility from the perspective of occupational pensions: the Safeguard Directive and the Supplementary Pension Rights Directive.

Other legislative acts borne out of these policy goals are the original IORP Directive and its successor, the IORP II Directive. One of the IORP (II) Directive's aims is to enable cross-border activity for pension providers with the intention of affording them the advantages of the Single Market. These advantages include investment freedoms, scale economies through international consolidation and competition-driven innovation, which in turn ought to bring new business opportunities for pension providers and higher pension results for scheme members.

Despite EU-level efforts, cross-border activity of IORPs remains limited and cross-border movement of workers remains problematic owing to obstacles caused by occupational pensions. Responding adequately to the aforementioned problems at the EU level appears difficult for two reasons. First, the occupational pension landscape in Europe is very diverse, preventing a one-size-fits-all-solution. That diversity makes it challenging to act at the European level, as legislation and preferences differ and, sometimes, collide. Second, the EU's specific prerogatives to regulate occupational pensions and the sensitivity of the topic make for a challenging legal and political arena in which to legislate. These two main themes serve as an assessment framework against which legislative measures will be discussed.

Consequently, the main question of this study is the following:

> *How does EU pension legislation secure the mobility of workers and the use of the advantages of the Single Market to the benefit of pension scheme members to achieve safe, adequate and sustainable pensions; and which alternatives are possible to remedy any weaknesses?*

The main research question can be answered with the help of the following **sub-questions**:
- What are the EU's prerogatives in the field of occupational pensions? (**Chapter 2**)
- What are the goals of EU pension policy generally, and the IORP (II) Directive specifically? (**Chapter 3**)
- From the perspective of a pension scheme member, how is the IORP II Directive's framework regarding cross-border IORPs to be assessed? For instance, to what extent does a cross-border IORP ensure mobility and how well suited is it to cross-border operation when the interests of scheme members are taken into account? (**Chapter 4**)

– If a cross-border IORP has certain benefits in terms of mobility and if it can offer certain efficiencies, how well is the legislative framework for cross-border IORPs tailored to cross-border operation from the perspective of a provider? (**Chapter 5**)
– If there are shortcomings to EU legislation regulating (the cross-border provision of) occupational pensions, what are the possibilities for the EU to legislate personal pension products in the third pillar? Could the legislation adopted in the third pillar be a solution to any shortcomings in the second pillar? (**Chapter 6**)
– Conclusion (**Chapter 7**)

Chapter 2: The EU and the Member States' Pension Systems: Legitimising EU Involvement with National Pension Systems

1   Introduction

As noted in Chapter 1, regulating pension systems of the Member States occurs primarily at the national level. However, EU law influences national pension systems in a multitude of ways.[202] This influence is exerted through positive and negative integration. Positive integration comes from EU legislative instruments and soft law and coordinative instruments like the Open Method of Coordination (OMC). Negative integration occurs through the prohibitions addressed at the Member States in the context of the "four freedoms"[203] enshrined in the Treaties – and the general principles enshrined in EU law that national pension systems must comply with. EU law is enforced by the European Court of Justice (ECJ).

Despite this assortment of sources of influence, integration in the realm of pensions "has been traditionally limited."[204] This chapter – along the subsequent chapter – shows that in spite of the many sources of EU influence on occupational pension systems, EU legislation adopted so far in this area has fallen well short of its initial objectives. Given the few direct competences to regulate occupational pensions,[205] its internal market powers have been dominant in its legislative efforts on occupational pensions and have left their marks on both the IORP (II) Directive and the proposed PEPP Regulation to be discussed in the next chapters.

---

202 See, for instance, H van Meerten, *EU Pension Law* (Amsterdam University Press 2019); M Haverland, 'When the welfare state meets the regulatory state: EU occupational pension policy' (2007) Vol 14 (6) Journal of European Public Policy 886; T van den Brink, H van Meerten & S de Vries, 'Regulating Pensions: Why the European Union Matters' (2011) Netspar Discussion Paper, available at ssrn.com/abstract=1950765 accessed 20 November 2019; M Hartlapp, 'Deconstructing EU old age policy: Assessing the potential of soft OMCs and hard EU law' (2012) European Integration Online Papers (EIoP), Special Mini-Issue 1, Vol 16, Article 3, available at eiop.or.at/eiop/texte/2012-003a.htm accessed 4 December 2019; M Lodge, 'Comparing Non-Hierarchical Governance in Action: the Open Method of Co-ordination in Pensions and Information Society' (2007) Vol 45 No 2 Journal of Common Market Studies 343.

203 The free movement of goods, persons, services (including establishment) and capital; Article 26(2) TFEU. As – for obvious reasons – only the last three freedoms are applicable to occupational pensions, the free movement of goods will not be discussed.

204 D Natali, *Pensions in Europe, European Pensions* (PIE Peter Lang 2008) 173.

205 K Kalogeropoulou, 'Addressing the Pension Challenge: Can the EU respond? Towards facilitating the portability of supplementary (occupational) pension rights' (2014) Vol 16 (4) European Journal of Law Reform 747, 758; H van Meerten, *EU Pension Law* (Amsterdam University Press 2019).

This chapter discusses EU influence on national occupational pension systems, what the available legal bases for action do and do not allow the EU to do and the rationale behind EU legislative action in occupational pensions. This chapter also shows that although it is frequently said that occupational pensions are the "full responsibility" of the Member States – even in EU directives – that notion is contestable given EU powers and existing regulatory initiatives in this field.[206] Finally, this chapter's inventory of EU powers in the field of occupational pensions places into perspective the objectives of the IORP II Directive and the proposed PEPP Regulation and is used in the conclusion to take stock of possible future avenues for EU occupational pension policy. The next chapter will consider in more detail the stated goals of EU pension policy. Together, Chapters 2 and 3 will argue that lacking EU powers in occupational pensions and political resistance from Member States and other interest groups have led to an imperfect system of EU occupational pension law.

2   THE EU AND OCCUPATIONAL PENSIONS

Since 1991, the Commission has repeatedly emphasised that it is the Member States' prerogative to organise their own pension systems.[207] Despite this, and as discussed throughout this book, the EU has influenced the Member States' pension systems over the years not only by adopting legislation that directly or indirectly influences these, but also through other measures that actively or passively affect Member States' pension systems. In fact, "the Member States' sovereignty and autonomy in the field of social policy and welfare has been 'eroded' though the process of European integration and the growing pressures from the goal of the completion of the internal market."[208]

---

206 For instance, Directive 2016/2341/EU of the European Parliament and of the Council of 14 December 2016 on the activities and supervision of institutions for occupational retirement provision (IORPs) [2016], OJ L 354/37 (IORP II Directive) and Directive 2014/50/EU of the European Parliament and of the Council of 16 April 2014 on minimum requirements for enhancing worker mobility between Member States by improving the acquisition and preservation of supplementary pension rights [2014] OJ L 128/1 (Supplementary Pension Rights Directive) note in their recitals that Member States should retain "full responsibility" for the organization of their pension systems while at the same time implementing rules that directly influence those systems.

207 See, for instance, Commission of the European Communities, 'Supplementary social security schemes: the role of occupational pension schemes in the social protection of workers and their implications for freedom of movement' (Communication from the Commission to the Council) SEC(91) 1332 final; European Parliament, *Report on the proposal for a European Parliament and Council directive on the activities of institutions for occupational retirement provision* (Session document 21 June 2001) A5-0220/2001 final, 9; EIOPA, EIOPA's Advice to the European Commission on the review of the IORP Directive 2003/41/EC (2012) EIOPA-BOS-12/015, 20, 26 and 293; European Council, *Common position adopted by the Council on 5 November 2002 with a view to the adoption of a Directive of the European Parliament and of the Council on the activities and supervision of institutions for occupational retirement provision* (2002) 3.

208 K Kalogeropoulou, 'Addressing the Pension Challenge: Can the EU respond? Towards facilitating the portability of supplementary (occupational) pension rights' (2014) Vol 16 (4) European Journal of Law Reform 747, 759.

The lack of explicit powers for regulating pension systems makes for fierce discussions whenever the EU takes legislative initiatives in this field, and the Member States "jealously" guard what they regard as their prerogatives.[209] The next chapter discusses some of those tensions specifically in the context of the IORP Directive. The previous chapter briefly named the Portability Directive[210] as another example.

As shown in this chapter, the EU has a generous regulatory and non-regulatory arsenal at its disposal to regulate occupational pensions in addition to its all-important prerogatives to regulate its internal market. Furthermore, the European Court of Justice has also played its part in cementing the EU's role as a driver of change in the Member States' pension policies. Finally, when organising their pension systems, there are also provisions in EU law that the Member States must observe.

So what are the powers on the basis of which the EU can act?

3   EU POWERS IN THE FIELD OF OCCUPATIONAL PENSIONS

As noted in the introduction, the EU's influence on national occupational pension systems comes from several sources. These are discussed in the following sections.

With respect to positive integration, we find the harmonisation achieved through EU legislative instruments, soft law and coordinative instruments such as the OMC and positive. Positive integration is an instrument that allows the EU legislator to bring the standards in the legal systems of the Member States closer together with the goal of alleviating large differences that form a barrier to freedom of movement within the EU. Large differences in regulatory standards between the Member States in fields such as consumer protection, health and safety or environmental standards can be a serious obstacle to offer goods or services in other Member States. Positive integration, which with occupational pensions is achieved by directives, aims to even out some of these differences.

Negative integration is achieved through certain prohibitions addressed at the Member States as well as by the general principles enshrined in EU law and negative integration. These prohibitions are contained in primary EU law: The Treaty of Lisbon. EU law, including the prohibitions contained therein, are enforced by the European Court of Justice. This type of integration abolishes barriers that hamper the free movement of goods, services, capital and persons because of their discriminatory nature or because they hinder market access in another way. An example of such a prohibition is Article 56 TFEU on the freedom to provide services, which stipulates that "restrictions on free-

---

209 J Woolfe, 'Letter from Brussels: Social and labour issues' (March 2013) Investment & Pensions Europe, available at www.ipe.com/social-and-labour-issues/50264.fullarticle accessed 4 December 2019; see also M Haverland, 'When the welfare state meets the regulatory state: EU occupational pension policy' (2007) Vol 14 (6) Journal of European Public Policy 886, 887.
210 Now the Supplementary Pension Rights Directive (see footnote 206).

dom to provide services within the Union shall be prohibited in respect of nationals of
Member States who are established in a Member State other than that of the person for
whom the services are intended."

4   POSITIVE INTEGRATION

4.1   Introduction

As a general principle the EU may only pass legislation in the areas in which it has been
explicitly granted such powers: Article 4 of the Treaty on European Union (TEU) stipulates that the competences not conferred upon the Union by the Treaties are to remain
with the Member States. Article 4 refers to Article 5 TEU in which the principle of conferral is enshrined. Under this principle, Article 5(2) TEU explains, the Union may act
only within the scope of the competences conferred upon it by the Member States.

In order to determine on what bases the EU may regulate occupational pensions, it is
necessary to take stock of the relevant EU Treaty articles. The Treaty on the Functioning
of the European Union contains an inventory list in Articles 3 to 6 of policy areas on
which the EU may act. It differentiates between exclusive, shared, coordinating and complementary competences.[211] Exclusive competences are those competences on which the
EU alone may legislate and adopt legally binding acts. Exclusive competences exist in the
fields of the customs union, the establishment of competition rules, the monetary policy
of the Euro countries, the conservation of marine biological resources under the common
fisheries policy and the common commercial policy.

Shared competences are those competences whereby both the Member States and the
EU may legislate. However, Member States may legislate only where the EU has not (yet)
chosen to exercise its legislative powers.[212] Thus, once the EU has legislated within a
specific area, the Member States lose their legislative prerogative. Once the EU ceases to
exercise its competence within a particular field, the Member States "shall again exercise
their competence".[213] Based on the definition of this article, it appears as though it would
be impossible for Member States to exercise any form of legislative power once the EU
has become active within a given field. However, this is not the case.[214] In practice,
Member States and the EU have legislated in the same field at the same time. Depending
on how the Union legislator has exercised its powers and the latitude leaves to the Member States, Union legislative action in a particular field need not always be pre-emptive.

---

211 Article 2 TFEU.
212 P Craig & G de Búrca, *EU Law: Text, Cases and Materials* (5th edn, Oxford University Press 2011), 83 et seq.
213 Article 2(2) TFEU.
214 R Schütze, 'EU Competences: Existence and Exercise' in A Arnull & D Chalmers (eds), *The Oxford Handbook of European Law* (Oxford University Press 2015), 86.

Policy areas that fall under this competence are, *inter alia*, the internal market, social policy, agriculture and fisheries (minus the conservation of marine biological resources), the environment, consumer protection, transport, energy etc.

Regarding the Union's coordinating competences, the Union may adopt guidelines and initiatives to ensure coordination, however the constitutional remit of this competence remains largely undefined.[215] Employment policies and the coordination of social policies fall under this competence.

Finally, the EU has complementary competences. The precise scope of these powers is, again, not entirely clear-cut but Article 2(5) TFEU at the very least excludes harmonisation on the policy areas listed in this article. The policy areas for this type of competence are listed – presumably exhaustively owing to their residual character[216] – in Article 6 TFEU.

The aforementioned Article 5 TEU also proclaims in paragraph 3 that using Union competences – also, necessarily, the powers it exercises in pensions – must be governed by the principles of proportionality and subsidiarity. This principle regulates the use of the powers that the EU has been given, and was introduced by the Maastricht Treaty to "curb the 'federalist' leanings of the Community."[217] This underlying rationale is that legislative action should be taken closest to those affected. This principle needs to be considered only where Union action concerns competences other than exclusive competences. In accordance with this principle, first, the EU legislator may act only if the objectives pursued cannot be addressed sufficiently by action at the level of the Member States. Second, the subsidiarity principle bars Union legislative action when it cannot be proven that EU action is appropriate due to the scale and effects. The final requirement set out by this action is that EU action should not go further than what is necessary to achieve the objective.

This third and final requirement is known as the proportionality test, and is enshrined in Article 5(4) TFEU.

4.2   *Legal Bases for Positive Integration*

The choice of legal basis is often a "controversial issue",[218] and the Court of Justice has developed criteria that must be satisfied if the basis upon which the legislative act is founded is to withstand judicial scrutiny.[219] These criteria do not, however, detract

---

215 ibid 87.
216 ibid.
217 P Craig & G de Búrca, *EU Law: Text, Cases and Materials* (5th edn, Oxford University Press 2011), 95.
218 H van Meerten, *EU Pension Law* (Amsterdam University Press 2019).
219 See H van Meerten, *EU Pension Law* (Amsterdam University Press 2019); P Leino, 'The Institutional Politics of Objective Choice: Competence as a Framework for Argumentation' in S Gerben & I Govaere (eds), *The Division of Competences Between the EU and the Member States: Reflections on the Past, Present and the Future* (Hart Publishing 2017).

from the fact that "the choice of legal basis is far from the objective, neutral or non-political exercise that the Court's jurisprudence claims it should be."[220] It appears as if the lack of a dedicated legal basis upon which to regulate occupational pensions, as well as resistance from the Member States and other interest groups has led to EU occupational pensions legislation to miss its initial goals. The following section examines a few of these legal bases, the next chapter will give more attention to the consequences of the legal basis chosen to underpin EU pension legislation, along with the political backgrounds of that legislation.

A   *The Internal Market*

According to Article 26 TFEU, the Union is to adopt measures with the goal of "establishing or ensuring the internal market, in accordance with the relevant provisions of the Treaties." This internal market is an area that is free from internal frontiers and in which goods, persons, services and capital can move freely. This provision is also necessary for the cross-border provision of pensions, as companies active in the market for pensions wishing to offer their services in another Member State may be hindered from doing this by national laws. The provisions on the free movement of goods, persons, services and capital, the famous four freedoms, contain provisions of negative integration. The EU may, however, also actively pursue positive harmonisation through secondary legislation to advance the goals of the internal market.

The legal basis for that is Article 114 TFEU,[221] and is one of the most frequently used Treaty provisions as a legal basis for EU legislative action.[222] According to that provision, the European Parliament and the Council shall adopt the measures for the approximation of laws of the Member States which have as their objective the establishment and functioning of the internal market. Of course, conditions apply here as well. The ECJ has reined in an overzealous European legislator by ruling that the measures adopted under Article 114 TFEU must contribute to the functioning of the internal market by removing appreciable obstacles; differences in legislation between the Member States do not qualify as such merely by themselves.[223] In the Tobacco Advertising case, the CJEU makes reference to the principle of conferral when it recalls that what is now Article 106 TFEU

---

220 P Leino, 'The Institutional Politics of Objective Choice: Competence as a Framework for Argumentation' in S Gerben & I Govaere (eds), *The Division of Competences Between the EU and the Member States: Reflections on the Past, Present and the Future* (Hart Publishing 2017), 230.

221 See H van Meerten, *EU Pension Law* (Amsterdam University Press 2019) for a more detailed discussion of the choice of a legal basis.

222 T van den Brink, H van Meerten & S de Vries, 'Regulating Pensions: Why the European Union Matters' (2011) Netspar Discussion Paper, 3, available at ssrn.com/abstract=1950765 accessed 20 November 2019; P Craig & G de Búrca, *EU Law: Text, Cases and Materials* (5th edn, Oxford University Press 2011) 582; I Maletić, *The Law and Policy of Harmonisation in Europe's Internal Market* (Edward Elgar Publishing 2013) 1.

223 T van den Brink, H van Meerten & S de Vries, 'Regulating Pensions: Why the European Union Matters' (2011) Netspar Discussion Paper, 4, available at ssrn.com/abstract=1950765 accessed 20 November 2019.

constitutes no general power to regulate the internal market, but that it may exercise only those powers conferred on it by the Treaties: "a measure adopted under Article 100a of the Treaty [now Article 114 TFEU] must genuinely have as its object the improvement of the conditions for the establishment and functioning of the internal market. If a mere finding of disparities between national rules and of the abstract risk of obstacles to the exercise of fundamental freedoms or of distortions of competition liable to result therefrom were sufficient to justify the choice of Article 100a as a legal basis, judicial review of compliance with the proper legal basis might be rendered nugatory."[224] While the Court is generally lenient when it comes to restricting the broad wording of the Treaty Articles, it has done so in the aforementioned case.[225]

Additionally, Article 48 TFEU provides that the European Parliament and the Council shall, acting in accordance with the ordinary legislative procedure, adopt such measures in the field of social security as are necessary to provide freedom of movement for workers.[226] The coordination regulations,[227] coordinating inter alia statutory pension systems, are based on this provision. In the field of occupational pensions, the Safeguard Directive[228] has as its legal bases Articles 48 and 352 TFEU.

B   Social Policy

Article 153 TFEU is a social policy legal basis which could serve to advance occupational pension legislation. That provision lists several social fields in which the EU "shall support and complement the activities of the Member States," which includes the social security and social protection of workers,[229] as well as the modernization of social protection systems.[230] The measures adopted under Article 153 TFEU, in which social security and social protection and occupational pensions are included, may not affect the Member States' rights to define themselves the "fundamental principles of their social

---

224 Case C-376/98 *Germany v. European Parliament and Council (Tobacco Advertising I)* [2000] ECLI:EU: C:2000:544.

225 P Craig & G de Búrca, *EU Law: Text, Cases and Materials* (6th edn, Oxford University Press 2015) 75-76.

226 That provision contains, in its second paragraph, a so-called emergency brake: "Where a member of the Council declares that a draft legislative act referred to in the first subparagraph would affect important aspects of its social security system, including its scope, cost or financial structure, or would affect the financial balance of that system, it may request that the matter be referred to the European Council. In that case, the ordinary legislative procedure shall be suspended."

227 Council Regulation EEC No 1408/71 of 14 June 1971 on the application of social security schemes to employed persons and their families moving within the Community [1971] OJ L 149/2 and Council Regulation 574/72 of 21 March 1972 fixing the procedure for implementing Regulation (EEC) No 1408/71 on the application of social security schemes to employed persons and their families moving within the Community [1972] OJ L 74/1, as well as their replacement Regulation (EC) No 883/2004 of the European Parliament and the Council of 29 April 2004 on the coordination of social security systems [2004] OJ L 166/1.

228 Council Directive 98/49/EC of 29 June 1998 on safeguarding the supplementary pension rights of employed and self-employed persons moving within the Community [1998] OJ L 209/46 (Safeguard Directive).

229 Article 153(1)(c) TFEU.

230 Article 153(1)(k) TFEU.

security systems and must not significantly affect the financial equilibrium thereof." The
required unanimity in the Council in the field of social policy and the reluctance of
Member States complicates the use of this legal basis for the adoption of formal legislation.[231]

C   Other Provisions

Other Treaty provisions are available besides Article 114 TFEU. While Article 114 TFEU
allows for "true legislation",[232] others allow the regulation of pensions via soft law measures. Article 148 TFEU allows the Council to examine the employment policies of the
Member States and to make recommendations. Article 136 TFEU, on the proper functioning of the economic and monetary union, allows the Council to adopt measures to
strengthen the coordination and surveillance of budgetary discipline of the Member
States and to set out economic policy guidelines for them. These measures can include,
"according to the pact of the Euro, aligning the pension system to the national demographic situation, for example by aligning the effective retirement age with life expectancy
or by increasing participation rates and limiting early retirement schemes and using
targeted incentives to employ older workers (notably in the age tranche above 55)."[233]

Over the past decades, the EU has increasingly become concerned with social policy.
To that end, Article 151 TFEU stipulates that the Union and the Member States are to be
fully aware of social rights and must promote "employment, improved living and working conditions, so as to make possible their harmonization while improvement is being
maintained, proper social protection" etc. To achieve that goal, Article 153 TFEU requires the EU to pursue that goal through the adoption of measures aimed at encouraging
cooperation between them and through the adoption of directives that set minimum
requirements.

---

231 W Baugniet, *The protection of occupational pensions under European Union law on the freedom of movement
for workers*, dissertation European University Institute Florence (2014) 192 et seq.
232 H van Meerten, 'The Scope of the EU 'Pensions'-Directive: Some Background and Solutions for Policymakers' in U Neergaard and others (eds), *Social Services of General Interest in the EU* (TMC Asser Press
2013) 421.
233 ibid.

D   *Specific Legislative Measures in the Field of Occupational Pensions*
The EU legislative measures concerning occupational pensions *directly*[234] were adopted
on the basis of its internal market powers. Their genesis also illustrates the "challenge of
legislating in the area of supplementary pensions."[235] These legislative measures – the
Safeguard Directive, the Supplementary Pension Rights Directive and the IORP II Directive – have been introduced in Chapter 1.[236]

4.3   *Alternatives to Legislation: Soft Governance and the Open Method of*
          Coordination

As indicated, as an alternative to legislative measures, the EU can use the Open Method
of Coordination enshrined in Article 153(2)(a) TFEU.[237] The Open Method of Coordination (OMC) provides a possibility for the EU to achieve common goals through the
coordination of policy efforts without using formal harmonisation, "with the eventual
indirect aim of converging national policies."[238] It was introduced as a new method of
governance at the Lisbon Summit in 2000 and can be applied in policy fields in which
"there are no explicit competencies at the EU level".[239] The Member States are steered
through policy guidelines and priorities as well as recommendations by the Council and
the Commission.[240]

---

234 These are the IORP II Directive (see footnote 206), the Safeguard Directive (see footnote 228) and the
    Supplementary Pension Rights Directive (see footnote 206). Legislative measures affecting occupational
    pension systems of the Member States *indirectly* are, for instance, Council Directive 2000/78/EC of 27 No-
    vember 2000 establishing a general framework for equal treatment in employment and occupation [2000]
    OJ L 303/16 and Directive 2008/94/EC of the European Parliament and of the Council of 22 October 2008
    on the protection of employees in the event of the insolvency of their employer [2008] OJ L 283/36.
235 E Oliver, 'From portability to acquisition and preservation: the challenge of legislating in the area of sup-
    plementary pensions' (2009) Vol 32 (4) Journal of Social Welfare & Family Law, 173.
236 See Chapter 1, section 4.2.
237 P Copeland & B ter Haar, 'The Coordinated governance of EU social security policy: Will there ever be
    enough?' in F Pennings & G Vonk (eds), *Research Handbook on European Social Security Law* (Edward
    Elgar Publishing 2015) 215.
238 P Copeland & B ter Haar, 'The Coordinated governance of EU social security policy: Will there ever be
    enough?' in F Pennings & G Vonk (eds), *Research Handbook on European Social Security Law* (Edward
    Elgar Publishing 2015) 201.
239 M Eckardt, 'The open method of coordination on pensions: an economic analysis of its effects on pension
    reforms' (2005) vol 15 (3) Journal of European Social Policy 247.
240 P Copeland & B ter Haar, 'The Coordinated governance of EU social security policy: Will there ever be
    enough?' in F Pennings & G Vonk (eds), *Research Handbook on European Social Security Law* (Edward
    Elgar Publishing 2015).

Specifically for pensions, the Open Method of Cooperation on Pensions[241] was launched in 2002 in order to coordinate pension reforms in the Member States, but – according to the Council – does "not alter in any way the distribution of responsibilities between the EU and the Member States or between government and the social partners."[242]

The OMC on Pensions was launched on the basis of eleven common objectives for national pension systems to achieve.[243] These are, *inter alia*, the prevention of social exclusion, enabling people to maintain their living standards and the promotion of solidarity.[244] For the OMC on pensions, the Member States were given non-binding rules, such as "open guidelines with the indication of broad goals to be achieved, leaving it up to member states to adopt specific reforms for their implementation."[245] Additionally, "Member states are asked to emulate each other in applying the guidelines, stimulating the exchange of best practices through periodic monitoring, evaluation and peer review accompanied by indicators and benchmarks."[246]

5   NEGATIVE INTEGRATION

This section discusses negative integration. This type of integration is achieved by the prohibitions addressed at the Member States barring them from keeping in place measures that obstruct the free flow of persons, services (including the freedom of establishment) and capital (Section 5.2). The prohibitions are enforced by the European Court of Justice (Section 5.1). However, some obstacles may be justified (Section 5.2.2). In the discussion in Chapter 3 of the IORP II Directive – which intends to promote the creation

---

241 See, *inter alia*, F Chybalski & M Gumola, 'The similarity of European pension systems in terms of OMC objectives: A cross⊠country study' (2018) Vol 52 Social Policy & Administration 1425, available at onlinelibrary.wiley.com/doi/epdf/10.1111/spol.12406 accessed 4 December 2019; M Lodge, 'Comparing Non-hierarchical Governance in Action: The Open Method of Co-ordination in Pensions and Information Society' (2007) Vol 45 No 2 Journal of Common Market 343; M Hartlapp, 'Intra-Kommissionsdynamik im Policy-Making: EU-Politiken angesichts des demographischen Wandels' in I Tömmel (ed), *Die Europäische Union: Governance und Policy-Making* (VS Verlag für Sozialwissenschaften 2007) 139; M Hartlapp, 'Deconstructing EU old age policy: Assessing the potential of soft OMCs and hard EU law' (2012) European Integration Online Papers (EIoP), Special Mini-Issue 1, Vol 16, Article 3, available at eiop.or.at/eiop/texte/2012-003a.htm accessed 4 December 2019.
242 Council of the European Union, 'Quality and viability of pensions – Joint report on objectives and working methods in the area of pensions' (2001) 10672/01 ECOFIN 198 SOC 272.
243 Commission of the European Communities, 'Joint report by the Commission and the Council on Adequate and sustainable pensions' (Draft) COM(2002) 737 final. On the goals of the OMC on pensions, see also Commission of the European Communities, 'Dealing with the impact of an ageing population in the EU (2009 Ageing Report)' (Communication from the Commission to the European Parliament, the Council, the European Economic and Social Committee and the Committee of the Regions) COM(2009) 180 final.
244 ibid.
245 D Natali, 'The Open Method of Coordination on Pensions: Does it De-politicise Pensions Policy?' (2009) Vol 32 (4) West European Politics 810, 816.
246 ibid.

of a single market for occupational pensions in which providers can freely offer their services Member States other than their own – it will be shown that certain obstacles to free movement can be justified. A good example is national social and labour law: legislation setting national parameters for occupational pensions.[247] Even though national social and labour legislation may obstruct either the freedom of services, persons or capital, there can be good reasons for Member States to keep these in place. The Court of Justice has accepted a number of these.[248]

EU law also influences national occupational pensions systems via the general principles enshrined in EU law that national pension systems must be in accordance with and these are discussed in the following section.

5.1 Judgments of the European Court of Justice

The case law of the European Court of Justice has shown significant influence of EU law on national pension systems. Its case law affecting occupational pension systems ranges from matters such as discrimination,[249] the implementation by Member States of EU legislation concerning occupational pensions,[250] and the manner in which the Member States are to organise their pension systems.

Regarding the latter point, in Kattner Stahlbau,[251] the Court decided that, while any EU prerogatives on the organization of social security systems are missing, the Member States are to exercise their prerogatives in accordance with Union law.[252] Consequently, the Treaty rules are not to be excluded, "in particular those relating to the freedom to provide services."[253] This judgment lays bare the seemingly inherent tension between the EU's ambitions of the achievement of a well-functioning single market (for occupational pensions) and the Member States' and balanced social protection.

In cases involving individuals, the influence of EU law becomes even more apparent when considering the recent judgment in *Faber*.[254] In that case, the Court clarifies that under certain circumstances, a national court must apply provisions of EU law of its own accord. This requirement applies in the same manner according to which a national court

---

247 See Chapters 4 and 5.
248 See Chapter 5.
249 See, for instance, Case C-476/11 *Experian* [2013] ECLI:EU:C:2013:590; Case C-149/77 *Defrenne* [1978] ECLI:EU:C:1978:130; Case C-152/84 *Marshall* [1986] ECLI:EU:C:1986:84; Case C-262/88 *Barber* [1990] ECLI:EU:C:1990:209.
250 Case C-343/08 *Commission v. Czech Republic* [2010] ECLI:EU:C:2010:14 concerning the Czech Republic's failure to fully implement the IORP Directive.
251 Case C-350/07 *Kattner Stahlbau* [2009] ECLI:EU:C:2009:127.
252 ibid para 74.
253 ibid para 75.
254 Case C-497/13 *Faber* [2015] ECLI:EU:C:2015:357.

is required to classify the matters of law and of fact which the parties in a given dispute have submitted to it for the purpose of identifying the applicable rule of national law.

The Court's case law relevant to occupational pensions is discussed throughout this book.

5.2 Negative Integration: The Fundamental Freedoms

5.2.1 The Fundamental Freedoms and Occupational Pensions: Establishment, Services, Workers and Capital

For occupational pension scheme members wishing to relocate within the EU – either as active employees or retirees – the free movement of persons, establishment and capital are important. Europeans who have found a new job in another Member State could be deterred from taking up this position if they face the loss of pension rights or cannot transfer their accrued pension rights to a new pension provider in another Member State. For example, the Commission requested the Netherlands in 2018 in a reasoned opinion to cease taxing "transfers of pension capital by mobile workers to the thirteen EU Member States which allow pension out-payments by pension funds in other forms than annuities. Under EU law, mobile workers are free to take up jobs in Member States that allow full or partial lump sum out-payments of pensions. The Dutch legislation is a restriction of the freedom of movement of workers (Article 45 TFEU), the freedom to provide services (Article 56 TFEU) and the free movement of capital (Article 63 TFEU)."[255]

For companies providing pension services within the EU, it is the free movement of services, the freedom of establishment and the free movement of capital that are important in the context of the provision of cross-border pension services. In accordance with these provisions, the Member States may not impede the provision of services across borders or the freedom of establishment. The ECJ gives further guidance on the application of those freedoms to social mechanisms in general and pension services in particular. For these free movement provisions to apply, there must be a cross-border element. This requirement is generally satisfied rather easily. For instance in *ING Pensii*,[256] with respect to mandatory affiliation to a pension scheme, the Court ruled that the services could be cross-border in nature if the persons who are under an obligation to affiliate themselves to one of the approved funds and their employers are established in different Member States, and the pension funds in a given country (in this case, Romania) belong to companies situated in other Member States.[257]

---

255 European Commission, 'July infringements package: key decisions' Press release 19 July 2018, available at europa.eu/rapid/press-release_MEMO-18-4486_en.htm accessed 11 December 2019.
256 Case C-172/14 *ING Pensii* [2015] ECLI:EU:C:2015:484.
257 ibid para 50.

A   *Freedom of Establishment*

The freedom of establishment is enshrined in Article 49 TFEU. It provides that;

"Within the framework of the provisions set out below, restrictions on the freedom of establishment of nationals of a Member State in the territory of another
Member State shall be prohibited. Such prohibition shall also apply to restrictions on the setting-up of agencies, branches or subsidiaries by nationals of any
Member State established in the territory of any Member State." The second
paragraph provides that "Freedom of establishment shall include the right to
take up and pursue activities as self-employed persons and to set up and manage undertakings, in particular companies or firms within the meaning of the
second paragraph of Article 54, under the conditions laid down for its own
nationals by the law of the country where such establishment is effected, subject
to the provisions of the Chapter relating to capital."

Article 54 TFEU extends the application of this right to companies or firms formed in
accordance with the law of a Member State and having their registered office, central
administration or principal place of business within the Union. Article 54 excludes
non-profit-making companies from the scope of the freedom of establishment. Companies are to be treated in the same way as the natural persons who are nationals of a
Member State.

This provision prohibits discrimination on the grounds of nationality. This prohibition encompasses direct and indirect discrimination and indistinctly applicable measures
that still cause constraints on the freedom of establishment.[258] Seminal cases in respect to
this Treaty provision are *Gebhard*[259] and *Reyners*.[260] In *Gebhard* the Court pointed out,
inter alia, that national measures liable to hinder or make less attractive the exercise of
fundamental freedoms guaranteed by the Treaty must fulfil four conditions: they must be
applied in a non-discriminatory manner; they must be justified by imperative requirements in the general interest; they must be suitable for securing the attainment of the
objective which they pursue; and they must not go beyond what is necessary to attain
it.[261] It also explained the purpose of the freedom of establishment: "The concept of
establishment within the meaning of the Treaty is therefore a very broad one, allowing
a Community national to participate, on a stable and continuous basis, in the economic
life of a Member State other than his State of origin and to profit therefrom, so contributing to economic and social interpenetration within the Community in the sphere of

---

258 F Weiss and C Kaupa, *European Union Internal Market Law* (Cambridge University Press 2014) 205.
259 Case C-55/94 *Gebhard* [1995] ECLI:EU:C:1995:411.
260 Case 2/74 *Reyners* [1974] ECLI:EU:C:1974:68.
261 ibid para 37.

activities as self-employed persons."[262] In *Reyners* the Court accepted the direct effect of what is now Article 49 TFEU. In *Commission v. Austria*[263] the Court held that Member States are prohibited from implementing conditions for the pursuit of activities for those persons exercising their freedom of establishment that differ from those that their own nationals are subject to.[264]

The freedom of establishment, however, not only covers protection against discriminatory national law, but also prohibits, in principle, restrictions on this freedom.[265] For instance, in *CaixaBank France*[266] and *Attanasio*[267] the Court ruled that French and Italian legislation that made it more difficult for foreign banks to enter the market was contrary to the freedom secured by Article 49 TFEU.

The differences between the right of establishment and the right to provide services are small. Both of these freedoms apply to the "business or professional activity pursued for 'profit' or 'remuneration'".[268] The key difference lies in the basis from which the activity is carried. The right to establish oneself in another Member State entails the right to "install oneself, to 'set up shop'" in another Member State permanently or semi-permanently.[269] No such settlement is required for the right to offer one's services in another Member State.

In the context of occupational pensions, this provision has as its consequence that occupational pension providers from another Member State may not be deterred from establishing themselves within the territory of a Member State.

For workers, this provision means that Member States may not deter workers or self-employed persons from relocating to another Member State by failing to safeguard accrued pension rights.

B   *Freedom to Provide Services*
The freedom to provide services is enshrined in Article 56 TFEU.

> "Within the framework of the provisions set out below, restrictions on freedom to provide services within the Union shall be prohibited in respect of nationals of Member States who are established in a Member State other than that of the person for whom the services are intended."

---

262 ibid para 25.
263 Case C-161/07 *Commission v. Austria* [2008] ECLI:EU:C:2008:759.
264 F Weiss and C Kaupa, European Union Internal Market Law (Cambridge University Press 2014) 205.
265 ibid.
266 Case C-442/02 *Caixa Bank France* [2004] ECLI:EU:C:2004:586.
267 Case C-384/08 *Attanasio* [2010] ECLI:EU:C:2010:133.
268 D Cahill and others, *European Law* (Oxford University Press 2011) 33.
269 ibid.

Article 57 TFEU defines services. The notion of a service is relatively young, emerging in the 1940s and 1950s as scholars began to recognise services as a distinct sector of the economy.[270] The establishment of a legal infrastructure for cross-border provision of services trailed that of goods. Services, explains Article 57 TFEU, are normally provided for remuneration, in so far as they are not governed by the provisions relating to freedom of movement for goods, capital and persons. It provides examples, citing the activities of an industrial or commercial character, the services provided by craftsmen and the activities of the professions. Pension services are considered services within the meaning of Article 57 TFEU. It also refers to the freedom of establishment, when it explains that "Without prejudice to the provisions of the chapter relating to the right of establishment, the person providing a service may, in order to do so, temporarily pursue his activity in the Member State where the service is provided, under the same conditions as are imposed by that State on its own nationals."

The direct effect of article 56 TFEU was established by the Court in *Van Binsbergen*.[271]

In its case law, the Court has made clear that any form of discrimination and any obstacle is contrary to the Treaty provisions on the freedom to provide services.[272] In paragraph 12 of its *Säger*[273] judgment, the Court explains that it "should first be pointed out that Article 59 EC [now Article 56 TFEU] requires not only the elimination of all discrimination against a person providing services on the ground of his nationality but also the abolition of any restriction, even if it applies without distinction to national providers of services and to those of other Member States, when it is liable to prohibit or otherwise impede the activities of a provider of services established in another Member State where he lawfully provides similar services." A conflict with the freedom to provide services exists even in instances where the provision of such services is made more burdensome for non-nationals. Thus, any obstacle is prohibited that "is liable to prohibit, impede or render less advantageous the activities of a provider of services established in another Member State where he lawfully provides similar services."[274]

The consequence of this provision is that the Member States may not keep in place any obstacles that keep pension providers from providing pension services in other Member States. The freedom to provide services in the context of occupational pensions will be discussed in more detail in Chapter 5.

---

270 F Weiss and C Kaupa, European Union Internal Market Law (Cambridge University Press 2014) 241.
271 Case 33/74 *van Binsbergen* [1974] ECLI:EU:C:1974:131.
272 H van Meerten, 'Vrij verkeer van diensten voor verzekeraars en pensioeninstellingen: Solvency II basic en de verplichtstelling' (2012) No 7/8 Tijdschrift voor Financieel Recht 290.
273 Case C-76/90 *Säger* [1991] ECLI:EU:C:1991:331.
274 Joined Cases C-369/96 *Arblade* and C-376/96 *Leloup* [1999] ECLI:EU:C:1999:575.

C   Free Movement of Workers

In accordance with Article 45 TFEU, "the freedom of movement for workers shall be secured within the Union."[275] That freedom of movement comprises not only an "abolition of any discrimination based on nationality between workers of the Member States as regards employment, remuneration and other conditions of work and employment",[276] but also entails the right to accept offers of employment in other Member States as well as to move freely within the EU for that purpose.[277]

With respect to pensions in particular, the Court has repeatedly held that "Articles [45 TFEU] and [49 TFEU] militate against any national measure which, even though applicable without discrimination on grounds of nationality, is capable of hindering or rendering less attractive the exercise by Community nationals of the fundamental freedoms guaranteed by the Treaty."[278] In that light, "measures which have the effect of causing workers to lose, as a consequence of the exercise of their right to freedom of movement, social security advantages guaranteed them by the legislation of a Member State have in particular been classed as obstacles."[279] In other words, the Member States must not have in place legislation that could hinder or deter the free movement of workers.

The ECJ held in the *Casteels* case that a loss of occupational pension rights in this case constitutes an obstacle to the freedom of movement of workers.[280]

As noted in the introduction, the mobility of workers was one of the key priorities of EU pension policy. Following the identification of the obstacles that mobile workers face regarding their occupational pension provision, the Safeguard Directive and the Supplementary Pension Rights Directive were both adopted on the basis of the freedom of movement of workers to aid the free movement of workers within the EU. They aim to achieve this by, *inter alia*, applying the principle of non-discrimination to the consequences of leaving an occupational pension scheme for workers who move to another Member State compared to those who change jobs within their own Member State[281] and by introducing maximum terms for waiting and vesting periods.[282] However, obstacles still remain, as will become apparent in the following chapters.

---

275 Article 45(1) TFEU.

276 Article 45(2) TFEU.

277 Article 45(3) TFEU.

278 See Case C-212/06 *Gouvernement de la Communauté française and Gouvernement wallon* [2008] ECLI:EU:
C:2008:178, para 45 and the case law quoted there; Case C-379/09 *Casteels* [2011] ECLI:EU:C:2011:131. See
also L van der Vaart & H van Meerten, 'De pensioen opPEPPer?' (2018) 1 Tijdschrift voor Pensioenvraagstukken 38.

279 Case C-212/06 *Gouvernement de la Communauté française and Gouvernement wallon* [2008] ECLI:EU:
C:2008:178, para 46.

280 Case C-379/09 *Casteels* [2011] ECLI:EU:C:2011:131, para 30.

281 Article 4 of Council Directive 98/49/EC of 29 June 1998 on safeguarding the supplementary pension rights
of employed and self-employed persons moving within the Community [1998] OJ L 209/46.

282 Article 4 Supplementary Pension Rights Directive (see footnote 206). A departure from an occupational
pension scheme before the end of the vesting period may result in the loss of pension rights.

D   *Free Movement of Capital*

In accordance with Article 63 TFEU, "all restrictions on the movement of capital between Member States and between Member States and third countries shall be prohibited." This freedom is not absolute, as the rest of the TFEU's Chapter on Capital and Payments indicates. For instance, Article 65 TFEU codifies the rights of the Member States to "apply the relevant provisions of their tax law which distinguish between taxpayers who are not in the same situation with regard to their place of residence or with regard to the place where their capital is invested"[283] or the right to "to take all requisite measures to prevent infringements of national law and regulations."[284] More general exceptions to the four freedoms are discussed in the next section.

It seems clear that the free movement of capital within the EU is of paramount importance for occupational pensions. It is important for employers, pension scheme members and pension providers for the reasons outlined here.

By enabling occupational pension funds to invest according to the so-called "prudent person rule", the original IORP Directive has brought "freedom of asset allocation that suits the precise nature and duration of the liabilities of IORPs,"[285] enabling IORPs to invest in assets anywhere in the EU, although some limitations still apply.[286] The prudent person principle does this by abolishing restrictive rules on asset allocation, potentially increasing returns on investment according to the Commission.[287] The Commission noted in 1991 that some Member States required pension institutions to invest in domestic government stocks or other particular category of assets, or to seek prior approval from the authorities for investments.[288]

In addition, in order for the internal market for occupational pensions to materialise – as envisaged by the IORP II Directive – it must be possible for pension assets to be

---

283 Article 65(1)(a) TFEU.

284 Article 65(1)(b) TFEU.

285 S Hooghiemstra, *Depositaries in European Investment Law: Towards Harmonization in Europe*, dissertation Utrecht University (Eleven International Publishing 2018) 462.

286 See recital 47 of the IORP II Directive: "[...] Member States should be given some discretion on the precise investment rules that they wish to impose on IORPs located in their territories. However, those rules should not restrict the free movement of capital, unless justified on prudential grounds."

287 Such rules can entail limitations on types and/or quantities of assets that IORPs may invest in. The Commission has noted that IORPs in Member States with more restrictive investment rules achieved lower returns on their investments: "Between 1984 and 1998, average annual real return on investments by IORPs was around 6% in the Member States with strict quantitative investment rules and more than 10% in Member States with rules that give managers more freedom. Lower returns mean lower pay-outs or higher contributions. The indirect cost of labour rises, as does the cost of financing retirement systems." See Commission of the European Communities, 'Proposal for a directive of the European Parliament and of the Council on the activities of institutions for occupational retirement provision' COM(2000) 507 final; S Hooghiemstra, *Depositaries in European Investment Law: Towards Harmonization in Europe*, dissertation Utrecht University (Eleven International Publishing 2018) 461.

288 European Commission, 'Commission proposes a directive on the investment and management of pension fund assets' Press release 16 October 1991, available at europa.eu/rapid/press-release_IP-91-919_en.htm accessed 11 December 2019.

transferred between providers across Member States. The IORP II Directive regulates such transfers,[289] and it is important from the perspective of this provision that Member States do not unjustifiably encumber such transfers.[290]

Pension scheme members benefit from the free movement of capital by, on the one hand, profiting from the higher returns thanks to the advantages of free asset allocation by IORPs, and on the other, by being able to move their pension pot through the EU in the event that they relocate to another Member State. As explained in the following chapters, the latter is still problematic with respect to occupational pensions.

5.2.2   Justifications to Obstacles to the Fundamental Freedoms

The ECJ has developed in its case law several criteria that may justify restrictions on the free movement clauses in the Treaty.[291]

In one case, *Gebhard*,[292] the Court noted that "national measures liable to hinder or make less attractive the exercise of fundamental freedoms guaranteed by the Treaty must fulfil four conditions: they must be applied in a non-discriminatory manner; they must be justified by imperative requirements in the general interest; they must be suitable for securing the attainment of the objective which they pursue; and they must not go beyond what is necessary in order to attain it."[293]

Further exceptions to the freedom to provide services and the freedom of establishment can be found in the Treaty itself. Article 51 TFEU disapplies the provisions on the right to establishment for activities connected with the exercise of official authority, and article 52 TFEU provides grounds for justification for "special treatment of foreign nationals on the grounds of public policy, public security or public health." The two aforementioned Treaty provisions apply also to the freedom to provide services by virtue of article 62 TFEU.

Article 52 TFEU justifies discrimination that is direct or indirect, as well as non-discriminatory measures.[294] The Court interprets the exceptions narrowly. However, it generally accepts that Member States have considerable discretion to define the requirements of public policy, public security and public health.[295] For instance, in the *Alpine Investments* case, the Court accepted that a measure implemented out of concern for the pro-

---

289 Article 12 IORP II Directive (see footnote 206).
290 See, for instance, H van Meerten & L Geerling, 'Build that wall? Het onderscheid tussen binnenlandse en grensoverschrijdende waardeoverdrachten van pensioenregelingen' (2019) No 2 Tijdschrift voor Recht en Arbeid; E Lutjens, 'Vragen over implementatie IORP Richtlijn: grensoverschrijdende uitvoering in discussie' (2018) supplement to parliamentary debate, available at www.eerstekamer.nl/overig/20181121/vragen_over_implementatie_iorp/document accessed 11 December 2019; Recital 37 et seq IORP II Directive (see footnote 206).
291 D Cahill and others, *European Law* (Oxford University Press 2011) 36.
292 Case C-55/94 *Gebhard* [1995] ECLI:EU:C:1995:411.
293 ibid para 37.
294 F Weiss and C Kaupa, *European Union Internal Market Law* (Cambridge University Press 2014) 209.
295 ibid.

tection of the reputation of the Dutch financial sector can be an acceptable justification for a restriction on the freedom to provide financial services.[296]

The exercise of official authority is interpreted narrowly by the Court; the mere circumstance that some tasks in a Member State are provided by public authorities cannot be used to successfully invoke Article 51 TFEU.[297] Rather, the activity must be connected directly and specifically with the exercise of official authority.

5.3 Fundamental Principles and Occupational Pensions

The guiding foundations and principles of European Union law also give hints as to how the pension systems in the European Union should be organised. The provisions of European law that are discussed first are addressed at the European Union, however under the principle of sincere cooperation, the Union and the Member States shall assist each other in carrying out tasks which flow from the Treaties.[298] In other words, "the Member States must refrain from doing anything that will jeopardize the achievement of the objectives of the EU."[299] This formula necessarily includes the organization of national pension systems. The following section considers some of the relevant beacons for the arrangement of pensions in Europe. These guidelines apply both at the national and EU level.

First, Article 3(3) TEU defines the objective of working for the sustainable development of the EU on the basis of economic growth and price stability. Article 3 TEU also mentions the promotion of social protection, as well as solidarity between generations. Social protection systems provide protection against, *inter alia*, unemployment, parental responsibilities, sickness and old age.[300] A pension system, in accordance with that provision, should therefore be tuned in such a manner that it maximizes its ability to serve its social protection and solidarity goals. The promotion of social protection should include continuous efforts to better attain this goal, taking into account relevant innovations, such as new manners of saving for retirement, but also changing parameters like population aging or economic difficulties.

Next, European pension systems must consider the relevant provisions of the Charter of Fundamental Rights of the European Union (the Charter). Article 6 TEU proclaims that the EU is to observe the provisions of the Charter. Fundamental rights were men-

296 H van Meerten & JC van Haersolte, 'Zelfrijzend Europees Bakmeel: de Voostellen Voor Een Nieuw Toezicht Op de Financiële Sector' (2010) No 2 Nederlands Tijdschrift voor Europees Recht 33, 34.

297 F Weiss and C Kaupa, *European Union Internal Market Law* (Cambridge University Press 2014) 210.

298 Article 4(3) TEU.

299 B Sjåfjell, 'Quo vadis, Europe? The significance of sustainable development as objective, principle and rule of EU law' in C Bailliet (ed), *Non-State Actors, Soft Law and Protective Regimes: From the Margins* (Cambridge University Press 2012) 278.

300 European Parliament, Directorate-General for Internal Policies, *EU Social and Labour Rights and EU Internal Market Law*, Study for the EMPL Committee (Publications Office of the European Union 2015) 18.

tioned explicitly in the Explanatory Memorandum to the IORP II proposal.[301] In a
"highly fundamental consideration",[302] the Commission explains that the proposal has
a positive impact on the rights codified in Articles 16, 25 and 38 of the Charter, on the
freedom to conduct business, the right of the elderly to lead a life of dignity and independence and on consumer protection, respectively. The freedom to conduct business is
served by the directive's intended removal of obstacles for the cross-border provision of
pension services. Member States' pension systems must, therefore, ensure that they do
not obstruct this right by setting up barriers to cross-border activity. Article 25 of the
Charter on the right of the elderly to live in dignity and independence can be interpreted
in the context of pensions as a requirement of pension adequacy: a sufficiently high
income is a prerequisite for a life of dignity and independence from, for instance, family
or the state. Article 38 of the Charter, which focuses on consumer protection, could entail
decent provision of information, the proper safeguarding of accrued pension rights and
good governance and oversight. National pensions systems should comply with all these
requirements so as not to frustrate the attainment of the goals of the European Union.

In fact, consumer protection, enshrined also in Articles 4(2)(f), 12, 114 and 169 TFEU
in the context of pensions has played an important role in several ECJ decisions.[303] In
Faber,[304] the ECJ decided that national courts must apply EU law *ex officio* in order to
determine whether an individual can be considered a consumer with commensurate
rights. In *Dansk Industri*,[305] the ECJ ruled that the general principle prohibiting discrimination on grounds of age – as a general principle of EU law – can be invoked in a
horizontal context between two individuals. The understanding of a consumer of a pension contract played a pivotal role in *Van Leeuwen*,[306] where the Court held that unwrit-
ten principles of national law can serve as a basis to require information from a pension
provider additional to written directives. A central consideration in all these cases is that
the consumer is in a disadvantaged position vis-à-vis the supplier or seller, and that he
must be protected accordingly.

Article 9 TFEU states that the Union, in defining and implementing its policies and
activities, shall consider, *inter alia*, the requirements for the promotion of a high level of

---

301 European Commission, 'Proposal for a directive of the European Parliament and of the Council on the
   activities and supervision of institutions for occupational retirement provision' COM(2014) 167 final, Paragraph 1.2.
302 P Borsjé & H van Meerten, 'A European Pensions Union: Towards a Strengthening of the European Pension
   Systems' in F Pennings & G Vonk (eds), *Research Handbook on European Social Security Law* (Edward Elgar
   Publishing 2015) 398.
303 H van Meerten & E Schmidt, 'Een overzicht van rechtspraak: consumentenbescherming als rode draad' in:
   O. de Lange (ed.), *Goud geld. De staat van de financiële sector* (Kluwer 2016) 139-144.
304 Case C-497/13 *Faber* [2015] ECLI:EU:C:2015:357.
305 Case C-441/14 *Dansk Industri* [2016] ECLI:EU:C:2016:278.
306 Case C-51/13 *van Leeuwen* [2015] ECLI:EU:C:2015:286.

employment, the guarantee of adequate social protection and the fight against social exclusion. This article is not just a "social rationale for more protective EU secondary legislation",[307] but also a requirement for "Member States to assess all their policies, laws and activities in light of their implications for the achievement of social goals. In combination with the Charter of Fundamental Rights and the future accession of the EU to the Convention for the Protection of Human Rights and Fundamental Freedoms, it may contribute to a fundamental reorientation of EU legislation and jurisprudence towards social aims."[308] The goal of sustainability (read: affordability) of a pension system can be read into this provision as a goal, on top of the requirements mentioned above. In this context, the European Commission's White Paper, titled "An Agenda for Adequate, Safe and Sustainable Pensions" treats pension adequacy and sustainability with importance.[309]

In accordance with Article 26 TFEU, the internal market for pensions must be one without internal frontiers in which the free movement of services and the freedom establishment is ensured. These freedoms will be introduced in some more detail in the following section, as they are the guiding principles for the rest of this book.

In accordance with Article 157 TFEU, no discrimination may take place as regards pay between workers based on gender. Specific rules are given in Directive 2006/54 (gender) and Directive 2000/78 (age) that apply (also) for occupational mentions. As a general principle of EU law, the prohibition of discrimination on gender and age are general principles of European law and can be invoked by an individual against another.[310] This is known as horizontal direct effect.[311]

6   CONCLUSION

This chapter discusses the EU's powers in the field of occupational pension systems. There are no direct powers in the EU Treaties that give the EU direct powers to regulate the pension systems of the Member States, save for Article 48 TFEU and 153 TFEU. Despite the absence of many direct powers, its internal market prerogatives and a variety of other options, such as negative integration, soft governance and the OMC, give it real influence over the pension systems of the Member States. Given those methods of influence, it appears clear that the Member States do not "retain full responsibility for the

---

307 W Baugniet, *The protection of occupational pensions under European Union law on the freedom of movement for workers*, dissertation European University Institute Florence (2014) 32.

308 P Vielle, 'How the Horizontal Social Clause can be made to Work: The lessons of Gender Mainstreaming' in N Bruun, K Lörcher & I Schömann (eds), *The Lisbon Treaty and Social Europe* (Hart Publishing 2012) 107.

309 European Commission, 'An Agenda for Adequate, Safe and Sustainable Pensions' (White Paper) COM (2012) 55 final.

310 Case C-555/07 *Kücükdeveci* [2010] ECLI:EU:C:2010:21.

311 Case C-476/11 *Experian* [2013] ECLI:EU:C:2013:590.

organisation of their pension systems."[312] Although the Member States can define, at least in respect of EU measures adopted under Article 153 TFEU, the fundamental principles of their social security systems, EU measures have provided the limits within which these systems may operate.

With its legislative as well as non-legislative instruments, the EU has had significant influence over the pension systems of the Member States. The abovementioned powers to regulate the Member States' social security systems cannot, however, be used against the will of the Member States. The latter have exerted their influence in order to shape the content of EU measures regulating occupational pensions. As will become apparent in the chapters to follow, this resistance from the Member States makes that the EU's influence is not sufficiently far-reaching to achieve all of the objectives envisaged. The next chapter discusses the history and objectives of the EU's involvement in occupational pensions.

It shows that *inter alia* the EU's limited powers in the field of occupational pensions, combined with resistance from the Member States, has led the Union to miss a number of goals. The result is that the legislation it has adopted regarding occupational pensions seems incomplete and appears to leave a few important obstacles.

---

312 See recital 19 of IORP II Directive 2016/2341/EU; Recital 9 of Supplementary Pension Rights Directive 2014/50/EU.

Chapter 3: The History and Goals of the EU's involvement in Occupational Pensions

1   Introduction

By 1991, only a handful of EU directives dealt with aspects concerning occupational pensions:[313] one on the protection of employees (and their occupational pension rights) in the event of a transfer of ownership of undertakings,[314] another dealing with employees' rights in case of the insolvency of an employer,[315] and finally a directive on the equality of treatment of men and women in occupational pension schemes.[316]

By contrast, the EU had been involved in regulating *statutory* pension schemes since 1958.[317] To boost both the European economies as well as the mobility and pension adequacy of Europeans, the EU began taking action on occupational pensions starting in the late 1980s. First with the Community Charter of Fundamental Social Rights for Workers[318] and a series of working documents to be discussed in this chapter, the Commission began setting out its envisioned policies.

By exploring the discussions that took place during the lengthy history of the EU's policies and legislatives instruments in the area of occupational pensions, this chapter aims to distil the goals of the EU's involvement in occupational pensions in order to see whether these goals have been met. The focus will be primarily on the IORP Directives, as

---

313 Commission of the European Communities, 'Supplementary social security schemes: the role of occupational pension schemes in the social protection of workers and their implications for freedom of movement' (Communication from the Commission to the Council) SEC (91) 1332 final (The 1991 Communication), 12.

314 Council Directive 77/187/EEC of 14 February 1977 on the approximation of the laws of the Member States relating to the safeguarding of employees' rights in the event of transfers of undertakings, businesses or parts of businesses [1977] OJ L 61/26. Currently Council Directive 2001/23/EC of 12 March 2001 on the approximation of the laws of the Member States relating to the safeguarding of employees' rights in the event of transfers of undertakings, businesses or parts of undertakings or businesses [2001] OJ L 82/16.

315 Council Directive 80/987/EEC of 20 October 1980 on the approximation of the laws of the Member States relating to the protection of employees in the event of the insolvency of their employer [1980] OJ L 283/23. Currently Directive 2008/94/EC of the European Parliament and of the Council of 22 October 2008 on the protection of employees in the event of the insolvency of their employer [2008] OJ L 283/26.

316 Council Directive 86/378/EEC of 24 July 1986 on the implementation of the principle of equal treatment for men and women in occupational social security schemes [1986] OJ L 225/40. Currently Directive 2006/54/ EC of the European Parliament and of the Council of 5 July 2006 on the implementation of the principle of equal opportunities and equal treatment of men and women in matters of employment and occupation (recast) [2006] OJ L 204/23.

317 Regulations 3 and 4 of 1958.

318 Available at www.eurofocend.europa.eu/observatories/eurwork/industrial- relations-dictionary/commu-nity-charter-of-the-fundamental-social- rights-of-workers accessed 3 January 2020.

it and the PEPP – to be discussed in Chapter 6 – are the focus of this research. Where appropriate, the Safeguard Directive[319] and the Supplementary Pension Rights Directive[320] are also discussed.

2   HISTORY OF THE EU'S INVOLVEMENT IN OCCUPATIONAL PENSIONS

This chapter considers the history of the EU's involvement in occupational pensions. The story begins with the 1991 Communication on Occupational Pensions,[321] announced by the 1989 Action Programme Relating to the Implementation of the Community Charter of Basic Social Rights for Workers,[322] a policy document in which the Commission discussed challenges and policy objectives in the area of occupational pensions. The chapter continues this history with the inception of the first IORP Directive in hand, tracing its lengthy legislative process from its beginnings in 1991 until its ratification in 2003. Paragraph 2.5 *et seq.* then assesses which of these ideas have been included in the Directive or other EU (legal) initiatives.

The European Union has been involved in the regulation of occupational pensions (second pillar) for nearly three decades. Long before that, in 1958, it has successfully adopted coordination regulations on statutory pensions in the form of Regulations 3 and 4 of 1958, which were subsequently succeeded by others in the 1970s.[323] The Regulations contained coordination rules of social security schemes for migrant workers, making it possible (*inter alia*) to aggregate the periods completed in another Member State for the purpose of fulfilling benefit conditions in the competent State, to determine the applicable legislation making clear where one is insured, to prohibit any discrimination on ground of nationality and to export acquitted rights. Such coordination was deemed

---

319 Council Directive 98/49/EC of 29 June 1998 on safeguarding the supplementary pension rights of employed and self-employed persons moving within the Community [1998] OJ L 209/46 (Safeguard Directive).
320 Directive 2014/50/EU of the European Parliament and of the Council of 16 April 2014 on minimum requirements for enhancing worker mobility between Member States by improving the acquisition and preservation of supplementary pension rights [2014] OJ L 128/1 (Supplementary Pension Rights Directive).
321 1991 Communication (see footnote 313).
322 Commission of the European Communities, 'Communication from the Commission concerning its Action Programme relating to the Implementation of the Community Charter of Basic Social Rights for Workers' COM(89) 568 final 22. This document also alludes to the changing dependency ratio and the resulting budgetary implications for the Member States.
323 Council Regulation EEC No 1408/71 of 14 June 1971 on the application of social security schemes to employed persons and their families moving within the Community [1971] OJ L 149/2 and Council Regulation 574/72 of 21 March 1972 fixing the procedure for implementing Regulation (EEC) No 1408/71 on the application of social security schemes to employed persons and their families moving within the Community [1972] OJ L 74/1, succeeded by Regulation (EC) No 883/2004 of the European Parliament and the Council of 29 April 2004 on the coordination of social security systems [2004] OJ L 166/1. The latter Regulation was revised by Regulation 988/2009 of the European Parliament and the Council of 16 September 2009 amending Regulation (EC) No 883/2004 on the coordination of social security systems [2009] OJ L 284/43 and supplemented by implementing Regulation 987/2009 OJ L 284/1.

essential to promote the free movement of workers by preventing the loss of their statutory pension rights. The exercise of the right to free movement is not just a fundamental right in EU law; free movement is also necessary for the Single Market to function efficiently and any loss of social security rights should be avoided.[324]

However, no legal framework exists for occupational pensions with respect to the rights of pension scheme members, or for the institutions to conduct their business in a cross-border context.[325] This lack of Community provisions protecting migrant workers against the loss of supplementary pension rights was a cause for concern for the Commission.[326] Its commitment to second-pillar retirement provision has been driven by the desire to facilitate labour mobility and to buttress retirement provision through the EU's internal market in the face of population ageing and strained public systems, as well as to provide for the conditions enabling pension institutions to provide their services in other Member States. Over time, the EU also appears to have begun to recognise the role of pension funds as institutional investors that play a key role in stimulating investment in the EU.

The emphasis of each of these concerns changes over time, as will become apparent in this chapter. The goals pursued by the EU *inter alia* reflect the interests on the one hand of pension scheme members and the social considerations that play a role from the perspective of labour mobility and pension adequacy, and on the other hand the interests of the pension funds as financial service providers. While these fulfil essential social tasks, they are also financial undertakings requiring a well-regulated internal market for financial services. The Commission's social affairs directorate was focused on occupational pensions from the social perspective, whilst the Commission's financial institutions directorate approached the subject from the perspectives of the freedom to provide services and the freedom of capital movements.[327]

2.1   *1991: Communication on Occupational Pensions and First Proposal for a Directive*

2.1.1   The 1991 Communication: Facilitating Worker Mobility

1991 saw one of the EU's first forays into regulating occupational pensions. In a Communication, the Commission that year identified legal divergences in social protection schemes as an obstacle to labour mobility.[328] It analysed occupational pensions from two

---

324 International Labour Organization, *Coordination of Social Security Systems in the European Union: An explanatory report on EC Regulation No. 883/2004 and its Implementing Regulation No. 987/2009* (ILO 2010).
325 1991 Communication (see footnote 313).
326 ibid.
327 K Lannoo, 'The Draft Pension Funds Directive and the Financing of Pensions in the EU' (1996) 21 The Geneva Papers on Risk and Insurance 114, 117.
328 1991 Communication (see footnote 313).

perspectives: first from the angle of their actual and potential contribution to the social protection of workers and second, from the perspective of the freedom of movement of workers. It was thus very much focused on the interests of the pension scheme member, and especially on the mobility of workers.

According to the Communication, cooperation at the Community level should lead to a greater convergence of national policies and systems in the field of pensions.[329] The Communication noted that the lack of Community involvement and resultant lack of coordination in the area of occupational pensions was still an obstacle to the free movement of workers. In particular, workers could be discouraged from moving to another Member State because there were no provisions protecting workers against the loss of their occupational pension rights.[330]

The Communication's aim was to spark a debate to explore what could be done to facilitate labour mobility, while recognising that each Member State "must remain free to choose amongst the different fundamental options (...)."[331] It outlined several obstacles – such as long vesting and waiting periods, calculations of transfer values that penalise scheme leavers and inadequate preservation of pension rights as well as taxation issues.[332] A vesting period is a period during which benefits are being accrued, but not yet vested, i.e. scheme members are not entitled to their benefits before the vesting period has elapsed. A waiting period is time an employee must work for an employer before he or she becomes eligible to participate in the pension scheme. Although both periods are important tools to foster employee loyalty, binding the employee to the employer and rewarding the employee for a long service, they can become an obstacle to take up employment in another Member State or to leave one's current employer: non-completion of the waiting and vesting periods could lead to a loss of pension rights. This would occur if the waiting and vesting periods exceed the term of employment.

For these problems, the Communication several possible solutions, including the possibility of 1) cross-border membership, 2) the facilitation of rights acquisition, 3) the protection of preserved rights, 4) fair transfer options and 5) better information on the financial consequences of a cross-border move, and 6) the avoidance of double taxation.

Cross-border membership (1) was defined as "the possibility to remain in the previous pension scheme, acceptance of the new employer to pay contributions to the employee's previous scheme, tax deductibility of these contributions and finally, the absence, both in the present and previous countries of employment, of legal obstacles prohibiting membership in a foreign fund."[333] Cross-border membership would avoid the need to change

---

329 ibid 3.
330 ibid 1.
331 ibid 2.
332 ibid 15-19.
333 ibid 19-21.

to a different pension scheme and the resultant losses in terms of social security rights, as well as the substantial administrative and financial burden involved.

However, the Commission noted that such cross-border membership would be difficult to achieve, given the "wide variety of pension arrangements" throughout the Member States, as well as the importance of "not undermining the social and political objectives pursued by these arrangements."[334] The possibility of cross-border membership came not with the IORP Directive, but with the Safeguard Directive,[335] and is available only to posted workers who work in another Member State for a limited amount of time. Nonetheless, the realization of cross-border membership remained a priority, and in 1992 the Commission published a working document on the cross-border membership of occupational pension schemes for migrant workers in September 1992. It proposed "that mobile employees, moving within the same group of companies, should be able to stay in their home country scheme during a period of maximum 5 years (an extension to 10 years should be negotiable)."[336]

Regarding the aims of the solutions 2 through 6, some of these were also dealt with by other EU directives (to some extent).

Regarding the facilitation of rights acquisition (2), the Commission noted in its 1991 Communication that "excessively long vesting and waiting periods can hinder labour mobility by linking an adequate pension level too strongly to long uninterrupted service periods with the same employer."[337] The Supplementary Pension Rights Directive reduces the maximum combined duration of waiting and vesting periods to three years.[338]

Regarding the protection of preserved pension rights (3), the Communication noted that "[t]he principal long-term objective in the area of supplementary pension schemes

---

334 ibid 20
335 Article 6 Safeguard Directive (see footnote 319):
    "1. Member States shall adopt such measures as are necessary to enable contributions to continue to be made to a supplementary pension scheme established in a Member State by or on behalf of a posted worker who is a member of such a scheme during the period of his or her posting in another Member State.
    2. Where, pursuant to paragraph 1, contributions continue to be made to a supplementary pension scheme in one Member State, the posted worker and, where applicable, his employer shall be exempted from any obligation to make contributions to a supplementary pension scheme in another Member State."
336 Lannoo (see footnote 327), 125.
337 1991 Communication (see footnote 313) 21. See also recital 17 of the Supplementary Pension Rights Directive (see footnote 320): "The fact that in some supplementary pension schemes pension rights can be forfeited if a worker's employment relationship ends before he or she has completed a minimum period of scheme membership ('vesting period'), or before he or she has reached the minimum age ('vesting age'), can prevent workers who move between Member States from acquiring adequate pension rights. The requirement of a lengthy waiting period before a worker can become a member of a pension scheme can have a similar effect. Such conditions therefore represent obstacles to workers' freedom of movement. By contrast, minimum age requirements for membership do not constitute an obstacle to freedom of movement, and are therefore not addressed by this Directive."
338 Article 4 Supplementary Pension Rights Directive.

should be to ensure that every scheme leaver is legally entitled to maintain acquired rights in a pension scheme until he/she retires."[339] The Safeguard Directive was the first EU initiative to deal with workers' rights to free movement in relation to occupational pensions.[340] It applies the principle of non-discrimination to workers leaving their Member State. Together with the aforementioned cap on waiting and vesting periods, the Safeguard Directive and the Supplementary Pension Rights Directive give a mobile worker some degree of protection, yet this group of EU citizens may still face pension-related obstacles beyond the scope of the directives, such as lacking options regarding transferability, waiting and vesting periods (shorter than the maximum of three years mandated by the directive), aggregation of periods of work[341] and an absence of a possibility of cross-border membership.[342] Part 2 of Chapter 4 looks at these issues in greater detail.

Finally, the provision of information on the financial consequences of moving to another Member State (5) is regulated in both the Safeguard Directive[343] as well as the Supplementary Pension Rights Directive.[344]

There is no EU legislation on fair transfer options (4) in the sense of an EU-regulated possibility for individual transfers of pension pots of European workers, but the IORP II Directive has introduced a provision regulating collective cross-border transfers between IORPs.

2.1.2 The First Proposal for an EU Directive in the Field of Occupational Pensions

The 1991 Communication also announced a proposal for a directive in the field of pension funds. It stated clearly that, while the Communication was imbued with considerations on occupational pensions from the perspective of labour mobility, the proposed directive would focus on pension funds as "financial institutions in the Internal Mar-

---

339 Commission of the European Communities, 'Supplementary social security schemes: the role of occupational pension schemes in the social protection of workers and their implications for freedom of movement' (Communication from the Commission to the Council) SEC (91) 1332 final 21.

340 W Baugniet, *The protection of occupational pensions under European Union law on the freedom of movement for workers*, dissertation European University Institute Florence (2014) 180.

341 ibid 210 et seq.

342 In this respect, Baugniet speaks of "untapped potential", and that "the internal-market rationale based on removing 'obstacles' to mobility has not delivered a system of legal protection that places migrant workers social protection rights at the heart of their fundamental freedom of movement." See Baugniet (see footnote 340) 335 and 337.

343 Article 7 Safeguard Directive (see footnote 319): "Member States shall take measures to ensure that employers, trustees or others responsible for the management of supplementary pension schemes provide adequate information to scheme members, when they move to another Member State, as to their pension rights and the choices which are available to them under the scheme. Such information shall at least correspond to information given to scheme members in respect of whom contributions cease to be made but who remain within the same Member State."

344 Article 6 Supplementary Pension Rights Directive (see footnote 320) specifies that scheme members may obtain information on how a termination of employment would affect their supplementary pension rights.

ket."[345] The institutions, instead of the scheme member, would from now on become the focal point of European efforts in occupational pensions.

Initially, the proposed directive focused also on the mobility of workers, however, the final proposal for the directive included no provisions on cross-border membership. These were stricken from an earlier draft in the interest of avoiding long negotiations on vesting and funding requirements, as well as harmonisation of taxation.[346]

The Proposal

On 12 November 1991, under the stewardship of Commissioner Sir Leon Brittan, the proposal for a directive heralded by the 1991 Communication was presented by the European Commission under the title "Proposal for a Council Directive relating to the freedom of management and investment of funds held by institutions for retirement provision".[347] It was to "free pension funds from arbitrary national restrictions"[348] relating to their management and investments. It sought to eradicate measures in place in Member States that, for instance, require pension institutions to invest in domestic government stocks or any other particular category of assets, or to seek prior approval from the authorities for investments. It was also to allow for the cross-border management of assets by asset managers. Sir Brittan noted the importance of the directive for the facilitation of cross-border pensions: It "marks a beginning in the Community's efforts to overcome the many practical problems which face companies with pension liabilities in several countries; and which face workers who move between Member States."[349] This proposed directive also contained the "prudent person" principle in the field of investments.

The Prudent Person Principle

The prudent person principle is a set of guidelines and principles for persons responsible for the operation of pension funds and investment activities, for instance fiduciary agents, trustees and asset managers.[350] The rules are qualitative rather than quantitative. "The aim is that the responsible persons behave as careful professionals in making investment

---

345 1991 Communication (see footnote 313) 3.
346 Lannoo (see footnote 327) 121.
347 Commission of the European Communities, 'Proposal for a Council Directive relating to the freedom of management and investment of funds held by institutions for retirement provisions' COM(91) 301 final.
348 European Commission, 'Commission proposes a directive on the investment and management of pension fund assets' Press release 16 October 1991, available at europa.eu/rapid/press-release_IP-91-919_en.htm accessed 11 December 2019.
349 ibid.
350 Commission of the European Communities, 'Towards a Single Market for supplementary pensions' COM (1999) 134 final (1999 Communication) 17.

decisions, but at the same time are aware of the need to earn an adequate return on investments. Prudent person principles require that the fund does not assume unnecessary risk. In fact, it aims at diminishing risk through diversification."[351] In a Communication published later, the Commission argues that experience has shown that "over-restrictive" investment rules have been detrimental to the yields of pension funds, resulting in lower benefits for scheme members or higher contributions. Academic literature appears to support the Commission's claim that, from an investment performance point of view, the prudent person principle is to be preferred over quantitative investment restrictions.[352]

Though the principle, as proposed in the 1991 proposal for a directive, would disgruntle several Member States – as we see below -, it was to remain part of the discussions and would become the standard for the 2003 IORP Directive and its revised form, the IORP II Directive.

The Commission, however, ran into "a great deal of opposition"[353] when it proposed the principle for the first time with this proposed directive. Though the proposal was "limited in scope and coverage", containing only provisions on management and investment of pension funds, it "raised the hopes of fund managers who seek new markets for their capital and investment expertise."[354] It did not address the issue of cross-border membership, considered by the 1991 communication, taxation or pension portability. It was significant, however, in that it attempted to end Member State investment restrictions and would give pension funds access to the services of fund managers from other Member States.[355]

Some Member States were wary of the proposed directive, as "it was seen by member states without significant funded pension plans as an offensive to impose a certain sys-

---

351 ibid.
352 See, for example, E P Davis, *Portfolio Regulation of Life Insurance Companies and Pension Funds* (OECD Insurance and Private Pensions Compendium for Emerging Economies, Book 2 Part 1:3)a, OECD 2001) 30-31. Available at: http://www.oecd.org/daf/fin/private-pensions/1815732.pdf. See also E P Davis, 'Prudent person rules or quantitative restrictions? The regulation of long-term institutional investors' portfolios' (2001) Vol 1 (2) Journal of Pension Economics and Finance 157; E P Davis & Y-W Hu, 'Should Pension Investing be Regulated' (2009) Vol 2 (1) Rotman International Journal of Pension Management 34; J Khort, 'Regulation of Pension Fund Investment Allocations in Private Equity; Analysis of the IORP Directive of 2003/41/EC Reform' (2015) Uppsala Faculty of Law Working Paper 2015:1, available at https://www.jur.uu.se/digitalAssets/585/c_585476-l_3-k_wps2015-1.pdf accessed 2 January 2020; L-N Boon et al, 'Pension Regulation and Investment Performance: Rule-Based vs. Risk-Based' (2014) Netspar Discussion Paper, available at https://ssrn.com/abstract=2414477 accessed 2 January 2020.
353 European Economic and Social Committee, Opinion on the 'Proposal for a Directive of the European Parliament and of the Council on the activities of institutions for occupational retirement provision', (2001/C 155/07), 2001. Available at http://eur-lex.europa.eu/legal-content/EN/TXT/?uri=celex:52001-AE0403 accessed 12 January 2020.
354 G Zavvos, 'Pension Fund Liberalization and the Future of Retirement Financing in Europe' (1994) Vol 31 (3) Common Market Law Review 609, 610.
355 ibid.

tem."[356] It was based on British principles, and France was the main opponent.[357] The French Government balked at relinquishing control over the investment decisions of its national pension funds without being replaced with a Community control.[358]

The proposal applied to all "institutions for retirement provision" including "institutions which operate essentially on a pay-as-you-go basis with compulsory membership and limited reserves",[359] barring those that are part of the social security system. This definition proved troublesome and would spark much disagreement during subsequent negotiations,[360] owing to the many shapes and sizes that occupational pension arrangements in the Member States come in. From the relatively unregulated UK funds, to underwritten-and-guaranteed-by state-funds institutions to those mandated by state legislation (France), there are many private/public hybrids that made their classification onerous.[361] Consequently, the proposal needed to be amended.

An Amended Proposal

The proposal for the directive was amended on 26 May 1993.[362] The definition "institutions for retirement provision" was clarified by a new one: "institutions for retirement provision means an institution or a fund, other than a statutory security body (...) including those (...) which constitute reserves which are capable of being invested in assets."[363] This definition, too, proved to be a ground for discord as the Member States began adding institutions[364] under the annex to the proposal which identified the exempted Social Security Bodies referred to in Article 2(a) of the revised proposal.[365]

The revised definition made that the directive primarily applied to funded supplementary pension plans and excluded pay-as-you-go, state-run social security funds.[366] However, pay-as-you-go (PAYG) plans that hold short term assets were held to be included in its scope, such as the French AGIRC and ARRCO.

---

356 Lannoo (see footnote 327) 122.
357 I Guardiancich & D Natali, 'The EU and Supplementary Pensions: Instruments for Integration and the Market for Occupational Pensions in Europe' (2009) 2009.11 ETUI Working Paper 11.
358 Lannoo (see footnote 327) 122.
359 Commission of the European Communities, 'Proposal for a Council Directive relating to the freedom of management and investment of funds held by institutions for retirement provisions' COM(91) 301 final 9.
360 Lannoo (see footnote 327) 122.
361 Zavvos (see footnote 354) 620.
362 European Commission, 'Amended proposal for a Council Directive relating to the freedom of management and investment of funds held by institutions for retirement provision' COM (93) 237 final.
363 ibid, Article 2.
364 Lannoo (see footnote 327) 122.
365 European Commission, 'Amended proposal for a Council Directive relating to the freedom of management and investment of funds held by institutions for retirement provision' COM (93) 237 final, Annex.
366 Zavvos (see footnote 354) 619.

The Netherlands attempted to make a case for the exemption of its civil servants' fund ABP, arguing that it is a statutory body.[367] The fund was, at the time, state-controlled and was required by law to invest 95% of its capital in the Netherlands (even 100% until 1988).[368] ABP expected the liberalization of investment rules to lead to a higher return on its investments.[369] However, the Dutch government did not wish to relinquish control over the ABP, as then-Minister of Finance Wim Kok argued that the government was responsible for the fund's financial health, and a say in the fund's investment strategy was necessary in order to retain control over the pension premiums for the fund, which premiums were also fixed by the government.[370] Kok therefore wanted to exempt the ABP from liberalisation until at least 1996, at which point the ABP was to be privatised. Despite the Netherlands' efforts, the Commission and other Member States refused because such an exemption would go against the spirit of liberalisation.[371]

Failure of the First Attempt at Regulating Occupational Pensions in the EU

This first attempt at regulating occupational retirement provision at EU level "failed miserably":[372] the proposal was ultimately retracted in 1994, as the Commission was not willing to pander to proposed amendments by Member States that effectively legitimised barriers to the freedom to provide services rather than getting rid of them.[373] The European Economic and Social Committee looked back on the negotiations in the early 90s: "The greatest stumbling block was the provision that pension institutions were only required to invest a certain percentage of their funds in assets denominated in their home currency. This watering down of the legal requirement was unacceptable to many Member States",[374] especially France.[375]

---

367 Lannoo (see footnote 327) 122.

368 'Brussel schenkt ABP vrijheid om meer in het buitenland te beleggen', *NRC Handelsblad* 17 October 1991. Available at http://www.delpher.nl/nl/kranten/view?query=abp+richtlijn&coll=ddd&identifier=KBNRC01%3A000029433%3Ampeg21%3Aa0127&resultsidentifier=KBNRC01%3A000029433%3Ampeg21%3Aa0127 accessed 2 January 2020.

369 ibid.

370 'Kabinet wil invloed op ABP niet prijsgeven', *Limburgsch Dagblad* 3 September 1993, available at: http://www.delpher.nl/nl/kranten/view?query=abp+richtlijn&coll=ddd&identifier=ddd%3A010637633%3Ampeg21%3Aa0590&resultsidentifier=ddd%3A010637633%3Ampeg21%3Aa0590 accessed 2 January 2020.

371 Zavvos (see footnote 354) 621.

372 Guardiancich & Natali (see footnote 357) 11.

373 Lannoo (see footnote 327) 123.

374 European Economic and Social Committee, Opinion on the 'Proposal for a Directive of the European Parliament and of the Council on the activities of institutions for occupational retirement provision', (2001/C 155/07), 2001. Available at http://eur-lex.europa.eu/legal-content/EN/TXT/?uri=celex:52001-AE0403 accessed 12 January 2020.

375 Lannoo (see footnote 327) 122.

After the Commission's withdrawal of the proposal, it issued a non-binding Communication covering, in essence, the same matters as the proposed directive.[376] This Communication sparked a row between the Commission and France, with the latter seeking to annul the document before the European Court of Justice with the support of Spain.[377] Although the Commission contended that the Communication was "not intended to have legal effects and that it did not intend to impose obligations on Member States",[378] the ECJ noted the "parallels"[379] between it and the withdrawn proposal and concluded that the communication was indeed intended to have legal effects of its own. The Court therefore annulled the Communication.[380]

2.2   1997: The Green Paper on Supplementary Pensions in the Single Market

Less than three months after the Court's decision in the aforementioned case, the Commission released a Green Paper on supplementary pensions.[381] It was – in light of the previously failed attempts – a cautious basis from which it would draw input from respondents, upon which it would propose new initiatives.[382] In the context of Europe's ageing population, the Green Paper combined the topics of the previous initiatives of worker mobility and investment freedom.

In light of population aging, the Commission anticipated a growth in supplementary pension provision in the second and third pillars in order to alleviate overburdened first pillars.[383] It focused on the role of occupational pensions for the maintenance of retirement income levels and how the Single Market could help in facilitating their growth. In this context, the Commission predicted that the role of second-pillar pensions would grow,[384] and recognised them not just as a way of maintaining Europeans' level of retirement income, but also as an opportunity for growth for the EU economy.

To that end, the Green Paper explored the possibility of creating a "real Single Market" for pension funds, in which their investments are free of excessive regulation (the

---

376 European Commission 'Commission Communication on the Freedom of Management and Investment of Funds held by Institutions for Retirement Provision: Communication on an internal market for pension funds' (94/C 360/08). Available at https://eur-lex.europa.eu/legal-content/EN/TXT/PDF/?uri=OJ: JOC_1994_360_R_0007_01&from=BG accessed 12 January 2020.

377 C Bittner, 'Occupational Pensions: a Matter of European Concern' (2001) Vol 2 (2) European Business Organization Law Review 401, 415.

378 Case C-57/95 France v. Commission [1997] ECLI:EU:C:1997:164, para 6.

379 ibid para 12.

380 ibid para 27.

381 Commission of the European Communities, 'Supplementary Pensions in the Single Market: A Green Paper' COM(97) 283 final.

382 P Pochet, 'Pensions: the European debate' in G L Clark and N Witheside (eds), Pension security in the 21st century (Oxford University Press 2003).

383 Commission of the European Communities, 'Supplementary Pensions in the Single Market: A Green Paper' COM(97) 283 final 1-14.

384 ibid 8.

prudent person principle) and in which they can engage in cross-border activity (harmonisation of supervisory law standards).[385]

It also focused on free movement of workers, identifying in particular the problem of losing pension entitlements, the issue of waiting and vesting periods, difficulties regarding cross-border transferability of pension pots emanating from Member State legislation or scheme rules and, finally, tax difficulties. According to the Green Paper, occupational pensions "can pose a significant obstacle" to worker mobility.[386] It said that the existing system of coordination that existed for statutory pensions was not appropriate for occupational pensions, given the "specific nature of many supplementary pension schemes and their extreme diversity at national level as regards their origin, their occupational and material scope, as well as their legal and technical forms."[387] It also made reference to the so-called High Level Panel on Free Movement of Persons chaired by Mrs. Simone Veil,[388] which advised to deal with mobility problems in the field of occupational pensions by a three-pronged approach. That approach encompassed the elements of 1) preservation of acquired rights based on equal treatment, 2) cross-border payments of pension benefits in retirement and 3) measures allowing workers temporarily seconded by their employer in another Member State to remain affiliated to the supplementary pension scheme in the country in which they were previously working.[389] These three elements were dealt with by Directive 98/49/EC.

Third, the Communication focused on fiscal barriers to the free movement of persons and services, and whether any measures at Community level could help. The matter of tax barriers was dealt with by the Commission a few years later in a separate Communication.[390]

The Green Paper's chapter on prudential rules was its centrepiece, and would be the core pillar of the later IORP Directive.[391] The Commission considered that, despite its previously failed efforts to convince Member States of its plans, the core of its considerations on prudential rules still stood. The Commission therefore felt that the "objectives of the withdrawn directive still need to be pursued". It still championed the removal of excessive rules on the investments for pension funds, and the replacement of those rules

---

385 ibid 15-21.

386 ibid III.

387 ibid 22.

388 European Commission, *Report of the High Level Panel on the free movement of persons chaired by Simone Veil* (Publications Office of the European Union 1998).

389 Commission of the European Communities, 'Supplementary Pensions in the Single Market: A Green Paper' COM(97) 283 final 23.

390 European Commission, 'Communication from the Commission to the Council, the European Parliament and the Economic and Social Committee - The elimination of tax obstacles to the cross-border provision of occupational pensions' COM(2001) 214 final.

391 2345th ECOFIN Council meeting, 7 May 2001, 9, available at http://data.consilium.europa.eu/doc/document/ST-8444-2001-INIT/en/pdf accessed 2 January 2020.

with the so-called prudent person principle.[392] Another of the Commission's objectives was to enable fund managers authorised in one Member State to offer their services all over the EU. These two objectives remain key features of the IORP II Directive today.

In its overview of responses to the Green Paper,[393] the Commission noted that there was "widespread agreement" among respondents that pension funds and pension-related life insurance funds would be a major growth market. Regarding prudential rules, the Commission stated that its suggestions were "extremely favourably received." Respondents expressed their approval with respect to the Commission's suggestions of requiring those pension fund managers and bodies taking investment decisions be approved by a supervisory authority, as well as for regular reporting obligations. The proposed prudent person principle also met with broad agreement among the respondents, though Southern European States would still continue to oppose it during later negotiations. The adoption of a directive for regulating prudential rules was the favoured method of the respondents. This call for a directive came to fruition in October 2000, while the other matters – the tax barriers and worker mobility – addressed by the Green Paper were dealt with in separate initiatives.[394]

On 3 December 1998, the European Parliament adopted a report (the Ferri report) containing a motion for a resolution, calling "on the Commission to adopt a proposal for a Directive"[395] for pension funds, including a "European passport"[396] that allows their cross-border operation.[397] This appears to have been the first time that such a passport was explicitly called for, with previous documents focusing on freedom of investment. According to the Ferri report, "(A)nyone in favour of Europe must also be in favour of the so-called 'European pass' for pension funds. This means that, as is the case with life insurance companies, any pension fund with prudential authorization in one country should receive prudential authorization throughout the internal market, but only if Europe-wide rules provide the security needed in this highly sensitive sector."[398] In response

---

392 See Section 2.1.2.

393 European Commission, 'Overview of the Responses to the Green Paper on Supplementary Pensions in the Single Market - COM(97) 283' of 6 April 1998.

394 The tax barriers were addressed in COM (2001) 214 final; worker mobility would eventually be dealt with by the Safeguard Directive (see footnote 319) and the Supplementary Pension Rights Directives (see footnote 320).

395 European Parliament, 'Report on the Commission Green Paper entitled 'Supplementary Pensions in the Single Market' (COM(97)0283 - C4-0392/97)', A4-0400/98, available at http://www.europarl.europa.eu/sides/getDoc.do?pubRef=-//EP//NONSGML+REPORT+A4-1998-0400+0+DOC+PDF+V0//EN accessed 2 January 2020, Point 2.

396 ibid, Point 11.

397 J Marshall & S Butterworth, 'Pensions Reform in the EU: The Unexploded Time Bomb in the Single Market' (2000) Vol 37 (3) Common Market Law Review 739, 745.

398 European Parliament, 'Report on the Commission Green Paper entitled 'Supplementary Pensions in the Single Market' (COM(97)0283 - C4-0392/97)', A4-0400/98, available at http://www.europarl.europa.eu/sides/getDoc.do?pubRef=-//EP//NONSGML+REPORT+A4-1998-0400+0+DOC+PDF+V0//EN accessed 2 January 2020, 27.

to the Green Paper on pensions, rapporteur Ferri remarked in the resolution that the
biggest problem is that there is no EU-wide legislative framework that applies to occupational pension funds, governing and liberalising their operations. This "lack of a single
internal market for supplementary occupational retirement provision is detrimental to
the financial markets in that funded occupational retirement provision schemes are
among the largest institutional investors, whose assets account for over 20% of the Union's annual GDP."[399] It is also detrimental to freedom of movement and worker flexibility.[400]

2.3   *1999: A New Communication from the Commission: "Towards a Single
        Market for Supplementary Pensions"*

In spite of the positive responses to the Green Paper on the subject, reaching agreement
on prudential rules turned out to be an onerous process. However, due to the responses to
the Green Paper and respondents' general agreement to the Commission's approach, the
Commission felt that revisiting the subject was justified, albeit in a new context.[401] In
"[d]rawing the lessons from the consultations", the Commission stated that a new proposal for a directive should place greater emphasis on fund security, rather than the 1991
proposed directive's focus on asset allocation.[402] Protecting beneficiaries "must remain
the cornerstone of the regulation" and "[a]ll conceivable steps must be taken to guarantee
the contractual benefits to future pensioners". It also pledged to be more ambitious than
the last time, and to create a proposal that will "take a first step towards creating the
conditions necessary for cross-border membership."[403] The Commission estimated that
the conditions created by the single currency and the greater consensus on the need for
pension reform should conspire to make for a more opportune environment in which to
present a new proposal for a directive.

---

399 European Parliament, *Report on the proposal for a European Parliament and Council directive on the activ-
    ities of institutions for occupational retirement provision* (Session document 21 June 2001) A5-0220/2001
    final, 57 (The Karas Report).
400 ibid.
401 1999 Communication (see footnote 350) 25.
402 ibid.
403 ibid. On the issue of cross-border membership, rapporteur Othmar Karas remarked at the EP Debate on
    2 April 2001 that; "Further Commission initiatives will have to follow [...] because we will not have trans-
    ferable pensions and mobility within the EU until the Member States agree on common taxation principles.
    We know that setting the tax rate is part of income tax and thus falls within the purview of the Member
    States. Nevertheless, in my view, a general shift to downstream taxation is necessary to avoid contributions
    and benefits being taxed twice or not at all." See http://www.europarl.europa.eu/sides/getDoc.do?pubRef=-//
    EP//TEXT+CRE+20010402+ITEM-007+DOC+XML+V0//EN&language=EN accessed 2 January 2020.

*In Favour of a Directive on Prudential Rules Creating a Single Market for Occupational
Pensions*

The Communication's purpose was to set out the policy conclusions drawn from the
consultations and to announce the measures for the creation of a single market for occupational pensions. It argued for the adoption of a directive on prudential rules for pension
funds that it should strive to attain the following goals: 1) to ensure the best possible
protection of beneficiaries, 2) to allow pension funds to profit fully from the single market
and the euro, 3) to guarantee equal treatment between occupational pension providers
and, finally, 4) to allow mutual recognition of prudential regimes to make cross-border
activity of IORPs possible, as when the Communication was written, "a pension fund
cannot have members in more than one Member State of the Union."[404] The IORP I
Directive would become that directive.

The Commission pointed out that the Green Paper was criticised for placing too
much emphasis on the role of pension funds as a tool to create European capital markets
instead of focusing on their social aspects. This criticism would, however, resurface during discussions by the European Parliament of the proposed IORP I Directive.[405] To
address that criticism, the Commission stressed in its Communication the protection of
participants' rights and the creation of a framework that aids in achieving a high level of
retirement benefits. A second point of concern was the security of pensions. The Commission pledged to address that point by proposing a prudential framework for pension
funds that has as its primary objective the protection of pension scheme members. However, "(n)otwithstanding these criticisms, the overwhelming majority of contributions
fully supported the Commission's analysis in the Green Paper." The Commission noted
that several Member States, social partners and almost the entire financial sector considered the lack of an EU-level legislative framework for pension funds to be a major omission in European financial services legislation.

In a chapter on prudential rules, the Commission emphasised the importance of asset
diversification, keeping of sufficient liquid assets, sound accounting, and authorisation
and oversight by a competent authority with a the aim of protecting pension beneficiaries.[406] Informing scheme members about the management of the fund is also identified
as a key component for the protection of their interests. The proposals on prudential
rules included in the Communication became the basis for the IORP I Directive.

Regarding the issue of worker mobility, the Communication intended to remove barriers in this field as problems will increase "if Member States choose to rely increasingly
on supplementary pensions".[407] To eliminate any measures by Member States likely to

---

404 1999 Communication (see footnote 350) 4.
405 See next section.
406 1999 Communication (see footnote 350) 11.
407 ibid 26.

impede or render less attractive the exercise by workers of fundamental Treaty freedoms, the communication lists a number of possible actions. These are the harmonization of qualifying conditions for acquiring occupational pension rights, the possibility of enabling cross-border affiliation for workers other than posted workers covered by Directive 98/49/EC and the transferability of pension rights. At the time the communication was written, Directive 98/49/EC was already in force, allowing posted workers to continue paying in to their existing pension schemes in their Member State of origin.

Regarding the harmonisation of qualifying conditions, the Commission concluded from the responses to the Green Paper that "a legislative framework seems to be premature."[408] It also expressed its commitment to addressing this problem, but it would take until 2014 until a solution came with the adoption of the Supplementary Pension Rights Directive by improving the acquisition and preservation of supplementary pension rights through setting maximum waiting and vesting periods.

On cross-border affiliation – that is, remaining in the same pension scheme while moving to a new job in another Member State – the Commission conceded that it would be difficult to implement cross-border membership. Such cross-border membership could be useful for some categories of migrant workers who work in another Member State for a short period and could avoid changes from one pension scheme to another and possible losses of pension rights. However, full-fledged cross-border membership turned out to be too challenging to achieve: the idea of allowing workers moving to another State to remain with their previous pension institution in the Member State they left – like keeping a bank account – appears to have been dropped from the Commission's agenda and does not appear to have been pursued in earnest since this Communication. It noted that cross-border membership "can only be a long-term aim"[409] because a number of conditions were not met. For this to be possible, the Commission noted that the mutual recognition of prudential regimes – for which purpose the IORP I Directive was adopted – the coordination of tax systems and social and labour laws of the Member States are required.[410] The IORP I Directive does not touch upon the latter two subjects, and these obstacles therefore exist to this day as the IORP II Directive brings no change in this regard. Directive 98/49/EC makes cross-border membership possible only for posted workers.[411]

Then Commissioner for Financial Services, Mario Monti, presented in May 1998 to the Council of Finance Ministers possible ways to improve the efficiency and flexibility of financial services markets. One possibility was the adoption of a directive tackling the restrictions on investments that pension funds experience. He recommended the adoption of a directive by the Commission: "I will (...) be recommending that the Commis-

---

408 ibid 28.
409 ibid 5.
410 ibid p.15.
411 Article 6 of the Safeguard Directive (see footnote 319).

sion proposes a Directive to establish an appropriate framework of prudential rules that sets minimum investment safeguards and tackles quantitative restrictions besides limits on investment in a company's own shares."[412]

The Commission's endeavour in occupational pensions was spurred along by the Lisbon European Council of 2000, at which the creation of efficient and integrated financial markets and the modernisation of social protection were named as goals.[413]

2.4   *Negotiations on the Proposed IORP I Directive: A Struggle for a More Social Directive*

Introduction: The Original Proposal for the IORP I Directive

Highlighting the urgency apparently felt to establish a legal framework governing IORPs at the European level, the Financial Services Action Plan of May 1999 – a roadmap for completing Europe's single financial market – rated the adoption of a directive on the prudential supervision of pension plans as a number 1 priority.[414]

Therefore on 11 October 2000, the Commission presented a proposal for a directive on the activities of IORPs, based on the Single Market provisions that are now enshrined in Articles 53, 62 and 114 TFEU.[415] The Commission presented the directive as a "liberalization measure" whose goal it was to let pension institutions enjoy single market advantages in a manner similar to other financial institutions.[416] The proposed directive allows pension institutions in one Member State to operate pension schemes and to accept pension contributions from another.

Relatedly, the proposed directive allowed undertakings to pay pension contributions to pension institutions in another Member State. For this cross-border activity to work, the proposal contains provisions for the mutual recognition by Member States of other States' supervisory regimes: pension institutions offering their services in other Member States (the host country) are under the supervision of their home state authorities, necessitating the host country to accept the supervisory regime of the home State as equivalent to its own. To this effect, the directive lays down minimum standards, "designed to ensure that occupational pension transactions attain a high level of security and effi-

---

412 European Commission, 'Supplementary Pensions: the next steps' Press release 19 May 1998, available at https://ec.europa.eu/commission/presscorner/detail/en/IP_98_447 accessed 2 January 2020.

413 European Parliament, Presidency Conclusions of the Lisbon European Council 23 and 24 March 2000, available at http://www.europarl.europa.eu/summits/lis1_en.htm

414 European Commission, 'Communication from the Commission implementing the Framework for Financial Markets: Action Plan' COM(1999) 232 final, 20.

415 Commission of the European Communities, 'Proposal for a directive of the European Parliament and of the Council on the activities of institutions for occupational retirement provision' COM(2000) 507 final.

416 M Haverland, 'When the welfare state meets the regulatory state: EU occupational pension policy' (2007) Vol 14 (6) Journal of European Public Policy 886, 894.

ciency", which in turn allow for mutual recognition.[417] Another principle is that pension providers operating schemes from other Member States must comply with the social and labour laws of the relevant host country. Neither the IORP I Directive nor the revised IORP II Directive, however, defines social and labour law, potentially leading to complications for pension scheme members as will be explained in Chapters 4 and 5.

The prudent person rule, which the Commission pursued since the early 1990s, was included in this proposal and – this time – would pass the scrutiny of the Council and the European Parliament. The Committee of Wise Men on the Regulation of European Securities Markets explained that proper regulation and integration the European financial market – of which implementing liberal investment rules for pension funds forms part – could lead to direct benefits for European citizens. Replacing "outdated investment rules for [...] pension funds"[418] would, according to the Committee, enable European pension funds to invest more freely and with modern investment techniques, in turn making a better pension yield possible.[419] There were, however, a few restrictions to the prudent person principle in the proposal, in that Member States would be allowed to adopt quantitative restrictions and more stringent investment rules in individual cases.[420]

Negotiations

The negotiations on the proposed IORP I Directive showed a difference in views between, on the hand, the European Parliament (EP) and, on the other, the Commission and the Council, with the former preferring more far-reaching integration between Member States' pension policies than the latter.[421] It also laid bare a rift *within* the EP between the parties which favoured a socially-oriented IORP Directive and those which supported a more liberal outlook.[422] While some parties within the EP were satisfied with the Commission's financial services approach, (some members of) other parties favoured a more social slant. A point of contention during the discussions in the European Parliament were provisions regarding solidarity, which were not part of the original proposal.[423] Such provisions concern rules with regard to risk-sharing – for instance, between young and old, men and women, high- and low income scheme members – and certain guar-

---

417 Commission of the European Communities, 'Proposal for a directive of the European Parliament and of the Council on the activities of institutions for occupational retirement provision' COM(2000) 507 final, Explanatory Memorandum.
418 'Final Report on the Committee of Wise Men on the Regulation of European Securities Markets (Lamfalussy Report)', Brussels, 15 February 2001, 12.
419 ibid, 74.
420 Commission of the European Communities, 'Proposal for a directive of the European Parliament and of the Council on the activities of institutions for occupational retirement provision' COM(2000) 507 final, Article 18.
421 Haverland (see footnote 416).
422 ibid.
423 ibid 894.

antees (such as return guarantees) and coverage of biometric risks (the risks of invalidity, longevity or death).[424]

The first reading of the proposed directive in the European Parliament on 3 July 2001 began with a dig at the Council and Commission, when Othmar Karas, rapporteur for the IORP Directive, noted that the IORP proposal and the Karas Report are a good example of successful dialogue on a legislative proposal and "of how seriously we take our work and of how we implement our projects, observing schedules, and also of how good we are at preparing decisions, unlike the Council."[425] MEP Kuckelkorn suggested that the Commission had U-turned on the issue of helping "the majority of Europe's citizens", instead favouring the interests of the financial industry, and that the text proposed by it "bears the hallmark of lobbyists."[426] The MEP appeared especially resentful at what he saw as the Commission's prioritizing of the investment sector over traditional second-pillar providers: "This is because you want to give financial products equal tax treatment but without obliging the financial sector to offer the same security as second pillar institutions, which in return benefit from their own security, that is to say from tax advantages." However, other MEPs viewed the proposal's social implications in a decidedly more positive light.[427]

As noted, the EP was "deeply divided as to whether the more integrationist solution should have a liberal or a social outlook."[428] Among the amendments by the more liberal parties was the introduction of a time limit for transitioning to an unrestricted prudent person rule to get rid of quantitative investment restrictions altogether. The time limit would be introduced to allow the different investment cultures in the Member States some time for adjustment, "(...) your rapporteur advocates a time-limit: Member States should indeed be given the option of retaining quantitative restrictions, but this option should apply only for an appropriate period, not exceeding ten years, in which time a Member State's 'supervisory culture and methods' can be brought into line with the qualitative approach."[429]

The IORP I Directive as adopted does not feature such a sunset clause.[430] The final version allows some quantitative restrictions; "[...] Member States may, for the institu-

---

424 M Draghi & R Pozen, 'US-EU Regulatory Convergence: Capital Markets Issues' (2003) Harvard Law School Discussion Paper No. 444, 10, available at https://ssrn.com/abstract=460560 accessed 2 January 2020.

425 Verbatim report of the European Parliament Debate on 3 July 2001 in Strasbourg, available at http://www. europarl.europa.eu/sides/getDoc.do?pubRef=-%2f%2fEP%2f%2fTEXT%2bCRE%2b20010703%2bITEM-007%2bDOC%2bXML%2bV0%2f%2fEN&language=EN accessed 2 January 2020.

426 ibid.

427 ibid.

428 Haverland (see footnote 416) 895.

429 The Karas Report (see footnote 399) 60.

430 Draghi & Pozen (see footnote 424) 10.

tions located in their territories, lay down more detailed rules, including quantitative
rules, provided they are prudentially justified, to reflect the total range of pension
schemes operated by these institutions."[431]

The same parties also wanted more lenient solvency requirements. Rather than the
requirement that "[i]n the event of cross-border activity the technical provisions must be
fully funded at all times to protect the interests of members and beneficiaries", these
MEPs desired to put in place a provision that applies the home country's solvency requirements.[432]

The European trade association for pension funds EFRP,[433] though highly critical of
the Parliament's more socially-oriented parties' proposals aiming to introduce more safeguards in pension products, welcomed this proposal.[434] As stated, the original Commission proposal also contained the prudent person principle, but allowed Member States to
introduce some permanent quantitative restrictions on investments within the margins
prescribed in the proposal.[435] The European People's Party and the Liberal Party aimed
to do away with these.

Another amendment, the result of a compromise between the liberal European People's Party group and the Socialist Party Group, contained a clause making it mandatory
for pension providers to offer their scheme members the cover of biometric risk – such as
through the payment of lifelong annuities, disability coverage and pension payments for
survivors.[436] This mandatory choice was inserted, since, according to the Karas Report,
"(p)ension schemes in the true meaning of the word have to cover biometric risks. Otherwise there is no clear line of distinction from e.g. life insurance products or investment
funds, which provide a pay out of the invested capital plus interest/profit share as a lump
sum or monthly payments from a given age or date on."[437] Another reason put forward
in the amendments was to encourage scheme members to "think carefully" about their
choices regarding retirement provision.[438]

Additionally, MEPs added amendments that pension funds must offer a minimum
return guarantee and that benefits should be lifetime benefits in lieu of lump-sums.[439]

---

431 Directive 2003/41/EC of the European Parliament and of the Council of 3 June 2003 on the activities and
supervision of institutions for occupational retirement provision [2003] OJ L 235/10 (IORP I Directive),
Article 17(5).

432 Haverland (see footnote 416) 895.

433 EFRP is now known as Pensions Europe.

434 EFRP, 'EP Karas-report on pension funds: EFRP welcomes reinforcement of prudent person rule', Press
Statement of 6 July 2001, available at https://www.pensionseurope.eu/system/files/Press%20release%20-%
20EP%20Plenary%20Karas%20final%202001-07-06.pdf accessed 2 January 2020.

435 Draghi & Pozen (see footnote 324).

436 Amendments 20 and 48 in the Karas Report (see footnote 399); See also Haverland (see footnote 416) 896;
A Hennessy, The Europeanization of Workplace Pensions: Economic Interests, Social Protection, and Credible Signaling (Cambridge University Press 2013) 71.

437 ibid, Amendment 20.

438 ibid, Amendment 48.

439 Haverland (see footnote 416) 896.

The Socialist Party ultimately went with these amendments, and the EP passed an amended version in July 2001.

The proposal therefore gained some social elements after the first reading, a development criticised by EFRP and deemed unworkable by the Commission[440] and later also the Council. The Commission already indicated at the Parliament's first hearing that "the directive cannot regulate the products offered by pension funds, nor can it define the precise arrangements for the payment of benefits which are often dependent on national tax, labour and social law".[441] Therefore, the Commission was not willing to accept amendments aiming at doing just that.

Commissioner Bolkestein explained that the proposal "has a limited ambition, namely the creation of a prudential framework with stringent prudential standards to ensure security and affordability and allow for mutual recognition." It was not intended to regulate the products offered by IORPs, and for that reason the Commissioner notes that the Commission cannot accept amendments with that aim. According to him, "the directive cannot regulate the products offered by pension funds, nor can it define the precise arrangements for the payment of benefits which are often dependent on national tax, labour and social law. Cover of biometric risks, in particular of longevity, is an important aspect of the fight against poverty and insecurity among elderly people. But this directive should not stipulate how and to what extent benefits ought to be paid out or which biometric risks need to be covered by the institution."[442]

The EFRP, in favour of the directive taking the form of a pure financial services directive, lamented that Parliament had in effect attempted "to oust the Commission proposal for a financial services directive" by trying to turn the proposal into a "social policy reform directive": "The EP has erred by proposing legislation for second pillar pension provision rather than addressing the needs of pension funds as financial institutions".[443]

The Council "appeared to have a totally different view on pensions issues than the European Parliament."[444] A number of southern European Member States opposed the prudent person rule while the northern European countries and Italy were in favour of it. Agreement was found by adding some margin of discretion to the prudent person rule. This eventually won over France – "the last large opposing member state"[445] – which gave up its opposition to allow the Council's Common Position on the directive to be

---

440 Verbatim report of the European Parliament Debate on 3 July 2001 in Strasbourg, available at http://www.europarl.europa.eu/sides/getDoc.do?pubRef=-%2f%2fEP%2f%2fTEXT%2bCRE%2b20010703%2bITEM-010%2bDOC%2bXML%2bV0%2f%2fEN&language=EN accessed 2 January 2020.

441 ibid.

442 ibid.

443 EFRP (see footnote 434).

444 F Betson, 'Member states are blocking "prudent man" directive' (Investment & Pensions Europe, 24 October 2001) available at https://www.ipe.com/member-states-are-blocking-prudent-man-directive/4578.article accessed 2 January 2020.

445 Haverland (see footnote 416) 897.

found. In the end, only Belgium was against the proposal. None of the EP's proposals for
more lenient solvency standards or more liberal investment rules were accepted (in particular, the Council rejected the proposal for a time limit to scrap investment restrictions). Moreover, the Council decided that host countries should be able to demand
more stringent investment rules than in the fund's home countries, undermining the
principle of mutual recognition. It also reaffirmed the Commission's requirement that
full funding is required in the event of cross-border activity and that a scheme's liabilities
must at all times be covered.

The Common Position also included no social issues and "lacked any reference to
solidaristic elements."[446] None of the Parliament's plans for biometric risks or guaranteed
returns were accepted. It followed the Commission's approach which allowed for the
payment of lump-sums "and it rejected the requirement that pension funds have to offer
the option of protecting against biometric risks and a return guarantee of the contributions paid."[447] The final directive provides Member States with the option to require the
option of biometric risk coverage.[448]

As neither the Council nor the Commission were prepared to accept the EP's "integrationist" stance, an informal trilogue was started between the Commission, the Greek
presidency and the rapporteur, Othmar Karas in order to fend off a conciliation procedure.[449] The goal was "that in its second reading the EP should only adopt amendments
that would be acceptable to the European Commission and the Council."[450] At second
reading, all 18 amendments proposed by the EP were accepted by the Commission and
the Council. The EP let go of its demand that pension providers must offer lifelong pay-
outs and its time limits on quantitative restrictions on investments. Criticism was levelled
at the Council by the EP for its defiance in dealing with the EP's amendments and its
tardy production of a common position; "Parliament's first reading produced 458 votes
in favour. If the Council had accepted this gesture of cooperation on our part, we should
already have had this directive long ago."[451] On 13 May 2003, the Council adopted the
text approved by the EP's second reading.[452]

---

446 ibid.
447 ibid 898.
448 Draghi Pozen (see footnote 424) 10.
449 Haverland (see footnote 416) 898-899.
450 ibid 899.
451 Verbatim report of the European Parliament Debate on 11 March 2003 in Strasbourg, available at http://
www.europarl.europa.eu/sides/getDoc.do?pubRef=-//EP//TEXT+CRE+20030311+ITEM-011+DOC+XML
+V0//EN&language=PL accessed 2 January 2020.
452 European Commission, 'Occupational pensions: Commission welcomes Council's definitive adoption of the
Pension Funds Directive' Press Release 13 May 2003, available at http://europa.eu/rapid/press-release_IP-
03-669_en.htm?locale=en accessed 2 January 2020.

2.5   *The IORP Directive: Analysis of Its Objectives and Adoption*

During the twelve years it took to bring about the first incarnation of the IORP Directive, the main premise upon which the EU became involved in regulating occupational pensions changed. This involvement was motivated initially by a desire to maximise the freedom of movement of workers by abolishing any obstacles in the area of occupational pensions these people faced when moving to another Member State to take up employment there. The loss of occupational pension rights, so the Commission argued, could deter workers from taking advantage of their rights of free movement just as it had with respect to statutory pension rights before these were regulated in the 1950s. In addition, the Commission wanted to make sure also that institutions providing occupational pensions could take full advantage of the EU's Single Market by liberalising investments by IORPs. The investment freedom of these institutions was often restricted by national laws of Member States to specific classes of assets or other rules that hampered their freedom of investment. After some years of being active on the subject, the Commission concluded that the Single Market should buttress the sustainability and adequacy of Member States' pension system in the face of population ageing, making cross-border activity of IORPs one of the key priorities in its policy. Towards the end of the 1990s, the need to provide such institutions with a "passport" was identified, to enable them to offer their services in other EU Member States.

In the end, not all of the ideas that were tabled during the discussions on the directive were translated into law.

The directive was proposed to fill the following lacunae in the EU legislative framework.[453] First, there were, before the advent of the directive, no rules on investment for IORPs: the directive aims to liberalise these so they can maximise returns, taking advantage of the free movement of capital. Second, because of the long-term nature of their investments, IORPs play a key role in the financing of private initiatives according to the Commission: a community framework can aid in the "efficient allocation of savings" and develop the EU economy in that manner. Third, the directive was to be the first step to the single market for occupational pensions. It therefore proposed to enable cross-border activities for IORPs, allowing them to take advantage of the freedom to provide services and the freedom of establishment. The explanatory memorandum to the proposal considered: "In the absence of proper coordination at Community level, IORPs are the only major financial institutions unable to provide their services in a Member State other than their own on the same conditions as banks, insurance companies and investment firms."[454] Enabling such cross-border activity is important for the efficiency of IORPs

---

453 Commission of the European Communities, 'Proposal for a directive of the European Parliament and of the Council on the activities of institutions for occupational retirement provision' COM(2000) 507 final, Explanatory Memorandum.
454 ibid.

since it would allow managing the pension schemes for multiple Member States from one home Member State. Finally, the directive also aims at facilitating the growth of IORPs: development of IORPs can alleviate Member State social security schemes.

After a "long and somewhat tortured" path "through the Commission, the European Parliament and the Council in the form of three separate proposals over a period of 12 years",[455] the directive was finally adopted in 2003. It was the "first step on the way to an internal market for occupational retirement provision organised on a European scale." This directive made the creation of pan-European pension funds simpler through, *inter alia*, the mutual recognition of prudential supervisory regimes: the host Member State recognises the home state's supervisory standards.

The resulting directive had a fairly limited aim, as conceded by the Commissioner Frits Bolkestein,[456] though it was decidedly more ambitious than the 1991 proposal that merely sought to harmonise investment rules. The IORP Directive's aim is to provide a framework for the activities of pension institutions wishing to provide cross-border occupational pension services.[457] "It makes no changes to national pension provision structures; it does not seek to require Member States to introduce specific types of pension arrangements; it does not introduce pan-European pensions, whereby an individual in one Member State may belong to a scheme set up in another Member State; nor does it introduce provisions affecting the tax treatment of contributions, funds or benefits."[458] However, the value of the directive lies in what it achieved for occupational pensions: its creation allowed for the first time the cross-border management of pension schemes, meaning various pension schemes (which need to comply with the social and labour law of the countries in which they operate) for various Member States can be managed by one institution in one Member State.

The directive provides for the mutual recognition of supervisory systems, the basic harmonization of prudential rules regarding fund investments and the introduction of a common system for the notification and cooperation between national supervisory authorities, all prerequisites for the cross-border management of occupational schemes.[459]

---

455 Draghi & Pozen (see footnote 424) 10.

456 Verbatim report of the European Parliament Debate on 3 July 2001 in Strasbourg, available at http://www.europarl.europa.eu/sides/getDoc.do?pubRef=-%2f%2fEP%2f%2fTEXT%2bCRE%2b20010703%2bITEM-010%2bDOC%2bXML%2bV0%2f%2fEN&language=EN accessed 2 January 2020.

457 S Arnot, *Directive 2003/41/EC on the Activities and Supervision of Institutions for Occupational Retirement Provision* (European Federation for Retirement Provision 2004).

458 ibid 4.

459 Commission of the European Communities, 'Proposal for a directive of the European Parliament and of the Council on the activities of institutions for occupational retirement provision' COM(2000) 507 final, Explanatory Memorandum, at 1.1 and 1.2.

The directive had seven stated objectives.[460] Some of the most significant ones include the facilitation of secure and efficient investment through principles rather than (potentially overly restrictive) quantitative requirements through implementing the prudent person principle. Additionally, "[b]y harmonising certain basic prudential rules, establishing mutual recognition of national prudential systems and proposing a system of notification and cooperation between competent authorities, this Directive removes all prudential barriers to cross-border management of IORP pension schemes."[461] Another important goal was the protection of the scheme member, about which the EP was adamant. This, as explained by commissioner Bolkestein, is a priority because "[f]ormer Commission initiatives in this area have been perceived as excessively focused on investment and management liberalization" and that there is now "a consensus between all parties" that pension security must come first through solid prudential regulation.[462] Another of the directive's goals is to support the creation of the single market for financial services and, finally, the creation of the single market for supplementary pensions. That said, the latter goal does not appear to have come to full fruition as will be discussed later.

The impression remains that the interests of pension scheme members – particularly mobile ones – have not been considered sufficiently. Abandoning the possibility for cross-border membership, as well as the absence of a provision for the individual transfer of accrued pension rights means that workers could face the loss of occupational pension rights. Chapter 4 will discuss these obstacles to worker mobility in more detail. Second, failing to include social elements in the IORP Directive seems like a missed opportunity in the protection of pension scheme members and could be a reason for the relatively low popularity of cross-border IORPs. The Commission and the Council were unwilling to include such elements, as a result of their focus on the role of IORPs as financial institutions. On the other hand, the inclusion of elements prescribing compulsory elements of pension scheme member protection arguably amounts to regulating Member States' social policy, and Article 153(4) TFEU prohibits the adoption of measures which define the fundamental principles of Member States' social security systems. Ultimately, the reluctance of the EU legislator to define such elements of social protection, such as pension security mechanisms, appears to have led to problems in a cross-border context, which the next two chapters explain.

The issue of pension taxation – the third of the suggestions of the 1997 Green Paper and the 1999 Communication on pensions – was dealt with separately from the IORP Directive. The Commission did not wish to frustrate the progress on IORP, as the

---

460 Commission of the European Communities, 'Proposal for a directive of the European Parliament and of the Council on the activities of institutions for occupational retirement provision' COM(2000) 507 final.

461 ibid.

462 European Commission, 'Frits Bolkestein, European Commissioner for the Internal Market Addressing the Challenges for European Pensions Royal Institute of International Affairs Chatham House, London' Speech 29 February 2000, available at http://europa.eu/rapid/press-release_SPEECH-00-60_en.htm accessed 2 January 2020.

chances of reaching unanimity on a pension taxation directive were assessed by Commissioner Bolkestein as being "similar to the prospects of a snowball in hell."[463] On 2 April 2001, at the EP Debate in Strasbourg on the future of pension systems, Bolkestein announced that the Commission will deal with tax matters in a communication "as a corollary to the pension fund directive". A communication was deemed an adequate manner to overcome, as "the most urgent obstacles to labour mobility and cross-border pension provisions can be overcome without secondary legislation, by enforcing the Treaty rules which are already in place."

This announcement drew the ire of impatient EP members, who had been expecting a "whole package necessary for an occupational pension" – including taxation – and could find "no sympathy" for the communication's tardy presentation of such a communication. The communication ultimately became a reality on 19 April 2001, in which it outlined its initiative to tackle tax obstacles that constitute a "major disincentive"[464] to persons who want to contribute pension schemes in other Member State or for pension institutions to provide their services in other Member States. The Commission pledges to monitor Member States' national rules and take the necessary steps to ensure effective compliance with EU law, including bringing non-compliant Member States before the European Court of Justice.[465] Several infringement procedures and ECJ cases have resulted from this policy.[466]

3   SINCE THE SAFEGUARD DIRECTIVE AND IORP I

Since the adoption of the 1998 Safeguard Directive and the 2003 IORP I Directive, the EU has published several new policy documents and adopted two new directives: the IORP II Directive,[467] which revised the first IORP directive, and the Supplementary Pension Rights Directive.

---

463 ibid.
464 European Commission, 'Commission to tackle tax obstacles to cross-border provision of occupational pensions' Press release 19 April 2001, available at http://europa.eu/rapid/press-release_IP-01-575_en.htm?locale=en accessed 2 January 2020.
465 European Commission, 'The elimination of tax obstacles to the cross-border provision of occupational pensions' COM(2001) 214 final.
466 See, for instance, Case C-136/00 *Danner* [2002] ECLI:EU:C:2002:558; Case C-422/01 *Skandia and Ramstedt* [2003] ECLI:EU:C:2003:380; Case C-520/04 *Turpeinen* [2006] ECLI:EU:C:2006:703; Case C-424/11 *Wheels* [2013] ECLI:EU:C:2013:144; Case C-464/12 *ATP PensionService* [2014] ECLI:EU:C:2014:139. See also European Commission, 'Pension taxation: Commission tackles discrimination against foreign pension funds in six Member States' Press release 5 February 2004, available at https://ec.europa.eu/commission/presscorner/detail/en/IP_03_179 accessed 1 January 2020; European Commission, 'Pensions taxation: Commission decides to refer Denmark to Court over discrimination and to open infringement procedures against the UK and Ireland' Press release 9 July 2003, available at https://ec.europa.eu/commission/presscorner/detail/en/IP_03_965 accessed 2 January 2020; For more information see https://ec.europa.eu/taxation_customs/individuals/personal-taxation/pension-taxation_en accessed 2 January 2020.
467 Directive 2016/2341.

Since the adoption of the IORP I Directive, the main topics of the EU's policies have
remained the improvement of worker mobility as well as the further expansion of the
single market for occupational pensions. The latter goal focused, again, on enhancing the
freedom of IORPs to provide services within the EU and the advantages the Single Market could bring to the safety, adequacy and sustainability of occupational pensions.

Two major publications on occupational pensions since the inception IORP I Directive were the 2010 Green Paper on pensions[468] (titled "Towards adequate, sustainable
and safe European pension systems") and the 2012 White Paper on pensions[469] (titled
"An Agenda for Adequate, Safe and Sustainable Pensions"), with the Green Paper consulting respondents on the course of action and the White Paper plotting a policy agenda.

With the financial and economic crisis as a catalyst for action, the Commission noted
that "[t]he crisis has revealed that more must be done to improve the efficiency and safety
of pension schemes."[470] In addition, demographic ageing is occurring faster than previously anticipated.[471] With these themes as the backdrop for new EU initiatives, the
two publications proposed to address adequacy (i.e. maintaining or improving of income
replacement in retirement by pension systems) and sustainability (i.e. the affordability of
pension provision) of occupational pension systems, as well as the opportunities for
mobility.

With these two publications, the EU has arguably strengthened its policy vision for
pension provision, including the goal of multi-pillar pension systems in the Member
States.[472] It seeks to foster this policy objective through intensifying its regulatory efforts,
which is partially driven by EIOPA.[473] In that context, the Commission sees the deepening of the single market for occupational pensions as one of the key ways of achieving
these goals. On the side of sustainability and adequacy, it notes that breaking down regulatory differences and legal uncertainties, "such as an unclear definition of cross-border
activity", and addressing "a lack of harmonisation of prudential regulation and complex
interaction between EU regulation and national law" can improve efficiency gains resulting from scale economies and competition.[474] Safer pension plans can be achieved
through closing regulatory gaps in EU pension law and improving solvency requirements
and information provision. The Commission therefore suggested revising the IORP Directive, and announced its course of action in the 2012 White Paper. The recast version of
the IORP I Directive, the IORP II Directive, was adopted in 2016.

---

468 European Commission, 'Green Paper towards adequate, sustainable and safe European pension systems'
   COM(2010) 365 final (Green Paper).
469 European Commission, 'An Agenda for Adequate, Safe and Sustainable Pensions' COM(2012) 55 final
   (White Paper).
470 Green Paper (see footnote 468) 2.
471 ibid.
472 M Reiner, 'Entwicklung und Probleme des europäischen Betriebspensionsrechts am Beispiel der Mobilitätsrichtlinie' (2017) Vol 1 (2) Journal für Arbeitsrecht und Sozialrecht 168, 169.
473 ibid.
474 Green Paper (see footnote 468) 11.

With respect to worker mobility, the Commission called for renewed action on the stalled negotiations on the Supplementary Pension Rights Directive to remove remaining obstacles to worker mobility created by occupational pensions,[475] and announced measures "that prevent supplementary pension schemes from being obstacles to professional mobility and labour market flexibility."[476] Those objectives would be carried out by the Supplementary Pension Rights Directive of 2014.

The IORP II Directive

The key goals of the revision of the IORP II Directive were to strengthen the provision of occupational retirement provision by "further facilitating the cross-border activity for IORPs and modernising their supervision."[477] Aided by EIOPA,[478] the Commission announced in its White Paper a revision of the IORP Directive[479] to address weaknesses within it to unlock what it saw as untapped potential "to realize further efficiency gains through scale economies, risk diversification and innovation."[480] It again emphasized the role of the Single Market to ensure the adequacy and sustainability of pensions.

The IORP Directive was to be revised so cross-border activity could be simpler.[481] As explained in the introduction, cross-border IORPs' operations are governed by their home Member State supervisory or prudential law, but their schemes offered in other Member States are governed by the applicable social and labour legislation of those host Member States. This regulatory setup is said to be complex and costly, "which prevents IORPs from fully benefiting from the Single Market."[482] The Impact Assessment accompanying the proposal for the revised IORP Directive noted that as of June 2012, "there were 84 cross-border IORPs, representing only 0.01% of IORPs with more than 100 members in the EU."[483] It attributed this in part to the complexity surrounding the procedure for cross-border activity.

The revised directive did not change this system, although it did clarify several remaining obstacles[484] in a bid to boost cross-border activity, but also "to facilitate the development of occupational retirement savings."[485] It did that by revising procedures

---

475 ibid 12.
476 White Paper (see footnote 469) 13.
477 ibid 13.
478 See, for instance, EIOPA, EIOPA's Advice to the European Commission on the review of the IORP Directive 2003/41/EC (2012) EIOPA-BOS-12/015; EIOPA, Report on QIS on IORPs (2013) EIOPA-BoS-13/124.
479 White Paper (see footnote 469) 17.
480 ibid 13.
481 European Commission, 'Impact Assessment Accompanying the document Proposal for a Directive of the European Parliament and of the Council on the activities and supervision of institutions for occupational retirement provision' SWD(2014) 103 final 3.
482 ibid 10. See also the case-studies in Annex E of the Impact Assessment.
483 ibid.
484 ibid 13-14.
485 ibid 24 et seq.

regarding cross-border activity by clarifying the definition of what constitutes cross-border activity and the applicable procedures.[486] It also clarified the procedure regarding the transfer of pension assets[487] and the scope of prudential rules.[488] The manner in which the directive approaches national social and labour law remains the same, while it – like its predecessor – fails to define social and labour law. The financing requirements for cross-border schemes also remain largely unchanged. The consequences of this are explained in Chapters 4 and 5.

The Supplementary Pension Rights Directive

In 2005, in a Communication to the Council and the Parliament the Commission announced a proposal for a directive that eventually became the Supplementary Pension Rights Directive.[489] This directive was to address obstacles that mobile workers faced regarding acquisition and preservation of pension rights, and would also create new rules regarding the transfer of pension pots.[490]

These were issues that the 1998 Safeguard Directive did not deal with, but still constituted significant obstacles for mobile workers as they could mean a loss of pension rights. The Safeguard Directive's major contribution to worker mobility was the application of the non-discrimination rule[491] to scheme-leavers; this is, however, not the only issue mobile workers face when changing jobs to another Member State. As explained previously, the harmonisation of waiting and vesting periods is also an important element for cross-border mobility of workers, as is the transferability and mobility of occupational pension rights.

As noted, the Supplementary Pension Rights Directive eventually featured rules to limit waiting and vesting periods, but in a watered-down form. It would include no provisions regarding the transferability of pension rights.[492] The consequences for the mobility of European workers of this directive are discussed in Part 2 of Chapter 4, Section 2.

---

486 Directive 2016/2341/EU of the European Parliament and of the Council of 14 December 2016 on the activities and supervision of institutions for occupational retirement provision (IORPs) [2016], OJ L 354/37 (IORP II Directive), Article 6(19).

487 ibid, Article 12.

488 ibid, Title V.

489 European Commission, 'Second Implementation Report of the Internal Market Strategy 2003-2006', COM (2005) 11 final, 40. See also European Commission, 'Communication from the Commission on the Social Agenda', COM(2005) 33 final 8.

490 European Commission, 'Second Implementation Report of the Internal Market Strategy 2003-2006', COM (2005) 11 final 40-41.

491 See paragraph 2.1.1.

492 For an in-depth discussion on the Supplementary Pension Rights Directive, see Baugniet (see footnote 340).

4   SUMMARY AND ANALYSIS

This chapter has taken a detailed look at EU pension policy and legislative action over the last three decades. Over the years, the rationale for the Commission's legislative efforts have shifted in focus. With this changing focus, the plans for regulating occupational pensions changed as well, leading to additions and omissions from previous plans. This section summarises the EU's plans and analyses which ideas did not (yet) make it into legislation.

Two main goals can be distilled from the EU's efforts in the field of occupational pensions. These are the 1) use of the single market for the safety, adequacy and sustainability of pensions and to 2) ensure the mobility of European workers from the perspective of occupational pensions.

1) The Use of the Single Market for Safe, Adequate and Sustainable Pensions

The first – modest – proposal for a directive for regulating occupational pensions, also dating from 1991, was focused on the pension institutions and their role in the EU's single market, with the interests of the scheme member only peripherally addressed from the perspective of the prudent investment of pension assets.[493] Certainly compared to the 2003 IORP Directive, this effort was "limited in scope and coverage",[494] as it contained merely seven articles focusing on pension institutions' freedom of investment and "the freedom to seek management advice from anywhere in the Community."[495] The issues of cross-border membership, taxation or portability were not included in the directive, and earlier iterations of the proposal included a clause on the centralized management of pension funds for multinationals, by which sponsoring undertakings of the same group would be able manage their investments on a group basis: "Centralized, in-house management of all related funds would reduce costs and increase investment flexibility by pooling assets."[496] However, the Member States removed this clause from the proposal before its demise in 1994. The failure of this first, modest proposal suggests that the early 1990s were an inauspicious time for legislative endeavours by the EU in the area of occupational pensions.

When the Commission gave the regulation of occupational pensions a fresh start in 1997, it approached the topic from a new angle: population aging. It drew attention to

---

493 Commission of the European Communities, 'Proposal for a Council Directive relating to the freedom of management and investment of funds held by institutions for retirement provisions' COM(91) 301 final.
494 Zavvos (see footnote 354) 609. For instance, the 1991 proposal "does not address pension portability or cross-border membership." It also did not address prudential supervision.
495 Lannoo (see footnote 327) 121.
496 Zavvos (see footnote 354) 621-622.

declining fertility rates and increasing life expectancy, resulting in pressure on statutory social security schemes and dependency ratios. In this context, it noted the importance of funded second-pillar pension schemes to ensure the adequacy of Europeans' retirement income. It discussed aiding the efficient operation of occupational pension institutions through, *inter alia*, the removal of investment restrictions, thereby enabling investments "on a continental scale [...] likely to improve their performance"[497] and the use of the expertise of appropriate investment managers – potentially from other Member States. Appropriate investment rules would also increase the security of pension rights. Another aim was the maintenance of retirement income levels through the growth of occupational pension funds in addition to statutory schemes. The possibility to achieve scale economies by being able to manage plans in more than one Member State would make them more cost-efficient.[498]

These goals could be achieved through the Single Market by creating a "real Single Market" for pensions. Though the IORP (II) Directive succeeded in removing certain barriers to the cross-border activities of IORPs and their investments and in that respect appears to have taken the first step towards the creation of the single market for occupational pensions, it has left in place some important barriers to the single market for occupational pensions. Chapters 4 and 5 will explain these barriers.

In all, the introduction of the IORP Directive was an important first step in creating the single market for pensions in that it has, *inter alia*, brought about cross-border operation of pension schemes and liberalisation of pension fund investments. But besides introducing some minimum harmonisation, this harmonisation does not extend beyond prudential, information and supervisory standards.

Before the IORP Directive came into being, the 1999 Communication on pensions outlined four goals[499] this directive should fulfil: 1) to ensure the best possible protection of beneficiaries, 2) to allow pension funds to profit fully from the Single Market and the euro, 3) to guarantee equal treatment between occupational pension providers and, finally, 4) to allow mutual recognition of prudential regimes.[500]

Addressing the first goal, the directive brought about a minimum harmonization of standards in information requirements, prudential standards and governance to the benefit of pension scheme members.[501] The aim of IORP II was to further bolster the protection of scheme members by introducing new governance requirements for key functions, significantly enhanced information requirements, provisions on remuneration policy,

---

497 1999 Communication (see footnote 350) 12.
498 ibid 4, 13 and 15.
499 ibid 4.
500 ibid.
501 European Commission, 'Report from the Commission on some key aspects concerning Directive 2003/41/EC on the activities and supervision of institutions for occupational retirement provision (IORP Directive)', COM(2009) 203 final.

self-assessment of the risk-management system of IORPs, the requirement to use a depositary in charge of safe-keeping of funds and enhanced powers for supervisors.[502]

In addressing second and fourth goals, the IORP Directive also largely freed pension institutions from restrictions on their investments, allowing them a flexible and efficient investment strategy not burdened by restrictions on the free movement of capital, except where justified on prudential grounds.[503] It has also made the cross-border activity of IORPs possible: they can operate pension schemes in all Member States, provided the schemes comply with the applicable social and labour legislation and fiscal provisions. Given the disappointing proliferation of cross-border IORPs, it appears that the directive has not entirely allowed pension institutions to profit *fully* from the Single Market.

2) Worker Mobility

At the very beginning of its attempts at regulating occupational pensions, the Commission named the divergences in social protection levels as obstacles to cross-border mobility of workers in its 1991 Communication.[504] Workers moving from one Member State to another could potentially lose their pension rights owing to differences in waiting and vesting periods, lacking or disadvantageous transfer rights and fiscal problems. The 1991 Communication considered the role of occupational pensions and their contribution to the social protection of workers and from the perspective of freedom of movement of workers. The Communication suggested enabling the possibility of cross-border membership (portability),[505] the facilitation of the acquisition of pension rights by addressing long waiting and vesting periods,[506] the availability of fair transfer options for accrued benefits to be transferred to a new scheme (as well as fair actuarial standards for calculating the value of transfers),[507] better information to the pension scheme member[508] and the avoidance of double taxation;[509] all very much proposals in the interest of scheme members. The issue of cross-border membership (portability) seems to have been abandoned by the time the proposal for the IORP Directive came along.

The Safeguard Directive adopted in 1998 and the Supplementary Pension Rights Directive addressed only a fraction of these goals. The Safeguard Directive applies the principle of non-discrimination to the consequences of leaving an occupational pension scheme for workers who move to another Member State compared to those who change

---

502 European Commission, 'Revision of the Occupational Pension Funds Directive – frequently asked questions', Memo 14/239, available at http://europa.eu/rapid/press-release_MEMO-14-239_en.htm accessed 3 January 2020.
503 Recital 32 of Directive 2003/41/EC.
504 1991 Communication (see footnote 313) 2.
505 ibid 19 et seq.
506 ibid 21.
507 ibid.
508 ibid 22.
509 ibid.

jobs within their own Member State. The Supplementary Pension Rights Directive improves worker mobility by introducing maximum terms for waiting and vesting periods. However, these waiting and vesting periods are laxer than the ones originally proposed.[510]

In sum, these directives give a mobile worker some degree of protection, yet mobile EU citizens may still face pension-related obstacles that are beyond these directives' scope, such as lacking options regarding transferability, waiting and vesting periods (shorter than the maximum of three years mandated by the directive), aggregation of periods of work and an absence of a possibility of cross-border membership.[511]

Although one of the stated goals of the IORP II Directive is to increase worker mobility, it deals primarily with the conditions under which pension providers (i.e. IORPs) can function in the internal market and its provisions do not seem to deal with worker mobility directly. However, its recitals mention worker mobility in several places and in different contexts. For instance, its provisions on governance, the provision of information and its aims of transparent and safe occupational retirement provision are touted by the directive's fourth recital as facilitating worker mobility. In addition, the possibility of cross-border service provision for IORPs should achieve that goal as well.[512]

Specifically, that provision aims to aid cross-border activity for groups of employees belonging to the same (corporate) group of employers.[513] When changing employer, the employee need not change pension provider and, accordingly, can forego potentially cumbersome and costly transfers of accrued pension rights: the RESAVER pan-European pension fund for researchers relies on this concept,[514] as do the cross-border pension funds of multiple multinational corporations. However, as it does not specifically focus on worker mobility, it has little to offer to other groups of mobile Europeans, owing to a lack of provisions on individual transferability of pension pots and no possibilities for cross-border membership.

The consequences of these omissions are discussed in Chapters 4 and 5.

---

510 The original proposal of the Directive mandated a maximum waiting period of one year and a maximum vesting period of two years. See Article 4(c) and (d) of COM(2005) 507. See also Part 2 of Chapter 4.

511 In this respect, Baugniet speaks of "untapped potential", and that "the internal-market rationale based on removing 'obstacles' to mobility has not delivered a system of legal protection that places migrant workers social protection rights at the heart of their fundamental freedom of movement." See Baugniet (see footnote 340) 335 and 337.

512 Recital 35 of the IORP II Directive.

513 M Reiner, 'Entwicklung und Probleme des europäischen Betriebspensionsrechts am Beispiel der Mobilitätsrichtlinie' (2017) Vol 1 (2) Journal für Arbeitsrecht und Sozialrecht 168, 180.

514 ibid; Chapter 1, Section 4.2.

5   CONCLUSION

The Member States closely guard their prerogatives in the field of pensions for which they are principally responsible. This is understandable given the tailor-made mix for each Member State between the pension pillars and the important ramifications that changes to a pension system can have for citizens. The organisation of the social security systems of the Member States is the result of decades-long political processes. Any (apparent) external threat to these systems heightens the tensions and awareness of the actors involved in the organisation of these national systems.

On the other hand, pension systems in the Member States are under severe strain and the EU aims to relieve some of the tension by developing ideas and solutions to some of these problems, but may only do so within the remits of the powers accorded to it. The discussion in Chapter 2 has shown that, although the EU has some powers to regulate occupational pensions, these prerogatives are largely limited to its internal market powers. For other instruments, such as to directly regulate or modernise pension systems, the (unanimous) consensus of Member States is needed and this is absent so far.

The IORP Directive has laid the foundations that enabled cross-border management of pension schemes. In that respect, the directive can be said to have made a significant contribution to the establishment of a European single market for pensions. The directive was and is a first step towards the creation of such a market and its success should therefore be assessed within the limitations of the EU's competences and the willingness of the Member States to agree to EU-level legislation in the field of occupational pensions. However, because some elements were not regulated in the IORP (II) Directive, a number of shortcomings appear to afflict this directive. The next two chapters will study these in more detail. The analysis of the Safeguard Directive and the Supplementary Pension Rights Directives paints a similar picture. Although they have both undoubtedly led to benefits for mobile workers, they have not been able to live up to the full extent of initial EU proposals.

Chapter 4: Cross-Border IORPs and the Pension Scheme Member

1   Introduction

The previous chapter studied the history of the EU's engagement with occupational pensions. It focused on the IORP Directives, and described a number of topics that – although discussed in the years during the Directive's germination – did not make it into either the IORP Directives or other EU legislative instruments. Among these topics were the possibility of cross-border membership, a harmonisation of security mechanisms such as a minimum return guarantee and the coverage of biometric risks. In addition, neither the IORP Directives nor the Safeguard Directive or the Supplementary Pension Rights Directive address the individual transferability of supplementary pension rights.

The aim of this chapter is to look into the consequences for pension scheme members of not regulating the aspects discussed in the previous chapter. It will do this by comparing the existing EU directives on occupational pensions – primarily the IORP II Directive, as well as the Safeguard Directive and the Supplementary Pension Rights Directive – to the EU's occupational pension policy objectives[515] of 1) using the EU's Single Market with a view to achieve safe, adequate and sustainable pensions and 2) facilitating the mobility of European workers from the perspective of occupational pensions. This chapter studies the position of pension scheme members of cross-border IORPs, while Chapter 5 will explore the position of cross-border IORPs as service providers on the EU's internal market.

The Structure of this Chapter

Accordingly, the chapter will be grouped into two parts: Part 1 on IORPs' use of the EU's Single Market with a view to achieve safe, adequate and sustainable pensions and Part 2 on mobility, both from the perspective from the scheme member. The following questions will be addressed in the subsequent sections.

Part 1. IORPs' use of the single market to the benefit of scheme members

This part will focus on the manner in which IORPs operate on a cross-border basis form a legal perspective. The IORP (II) Directive makes cross-border activity of IORPs possi-

---

515 See Chapter 1.

ble. It appears that the framework within which that is made possible can have undesirable consequences for pension scheme members. These potential undesirable consequences, each to be discussed in their own sub-sections, are: a) uncertainty as to the security mechanisms of a pension scheme, thereby affecting retirement income security and b) consequences caused by the application to the IORP of another Member State's prudential legislation. Finally, c) the IORP II Directive's support for the social function of occupational pensions will be given attention.

a. Retirement Income Security

Retirement income security is perhaps the single most important concern for pension scheme members: will the managing institution handle my money responsibly? Will my pension be sufficient to maintain my standard of living? Will I get a pension at all? Pension security mechanisms, such as a guaranteed pension benefit or an obligation for an employer to compensate a funding shortfall, serve to protect the scheme against potential dangers, such as low interest rates and disappointing investment returns. These mechanisms will be taken into consideration for the overall assessment of cross-border IORPs. These security mechanisms – they will be discussed in Section 3 – are to the benefit of pension scheme members, as they can help to achieve a promised level of pension benefits, and are therefore important for scheme members' financial position.

However, as these security mechanisms have been left largely unregulated by the IORP II Directive, it appears that pension scheme members whose schemes are operated by cross-border IORPs could be faced with legal uncertainty or even the potential loss of the application of such security mechanisms. This section will take a closer look at the operation of security mechanisms in a cross-border context.

b. Prudential Supervision of Cross-Border IORPs

In cross-border situations, IORPs are subject to the prudential supervision of their home Member State. The pension rights of scheme members of a cross-border IORP are subject to a foreign country's prudential regulations and governance requirements. This can have potentially far-reaching consequences, for instance with respect to the funding requirements of IORPs. This section will study these consequences as well as to what extent the IORP II Directive protects pension scheme members of cross-border IORPs against unforeseen consequences of their pension entitlements being subject to another Member State's prudential legislation.

c. The Social Function of Occupational Pensions

The social function of occupational pensions is to provide an income in retirement. But current trends are shifting more responsibility for the risks surrounding occupational pensions – such as investment and biometric risks – to pension scheme members, away from employers and/or pension scheme providers. At the same time, a retrenchment of the public retirement system can be identified in many Member States.

The aim of cross-border IORPs is to take advantage of scale economies and, by doing so, support the creation of safe, adequate and sustainable pensions. Can the cross-border IORP keep this promise?

Part 2. Worker Mobility

The main obstacles preventing worker mobility from an occupational pensions perspective identified by the Commission are complications related to the taxation, acquisition, preservation and transfer of pension rights.[516] This part will analyse current EU pension law on its ability to facilitate the mobility of European workers.

PART 1: CROSS-BORDER IORPS' USE OF THE EU'S SINGLE MARKET WITH A VIEW TO ACHIEVE SAFE, ADEQUATE AND SUSTAINABLE PENSIONS

This part will focus on the IORP II Directive's framework making cross-border activity for IORPs possible, and how IORPs operate on the Single Market with a view to achieving safe, adequate and sustainable pensions. Chapter 1 studied a few of the potential benefits of cross-border IORPs. For instance, the Commission's view was that the Single Market could bring scale economies, which in turn could yield lower costs and/or a better pension result. This would benefit employers and their employees alike. There are currently a number of employers who are reaping the benefits of the single market in respect of their pension schemes.

SECTION A: RETIREMENT INCOME SECURITY

Retirement income security is "the primary economic function" of old age pensions;[517] it is "the degree to which a person's customary standard of living is protected from the ups

---

516 European Commission, 'Commission Staff Working Document. Annex to the: 'Proposal for a Directive of the European Parliament and the Council on the Improvement of Portability of Supplementary Pension Rights', SEC(2005) 1293.

517 Z Bodie, 'Pensions as retirement income insurance' (1989) National Bureau of Economic Research Working Paper No. 2917, 2.

and downs of economic circumstance."[518] In other words, it is the notion that sufficient money will be left after retirement. In the Netherlands, for instance, most pension schemes are geared towards achieving a replacement rate of 70% of a scheme member's average salary.[519]

Employer-sponsored pension plans can be seen as a savings scheme that provides income security in retirement.[520] A pension scheme also provides insurance against the many risks associated with saving for retirement.[521] Typically, pension assets in funded occupational schemes[522] are invested over a period of time in order to reap yields on financial markets. In this case, the pension assets are exposed to market risks: the risk that the value of invested assets fluctuate with changes in interest rates (interest rate risk), exchange rates or stock markets (investment risk).[523] Other risks include longevity risk if the scheme member lives longer than anticipated, inflation risk, liquidity risk if certain investments cannot be liquidated sufficiently quickly by the pension institution to pay benefits and the risk of a sponsor's default.[524] These risks ultimately need to shouldered by one of the pension institution's stakeholders.[525] Those stakeholders can be, for instance, the pension institution itself, the employer or the scheme members.

A number of factors that are involved in achieving retirement income security will be discussed in this section. First, Section 1 will focus on the types of pension schemes available and how they allocate risks between the stakeholders and what – if anything – they promise the scheme member. After that, Section 2 will discuss the pension security mechanisms that are meant to secure the pension promise, and therefore aid in the achievement of retirement income security. The IORP II Directive itself does not regulate the pension schemes offered in the Member States or their details, but contains a number of general provisions for the operation of pension *institutions* that also have their effect on the (security of) schemes they administer.

---

518 R Atchley, 'Retirement Income Security: Past, Present and Future' (1997) Vol 21 (2) Generations.

519 M. Knoef et al, 'Nederlandse pensioenopbouw in internationaal perspectief' (2015) Netspar Industry Series Paper, 18, available at https://www.netspar.nl/assets/uploads/Netspar_design_41-WEB-1.pdf accessed 3 January 2020.

520 Bodie (see footnote 517).

521 For a more complete overview of the risks involved in the generation of retirement income, see D Blake, 'We Need a National Narrative: Building a Consensus Around Retirement Income' (2016) Report: Independent Review of Retirement Income.

522 Scheme funding is required by the IORP Directive, and full funding is required in the event of cross-border activity.

523 D Franzen, 'Managing Investment Risk in Defined Benefit Pension Funds' (2010) OECD Working Papers on Insurance and Private Pensions No 38.

524 D Broeders & A Chen, 'Pension Benefit Security: A Comparison of Solvency Requirements, a Pension Guarantee Fund and Sponsor Support' (2013) Vol 80 (2) The Journal of Risk and Insurance 239, 240.

525 ibid.

1   PENSION SCHEME TYPES: DEFINED BENEFIT TO DEFINED CONTRIBUTION AND
     EVERYTHING IN BETWEEN

Put simply, the division between defined benefit (DB) and defined contribution (DC) plans is remembered easiest with the division of risks borne in mind. In a DB plan, the risk bearer is usually an employer and/or a pension provider (such as a pension fund or an insurance company),[526] and the level of benefits to be received in retirement by the scheme member is determined in advance and is – in principle – guaranteed. In a pure DC scheme, it is the contributions to be paid by the scheme member and/or the employer, rather than the level of benefits to be received, that is fixed. The risks are borne by the pension scheme members themselves: the pension benefits are determined by what has been paid into the scheme and the investment yield, minus costs. While there seems to be a general consensus on the classifications of the two scheme archetypes, this distinction sometimes becomes muddled under the application of European and national pension legislation.[527] The section below will set out the different types of pension schemes and their various sub-types, which often combine elements of both DB and DC schemes. The division between the sub-types is not always very clear, but is classified here as sub-types of DC or DB plans, and will be discussed in the following section. The scheme types are depicted graphically in the conclusion to this section on Section 1.3.

1.1   *Defined Contribution (DC) Plans*

A. *The Archetype: Pure/Individual Defined Contribution (IDC) Plans*

Per the OECD's "Pensions Glossary", Defined Contribution (DC) plans are: "Occupational pension plans under which the plan sponsor pays fixed contributions and has no legal or constructive obligation to pay further contributions to an ongoing plan in the event of an unfavourable experience."[528] In this type of pension plan, it is the contribution that is agreed on (defined), and the level of the pensions is not known in advance.[529] In other words, the employer pays a contribution that does not change depending on the financial situation of the pension provider,[530] and the employees' eventual pension income is based directly on what has been paid into the plan. The employee is the one who

---

526 European Parliament, Directorate-General for Internal Policies, *Pension Schemes*, Study for the EMPL Committee (Publications Office of the European Union 2014), 20.

527 H van Meerten & P Borsjé, 'Pension Rights and Entitlement Conversion ('invaren'): Lessons from a Dutch Perspective with Regard to the Implications of the EU Charter' (2016) 18 (1) European Journal of Social Security 46, 49.

528 OECD, *Private Pensions: OECD Classification and Glossary* (OECD Publishing 2005) 14.

529 M Heemskerk, *Pensioenrecht* (Boom Juridische Uitgevers 2015) 57.

530 This is not to say that premiums cannot be adjusted at all: these are typically reviewed every few years.

bears the "risk" of longevity and the resulting lowering of benefits to finance the longer-than-expected life expectancy, as well as risks related to, for instance, fluctuating interest levels and stock market yields.

There are a number of variations on this type of pension plan, ranging from *pure* or *individual* DC plans, in which the employee bears all the risk individually (longevity, investment, interest etc.) to DC plans that share or provide insurance against some number of risks that can occur during the accrual phase and/or the payout phase.

B. Sub-Type 1: Collective Defined Contribution (CDC) Plans

A Collective Defined Contribution plan is a hybrid plan that combines elements of defined benefit and defined contribution schemes. This scheme has main characteristics: 1) a maximum premium for the employer is set for a period of five years,[531] which is typical of a defined contribution plan, 2) the level of pensions is defined in advance, which is typical for a defined benefit plan, but as a target and not as a hard promise and 3) the level of the pension is guaranteed only to the extent that the premiums paid are sufficient is clearly disclosed. Benefits from a CDC scheme can be based on average career earnings – with the pension agreement between the employer and employee clearly stating that no guarantees are given as to the achieved level of benefits – or on the basis of an annual assessment of the pension 'rights' that can be purchased on the basis of the collectively fixed pension contributions.[532]

In a CDC scheme the employer, in principle, bears no economic or legal risk in the event that the agreed level of benefits is not attained.[533] The 'collective' in a Collective Defined Contribution scheme refers to collective pooling of the assets: this allows for risk sharing between members.[534] For instance, if one scheme member lives longer than expected, the increased cost of that scheme member's stroke of luck can be financed through another's misfortune of living shorter than expected. This type of scheme can be contrasted to a "pure" IDC scheme, in which the scheme member *individually* bears all types of risk relating to the pension.[535]

---

531 R Gradus, 'Bouwstenen voor een toekomstbestendig pensioenstelsel' (2014) Vol 19 (4) PensioenMagazine 30.

532 E Schols-Van Oppen, 'De collectieve beschikbarepremieregeling' in *De CDC-Regeling: stand van zaken anno 2008* (Sdu Fiscale & Financiële Uitgevers 2008) 9-11.

533 Heemskerk (see footnote 529) 59. In the Netherlands, CDC plans *can* also qualify as defined benefit schemes if there is a sufficient amount of certainty that the agreed upon level of pensions will be attained.

534 D Blake, 'We Need a National Narrative: Building a Consensus Around Retirement Income' (2016) Report: Independent Review of Retirement Income 492.

535 CDC schemes share the surpluses or deficits in the funding process between young, old and future generations "by adjusting either contributions, or benefit levels or a both, which leads to intergenerational transfers." See J Cui, F de Jong & E Ponds, 'Intergenerational risk sharing within funded pension schemes' (2011) Vol 10 (1) Journal of Pension Economics and Finance 1, 4.

C. Sub-Type 2: Collective Individual Defined Contribution (CIDC) Plans

DB and CDC plans, by their collective nature, leave relatively little room for individual wishes or needs.[536] Traditional IDC plans afford scheme members more latitude for their own decisions, but provide no protection against the myriad of complex decisions pertaining to their retirement planning,[537] while the future consequences of decisions made in the present are difficult to foresee: individuals are left to invest in the "unknown and unknowable".[538]

CIDC plans have been presented as a manner of retaining the desirable aspects of CDC and IDC schemes, with improvements to the less desirable features.[539] A CIDC scheme features a fixed premium and collective asset management (as in a CDC scheme), but with individual pension accounts. Therefore, "[a]n important advantage of CIDC schemes compared to traditional occupational plans is that the ownership of the financial assets lies unambiguously with the members of the pension fund through individual accounts."[540] The individual account allows for clear definition and individualization of the accrued rights and the risks involved. The achieved level of pension benefits is a direct and individual consequence of the premiums paid, and the scheme gives an indication of the expected return on the pension assets.[541]

The drawbacks to the IDC and CDC schemes are addressed in a CIDC scheme in the following ways.[542] The drawbacks of a CDC scheme are mitigated by the introduction of 1) individual property rights through individual accounts, 2) individual risk management through tailored investments, enabled by individual accounts and 3) a simplified (and therefore more understandable) scheme. The drawbacks of an IDC scheme are mitigated by 1) mandatory participation, 2) collective management of assets, leading to scale economies and 3) sharing of risks, such as investment and longevity risks. Longevity risk is shared by redistributing leftover funds from scheme members who pass away early into a "collective pool", to the benefit of surviving scheme members.[543] Like a DC scheme, a CIDC scheme is fully funded per definition.

---

536 L Bovenberg & R Gradus, 'Reforming occupational pension schemes: the case of the Netherlands' (2015) Vol 18 (3) Journal of Economic Policy Review 244, 250.

537 ibid 250.

538 R Zeckhauser, 'Investing in the Unknown and the Unknowable' in F Diebold, N Doherty & R Herring (eds), *The Known, the Unknown, and the Unknowable in Financial Risk Management: Measurement and Theory Advancing Practice* (Princeton University Press 2010) 304-346.

539 G Beechinor & C Hoekstra, 'CDC Focus: Has CDC already had its day?' (2014) UK Plansponsor.

540 ibid.

541 R Gradus, 'Bouwstenen voor een toekomstbestendig pensioenstelsel' (2014) Vol 19 (4) PensioenMagazine 30.

542 ibid.

543 Bovenberg & Gradus (see footnote 536) 251.

1.2 Defined Benefit (DB) Plans

Defined benefit (DB) plans are available in one form or another in nearly all EU Member States.[544] Defined benefit plans are occupational pension plans "other than defined contributions plans. DB plans generally can be classified into one of the three main types, "traditional", "mixed" and "hybrid" plans."[545]

In this type of scheme, the employer and the employee/scheme member have agreed upon a particular level of pensions.[546] The risks are borne by the employer and/or the pension institution, and not by the scheme member. The level of the pension benefits can be based on the final salary or average salary; the level of pensions is tied to the number of years spent working and the salary. It is important to note here that the benefits are not necessarily conditional on the amount contributed; it is the level of benefits agreed upon that is decisive, rather than the value of the contributions.[547]

Again, the design of such schemes may vary. There are variations such as final salary and average salary schemes. In principle, "the annuity promised to the employee is the employer's liability. The present value of this liability represents the amount of money that the employer must set aside today in order to fund the deferred annuity that comes upon the employee's retirement."[548] However, the "promise" of a defined benefit scheme, namely the level of benefits for the employee agreed upon, is not necessarily absolute.

---

544 European Parliament (see footnote 526) 21.
545 OECD, 'Pension Country Profile: Denmark' in: OECD Private Pensions Outlook 2008 (OECD Publishing 2009).
546 Heemskerk (see footnote 529) 55.
547 European Parliament (see footnote 526) 21.
548 Bodie (see footnote 517) 7.

1.3   Taking Stock of the Scheme Types

Figure 3

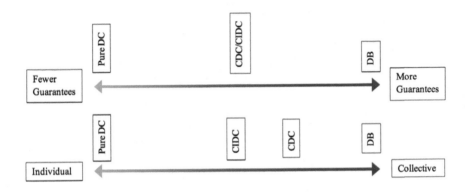

The previous discussion of the types of pension schemes has illustrated where the risks lie and who is to carry them. Section 2 will discuss the mechanisms that exist for dealing with the various risks associated with pension management. In a DC scheme, the 'pension promise' is the payment by the employer of the pension contributions. "Once made or accrued, the employer has no further obligation for the value of the assets held by the plan or for the sufficiency of fund assets for payment of the benefits, absent any violation of the terms of the agreement by the employer."[549] The employee and/or employer pays the required contributions and when it is time for the employee to retire, the level of benefits is determined, in principle, solely by what was paid in, plus or minus investment yields and charges. Some Member States feature additional rules, such as a guaranteed rate of return or an indexation guarantee, making the distinction of such schemes from DB schemes somewhat murky.

In a DB scheme, "the employer (sponsor) is responsible not merely for the current contribution to be made to the plan on behalf of participants, but additionally for the sufficiency of the assets in the plan for the ultimate payment of benefits promised to the participants. Thus the current contribution is at best a partial satisfaction of his obligation, and the amount of actual cost incurred is not measured by this alone."[550] The payments are estimated by actuaries who take into account factors such as mortality of scheme members/beneficiaries, salary levels at which they retire, financial market performance etc.

---

549 B. Mackenzie et al, *Wiley Interpretation and Application of International Financial Reporting Standards* (Wiley 2014) 460.
550 ibid.

As explained in the previous paragraph, "The nature of the insurance provided under a defined benefit plan varies with the specific type of plan and benefit formula."[551] The guarantee is in principle unconditional, which sets a DB scheme apart from the others. In CDC and CIDC schemes a maximum premium is set, but an indicated pension benefit is given. There is no legal obligation for a scheme sponsor or the fund to actually pay out such a level of benefits.

The next section will study the security mechanisms in place to secure the promises made in the context of these pension schemes. These mechanisms serve to ensure the financial soundness of the pension scheme, the pension fund or both.

2   SECURING THE 'PROMISE': SECURITY MECHANISMS AND IORP II

2.1   Introduction

The previous part considered the agreements under the various types of pension schemes. This part will explain some of the mechanisms in place that can aid in securing the pension promise – achieving retirement income security – and their interaction with the IORP II Directive. Guarantees and benefit adjustment mechanisms may either serve to enhance the financial outcome for the scheme member, such as in the case of an obligation on the employer to make up funding deficits of the pension scheme, or work to their detriment, such as in the case of pension benefit cuts. They also have the effect of altering the position that a pension scheme takes up on the DB-DC spectrum: a DC scheme with some additional guarantees – such as guaranteed indexation or a guaranteed investment yield – would move the scheme closer towards the DB end of the spectrum, whereas a DB scheme with conditional indexation or the possibility to reduce benefits would move the DB scheme closer towards the DC end of the spectrum. Section 2.2 will describe some of the security mechanisms available to secure pension promises.

Chapter 3 explained that neither the Commission nor the Council wished to harmonise occupational pension schemes, as a consequence of which any provisions mandating security mechanisms such as the mandatory coverage of biometric risks or minimum return guarantees were stricken from the proposals. The security mechanisms and valuation methods used by the Member States differ significantly,[552] which is likely one of the reasons that harmonisation of such security mechanisms was deemed undesirable by the Commission and the Member States. In the case of the operation of a pension scheme by a cross-border IORP, the consequences for pension scheme members of the decision to

---

551 Z. Bodie, 'Pension funds and financial innovation' (1989) National Bureau of Economic Research Working Paper No. 3103, 7.
552 CEIOPS, 'Survey on fully funded, technical provisions and security mechanisms in the European occupational pension sector' (2008) CEIOPS-OPSSC-01/08 Final 4.

not harmonise these security mechanisms in the IORP II Directive will be discussed in Section 3.

2.2 Security Mechanisms

A. Scheme Funding

Appropriate funding requirements are arguably one of the most important security mechanisms for a pension scheme: the presence of sufficient assets to back pension entitlements appears to be the most valuable mechanism available to scheme members. Underfunding in pension schemes in the EU and beyond has been featured prominently in recent news items.[553] After a "golden age" for pension funds, in which they benefited from high investment returns and funding surpluses, the start of this millennium saw the start of a more troubled period.[554] Thereafter, the financial crisis and subsequent low-interest-rate environment has placed pension scheme operators in a difficult position. The crisis led to major pension losses across the EU: "Funded pension systems in OECD countries lost US$5.4trn with an average reduction of 20–25 percent in the value of the assets."[555] It appears that the aftermath of this period is not yet in the past.

A pure defined contribution plan with no additional guarantees is fully funded by definition: the contribution paid into the scheme, plus or minus investment results and fees, is what defines the pension benefit. In other words, "In defined contribution plans, the value of the benefits equals that of the assets and so the plan is always exactly fully funded."[556] On the other hand, a defined benefit plan presents a more complex situation: the funding of such schemes occurs on the basis of formulas that aim to achieve the promised benefits to be paid after retirement. These formulas take into account years of service and the employees' salary.[557] Financing those benefits can be done in a variety of

---

553 EIOPA reports that "cover ratios close to or below 100 per cent remain a concern for the sector if low interest rates persist", see EIOPA, *Financial Stability Report December 2018,* 41, available at eiopa.europa.-eu/Publications/Reports/EIOPA%20FSR%20December%202018.pdf accessed 3 January 2020. See also the various news contributions on the funding situation of pension funds, for instance C Pelgrim, 'DNB: korting dreigt bij 60 procent van de pensioenen', *NRC* 3 June 2019; G. Topham, 'Pension deficit of UK's leading companies equivalent to 70% of their profits', *The Guardian* 29 August 2017; C. Weston, 'Deficits in traditional company pension plans rise to €1.6bn', *The Independent* 31 January 2019; S Pollak, 'Ageing population leading to 'significant annual deficits' in pension fund', *The Irish Times* 29 November 2018; M. Frühauf, 'Anlegen wie die Grossen: So machen's die Pensionskassen', *Frankfurter Allgemeine* 14 January 2018.

554 F Stewart, 'Benefit Security Pension Fund Guarantee Schemes' (2007) OECD Working Papers on Insurance and Private Pensions No 5, 4.

555 B Ebbinghaus & T Wiß, 'Taming Pension Fund Capitalism in Europe: Collective and State Regulation in Times of Crisis' (2011) Vol 17 (1) Transfer 15, 24.

556 Z Bodie & O Mitchell, 'Pension Security in an Aging World' in Z Bodie, O Mitchell & J Turner (eds), *Securing Employer-Based Pensions: An International Perspective* (University of Pennsylvania Press 1996) 10.

557 ibid 9.

ways: unfunded, underfunded or funded. As noted, the methods determining the funding situation differ per Member State, and therefore, with regard to the security of any accrued retirement benefits, the Member State in which an IORP is located matters for a pension scheme member.[558]

Full funding can be seen as an appropriate measure to secure the pension promise, as "without full funding, what is the guarantee worth anyway?"[559] The assets present on a pension fund's balance sheet "provide collateral" for the plan beneficiaries.[560] There are multiple reasons why employers fund their DB schemes: 1) security of benefits in case there is no (or only partial) government insurance, 2) a statutory funding obligation such as that in the Netherlands, or 3) tax incentives that incentivise scheme funding.[561]

It may also be the case that there are no assets to back the benefits at all, in which case the scheme is unfunded. German book reserve schemes are an example.[562] This is not an insurance policy, but rather a direct commitment by the employer to the benefit of the employee to provide him or her with retirement benefits. The employee possesses a legal right to claim these benefits from the employer without the interference of an external pension provider. The employer may use the retained salaries for his or her business ventures, and this possibility is widely used. In the past decades, however, employers have begun to accumulate reserves that protected from insolvency and legally separated from the employer's business.[563]

B. Additional Financing Mechanisms

In the event of a funding shortfall, a pension scheme offering guarantees, such as a DB scheme, may require additional funding from the scheme sponsor (e.g. the employer), the scheme member or an external party. Additional financing mechanisms can take a number of forms, such as an increase in pension contributions or another kind of additional funding obligation for the employer to make up any shortfalls in the funding of the scheme.[564] They provide additional assets to buttress the financial position of the pension scheme. Such support is legally enforceable if the sponsor is legally required to provide extra funding to the scheme. In other words, the sponsor can be compelled to support the

---

558 CEIOPS, 'Survey on fully funded, technical provisions and security mechanisms in the European occupational pension sector' (2008) CEIOPS-OPSSC-01/08 Final 4

559 R. Goode, 'Occupational Pensions: Securing the Pension Promise' (1994) Vol 9 (1) The Denning Law Journal 15, 18.

560 Bodie & Mitchell (see footnote 556) 10.

561 ibid 11.

562 A Hennessy, *The Europeanization of Workplace Pensions: Economic Interests, Social Protection, and Credible Signaling* (Cambridge University Press 2013) 122.

563 J Clemens & T Förstemann, 'Das System der betrieblichen Altersversorgung in Deutschland' (2015) Vol 95 (9) Analysen und Berichte Rentenpolitik 628.

564 EIOPA, EIOPA's Advice to the European Commission on the review of the IORP Directive 2003/41/EC (2012) EIOPA-BOS-12/015, 126-127.

scheme either by an IORP or the scheme members and/or beneficiaries. Such an obligation can arise from national legislation as well as contractual obligations between the IORP and the sponsor or between the sponsor and members and beneficiaries.[565] In the case of a contractual obligation, it should be clear under which circumstances a security mechanism applies and who is to foot the bill.

C. Benefit Adjustment Mechanisms & Guarantees

Contrary to the additional financing mechanisms that infuse a pension scheme with additional funding (assets), benefit adjustment mechanisms alter the liabilities of the scheme. A benefit adjustment mechanism that could potentially have serious consequences for scheme members is the cutting of benefits. Although in principle DB plans guarantee a promised level of benefits, a number of EU Member States allow for – or even require – the reduction of pension benefits. Benefit reduction mechanisms are an important feature of the benefit promise as a way to "keep alive" a DB pension scheme,[566] and can take different forms and may be done under a variety of circumstances. Under Dutch law, for instance, a pension institution may cut pension entitlements and pension benefits under strict conditions.[567]

Other benefit adjustment mechanisms are (the suspension of) indexation and guarantees, such as minimum return guarantees or a guarantee of a lifelong payment of pension annuities. Some Member States have legislation in place guaranteeing a minimum return on the pension assets. For instance, the UK, where DB schemes in payment are indexed "in line with inflation".[568] In Belgium, pensions assets have a minimum employer-guaranteed return in accordance with Article 24 of the Belgian 2003 Act on Supplementary Pensions.

With respect to indexation of pension benefits, some Member States feature statutory indexation rules, while others do not. In the Netherlands, indexation for occupational plans can be either conditional or unconditional. If a conditional indexation has been agreed on, this indexation is legally not part of the pension entitlement.[569] The pension participant must, by law, be duly informed of the conditional nature of the applicable indexation policy. This is not a mandatory indexation. In contrast, Germany features a – conditional – mandatory indexation mechanism for occupational pension benefits currently in payment – meaning that indexation comes into effect in the payout phase. Article 16 of the German Company Pensions Act[570] requires the employer to assess a

---

565 ibid 129 et seq.
566 ibid 281.
567 Article 134 of the Dutch Pensions Act
568 D Thurley, 'Occupational Pension Increases', Briefing Paper CBP-05656 of 21 June 2017, House of Commons Library.
569 C. Luijken, 'Fiscaal kader voor indexatie van pensioenen' (2015) *NTFR Beschouwingen*.
570 Gesetz zur Verbesserung der betrieblichen Altersversorgung (BetrAVG)

possible indexation of the pension benefits every three years. He is to decide in accordance with his "reasonable discretion" whether or not the indexation is to be executed. Factors such as the scheme member's interests, but also the employer's financial health are factors in this decision.[571] Here, again, the same potential uncertainty regarding the question whether these mechanisms are couched in social and labour law, prudential law or perhaps both could apply to benefit reduction mechanisms.

3   SECURITY MECHANISMS AND CROSS-BORDER IORPs

3.1   Introduction

The security mechanisms discussed above are tools used to ensure the preservation of the financial soundness of a pension scheme and/or an IORP. They are therefore essential to pension scheme members, as these security mechanisms can ensure that the promises under the respective pension schemes discussed in Section 1 are kept.

Of particular interest is the operation of these security mechanisms in the case of cross-border IORPs from the perspective of pension scheme members. For pension schemes operated across borders, the IORP II Directive requires the application of the host Member State's social and labour legislation. This is, in most cases, the same jurisdiction as that of the Member State in which the pension scheme participant resides. The IORP II Directive therefore appears to aim for equal protection of pension scheme members irrespective of whether their scheme is operated by an IORP from their own Member State or one from another Member State. Such an obligation seems not only important for the financial position of a pension scheme member – the availability of a guarantee, indexation mechanism or sponsor support obligation can be significant contributors to the likelihood of achieving a good pension result – but also appears to be important for the acceptance of cross-border IORPs: the legislation that applies to the pension schemes offered within a Member State is in principle the same, regardless from where in the EU the scheme is operated. It would seem problematic for workers if their employers could escape the application of legal norms protecting pension scheme members by simply moving their pension schemes to other Member States with lower – and therefore less costly – demands regarding scheme member protection. There are therefore numerous reasons as to why the application of social and labour legislation protecting scheme members in a cross-border context should be considered important.

Security mechanisms protecting pension scheme members are often enshrined in Member States' social and labour and prudential legislation.[572] In particular, the question

---

571 B. Uebelhack, *Betriebliche Altersversorgung – Grundlagen und Praxis* (C.F. Müller 2011), 80-81.
572 CEIOPS, 'Survey on fully funded, technical provisions and security mechanisms in the European occupational pension sector' (2008) CEIOPS-OPSSC-01/08 Final 12.

in a cross-border context is to which category (e.g. social and labour law or prudential law) any of these security mechanisms belong. It was noted in Chapter 1 that cross-border IORPs are subject to their home Member State's prudential legislation while having to ensure that the schemes they operate comply with the social and labour legislation of the respective host Member States. The allocation of a security mechanism to one category or the other therefore has consequences for its applicability.

The original IORP Directive contained little to no guidance on what social and labour law and prudential regulation are,[573] and consequently there was no clear distinction between the two. In fact, The Commission noted in 2014 – in its impact assessment on the proposed-at-the-time revision of IORP I – that the "scope of prudential regulation rules applicable in [Member States] is uncertain."[574] IORP II has now, in an attempt to clarify this distinction, been endowed with a provision defining prudential requirements in its new Article 46. That provision lists matters such as the funding requirements of an IORP, investment rules and the system of governance that applies to IORPs. Yet despite the fact that the unclear scopes of prudential regulation and social and labour law have been explicitly problematised in the Impact Assessment to the proposal for IORP II[575] as well as the directive's recitals[576] – and despite the fact that respondents to the Green Paper on Pensions explicitly called for clear definition of the scope of social and labour legislation and its interaction with prudential regulation[577] – the final version of the IORP II Directive fails to provide a clearer definition of social and labour law.

Consequently, security mechanisms enshrined in national legislation may be qualified by the Member State authorities themselves: they may decide what counts as social and

---

573 P Borsjé & H Van Meerten, 'A European Pensions Union' (2014) National Bank of Slovakia Series 2014, 15–21.

574 See European Commission, 'Impact Assessment Accompanying the document Proposal for a Directive of the European Parliament and of the Council on the activities and supervision of institutions for occupational retirement provision' SWD(2014) 103 final Part 1/2, 13. In addition, EIOPA found in 2012 that "many member states do not even make a distinction between prudential regulation and [social and labor law] in their legislation", and that there could be gray areas which could either be "an overlap of prudential regulation and [social and labor law]" or a "tertium genus and could create a situation of conflicting laws as well as uncertainty about Home/Host responsibilities" See EIOPA, EIOPA's Advice to the European Commission on the review of the IORP Directive 2003/41/EC (2012) EIOPA-BOS-12/015, 57-58.

575 European Commission, 'Impact Assessment Accompanying the document Proposal for a Directive of the European Parliament and of the Council on the activities and supervision of institutions for occupational retirement provision' SWD(2014) 103 final Part 1/2, 13; See also European Commission, 'Impact Assessment Accompanying the document Proposal for a Directive of the European Parliament and of the Council on the activities and supervision of institutions for occupational retirement provision' SWD(2014) 103 final Part 2/2, 3.

576 See recital 70 of Directive 2016/2341/EU of the European Parliament and of the Council of 14 December 2016 on the activities and supervision of institutions for occupational retirement provision (IORPs) [2016], OJ L 354/37 (IORP II Directive), which notes that "[t]he scope of prudential supervision differs between Member States. This can cause problems where an IORP needs to comply with the prudential regulation of its home Member State whilst simultaneously complying with the social and labour law of its host Member State."

577 Impact Assessment Part 2/2 (see footnote 575), 4.

labour legislation and prudential legislation, within limits set by Article 46. However, this provision is non-exhaustive and still appears to leave room for ambiguity,[578] and it is not said that the qualification of a certain security mechanism as a provision of social and labour law necessarily precludes it from *also* being a provision of prudential requirements or vice versa. And even if a Member State settles for one classification or the other, "the European Court of Justice might think otherwise on the basis of overruling European law."[579] Accordingly, Stevens concludes that the "notion of 'social and labour law' is (1) polysemic [in the sense that every Member State has its own, or even multiple, conceptions of social and labour law], (2) non concurrent between Member States [in the sense that the definitions do not overlap] and (3) evolves permanently within these Member States."[580] The inclusion of Article 46 IORP II is therefore at best a partial solution, as it does not definitively settle the question around the scope of social and labour law and prudential law.

This ambiguity could lead to potentially undesirable outcomes for pension scheme members, as the discussion of the security mechanisms within a cross-border in the next section context will demonstrate. A solution to this problem will be suggested in Section 3.3.

---

578 According to Article 46 of the IORP II Directive, prudential supervision "*includes*": conditions of operation, technical provisions, funding of technical provisions, regulatory own funds, available solvency margin, required solvency margin, investment rules, system of governance and information to be provided to members and beneficiaries.

579 Y Stevens, 'The meaning of "national social and labour legislation" in directive 2003/41/EC on the activities and supervision of institutions for occupational retirement provision' (2004) Research report commissioned by the European Association of Paritarian Institutions (AEIP) 8.

580 Stevens 2004 (see footnote 579) 31. See also Y Stevens, 'The development of a legal matrix on the meaning of "national social and labour legislation" in directive 2003/41/EC with regard to five member states: Belgium – France – Germany – Italy – Netherlands' (2006) Research report by the European Association of Paritarian Institutions (AEIP).

3.2   *The Classification of Security Mechanisms in the Case of Cross-Border*
          IORPs

A Close Connection between Prudential Law and social and Labour Law

Although the IORP II Directive requires cross-border IORPs to be fully funded *at all times*,[581] the substance of these funding requirements is determined by the Member States themselves.[582] Therefore, this provision adds a measure of security for pension scheme members whose pension schemes are being operated by an IORP from another Member State, but that is not to say that all Member States' requirements provide scheme members the same level of protection. Section b will discuss the consequences of the application of another Member State's prudential supervision in more detail.

More relevant for this section is the relationship between funding requirements and the other security mechanisms. The funding requirements of an IORP are considered by the IORP II Directive to fall under prudential supervision: Article 46 IORP II includes as part of prudential legislation the technical provisions of an IORP,[583] the funding of the technical provisions,[584] regulatory own funds, available solvency margin, requirements on investment rules and management, the IORP's system of governance and the information to be provided to scheme members. The security mechanisms discussed above – such as additional finance mechanisms, guarantees, reductions of benefits and indexation – are also of direct consequence for the funding position of the IORP: these security mechanisms can be costly items on the balance sheet and may require additional financial reserves. There is therefore a close interaction between prudential legislation and social and labour law.[585] In a cross-border context, the classification of a security mechanism as either social and labour law or prudential law can lead to the application of either home

---

581 Article 14(3) IORP II. The IORP II Directive has relaxed this requirement somewhat vis-à-vis IORP I by changing this requirement so that temporary periods of underfunding are allowed, provided that the IORP immediately draws up appropriate measures and implement them without delay in a way that members and beneficiaries are adequately protected.

582 See, on this, CEIOPS, 'Survey on fully funded, technical provisions and security mechanisms in the European occupational pension sector' (2008) CEIOPS-OPSSC-01/08 Final 14: "It should be noted that the current IORP Directive, while setting out some principles for calculation of technical provisions (recognised actuarial methods, prudence, reference points for rates of interest and biometric tables), does not mention specific rules or parameter values to be used. For that reason, currently technical provisions tend to be defined differently across Member States using different underlying principles and assumptions resulting in divergent sizes of technical provisions. While countries have adopted the principles set out in the Directive, differences exist as regards the method by which technical provisions are calculated."

583 See, on this, Article 13 IORP II, requiring "IORPs operating occupational pension schemes [to] establish at all times in respect of the total range of their pension schemes an adequate amount of liabilities corresponding to the financial commitments which arise out of their portfolio of existing pension contracts."

584 See, on this, Article 14 IORP II, requiring Member States to oblige "every IORP to have at all times sufficient and appropriate assets to cover the technical provisions in respect of the total range of pension schemes operated."

585 CEIOPS (see footnote 582) 12-13.

or host Member State law. Any confusion over that question can lead to the (in)applica-
tion of a certain security mechanism. This can be problematic for pension scheme members. This will be explained below.

The case of sponsor support is a good illustration of the uncertainty that the IORP II
Directive leaves by not clearly defining the two concepts. In the Netherlands there is no
statutory obligation for the employer to make up any shortfalls in the funding of the
scheme. Such an obligation is optional, and would be a contractual obligation included
in the pension fund administration agreement (*uitvoeringsovereenkomst*).[586] In Belgium,
a *statutory* funding obligation is in place for Belgian pension schemes.[587]

In the case of a *statutory* sponsor support obligation, it seems not entirely clear
whether such an obligation lies within social and labour law or prudential law. On the
one hand, the existence of a sponsor support obligation has direct consequences for the
funding situation of the IORP – an argument for its classification as prudential law –
while it also serves to protect the interests of pension scheme members – an argument
in favour of a classification as social and labour law. This uncertainty could be problematic for pension scheme members, as its qualification has consequences for members of
schemes from outside Belgium operated by Belgian IORPs: a qualification as Belgian
social and labour legislation would mean that scheme members outside Belgium would
be deprived of its application, whereas a qualification as Belgian prudential legislation law
means that even non-Belgian employers whose pension schemes are operated in Belgium
are obliged to make up funding shortfalls to the advantage of scheme members.

Consequences for Pension Scheme Members

This uncertainty can be problematic for pension scheme members for a number of reasons. First, there is the risk that a financially strained employer or IORP seeks to exploit
this ambivalence by arguing that a security mechanism is part of a cross-border IORP's
home State social and labour law or a host State's prudential law, rendering the mechanism inapplicable to a scheme operated across borders. Second, supervision of cross-
border IORPs' compliance with social and labour legislation can be made more strenuous. Section b will show that the supervisory authority of a cross-border IORP's home
Member State monitors the IORP's compliance with that state's prudential standards,
while the host Member State's authorities monitor the compliance of its activities with
the host State's social and labour law. If the sponsor support obligation is said to be
Belgian social and labour legislation, this security mechanism falls neither within the
purview of the Belgian authorities – they monitor only the IORP's compliance with Belgian prudential law – nor within the supervisory purview of Dutch authorities – these

---

586 M Minnaard, 'Bijstorting: wettelijke of contractuele plicht?' (2013) PensioenMagazine.
587 Articles 24 and 30 of the 2003 Belgian Act on Supplementary Pensions.

monitor only whether the IORP's activities in the Netherlands are compliant with *Dutch* social and labour law.[588] Vice versa, if home and host state authorities both find a security mechanism to be within their remit of supervision – for instance if the host Member State's authorities find an indexation mechanism to be part of their Member State's prudential legislation while a host State authority considers a similar mechanism to be part of its social and labour legislation – a conflict between the supervisory authorities could arise.

The question of the qualification of the sponsor support mechanism did indeed arise in practice in the context of discussions over what is termed in The Netherlands as the 'Belgium-route'. The term Belgium-route signifies a relocation of Dutch pension schemes from a Dutch IORP to one located in Belgium. SEO, an economic research agency, reported in December 2016 that 19 Dutch pension schemes covering around 10,400 Dutch workers are being operated in other Member States, mainly in Belgium.[589] This development caused concern among Dutch MPs and, in a letter written to the State Secretary of Social Affairs and Employment, these MPs asked questions *inter alia* about sponsor support.[590] In one instance,[591] a Dutch MP asked to what extent Dutch employers would be liable for this Belgian requirement. Belgian law makes the sponsor support obligation mandatory for employers. There is no such obligation under Dutch law, although Dutch employers who have relocated their pension scheme(s) to Belgium may contractually obligate themselves to this sponsor support obligation. There appeared to be some confusion as to which effects this sponsor support obligation would have for Dutch employers, given that it seems unclear whether this obligation is part of social and labour law or prudential law.[592] The Belgian funding requirements for IORPs depend on this sponsor support obligation, which is used as one of the criteria for the calculation of the required financial reserves.[593]

Although in this particular instance the Dutch State Secretary answered that the Belgian sponsor support obligation forms part of Belgium's social and labour law, as a consequence of which Dutch employers would not be bound by it, she also conceded that it would be uncertain what the consequences would be in the event that a Dutch employer did not contractually assume responsibility for it. This lays bare the sometimes intricate link between social and labour law and prudential law and the IORP II Directive's sometimes conflicting architecture: funding requirements are a part of prudential law, whereas the protection of pension scheme members is part of social and labour law. The case could be made that the sponsor support obligation falls under both – the presence of a sponsor support obligation is relevant to the IORP's funding requirements while it also

---

588 E Schop, 'België-route niet omstreden, wel lastig' (2015) *PensioenAdvies*.
589 L Kok & H Geboers, *Grensoverschrijdende Pensioenuitvoering* (SEO Economisch Onderzoek 2016) 15 et seq.
590 *Aanhangsel Handelingen II* 2013/14, 2319; *Aanhangsel Handelingen II* 2014/15, 2169.
591 *Aanhangsel Handelingen II* 2013/14, 2319.
592 Schop (see footnote 588).
593 Kok & Geboers (see footnote 589) 9 et seq.

protects scheme members' pension entitlements. The Belgian supervisory authority – the FSMA – explained in a 2013 annual report that a case-by-case approach is necessary in the event that there is any uncertainty regarding the role of a scheme sponsor in the context of a sponsor support obligation.[594] Section 3.3 will present a possible solution for this problem.

It seems that the same discussion can also be held in respect of the other security mechanisms, such as for guarantees and insurances provided in the context of the pension scheme, such as investment risk, inflation risk and biometric risk.[595] Regarding minimum return guarantees, Stevens notes that it is possible to argue that these fall under social and labour law, as that mechanism is "meant to protect the members of the pension scheme and should therefore always be considered as part of social law", yet that it seems equally possible to argue that it does not.[596] On the one hand, such guarantees and insurances can be said to hold a "significant socio-political element", and should therefore be categorised as social and labour law.[597] On the other hand, it could also be argued that insurance mechanisms are the "traditional core focus of financial supervision".[598]

Based on the discussion above, it appears that the guarantees, benefit adjustment mechanisms and financing mechanisms cannot always be labelled clearly as either social and labour law or prudential law. This is because these mechanisms in most cases clearly encapsulate elements of both. For pension scheme members, the unfortunate situation could arise in which such mechanisms end up in a grey area and give rise to legal uncertainty or, after a long legal dispute, be rendered completely inapplicable. This could have serious consequences for their financial position. The next section will offer a solution for this problem.

3.3   Towards a Solution

There can be no disputing the importance of the legislation protecting the interests of pension scheme members. Guarantees and other instruments arising from national law that protect pension scheme members by making their schemes safer are – barring any legal conflicts that could arise – to the obvious benefit of these individuals. In light of the discussion above, it seems that the ambivalence of the operation under IORP II of the security mechanisms meant to secure the promises made under the various pension scheme types seems to go beyond mere legal uncertainty. Therefore, if cross-border oc-

---

594 FSMA, *Jaarverslag 2013* (2013) 72, available at https://www.fsma.be/nl/news/fsma-publiceert-jaarverslag-2013 accessed on 3 January 2020.
595 M Reiner, 'Strukturfragen zum Zusammenspiel von Aufsichts- und Arbeitsrecht im europäischen Pensionsfondsgeschäft gemäß IORP II' in D Krömer and others (eds), *Arbeitsrecht und Arbeitswelt im Europäischen Wandel* (Nomos 2016) 213.
596 Stevens 2004 (see footnote 579) 8.
597 Reiner (see footnote 595), p. 214.
598 ibid 215.

cupational pension provision is to develop further, it seems worthwhile to strive to re-move as many causes for conflict as possible while ensuring pension scheme security. That seems important not only for IORPs' ease of engaging in cross-border activity, but especially for pension scheme members who would obviously benefit from greater legal certainty.

It therefore seems useful to introduce some extra guidance in EU legislation that could lead to a more secure legal position for pension scheme members. This section will con-sider a possible solution to the uncertainty caused by the IORP II Directive's current architecture.

A Provision that Exhaustively Lists Categories of Social and Labour Law

It seems that the inclusion in the IORP II Directive of an exhaustive list of a core cate-gories of social and labour legislation could contribute to resolve some of the problems described in the previous sections. Together with the IORP II Directive's Article 46, list-ing aspects of prudential law, extra guidance in what constitutes social and labour law and what constitutes prudential law would seem to be helpful for pension scheme members, employers and IORPs alike, as it would clarify which elements of host State legislation apply to the pension scheme. Whereas under the current IORP II Directive, certain pen-sion security mechanisms could be argued to fall under either category – or both cate-gories – a provision listing which security mechanisms belong to social and labour law appears to settle such debates. The proposed contents of such a provision, as well as its implementation, will be discussed in the next sub-section.

Since the IORP II Directive applies to pension schemes the existence of which can easily span decades, it is of paramount importance that pension scheme members receive adequate protection. The results of improper protection of pension scheme members could result in potentially disastrous outcomes for these individuals and, in the worst case, leave them destitute in retirement. It therefore seems fitting that scheme members within a given Member State must be subject to the same standard of protection irrespec-tive of where the IORP operating their pension scheme is located. In addition, any provi-sion prescribing what is social and labour law must be respectful of the great diversity of social and labour legislation in the Member States, as well as the interaction of occupa-tional pension schemes with other pension pillars. The protection of pension scheme members' pension rights must not be sacrificed for IORPs' freedom to provide services.

For these reasons, a provision in the IORP II Directive listing categories of social and labour law must on the one hand enhance the legal certainty of pension scheme members and, on the other, avoid an overly restrictive prescription of legislative categories. This could be done by including categories of social and labour legislation that are formulated broadly, so that the categories are inclusive enough to accommodate the whole of Mem-ber States' applicable social and labour legislation. The purpose of such a provision would not be to limit the application of social and labour legislation in cross-border situations, but merely to clarify which items belong to social and labour law and which belong to prudential law, and therefore which Member State's legislation is applicable to the scheme.

Which Categories Should Be Considered Social and Labour Legislation?

The next question is which categories should be listed as being social and labour legislation in the new provision. Regarding specifically the security mechanisms discussed in this chapter, an answer to that question could be to consider the primary purpose of such mechanisms. In the case of sponsor support obligations, guarantees and risk coverage for scheme members, for instance, it seems obvious that the protection of pension scheme members is the primary goal. Such security mechanisms *directly* ensure that any promises made under the pension scheme are kept, ensuring the security of the pension scheme for scheme members. It is therefore important that such mechanisms are applied in accordance with the legislation of the host Member State of an IORP, so that, first, pension scheme members whose pension scheme is operated by an IORP from another Member State can expect to rely on the same type of security mechanisms as other workers from the same Member State whose pension scheme is operated by a domestic IORP. Second, such a mechanism would also prevent employers from relocating a pension scheme to an IORP in another Member State in order to escape security mechanisms that can be costly for the employer, but beneficial to pension scheme members. Therefore, despite their evident consequences for the funding position of an IORP, security mechanisms with the primary goal of protecting pension scheme members should be considered to fall under the scope of social and labour law. On the other hand, mechanisms such as benefit cuts and the suspension of indexation appear to have as their primary goal the safeguarding of the financial stability of the IORP, and should therefore be considered prudential law.

Of course, the body of social and labour of the Member States goes beyond security mechanisms. In order for the provision to be complete and the full body of Member States' social and labour legislation remains applicable in a cross-border scenario, that legislation must be reviewed and categorized. EIOPA keeps a registry of Member States' applicable social and labour law.[599] A review of the applicable social and labour legislation provided by Member States yields a number of other categories. These categories are the following: the conditions for establishment of and participation in an occupational pension scheme,[600] provisions governing vesting and waiting periods, provisions regarding contributions, provisions regarding benefits and the transferability of pension rights.

---

599 See EIOPA 'Social and Labour Law', available at https://eiopa.europa.eu/regulation-supervision/pensions/occupational-pensions/social-and-labour-law accessed 3 January 2020.
600 Such as Austria's §3 BPG, Belgium's Articles 5 and 7 WAP, the Netherlands' Art. 23 Pensions Act.

In addition, the IORP II Directive itself gives as examples of national social and labour law compulsory membership,[601] the outcomes of collective bargaining agreements[602] as well as the definition and payment of retirement benefits and the conditions for transferability of pension rights.[603] Because the lists provided by the Member States on EIOPA's website are often outdated and incomplete, the items proposed here should not be considered to be conclusive, but rather as a suggestion.

Finally, it was noted in Section 3.2 that there is a close connection between a Member State's social and labour law, on the one hand, and prudential law on the other. The IORP II Directive causes, in the case of the cross-border operation of a pension scheme, a situation in which the host Member State's social and labour legislation defines the contents of a pension scheme that must subsequently be achieved under another Member State's prudential requirements. Under the solution presented above, a situation could arise in which a pension scheme is moved to an IORP in a Member State where there is a statutory sponsor support obligation – which under the solution provided above would be considered social and labour law – but the prudential requirements are less strict than those of the Member State from where the scheme was previously operated. As a consequence, pension scheme members cannot make use of the sponsor support obligation enshrined in the new home IORP's Member State's social and labour law if the scheme is underfunded, while the new IORP operating the scheme is subject to less strict prudential requirements than previously. At first glance, that appears problematic. However, the IORP II Directive's Title II requires the host home Member State's prudential system to (indirectly) take into account the social and labour law of the host state.[604] This means that the funding requirements of an IORP are influenced by the obligations arising from another Member State's social and labour law to which a pension scheme operated by the IORP is subject. Section b will explain that the IORP II Directive also provides other safeguards protecting pension scheme members whose scheme is operated by an IORP in another Member State.

An Amendment to the IORP II Directive

I suggest that the categories of law relating to pensions that are defined as part of social and labour legislation for the purposes of the cross-border activity of IORPs could be

---

601 See recital 35 IORP II.

602 ibid.

603 See recital 36 IORP II.

604 See, for instance, Article 13(1) IORP II, which requires that "The home Member State shall ensure that IORPs operating occupational pension schemes establish at all times in respect of the total range of their pension schemes an adequate amount of liabilities corresponding to the financial commitments which arise out of their portfolio of existing pension contracts," or Article 14(1) IORP II, which requires that "The home Member State shall require every IORP to have at all times sufficient and appropriate assets to cover the technical provisions in respect of the total range of pension schemes operated."

integrated into the IORP II Directive by amending the directive. This amendment could produce, inter alia, a new Article 12 in the directive listing the categories of social and labour legislation. The text of that provision could read as follows: "The social and labour law referred to in Article 11 comprises the following categories:

- the conditions for establishment of and participation in an occupational pension scheme
- provisions governing vesting and waiting periods
- provisions regarding contributions
- provisions regarding benefits
- transferability of pension rights
- pension security mechanisms whose goal is the safeguarding of scheme members' accrued pension rights, including sponsor support obligations, guarantees and risk coverage for scheme members."

In addition, Article 46 IORP II should be amended to include a new item (k), reading: "security mechanisms whose goal it is to ensure the financial stability of the IORP, including benefit cuts and the suspension of indexation."

The Directive's current legal bases of Articles 53, 62 and 114 TFEU appear to provide appropriate legal bases. Those provisions provide the legal basis for legislation on the freedom to provide services and the freedom of establishment, as well as for the adoption of measures for the approximation of laws which have as their object the establishment and functioning of the internal market. The inclusion of a provision clarifying the scope of social and labour legislation could be argued to enhance the operation of the single market for occupational pensions, while at the same time advancing the goal of consumer protection, which Article 169 TFEU seems to call for.

Applying a solution such as the one suggested above also appears to prevent debates over the EU's competence and subsidiarity, as it would merely list categories of legislation that are to be considered social and labour legislation without defining the substance thereof. A similar solution was adopted in the Posted Workers Directive (PWD),[605] which requires the application to posted workers of "a nucleus" of a host state's mandatory rules protecting workers.[606] This nucleus of applicable legislation is listed exhaustively in Article 3 of that directive, and includes items such as maximum work periods and minimum rest periods, remuneration, as well as standards on health, safety and

---

605 Directive 96/71/EC of the European Parliament and of the Council of 16 December 1996 concerning the posting of workers in the framework of the provision of services, [1997] OJ L 18/1 (Posted Workers Directive), recently amended by Directive 2018/957/EU of the European Parliament and of the Council of 28 June 2018 amending Directive 96/71/EC concerning the posting of workers in the framework of the provision of services [2018] OJ L 173/16.

606 C Jacqueson & F Pennings, 'Equal Treatment of Mobile Persons in the Context of a Social Market Economy' (2019) Vol 15 (2) Utrecht Law Review 64, 76.

hygiene at work.[607] The PWD seems to have found a solution to the problem of competence by including a list of items that host Member States guarantee the application of to workers posted in their territory, without defining their substance.[608] So within the boundaries of the list of applicable categories social and labour legislation, Member States would be free to interpret the provisions as they wish, as is also the case under the PWD. For the IORP II Directive, such an approach would mean avoiding (politically) highly sensitive discussions on the EU's defining of – and thereby harmonising – aspects of Member States' substantive pension legislation. This sensitivity was discussed in Chapter 3. Given the importance of social and labour legislation – an importance derived not in the last place from its protection of pension scheme members' pension rights it would seem wise – and indeed in line with the principle of subsidiarity – to leave the definition of social and labour legislation to the Member States. This seems all the more true when considering the intricate balance between Member States' pension pillars, the role and powers of the social partners and the social importance and sensitivity of pension systems. Finally, given the challenges and watering-down of current EU occupational pension legislation (see Chapter 3), it seems unavoidable that some Member States and other stakeholders will fiercely oppose any such effort.

Opposition seems especially likely for Member States with well-developed occupational pension systems, who could fear a restriction in the cross-border application of the social and labour law protecting workers in their territory. However, the case of the PWD shows that such a provision can be implemented in practice, and in the interest of the protection of pension scheme members it is to be hoped that more clarity in the IORP II Directive can be achieved.

4   CONCLUSION TO SECTION A

Retirement income security is "the degree to which a person's customary standard of living is protected from the ups and downs of economic circumstance."[609] In other words, it is the notion that sufficient money will be left after retirement. Defined Benefit schemes can provide a pension scheme member with a great luxury: the amount of the benefits is defined in advance and the employer and/or the pension institutions – in principle – bear the burden of honouring that promise. The scheme member has an enforceable right. A Defined Contribution scheme does not provide that type of guarantee, though it should not be said that this scheme type cannot provide equally favourable end results. It is, however, the legally enforceable right to the amount of benefits that is

---

607 Article 3 Posted Workers Directive.
608 M Houwerzijl & H Verschuren 'Free Movement of (Posted) Workers and Applicable Labour and Social Security Law' in T Jaspers, F Pennings & S Peters (eds), *European Labouw Law* (Intersentia 2019).
609 R Atchley, 'Retirement Income Security: Past, Present and Future' (1997) Vol 21 (2) Generations.

absent in a pure DC scheme. On the other hand, the discussion of the various scheme options has shown that there is plenty of room for manoeuvre between a pure DC scheme and a DB scheme, that more than a mere investment account is offered, but less than an all-risks-covered defined benefit pension.

With respect to the security mechanisms that secure the promises made under the respective pension schemes, this section has shown that the IORP II Directive has, despite its intentions of clarifying which areas are to be considered part of prudential supervision, seemingly not succeeded in avoiding potential conflicts between national social and labour law and prudential law. Though it has added a new (non-exhaustive) provision, defining what prudential supervision is, there appears to be some overlap between social and labour law and prudential provisions. This overlap is not in the interest of scheme members, because conflicts arising from this lacking clarity could be detrimental to their position.

The result of this uncertainty is the open question whether a national standard that is branded as social and labour law preclude it from *also* being prudential law under certain circumstances. The national supervisory authorities are to ensure *inter alia* the solvency of IORPs and the valuation of assets depends also on the availability on such mechanisms as benefit adjustment tools and sponsor support obligations, typically ascribed to social and labour law. Such mechanisms appear to fit into the definition given by IORP II of prudential supervision,[610] as they have effects on – for example – technical provisions. The definitions are still largely up to the Member States.

As noted in the previous chapter, neither the Commission, the Council or other stakeholders were in favour of harmonizing such aspects of pension schemes. The question of the EU's competence and subsidiarity aside, it seems evident that this omission has not helped in creating more certainty in cross-border situations. The confusion surrounding sponsor support in the case of the relocation of Dutch pension schemes to Belgium has made clear that this uncertainty is not merely theoretical. It is therefore to be considered a shortcoming in the IORP II Directive's architecture that needs correcting.

A possible solution to this problem might be offered by the approach taken in the Posted Workers Directive. That directive includes a list of a "hard core" of labour law to be applied to posted workers in the territory of the host state. The IORP II Directive could be amended to include a list of categories of provisions that are to considered social and labour law. In particular, that list, as well as an amendment to Article 46 of the IORP II Directive defining prudential supervision, could help resolve some of the ambivalence found in the case of security mechanisms. This would clarify whether these security mechanisms are to be considered social and labour legislation or prudential law, without prescribing to the Member State what is and is not allowed. After all, social and labour legislation is there to protect pension scheme members, as well as the cohesiveness of

---

610 Article 46 IORP II.

national pension systems, and it would therefore seem unwise to include mandatory definitions in the IORP II Directive harmonising elements of social and labour for both cross-border as well as national circumstances.

SECTION B: PRUDENTIAL SUPERVISION OF CROSS-BORDER IORPs

1   INTRODUCTION

IORPs are subject to the prudential standards of their home Member State, regardless of whether they are operating a pension scheme from another Member State. This section studies to what extent pension scheme members of cross-border IORPs are protected against unforeseen consequences of their pension entitlements being subject to another Member State's prudential legislation. Such legislation includes financial solvency requirements, investment rules, pension fund governance provisions and the information to be provided to members and beneficiaries.[611]

The competent authorities of the host Member State recognise the prudential standards of the home Member State of the cross-border IORP. This mechanism is essential for the internal market for cross-border IORPs to function. Indeed, the proposal for the IORP I Directive called the mutual recognition of these supervisory systems "a prerequisite for cross-border management of occupational schemes."[612] The IORP II Directive sets minimum standards for national prudential regimes, respecting the diversity of Member States' pension systems, but at the same time setting the required minimum standards necessary to allow for a system of mutual recognition to exist.[613]

With respect to the prudential supervision of cross-border IORPs, it is the supervisory authorities of the IORP's home Member State that are charged with the supervision of the IORP.[614] The host Member State supervisory authorities are responsible for the IORP's "compliance of its activities with the host Member State's requirements of social and

---

611 Article 46 IORP II.
612 Commission of the European Communities, 'Proposal for a directive of the European Parliament and of the Council on the activities of institutions for occupational retirement provision' COM(2000) 507 final.
613 ibid. The Explanatory Memorandum notes:
    "IORPs operate very differently from one Member State to another. In some Member States, they resemble life-assurance companies. In others, they are more like investment funds. The Directive proposed takes account of these differences, which are often linked to tax and social security legislation in the Member States. It cannot seek to harmonise in detail the conditions under which IORPs operate.
    Their diversity also necessarily restricts the degree of prudential harmonisation that can be attained by this initial proposal for a Directive. However, an extremely rigorous approach has been adopted for the most crucial prudential aspects (financing liabilities, diversification of assets, information to be provided to the supervisory authorities, members and beneficiaries). This should enable the fundamental objective of a high level of protection for the rights of present and future pensioners to be attained and to permit mutual recognition."
614 Article 47(1) IORP II.

labour law relevant to the field of occupational pension schemes and of the host Member
State's information requirements".[615] In the event that the host Member State authorities
find irregularities, they are to inform the home Member State's authorities. The latter will
then, "in coordination with the competent authority of the host Member State", take the
necessary measures to ensure that the IORP ends the detected breach.[616] The directive
also contains minimum requirements regarding the powers of intervention and supervisory duties of the competent authorities,[617] as well as the supervisory review process.[618]

The consequence of this system for pension scheme members of a foreign cross-border IORP is that the pension scheme that they are a member of is being operated by an
IORP from another Member State, which itself is subject to foreign prudential legislation
and under the supervision of a foreign supervisory authority. This means that pension
scheme members of cross-border IORPs are subject to prudential conditions that they
would not have been subject to had their scheme been operated by a domestic IORP.
Specifically, although the IORP II Directive sets minimum standards, this could mean
that the solvency requirements or the governance standards their IORP is subject to are
laxer than those of their own Member State. It could, of course, also mean that the
protection scheme members enjoy is superior to that of their own Member State's prudential regulations. An illustration follows in the next paragraph.

1.1   An Illustration

Again, the so-called "Belgium-route", which has caused a lasting stir in Dutch politics,
can serve as an example.[619]

One of the central arguments given by multinationals that have relocated their Dutch
pension schemes to Belgium is the desire to benefit from the scale economies resulting
from accommodating the pension schemes from multiple countries in one pension
fund.[620] This allows for saving costs *inter alia* on governance and asset management.
Other benefits named by employers who have moved their schemes to Belgium are that
the consolidation of pension schemes from multiple countries avoids the need for a local
fund in each country, with its own offices, administration, management and supporting

---

615 Article 11(10) IORP II.
616 ibid.
617 Article 48 IORP II.
618 Article 49 IORP II.
619 Dutch MPs have asked parliamentary questions about the issue from at least 2007 up until 2018. See, for
    instance, for the year 2007: *Aanhangsel Handelingen II* 2006/07, 1182; for 2014: *Aanhangsel Handelingen II*
    2013/14, 2319; for 2015: *Aanhangsel Handelingen II* 2014/15, 2169; for 2016: *Aanhangsel Handelingen II*
    2015/16, 2759, *Aanhangsel Handelingen II* 2015/16, 2757 as well as *Aanhangsel Handelingen II* 2016/17, 871,
    Aanhangsel Handelingen II 2016/17, 872 as well as *Aanhangsel Handelingen II* 2016/17, 896; for 2018:
    Aanhangsel Handelingen II 2017/18, 3196 as well as *Aanhangsel Handelingen II* 2018/19, 210.
620 Kok & Geboers (see footnote 589) 16 et seq.

personnel. Costs can also be saved on accountants', actuaries' and consultants' fees.[621] The administration of pension schemes from several Member States can also be made easier for a multinational by having only one set of applicable funding requirements to deal with.[622] Other arguments provided by these multinationals are the desire to avoid the relatively strict Dutch funding requirements as well as the complexity of Dutch governance rules.[623] Medium-sized enterprises were also included in the report. They present as a major reason for moving their pension schemes to another Member State the end of an insurance contract. A new contract could entail less favourable conditions than the old contract due to decreased interest rates and increased life expectancy, prompting a search in other Member States for better terms. Such enterprises could opt for a so-called open-ended IORP, operating schemes for a variety of employers, outside their own country. Other reasons for medium-sized enterprises to move their pension schemes outside the Netherlands include the poor financial position of their company pension fund as well as high administrative costs.[624]

Dutch politicians voiced concerns over the move of Dutch pension schemes to Belgium, mostly because in their eyes pension scheme members could be placed in an inferior position compared to a Dutch pension scheme being operated in the Netherlands by a Dutch provider.[625] Dutch politicians regarded the transfer by Dutch employers of their pension schemes to Belgium as an attempt to escape the strict Dutch funding requirements for pension funds.[626] Belgium is represented by some Dutch politicians and in news coverage – incorrectly[627] – as a Member State with laxer funding and governance requirements.[628] Specifically regarding the funding requirements, a Dutch MP asked the Minister of Social Affairs and Employment a number of questions[629] following a transfer of a pension fund to Belgium. The MP noted that, as a consequence of the transfer, the coverage ratio of the specific fund at issue increased by 11% as a consequence of the application of Belgian funding requirements, and that the fund was now allowed to index the pension benefits – something it would not have been allowed to do under Dutch funding requirements. In addition, the actuarial interest rate with which the fund calculates its required future assets was set by the Belgian supervisory authority at 3.5%, whereas in the Netherlands the prescribed percentage is 1%, resulting in a lower demand

---

621 ibid 17.
622 ibid.
623 ibid.
624 ibid 20 et seq.
625 Then Finance Minister Jeroen Dijsselbloem called the Belgium-route "irresponsible". See 'Dijsselbloem: verhuizen pensioenfondsen naar België onverantwoord', (*Financieel Dagblad* 6 May 2014); see also the Parliamentary Questions referred to in footnote 619.
626 E Schop, 'België-route niet omstreden, wel lastig' (2015) *PensioenAdvies*.
627 ibid. See also Kok & Geboers (see footnote 589) 8.
628 See, for instance, *Aanhangsel Handelingen II* 2017/18, 3196; Financieel Dagblad, 'Dijsselbloem: verhuizen pensioenfondsen naar België onverantwoord', 6 May 2014.
629 See, for instance, *Aanhangsel Handelingen II* 2017/18, 3196.

on current assets held by the fund. The different actuarial interest results from the fact that Belgian legislation on this matter is more principle based, whereas Dutch legislation sets more rigid boundaries. The responding minister noted that the interest rate determined by the Belgian authorities is not considered a prudent interest rate by Dutch standards.[630]

The concerns expressed by Dutch politicians over the transfer of pension schemes to an IORP in another Member State illustrates the many aspects of pension scheme operation that are affected by such a move. Although such a move can be attractive for employers as pension scheme sponsors, the consequences for pension scheme members can be severe. Other Member States have, for instance, different funding requirements, governance requirements and different rules regarding scheme member representation in the IORP.

2   Safeguards in the IORP II Directive

In order to address the concerns described in the final part of the previous paragraph, the IORP II Directive contains a few measures strengthening the position of pension scheme members whose pension scheme is operated by an IORP in another Member State – and therefore subject to another Member State's prudential supervision. There can be two cases in which such protection is needed: 1) a worker is a member of a pension scheme or fund which is moved to another Member State, and 2) a worker joins a pension scheme that is already being operated from another Member State. The latter case could concern, for instance, new workers who join an employer who already has a pension scheme which is being operated from another Member State.

In either case, the IORP II Directive ensures that the social and labour law of the worker's own Member State remains applicable to the scheme. This means that the legislation applicable to the scheme governing matters such as vesting and waiting periods, provisions regarding pension contributions, accrual and benefits, contract law, legislation on guarantees and risk sharing and pension transfers remain that of the IORP's host Member State.[631] The compliance by the IORP operating the scheme with this legislation is ensured by the competent authorities of the Member State in which the worker resides. As noted in Section a, the social and labour legislation applicable to a pension scheme plays an important role in the protection of scheme members. Other mechanisms in the directive ensure a floor of prudential standards that ensure the proper operation of pension schemes, wherever in the EU they are operated from. The sections below will explain these.

---

630 ibid.
631 EIOPA 'Social and Labour Law', available at https://eiopa.europa.eu/regulation-supervision/pensions/occupational-pensions/social-and-labour-law accessed 3 January 2020.

2.1   New Requirements in the IORP II Directive

In order to avoid differences in scheme member protection across the Member States, the IORP II Directive has shored up the standards of governance and information provision vis-à-vis the IORP I Directive. During the revision process of the IORP I Directive, the Commission identified four[632] specific problems, three of which concerned the protection of pension scheme members. These three problems concerning the position of pension scheme members were, first, that insufficient governance and risk management requirements cause so-called principal-agent problems in the sense that those who effectively manage IORPs might not necessarily act in the best interest of the scheme members or beneficiaries. Second, the information to scheme members was considered insufficient and third, the supervisory powers were considered insufficient by the Commission to effectively ensure that IORPs comply with the prudential standards and information disclosures. The other (fourth) problem was that cross-border activity was still considered expensive and complex for employers. Chapter 5 will discuss this problem in more detail.

The IORP II Directive aims to address these problems by adding an entire Title governing the activity of IORPs,[633] containing new requirements on governance, as well as one on information requirements,[634] bringing the governance of IORPs and the information they provide to a more uniform level throughout the EU. The IORP II Directive has also introduced a Title on prudential supervision, containing new provisions on the prudential supervision which includes powers of intervention for the supervisory authorities.[635] Although these new rules seem to mean by no means an equally high level prudential supervision, these new provisions introduce a floor of prudential standards across all European Member States, equalizing these standards to some extent. Avoiding so-called "regulatory arbitrage", which could strengthen the "incentive to locate IORPs in a MS that has laxer rules", was a priority in the revision of the IORP Directive.[636] These new requirements will be discussed in the following sections. First, another important element in the prudential supervision of IORPs will be discussed: the quantitative requirements in the IORP II Directive.

2.2   Quantitative Requirements

All IORPs are subject to the so-called quantitative requirements of the IORP II Directive. These requirements, enshrined Title II of the directive, set the requirements for the fund-

---

632 See Impact Assessment Part 1/2 (see footnote 575) 10.
633 See Title III IORP II.
634 See Title IV IORP II.
635 See Title V IORP II.
636 See Impact Assessment Part 1/2 (see footnote 575) 22-23.

ing of an IORP. While the specifics of the funding requirements are determined at national level, the provisions of Title II of the directive require that the financial reserves of the IORP are, in principle, "sufficient and appropriate assets to cover" at all times the financial obligations arising out of the pension schemes the IORP operates. All IORPs engaged in cross-border activity face a stricter requirement imposed by the directive: as noted in Section 3 of Section a, these must be fully funded, meaning that every Euro owed by the IORP must be covered by a Euro in its coffers. This requirement for full funding appears to give extra security to pension scheme members of cross-border IORPs, as their schemes are at all times backed by sufficient financial reserves. While the it is determined at national level what constitutes full funding – this involves complex calculations taking into account a pension scheme's future obligations – this requirement for cross-border IORPs also seems to be an important aspect making the mutual recognition of prudential regimes possible. Any differences in the standards for IORPs' prudential supervision across the EU seem to be relatively less concerning for the protection of pension scheme members if cross-border IORPs are always required to be in a position to meet their financial obligations.

2.3   Governance and Risk Management

With a view to addressing weaknesses in the governance of IORPs, the IORP II Directive has introduced a system of governance for all IORPs (not just cross-border IORPs) that is modelled after the requirements of other financial sectors.[637] The aim of the new governance requirements is the "adequate management of risk and the protection of members and beneficiaries."[638] The functions, as will be described below, serve to enhance the position of scheme members of IORPs where scheme member protection is not yet at the level prescribed by the directive.

The IORP II Directive requires that all IORPs must have a governance system in place that provides for "sound and prudent management of their activities."[639] The Directive furthermore requires that that system must include an "adequate and transparent organisational structure with a clear allocation and appropriate segregation of responsibilities" as well as "an effective system for ensuring the transmission of information."[640]

A central aspect of these new provisions is the introduction of three key functions: a risk-management function, an internal audit function, and, where applicable, an actuarial

---

637 The supervisory in IORP II requirements bear many resemblances with the requirements in the Solvency II
   Directive for the insurance sector, the CRD IV for the banking sector and the MiFID for investment firms
   and the AIFM Directive for managers of alternative investment funds.
638 Recital 52 IORP II
639 Article 21(1) IORP II.
640 ibid.

function.[641] The persons in charge of running the IORP as well as those who carry out functions must be qualified, knowledgeable and experienced to properly carry out their tasks and must also be of good repute and integrity. These are the so-called requirements for fit and proper management.[642]

Regarding the key functions specifically, the risk management function's task is "to facilitate the function of risk management". In particular, the function is to oversee risks related to underwriting and reserving, asset-liability management, investments, liquidity risk management etc.[643]

The actuarial function must be present in case an IORP itself provides cover against biometric risks or guarantees either an investment performance or a given level of benefits. It is in charge of ensuring *inter alia* that the methodologies and underlying models used in the calculation of technical provisions and the assumptions made are appropriate and to inform the administrative, management or supervisory body of the IORP of the reliability and adequacy of the calculation of technical provisions.[644]

Finally, the internal audit function's task is, as the name suggests, to evaluate the adequacy and effectiveness of the internal control system and other elements of the system of governance, including, where applicable, outsourced activities. This includes oversight over the other key functions.[645]

2.4   *Information Requirements*

In addition to the social and labour law remaining applicable, the IORP II Directive also requires that the information to be provided to pension scheme members and beneficiaries, although confusingly considered by the IORP II Directive to be part of the prudential requirements,[646] must comply with the requirements of the Member State whose social and labour law is applicable to the scheme.[647]

Title IV of IORP II contains the requirements for information to be given to (prospective) scheme members and beneficiaries (i.e. a person receiving retirement benefits).

For active scheme members, such information must contain, *inter alia*, the name of the IORP, the Member State in which the IORP is registered or authorised and the name of its competent authority (i.e. the authority responsible for the prudential supervision of the IORP[648]).[649] In addition, IORPs must inform scheme members about the specific

---

641 Article 24(1) IORP II.
642 Article 22 IORP II.
643 Article 25 IORP II.
644 Article 27 IORP II.
645 Article 26 IORP II.
646 Article 46(j) IORP II.
647 Article 11(6)-(11) IORP II, as well as Title IV IORP II.
648 Article 47(1) IORP II.
649 Article 37(1) IORP II.

nature of national pension systems and of relevant national social, labour and tax law.[650] The information to be received is also to contain information about *inter alia* the pension scheme and the investment profile, the nature of financial risks borne by members and beneficiaries, costs, guarantees (if any) and mechanisms protecting accrued entitlements or the benefit reduction mechanisms.[651]

For prospective scheme members (i.e. those who have not yet joined the scheme but are eligible to join it[652]), the IORP II Directive stipulates that such persons are to be given all the necessary information to make an informed choice. Where prospective members do not have a choice and are automatically enrolled in a pension scheme – for instance in the case of compulsory membership – the IORP should provide them with the key relevant information about their membership promptly after enrolment.[653]

Prospective scheme members are to be given "at least"[654] the information about the options within their pension scheme (including investment options), the relevant features of the pension scheme including the kind of benefits, information on whether and how environmental, climate, social and corporate governance factors are considered in the investment approach.[655] In case prospective pension scheme members are to bear investment risks or can take investment decisions, the IORP must provide information past performance of investments.[656]

2.5 Powers of Intervention for Supervisory Authorities

According to Article 45 of the IORP II Directive, the objective of prudential supervision is "to protect the rights of members and beneficiaries and to ensure the stability and soundness of the IORP."[657] To that end, the Member States must ensure that the competent authorities are provided with the necessary means, and have the relevant expertise, capacity, and mandate to achieve the objective of prudential supervision.[658] Prudential supervision includes the supervision of the funding requirements of the IORP,[659] the IORP's

---

650 Article 38(1) IORP II.
651 For a complete overview of the information to be given to active scheme members, see Articles 36 to 40, 42 and 44 IORP II.
652 Article 6(7) IORP II.
653 Recital 65 IORP II. See also Article 36 and 41 IORP II.
654 Article 36(1)(a) IORP II.
655 Article 41(1) IORP II for prospective scheme members who are not automatically enrolled in a pension scheme or 41(3) IORP II for prospective scheme members who are automatically enrolled in a pension scheme.
656 Article 41(2) IORP II.
657 Article 45(1) IORP II.
658 Article 45(2) IORP II.
659 This includes supervision of the technical provisions, the funding of technical provisions, regulatory own funds, the available solvency margin and the required solvency margin. See Article 46 IORP II.

adherence to the investment rules and management, its system of governance and the information to be provided to scheme members.[660]

In order to ensure compliance with the requirements of the Directive, national competent authorities are vested with several powers. Their supervision of IORPs within their territory must be "forward-looking and risk-based"[661] and is to "comprise an appropriate combination of off-site activities and on-site inspections."[662] It must also be "timely and proportionate to the size, nature, scale and complexity of the activities" of an IORP.[663]

In the case of cross-border IORPs, these are under the ongoing supervision by the competent authority of the host Member State as to the compliance of the IORP's activities with the host Member State's requirements of social and labour law and of the host Member State's information requirements.[664] In the event of any breaches, the host Member State authorities inform the home Member State's authorities, in which case the latter is to take "the necessary measures to ensure that the IORP puts a stop to the detected breach" in coordination with the authorities of the host State.[665] If the home State authorities do not take (adequate) measures or if the IORP fails to stop breaching social and labour law and/or information requirements, "the competent authority of the host Member State may, after informing the competent authority of the home Member State, take appropriate measures to prevent or penalise further irregularities, including, insofar as is strictly necessary, preventing the IORP from operating in the host Member State for the sponsoring undertaking."[666]

The powers of intervention for the home State's competent authorities are listed in Article 48 IORP II. The competent authorities must require every IORP registered or authorised in their territories to have sound administrative and accounting procedures and adequate internal control mechanisms. The Directive also requires Member States that competent authorities may impose administrative sanctions and other measures applicable to all infringements of the national provisions implementing the Directive, and those sanctions must be made public.

More far-reaching powers of intervention include the power to "restrict or prohibit the free disposal of the IORP's assets"[667] when the IORP fails to meet the funding requirements and the power to transfer the power from persons who are running an IORP registered or authorized in the competent authorities' territories in accordance with the law of the home Member State wholly or partly to a special representative who is fit to exercise those powers. The activities of an IORP may be restricted in case it fails to

---

660 Article 46 IORP II.
661 Article 47(2) IORP II.
662 Article 47(3) IORP II
663 Article 47(4) IORP II.
664 Article 11(10) IORP II.
665 ibid.
666 Article 11(11) IORP II.
667 Article 48(6) IORP II.

protect adequately the interests of scheme members and beneficiaries, no longer fulfils the conditions of operation or fails seriously in its obligations under the rules to which it is subject. In addition, the home state competent authorities may also restrict the operation of cross-border IORPs established in their jurisdiction if the IORP does not respect the requirements of social and labour law of the host Member State relevant to the field of occupational pension schemes.

2.6   *Conditions Applicable to Cross-Border Transfers*

Any cross-border transfer of existing pension schemes is subject to the prior approval by a majority of members and a majority of the beneficiaries concerned or, where applicable, by a majority of their representatives.[668] What constitutes a majority is to be defined by national law. The information on the conditions of the transfer shall be made available to the members and beneficiaries concerned and, where applicable, to their representatives before the application for a transfer is submitted. The sponsoring undertaking, if there is one, must also give its approval to the transfer.[669]

Additionally, both the home Member State as well as the host Member State competent authorities must give their approval to the transfer of all or a part of a pension scheme's liabilities, technical provisions, and other obligations and rights, as well as corresponding assets or cash equivalent thereof. Transfers between IORPs shall be subject to authorisation by the competent authority of the home Member State of the receiving IORP after obtaining the prior consent of the competent authority of the home Member State of the transferring IORP.[670] The authorities of the home Member State of the receiving IORP must assess, *inter alia*, the administrative structure and financial situation of the receiving IORP and the qualifications or experience of the persons running the receiving IORP, and whether both the receiving IORP as well as the pension scheme to be received by it are fully funded.[671] The competent authorities of the transferring IORP are to ensure that the individual entitlements of the members and beneficiaries are at least the same after the transfer and that the assets corresponding to the pension scheme to be transferred are sufficient to satisfy the rules of the home Member State of the transferring IORP.[672] Consequently, the IORP II Directive does not appear to allow competent authorities of a sending IORP's home Member State to block a transfer over concerns regarding the prudential standards of a receiving IORP's Member State. This would be irreconcilable with the system of mutual recognition of Member States' prudential regimes, on which the IORP II Directive's system enabling the cross-border activity of IORPs relies.

---

668 Article 12(3)(a) IORP II.
669 Article 12(3)(b) IORP II.
670 Article 12 IORP II.
671 Article 12(7) IORP II.
672 Article 12(8)(b) and 12(8)(c) IORP II.

While the possibility for the competent authorities of a sending IORP's home Member State to block a transfer over concerns regarding the system of prudential supervision in the receiving IORP's home Member State would seem to add an extra layer of protection for pension scheme members, the directive contains safeguards that alleviate those concerns to a significant extent, as discussed in this and the previous sub-sections. Not only has the IORP II Directive introduced minimum standards regarding governance, funding and information requirements for IORPs, cross-border IORPs are under the ongoing supervision of both the home and host Member State's competent authorities and must, in principle, be fully funded. Finally, the rules on pension scheme transfers give the sponsoring undertaking, the scheme members and beneficiaries or their representatives the possibility to block a transfer if the transfer is not in their long-term interests.[673]

These requirements do not, however, seem to make entirely clear whether they apply also to a second transfer between two IORPs in another Member State. For example, a company located in Member State A transfers its pension scheme to an IORP in Member State B. In this case, the IORP II Directive's Article 12 on cross-border transfers applies. Consequently, the scheme members and beneficiaries or their representatives must give their prior approval for the scheme to transferred to another Member State's prudential jurisdiction. Sometime later, the undertaking wishes to transfer the scheme to another IORP, also located in Member State B. Does Article 12 apply? It appears that is does not. First, there is the obvious argument that the title of the provision "Cross-border transfers", suggesting that only transfers *between* Member States are within its scope. A literal reading of the provision seems to support that finding: the text of the provision provides that Member States are to allow IORPs to transfer their schemes to "a receiving IORP". Article 6(13) defines a receiving IORP as an IORP receiving all or a part of a pension scheme's liabilities, technical provisions, and other obligations and rights, as well as corresponding assets or cash equivalent thereof, from an IORP registered or authorised in another Member State". The Article's purpose appears to be to let pension scheme members have a say in the transfer of their scheme to another prudential jurisdiction. That protection, therefore, seems no longer required once the initial transfer to the receiving Member State has taken place, and is therefore no longer applicable to following transfers within the receiving Member State's jurisdiction.

An argument against the provision's non-application in the case of transfers within the same receiving Member State would be that there is still a transfer taking place between a host and a home Member State, albeit the same ones as a previous transfer. Protection of scheme members in such instances still seems important, as the performance and security of IORPs differs, affecting the position of scheme members. However, transfers within the receiving Member States are governed by that Member State's own

---

673 In accordance with Article 12(3) IORP II.

legislation on transfers, protecting the scheme members. Nevertheless, this provision in the IORP II Directive appears to concern only cross-border transfers.

Arguably, IORP II's provisions on the transfer of pension schemes strengthen the position of pension scheme members who do not wish to see their pension scheme being relocated to an IORP in another Member State. The Directive does this by giving scheme members and/or their representatives a vote before the transfer. In addition, both the home and host state competent authorities are involved in the transfer, and must both authorise the transfer.

3   CONCLUSION TO SECTION B

While it is true that pension scheme members of foreign cross-border IORPs are subject to another Member State's prudential requirements, including funding requirements, investment rules, pension fund governance provisions, the IORP II Directive provides a number of provisions protecting the position of prospective members and active members. Not only does the directive foresee that the same social and labour law requirements remain applicable to the pension scheme, it also prescribes rigorous information requirements both for prospective scheme members as well as active scheme members facing a cross-border transfer of their scheme. Its new requirements for governance protect scheme members not only of cross-border IORPs, but all IORPs. These requirements ratchet up the minimum standards of protection of pension scheme members, *inter alia* by introducing dedicated functions in charge of monitoring specific risks and potential shortcomings in the governance of an IORP, ultimately with the goal of ensuring that pension scheme members' accrued rights are safely and soundly cared for. The respective competent supervisory authorities have also been equipped with far-reaching powers of intervention should the IORP's operations not be in line with legislative requirements.

Finally, a cross-border transfer of pension schemes requires the consent of pension scheme members, the employer as well as the home and host state supervisory authorities who are to consider *inter alia* the long term interests of pension scheme members and whether entitlements of the members and beneficiaries of the scheme to be transferred are at least the same after the transfer. Although those requirements have their critics,[674]

---

[674] See L Weymouth, 'IORP II will 'kill off' DB cross-border arrangements, ACA says', (*European Pensions* 13 January 2015), available at http://www.europeanpensions.net/ep/IORP-II-will-kill-off-DB-cross-bord er-arrangements-ACA-says.php accessed 3 January 2020; H van Meerten & L Geerling, 'Build that wall? Het onderscheid tussen binnenlandse en grensoverschrijdende waardeoverdrachten van pensioenregelingen' (2019) No 2 Tijdschrift voor Recht en Arbeid; E. Lutjens, 'Vragen over implementatie IORP Richtlijn: grensoverschrijdende uitvoering in discussie' (2018) Report attached to parliamentary document, available at https://zoek.officielebekendmakingen.nl/blg-863202 accessed 3 January 2020; Recital 37 et seq. IORP II.

since they can unjustifiably[675] stifle cross-border transfers, they can serve to protect the position of pension scheme members if used correctly.

The fact, however, remains that membership to a foreign IORP means the application to another Member States' prudential requirements, and that can have unexpected and unforeseen consequences. For instance, it seems nearly impossible to inform pension scheme members of all the details and consequences of membership of an IORP in another Member State. The same could, however, be argued in respect of pension scheme members of IORPs in their own Member State, given the myriad of aspects that are involved in pension provision. But the information that is to be given to scheme members as a consequence of the requirements of the IORP II Directive appears to focus on the most important aspects, and sets requirements for the clarity and quality of that information.[676] The IORP II Directive also provides a minimum level of harmonisation concerning prudential requirements. The fact that national social and labour law remains applicable is an additional safeguard.

The extensive and at times far-reaching powers of intervention of the national competent authorities can only be of any use to pension scheme members if those authorities are competent and capable of performing their tasks. For instance, the option to prohibit or restrict the activities of a cross-border IORP that does not respect the requirements of social and labour law of the host Member State requires good communication between the home and host state authorities, and the IORP's home Member State's authorities must be willing and able to intervene in a timely and appropriate manner. This is another reason why the consequences of membership of an IORP from another Member State can be difficult to anticipate.

In addition, the safeguards contained in the directive cannot alter the fact that under some circumstances, the Directive's distinction between social and labour law on the one hand, and prudential law on the other, could mean that pension scheme members could find that certain guarantees or protective mechanisms intended to protect them can be (unexpectedly) rendered inaccessible, as was shown in Section 3.2 of Section a. The risk of that happening seems all the more real given the relatively few cross-border IORPs and therefore relatively new subject matter for national supervisory authorities. This means that (prospective) scheme members to schemes operated by foreign IORPs must be made aware that such risks could, at least in theory, arise.

In sum, although pension scheme members of cross-border IORPs are exposed to another Member State's prudential supervision, the safeguards in the IORP II Directive appear – at least from the perspective of a pension scheme member – to provide ample

---

675 Van Meerten & Geerling (see footnote 674) and Lutjens (see footnote 674) argue quite correctly that the requirement contained in the IORP II Directive for the approval of pension scheme members before a transfer can be in contravention of EU primary law, as it can cause different requirements for domestic versus cross-border transfers.

676 Article 36(2) IORP II.

protection. The concern expressed by Dutch politicians over Dutch pension schemes being relocated to Belgium therefore seem to require placing into perspective.

SECTION C: THE SOCIAL FUNCTION OF OCCUPATIONAL PENSIONS

1   INTRODUCTION

This section will focus on the social function of occupational pensions and to what extent cross-border IORPs can support this social function. Ostensibly, the main traditional (social) function of (occupational) pensions is to provide scheme members with an income in their retirement.[677] That social function was also recognised by the ECJ in its case law[678] and is expressed in the IORP II Directive's recitals.[679]

Currently in many EU Member States, the role of occupational pensions in the provision of retirement income of Europeans is increasing as public retirement systems are under pressure and becoming less generous. This trend, called privatisation, will be discussed in the next section, together with the trend of marketisation, whereby the responsibilities for an adequate retirement income are being shifted from employers and/or pension providers to pension scheme members. The trend of pension privatisation brings as a consequence that the social function of other pension pillars as sources of retirement income is becoming stronger.

One of the stated goals of cross-border IORPs is to contribute to adequate, safe and sustainable pensions. The safety, adequacy and sustainability of occupational pensions seems inseparable from the social function of occupational pensions: a pension scheme can only be of any meaningful use – i.e. fulfil a social function – to a scheme member if it safely provides an adequate retirement income, and if that income can be sustainably financed in the long term. Given the aforementioned trends, an effort supporting that tripartite goal seems more urgent than ever. How is the cross-border IORP to be seen in the light of these trends?

---

677 This definition of a pension scheme as providing insurance against outliving one's resources is well established in the academic literature, see, e.g., Z Bodie, 'Pensions as retirement income insurance' (1989) National Bureau of Economic Research Working Paper No. 2917 28-49; N Barr & P Diamond, *Reforming Pensions: Principles and Policy Choices* (Oxford University Press 2008); Bodie & Mitchell (see footnote 556) 1; Blake (see footnote 534) 29.

678 See, for instance, Joined Cases C-159/91 and C-160/91, *Poucet & Pistre* [1993] ECLI:EU:C:1993:63, para 9; Joined Cases C-430/93 and C-431/93, *Van Schijndel* [1995] opinion of AG Jacobs ECLI:EU:C:1995:185, para 62; Case C-244/94 *Fédération Française des Sociétés d'Assurance (FFSA)* [1995] ECLI:EU:C:1995:392; Case C-67/96, *Albany* [1999] ECLI:EU:C:1999:430; Joined Cases C-115/97, C-116/97 and C-117/97, *Brentjens'* [1999] ECLI:EU:C:1999:434; Case C-219/97, *Drijvende Bokken* [1999] ECLI:EU:C:1999:437; Joined Cases C-180/98 to C-184/98, *Pavlov and others* [2000], ECLI:EU:C:2000:428; Case C-271/08, *Commission v. Germany* [2010] ECLI:EU:2010:426.

679 See recitals 25 and 32 IORP II.

1.1   Context – An Increasing Social Role for Occupational Pensions

The trend of privatisation and marketisation of (occupational) pension systems is well-documented.[680]

Privatisation entails the shift from public pensions to a multi-pillar system (with increased reliance on, *inter alia*, pre-funded occupational pensions), whereas marketisation describes a commodification of pensions; "they become dependent on market logic, be it through tighter coupling of benefits with contributions or financial returns on investments."[681] Pension privatisation – or individualization[682] – individualizes risk and returns[683] and "creates 'funded,' 'defined contribution' pension systems to fully or partially replace social security and other 'defined benefit' systems (such as those provided in the past by many U.S. and European employers)."[684] Both Member States that rely primarily on public pensions as well as those that rely primarily on occupational pensions are undergoing such changes "because of the already enacted or further planned retrenchment of public pensions (marketization) and the shift toward private funded pensions (privatization), both advocated by a sustainability rationale."[685]

While the importance of second and third pillar pension provision is on the rise throughout the EU in the context of pension privatisation, the trend of marketisation of occupational pension schemes sees businesses moving away from defined benefit pension schemes towards defined contribution schemes or a hybrid form.[686] This trend from defined benefit to defined contribution plans is attributable mainly to the desire of employers to reduce the risk of an underfunded pension plan. Defined benefit plans, in which the employer or the pension institution guarantees a certain level of pensions, entail substantial funding obligations for employers.[687] Successive financial crises and

---

680 See, for instance, B Ebbinghaus, 'The Privatization and Marketization of Pensions in Europe: A Double Transformation Facing the Crisis' (2015) Vol 1 (1) European Policy Analysis 56; A Zaidi, A Grech & M Fuchs, Pension policy in EU25 and its possible impact on elderly poverty (2006) Centre for Analysis of Social Exclusion paper 116; M Orenstein, 'Pension privatization in crisis: Death or rebirth of a global policy trend?' (2011) Vol 11 (3) International Social Security Review 65; S Brooks, 'Interdependent and domestic foundations of policy change: The diffusion of pension privatization around the world' (2005) Vol 49 (2) International Studies Quarterly 273; B Palier (ed), *A Long Goodbye to Bismarck?: The Politics of Welfare Reform in Continental Europe*, (Amsterdam University Press 2010); R Holzmann, 'Global pension systems and their reform: Worldwide drivers, trends and challenges' (2013) Vol 66 (2) International Social Security Review 1.
681 Ebbinghaus 2015 (see footnote 680) 57.
682 Y Stevens, 'The silent pension pillar implosion' (2017) Vol 19 (2) European Journal of Social Security 98.
683 M. Orenstein, *Privatizing Pensions: The Transnational Campaign for Social Security Reform*, (Princeton University Press 2008) 15.
684 ibid 16.
685 Ebbinghaus 2015 (see footnote 680) 67.
686 See also See Impact Assessment Part 1/2 (see footnote 575) 9.
687 J. Arts, DC *Defaults & Heterogeneous Preferences* (MSc Thesis, Tilburg University 2015) Netspar Academic Series, 7, available at https://www.netspar.nl/assets/uploads/017_-_MSc_-_Arts.pdf accessed 3 January 2020.

changes in accounting rules have led to sometimes significant underfunding. This under-funding was aggravated by, among other things, declining interest rates, causing the de-clining value of pension fund assets to shrink while increasing the value of liabilities. "Due to the large impact of the financial crisis, employers have come to realize that they are tied to guarantees that they can no longer make, nor are willing to make,"[688] leading to an accelerated shift to DC plans.

In those Member States that have a significant number of defined benefit schemes, the share that such schemes enjoy is being encroached upon by defined contribution schemes, although DB schemes still currently dominate the European occupational pen-sion fund sector in terms of assets.[689] In 2014, the Commission reported[690] in its impact assessment for the proposed-at-the-time IORP II Directive that "[s]ince the adoption of the [IORP] Directive more than 10 years ago, the importance of DC and hybrid schemes has increased [...] and it is expected that this trend will continue." The Commission gave as reasons for this trend the fact that "traditional final-salary DB schemes have become unaffordable for many sponsoring employers and are increasingly providing DC and hybrid schemes, either to replace existing DB Schemes or when creating new IORPs."[691] In addition, it names labour market changes and technological progress as reasons.

In the EU, this trend appears to have started in the UK in the 1980s when the Thatch-er government made efforts to face the UK's impending pensions crisis.[692] Employees were offered subsidies to contract-out of occupational cover and into DC personal pen-sion plans. In the wake of the dot.com bubble burst and the advent of the IAS 19 account-ing standards – which require corporations to divulge their pension deficits in their an-nual accounts – British businesses moved away from DB schemes.[693] Since 2000, this trend has accelerated, and the Pensions Commission estimated that active membership in DB plans has fallen 60% between 1995 and 2004.[694] Public-sector DB schemes are currently under review. In Ireland, this trend is also perceptible. In Sweden, too, both the statutory as well as occupational pensions were gradually converted from DB to DC.[695] In the Netherlands, occupational pension schemes are still overwhelmingly DB;

---

688 ibid.

689 EIOPA, *Financial Stability Report June 2017*, available at https://eiopa.europa.eu/Publications/Reports/Fi-nancial_Stability_Report_June_2017.pdf accessed 3 January 2020.

690 Impact Assessment Part 1/2 (see footnote 575) 9.

691 ibid.

692 D Blake, 'Two Decades of Pension Reform in the UK: What Are the Implications for Occupational Pension Schemes?' (2000) Vol 22 (3) Employee Relations 223.

693 B Ebbinghaus & N Whiteside, 'Shifting responsibilities in Western European pension systems: What future for social models?' (2012) Vol 12 (3) Global Social Policy 266, 275.

694 J Broadbent, M Palumbo & E Woodman, 'The Shift from Defined Benefit to Defined Contribution Pension Plans – Implications for Asset Allocation and Risk Management' (2006) Paper prepared for a Working Group on Institutional Investors, Global Savings and Asset Allocation established by the Committee on the Global Financial System 15.

695 K Anderson, *Occupational Pensions in Sweden* (Friedrich Ebert Stiftung 2015), available at http://library.fes.de/pdf-files/id/12113.pdf accessed 3 January 2020.

90% of participants is enrolled in a DB scheme.[696] However, Dutch employers are also increasingly unwilling to shoulder uncertain pension expenses and to include such expenses on their balance sheets.[697] Social partners increasingly opt for DC schemes because of increases in life expectancy, low interest rates and increasing pension premiums. These factors all conspire to make the obligation of paying a lifelong, guaranteed pension dearer.

But this shift seems to affect not just Member States with DB pension plans, but also those with a generous public pension pillar where occupational pensions play a comparatively modest role. This development towards more private pension responsibility has been driven in those countries mainly by "the pressure to contain PAYG public pension costs faced with demographic challenges, falling contributions and public debt in a context of sluggish economic growth and public expenditure constraint."[698] Indeed, "[n]early everywhere in Europe the pension systems transformed their public-private mix through privatization."[699] To be sure, in theory, a well-managed DC scheme need not leave a pension scheme member worse off than a DB plan. However, the (legally enforceable) guarantees that are enjoyed by DB plan participants are, in principle, not available to DC scheme members.

In conclusion, the role of occupational pension provision in the EU has been steadily growing over the last decades in the face of retrenching public pension schemes – the privatisation of pensions. It therefore seems that the social role of occupational pensions – that of providing an income in retirement – is on the rise in all Member States. But this increasingly important social role comes at a time when pension scheme members must increasingly bear the risks associated with pensions themselves. This trend is described in literature as the marketisation of pensions: a commodification of pensions; "they become dependent on market logic, be it through tighter coupling of benefits with contributions or financial returns on investments."[700] In many Member States, DB pensions are being replaced with DC schemes, placing more risk on the shoulders of workers instead of the employer and/or the pension provider.

It seems that in this context, the aim of cross-border IORPs to stimulate safe, adequate and sustainable pensions is more important than ever. The following section will study whether the IORP II Directive's provisions on cross-border IORPs can facilitate the achievement this aim.

---

696 K Goudswaard, 'Blijft het Nederlandse pensioenstelsel bijzonder?' in R Bijl et al (eds) *Opvallend gewoon. Het bijzondere van Nederland* (Sociaal en Cultureel Planbureau 2013) 18-24. It is worth mentioning that, since Dutch pension schemes allow for benefit reductions as well as conditional indexation, Dutch DB schemes may not be recognized as such in other jurisdictions.
697 P Kiveron & H van Meerten, '"DBization", a continuing story' (2014) Pensioen Magazine 30, 31.
698 Ebbinghaus & Whiteside (see footnote 693) 267.
699 Ebbinghaus 2015 (see footnote 680) 60.
700 ibid 57.

2   THE FULL FUNDING REQUIREMENT: DOES THE IORP DIRECTIVE ENCOURAGE
     CROSS-BORDER PROVISION OF DC OVER DB SCHEMES?

2.1   *Funding a Cross-Border Scheme*

As noted in Section b, the IORP II Directive requires that cross-border IORPs are, in principle, fully funded at all times. The funding requirements of the IORP II Directive are more demanding for pension institutions that operate defined benefit (DB) schemes than for those who operate defined contribution (DC) schemes. Article 14(3) of the IORP II Directive stipulates that the technical provisions of cross-border IORPs must be fully funded.

Article 13 of IORP II gives qualitative prudential guidelines for the calculation of the technical provisions. Technical provisions are a valuation of the scheme's liabilities. An IORP must have sufficient assets to cover its technical provisions. The technical provisions are reserves the pension fund keeps in order to be able to cover the fund's liabilities, which are its current and future benefit payment obligations. According to the fourth paragraph of Article 13, the calculation of the technical provisions must be done according to "actuarial methods recognised by the competent authorities of the home Member State". The technical provisions must be sufficient to perform the payments of pensions and benefits that are already in their payout phase, "and to reflect the commitments which arise out of members' accrued pension rights". The rates of interest that are used to calculate the technical provisions must be in accordance with the rules of the home Member State. The article also states that that "The home Member State may make the calculation of technical provisions subject to additional and more detailed requirements, with a view to ensuring that the interests of members and beneficiaries are adequately protected."

What is required for certain IORPs in addition to the technical provisions are the so-called regulatory own funds. This is because "in some cases, it is the IORP itself which provides such cover or guarantees and the sponsor's obligations are generally exhausted by paying the necessary contributions. In those circumstances, the IORP concerned should hold own funds based on the value of technical provisions and risk capital."[701] In other words, an IORP must hold such funds if it, and not the sponsoring undertaking, takes on liability for the coverage of – for example – biometric risk, guarantees a certain investment performance or a certain level of benefits. This would be the case for an IORP operating a DB scheme or any other scheme featuring guarantees for which no external sponsor bears risk. To this end, article 15 of IORP II stipulates that such IORPs must "hold on a permanent basis additional assets above the technical provisions as a buffer."

---

701 Recital 44 of the IORP II Directive

The amount of the required buffer is calculated on a remnant of the old Solvency I framework that has been replaced in 2009 by Solvency II. IORP I originally referred to the articles 27 and 28 of the old Solvency I Directive. When that Directive was replaced by Solvency II, the latter transposed some of the old Solvency I articles into the IORP I Directive, adding articles 17a-d, so that IORPs would not be affected by the new Solvency II legislation. "These articles deal in broad terms with the eligible assets to cover the solvency margin (assets above technical provisions) and the level of the required solvency margin."[702] When IORP I itself was replaced, IORP II made small changes to the requirements for regulatory own capital. Although no new solvency standards were added (which would likely have meant significant costs to DB schemes[703]), the old article 17a (5) on the possibility for the Commission to adopt implementing measures and the entire old article 17c on guarantee funds were stricken.

2.2   No Removal of the Requirement, but a Compromise?

This requirement was to be removed by the IORP II Directive. The Commission, in its Impact Assessment for the IORP II Directive, noted that retaining the requirement that cross-border IORPs be fully funded "will not help attain the objective and would hamper IORPs' willingness to engage in cross-border activities."[704] The preferred option was the removal of the "additional requirements" for cross-border activity from the Directive. This would have meant that cross-border IORPs would have been treated in the same way as IORPs that do not engage in cross-border activity: "The same regulatory oversight should apply to IORPs which operate domestically or across borders. This would avoid regulatory arbitrage between the IORPs, regardless of how and where they operate."[705] The Commission also stated that "The removal of the full funding requirements contained in Article 16(3) make cross-border IORPs less expensive and less burdensome by aligning the rules to those for domestic IORPs. Respondents to the Green Paper on pensions mentioned that the full funding requirement is a major obstacle to cross-border activity."

However, the funding requirement was ultimately retained. Several stakeholders have expressed their disappointment at this. BusinessEurope lamented the failure to abolish the full funding requirement, and contended that: "This is all the more surprising as it is

---

702 European Commission, *Annex to the Call for Advice from EIOPA for the review of Directive 2003/41/EC (IORP II)* (2011), available at https://eiopa.europa.eu/Publications/Requests%20for%20advice/20110409-a-389075-Letter-to-Bernardino-Annexe.pdf accessed 3 January 2020.
703 Arbeitsgemeinschaft für betriebliche Altersversorgung, 'aba Analyse zum Kompromisstext für die EbAV-II-Richtlinie' (2016) available at http://www.aba-online.de/docs/attachments/9b4b65a7-c2f0-4cf0-91b6-3c42 2d1e426b/20160810-EbAV-II-Trilogkompromiss-aba-Analysepapier.pdf accessed 3 January 2020.
704 Impact Assessment Part 2/2 (see footnote 575) 2.
705 ibid.

noted in the Commission's impact assessment as one of the important prudential barriers restricting cross-border operation of IORPs."[706] BusinessEurope agreed with the Commission's apparent earlier point of view, stating that a reason as to why there is a "low number of cross-border" IORPs could be due to the reduced cost-efficiency possibly caused by the fully-funded requirement. PensionsEurope, a representative organisation of national associations of occupational pension institutions, stated that the full funding requirement for cross-border IORPs should be dropped.[707] In addition, PensionsEurope calls this full finding requirement "a major barrier to the development of cross-border pension schemes."[708]

As a compromise, the requirement that cross-border IORPs be fully funded *at all times* was abated. IORPs that are active on a cross-border basis may now be underfunded temporarily. The text of the funding requirement was changed from "In the event of cross-border activity […], the technical provisions shall at all times be fully funded in respect of the total range of pension schemes operated. If these conditions are not met, the competent authorities of the home Member State shall intervene in accordance with Article 14. To comply with this requirement the home Member State may require ring-fencing of the assets and liabilities."

Although this textual change makes temporary underfunding possible, it does not alter the fact that, in principle, a cross-border IORP must be fully funded at all times. While it is therefore questionable whether it will have any consequences in practice for the cross-border activity of IORPs, the upholding of the full funding-requirement shows that the funding security of pension schemes has remained a top priority during the directive's revision. As noted in section b, it also seems to make up for any differences between Member States' prudential systems.

2.3 Does the Requirement Make It More Difficult to Operate DB Schemes Across Borders?

The requirement that cross-border IORPs be fully funded at all times makes the cross-border operation of any scheme more generous scheme than a pure DC scheme more difficult. Pure DC schemes are, after all, fully funded by definition whereas DB schemes require complex actuarial calculations and prudent investment to ensure that the promised benefit can be met.

Although the implicit promise of a certain level of benefits would suggest the assurance that such promises can be kept – either through full funding or external mechanisms

---

706 BusinessEurope, 'Proposal for the revision of IORP Directive' (2014) Position Paper available at https://www.businesseurope.eu/sites/buseur/files/media/imported/2014-00629-E.pdf accessed 3 January 2020.
707 ibid.
708 ibid.

such as pension guarantee funds – the reality is that many DB funds are in fact under-funded, making their transfer to a cross-border IORP a challenge. In addition, it is the national legislation of the Member States which determines the funding requirements for the technical provisions[709] as well as the regulatory own funds required for IORPs oper-ating schemes where the IORP itself, rather than the sponsoring undertaking assumes liability for certain guarantees.[710]

A number of multinationals have set up cross-border DB funds,[711] but the full fund-ing requirement reportedly "has been a major brake on development of cross-border defined benefit pension plans since it requires a higher standard of funding for them than single-country arrangements. Whilst the requirement does seem to have been sof-tened, any practical effect of the new wording will depend on how each country's legis-lators and regulators interpret it."[712] The requirement of full funding is considered by "many in the European pension market [...] as one of the greatest obstacles facing IORPs in developing *cross-border activities* between Member States."[713]

3 CONCLUSION TO SECTION C: THE SOCIAL FUNCTION OF OCCUPATIONAL PENSIONS

From the perspective of a pension scheme member, the idea that a cross-border IORP is more suited to operating a DC scheme than a DB scheme may at first glance seem pro-blematic in the light of occupational pensions' social function of offering an income in retirement. In principle, DB schemes offer a guaranteed pension result, as well as greater security due to a greater number of enforceable guarantees.

Although the IORP II Directive is in principle neutral towards scheme types, it ap-pears that its architecture does indeed make cross-border IORPs more adept at operating

---

709 Article 14(1) of the IORP II Directive stipulates that: "The home Member State shall require every IORP to have at all times sufficient and appropriate assets to cover the technical provisions in respect of the total range of pension schemes operated."

710 Article 15(1) stipulates that: "The home Member State shall ensure that IORPs operating pension schemes, where the IORP itself, and not the sponsoring undertaking, underwrites the liability to cover against bio-metric risk, or guarantees a given investment performance or a given level of benefits, hold on a permanent basis additional assets above the technical provisions to serve as a buffer. The amount thereof shall reflect the type of risk and the portfolio of assets in respect of the total range of schemes operated. Those assets shall be free of all foreseeable liabilities and serve as a safety capital to absorb discrepancies between the anticipated and the actual expenses and profits."

711 S Baxter, 'IORP II proposal would "kill" European DB cross-border schemes' (*Professional Pensions*, 13 Jan-uary 2015) available at https://www.professionalpensions.com/professional-pensions/news/2390004/iorp-ii-proposal-would-kill-european-db-cross-border-schemes accessed 3 January 2020.

712 Willis Towers Watson, 'Perspectives: IORP II – what it means for cross-border pensions' (2016). See also 'Is the Future of European Cross-Border Pensions in DC?' (*Chief Investment Officer* 25 July 2013) available at https://www.ai-cio.com/news/is-the-future-of-european-cross-border-pensions-in-dc/ accessed 3 January 2020.

713 Borsjé & H Van Meerten, 'A European Pensions Union' (2014) National Bank of Slovakia Series 2014, 18.

pure DC schemes rather than DB schemes, owing to its deference to national social and labour law and the funding requirements it imposes on DB schemes. For an IORP, complying with all the local legislative requirements applying to DB schemes set by Member States – however important these requirements are for the protection of scheme members – can be complex, time-consuming and costly.[714] Of course, from the perspective of pension scheme members, the compliance of the scheme with all applicable local legislation is an important element in the protection of their pension rights.

In conclusion, then, does the IORP II Directive's architecture, which is apparently more favourable to the cross-border operation of DB schemes, mean that it places the social function of occupational pensions under pressure? First, EIOPA's 2017 market development report does show that cross-border provision of Defined Benefit plans is not impossible: more than half of cross-border IORPs (53%) operate Defined Benefit schemes.[715] Though it must also be said that this cross-border activity is largely between the UK and Ireland where similar legal systems facilitate such activity.[716] Second, it was shown in Section a of this Chapter that DB schemes are not always as secure as they might seem. Certainly in the event that indexation is conditional on the funding position of the risk-bearer (which could be the employer and/or the IORP), and if there is a possibility to reduce the pension benefits promised in the DB scheme, it cannot be reasonably argued that DB schemes per definition lead to a better pension outcome than DC schemes. The discussion in Section a of the pension scheme types also illustrated that the distinction between the scheme types is not always clear due to the myriad different features. Accordingly, it is difficult to say as a rule whether one pension scheme necessarily provides a better or worse pension outcome than another. Nonetheless, there is in any case a relative difference between scheme archetypes, as DB schemes offer scheme members (contractually or statutorily) enforceable rights to a promised level of benefits than pure DC schemes.

Consequently, it seems that drawing a general conclusion on whether the IORP II Directive contributes to the social function of occupational pensions cannot be done. While on the one hand the IORP II Directive's architecture seems to be more conducive to the cross-border operation of simplified DC schemes, DB schemes do not, as a rule, seem to provide better pension outcomes. There does seem to be some risk, however, employers exploit the possibility of finding an IORP in a Member State with more lenient prudential standards, bringing lower costs of pension provision together with a pension scheme providing less security for pension scheme members. But the instruments dis-

---

714 See Chapter 5.

715 EIOPA, '2017 Market development report on occupational pensions and cross-border IORPs' (2018) EIOPA-BOS-18/013, 26, available at eiopa.europa.eu/publications/reports accessed 3 January 2020.

716 C Senior, 'Stumbling block' (*European Pensions* April 2012) available at https://www.europeanpensions.net/ep/april-stumbling-block.php accessed 12 January 2020; E-mail enquiry sent to EIOPA.

cussed in Section b, among which is the requirement of full funding for cross-border IORPs, should be an adequate safeguard against such developments.

CONCLUSION TO PART 1

The goal of Part 1 was to assess how a cross-border IORPs' use of the internal market is to be seen from the perspective of a pension scheme member. In order to answer this question, Part 1 studied the possibility for cross-border IORPs to contribute to retirement income security, the effects of the IORP II Directive's system of prudential supervision, as well as the Directive's effects on the social function of occupational pensions. The outcome of this Part produced mixed results.

With respect to retirement income security, Part 1 studied the various pension scheme types and the security mechanisms available to secure the promises under the respective scheme types. It also concluded that, although indisputably important in the protection of pension scheme members, the security mechanisms emanating from national legislation applicable to pension schemes seem to be able to cause legal uncertainty in a cross-border pension context. It is especially because of the importance of these security mechanisms that a solution must be found to continue to ensure their effectiveness also in cross-border situations. This is because the IORP II Directive defines neither what social and labour law is, nor does it definitively define what is prudential legislation. As a consequence, it appears that in many cases, security mechanisms meant to protect the pension scheme member could be said to have features of both social and labour law as well as prudential legislation. It therefore seems that disputes could arise as to whether a certain security mechanism is applicable to a pension scheme operated by an IORP in another Member State: is the security mechanism part of the scheme's host State's social and labour legislation, in which case it would be applicable? Or is it part of the host State's prudential legislation, in which case the IORP would not be bound by it as it is located in another Member State?

A possible solution to this problem could be the inclusion in the IORP II Directive of a provision defining which categories of security mechanisms are to be regarded as social and labour legislation, without defining the substance of these categories. Such an approach would avoid harmonization of national legislation, but would instead merely give extra guidance as to which aspects are to be considered prudential and which are to be consider social and labour law. A less restrictive option would be to oblige Member States to provide comprehensive and up-to-date information on their social and labour law requirements.

With respect to the prudential supervision of cross-border IORPs, Part 1 looked at some of the implications for pension scheme members of being a member of a cross-border IORP. Requirements of scheme funding and governance of the IORP are all governed by legislation of a Member State the scheme member is not a resident of, and might therefore not be familiar with. This could mean that the prudential standards applicable to the cross-border IORP are of a lower – or, ideally, higher – standard than those of the scheme member's own Member State. In order to counter some of the negative effects, the IORP II Directive contains a number of safeguards. First, the social and labour legislation of the Member State in which the scheme member works remains applicable to the pension scheme, and the supervisory authorities of both the home and host Member State of the IORP have been equipped with extensive powers to ensure compliance with all applicable legislation. Second, the IORP II Directive has shored up the standards of governance and information to create a more uniform level of governance across EU Member States. Third, any cross-border transfer of existing pension schemes is subject to the prior approval by a majority of pension members and beneficiaries. Finally, both the home Member State as well as the host Member State competent authorities must give their approval to the transfer of a pension scheme. It therefore seems that the IORP II Directive contains sufficient safeguards to inform and protect pension scheme members.

Finally, in Section c, the social function of occupational pensions was discussed and how the cross-border IORP is to be seen in the light of the increasing importance of supplementary pension provision caused by declining generosity in first-pillar pension provision. This section concluded that, although the IORP II Directive does appear to make the cross-border provision of DB schemes more challenging than DC schemes, giving scheme members fewer guarantees, it cannot be said that this fact alone makes that the IORP II Directive has a detrimental effect on the interests of pension scheme members. While the IORP II Directive's architecture could have as a consequence that besides the cross-border activity between the UK and Ireland – where DB schemes are operated more easily by cross-border IORPs due to similarities in the two Member States' legal systems – DC schemes will be the more likely option for employers to operate across borders, DB schemes in and of themselves do not appear per definition to yield poorer pension results than DB schemes. However, there does appear to be a risk of employers using the possibility to find an IORP in another State in order to find a more lenient prudential regime – with laxer governance and funding standards – allowing cost savings for the employer that could come at the cost of the pension result and the scheme's security. The instruments discussed in Section b are an important and, so it seems, an adequate, bulwark against such threats.

In sum, the IORP II Directive appears to complement the promise of safe, adequate and sustainable pensions with the necessary mechanisms that protect scheme members against possibly negative effects of a membership to a pension scheme that is being operated by an IORP in another Member State. On the other hand, the score is not perfect: the directive does not take away all legal uncertainty that can arise in the case of pension scheme security mechanisms since the definition of these has been left largely to the

Member States, though it seems that this can be remedied with reasonable effort. Finally, the possibility for employers of selecting an IORP in another Member State also seems to bring with it the option of "shopping around" for a Member State with lower prudential standards.

Part 2 will continue scrutinising the cross-border IORP, now from the perspective of worker mobility.

PART 2: WORKER MOBILITY

One of the priorities of the Commission's pension policy was to promote the mobility of European workers. Starting in 1989, the Action Programme Relating to the Implementation of the Community Charter of Basic Social Rights for Workers[717] identified the co-ordination of "supplementary social security" as an important prerequisite for freedom of movement of workers. According to the Commission, the problems related to a loss of pension rights when moving to another Member State represented a problem for an increasingly mobile workforce. In particular, workers could be discouraged from moving to another Member State because there were no provisions protecting them against the loss of their occupational pension rights. Subsequent Commission documents[718] retained this focus, and it has remained a policy goal of the Commission to this day.[719] This section will show that although cross-border IORPs offer improved mobility to some categories of workers, there are other sources of EU law that have made meaningful contributions to the position of mobile European workers.

---

717 European Commission, 'Communication from the Commission concerning its action programme relating to the implementation of the Community Charter of Basic Social Rights for Workers' COM(89) 568 final.

718 See European Commission, 'Supplementary social security schemes: the role of occupational pension schemes in the social protection of workers and their implications for freedom of movement' (Communication from the Commission to the Council) SEC(91) 1332 final (the 1991 Communication); European Commission, 'Report from the Commission concerning social protection in Europe 1993' COM(93) 531 final; European Commission, *Report of the High Level Panel on the free movement of persons chaired by Simone Veil* (Publications Office of the European Union 1998).

719 See, inter alia, EIOPA, *Seventh Consumer Trends Report* (Publications Office of the European Union 2018) 49; EIOPA, 'Final Report on Good Practices on individual transfers of occupational pension rights' (2015) BoS-15/104, available at eiopa.europa.eu/Publications/Reports/EIOPA-BoS-15-104_Final_Report_on_Pensions_Transferabity.pdf accessed 3 January 2020.

1   INTRODUCTION: THE OBSTACLES TO WORKER MOBILITY AND TERMINOLOGY

As noted in Chapter 3, the coordination of statutory pensions began at the end of the 1950s. Non-statutory social security, including occupational pensions, is excluded from this framework.[720]

The main obstacles preventing worker mobility from an occupational pensions perspective identified by the Commission are complications related to the taxation (beyond the scope of this study), acquisition and preservation (Section 3) and transfer of pension rights (Section 4).[721] The Commission calls these the obstacles to portability (Section 2) in an annex to the first proposal on the Supplementary Pension Rights Directive.[722] In this document, the Commission provided the following example, illustrating the consequences national legislation and pension scheme rules could have for a mobile worker's pension entitlement:[723]

> *We assume that all employers offer a pension worth 1% of final earnings for each year of employment. The employee earns €10000 per year during a career starting at 25 and ending at 65 (40 years). There is no inflation.*
>
> *Employee A remains with the same employer during the entire career: the pension will amount to €4000 per year.*
>
> *A mobile career can result in significantly lower pension entitlement.*

---

720 F. Pennings, *European Social Security Law* (Intersentia 2015) 231. See also I Guardiancich, 'The "Leap" from Coordination to Harmonization in Social Policy: Labour Mobility and Occupational Pensions in Europe' (2016) Vol 54 (6) Journal of Common Market Studies 2016 1313, 1313-1314.

721 European Commission, 'Commission Staff Working Document. Annex to the: 'Proposal for a Directive of the European Parliament and the Council on the Improvement of Portability of Supplementary Pension Rights', SEC(2005) 1293.

722 ibid.

723 ibid.

> *Suppose employee B works between 25 and 28 in a scheme where pension rights only vest at 30; for the next 7 years, B works for another employer with a scheme with a 10-year vesting period. At 36 years of age B still has not earned any pension rights. The third job, held between 37 and 49 (13 years) gives rise to pension rights for 11 years because of a waiting period of 2 years before being admitted into the pension scheme. A fourth job held between 50 and 55 gives rise to no pension entitlement because the employee has to be in the company at the moment of retirement in order to obtain a pension. The last job, between 56 and 65, is covered by a scheme with a waiting period of one year.*
>
> *The resulting pension at the end of employee B's career would amount to only €1900 per year. B has worked during 40 years, but only less than half of this period counted for the building up of pension rights (19 years).*

In order to address such challenges faced by mobile workers, the Commission endeavoured to adopt a Directive easing worker mobility from the perspective of occupational pensions. That Directive and its fate will be discussed below.

What Is Meant by the Word "Portability"?

In the interest of clarity for the following discussion, it is important to stress that the term portability has been used in different ways by the EU legislator. For the purposes of the Supplementary Pension Rights Directive, the first proposal defined the term "portability" as "the option open to workers of acquiring and retaining pension rights when exercising their right to freedom of movement or occupational mobility."[724] In other words, it appears that portability in the sense of this proposal meant "the possibility for EU workers to move either within the same or to a different Member State, for employment reasons, without losing or being disadvantaged in relation to their supplementary pension benefits."[725] The later version of the proposal deleted all references to portability, with the Commission clarifying that the amendments made by the European Parliament "shift the focus of the Directive onto the acquisition and preservation of dormant rights and

---

724 Commission of the European Communities, 'Proposal for a Directive on improving the portability of supplementary pension rights' COM(2005) 507 final, Article 3(g).
725 K. Kalogeropoulou, 'European Governance after Lisbon and Portability of Supplementary Pensions Rights' (2006) Vol 2 (1) Journal of Contemporary European Research 75, 76.

away from provisions for transfers."[726] The provision on compulsory transfers was also stricken, giving the impression that portability was equated with transferability.

This book distinguishes portability from transferability. Portability in this dissertation shall mean what the Commission's earlier documents called cross-border membership, meaning that a pension scheme member can remain a member of a pension scheme even when he or she changes employer and/or Member State of residence.[727] A pension scheme member would be entitled to continue using his or her current occupational pension scheme, regardless of employer or Member State of residence, making the scheme itself portable. Such a definition also seems consistent with the definition of portability in the PEPP Regulation (to be discussed in Chapter 6).

Transferability, on the other hand, means the transfer of accrued pension assets – either collectively for an entire pension scheme and all of its members or individually per scheme member – to another pension scheme and/or provider.

Taking into account the distinction between portability and transferability, it appears that there would be five obstacles to worker mobility: taxation, acquisition, preservation and transfer of pension rights as well as the absence of a possibility for portability/cross-border membership.

2   PORTABILITY IN CURRENT EU OCCUPATIONAL PENSION LAW

As noted in Chapter 3, there is currently no provision in EU law providing for the possibility of cross-border membership (portability) of pension schemes. The possibility to remain with the same pension scheme when moving to another Member State would avoid "the many legal and practical problems which may result from a change of membership in occupational pension arrangements, caused by moving abroad to work."[728]

---

726 European Commission, 'Amended proposal for a Directive of the European Parliament and of the Council on minimum requirements for enhancing worker mobility by improving the acquisition and preservation of supplementary pension rights' COM(2007) 603 final.
727 This is also the definition of portability used by the PEPP Regulation. See Chapter 6.
728 European Commission, 'Supplementary Pensions in the European Union: Development, Trends and Outstanding Issues' (1994) Report by the European Commission's Network of Experts on Supplementary Pensions 116, available at http://aei.pitt.edu/33750/4/A310.pdf accessed 3 January 2020.

Although frequently discussed during the EU's involvement in the regulation of occupational pensions, cross-border membership has not made a meaningful entry into current EU legislation. The possibility of such cross-border membership was discussed throughout the 1990s, and in 1999 the Commission noted that "cross-border membership would facilitate the mobility of workers in the Union: the consultations showed without ambiguity that the impossibility of any cross-border membership constituted a major obstacle to such mobility."[729]

The Pensions Forum – established by a Commission Decision with a view to aid the Commission in finding solutions to obstacles related to occupational pensions facing mobile workers[730] – echoed that finding, calling taxation the most significant obstacle to the possibility of cross-border membership.[731] This is because the typical tax exemption that contributions to occupational pension schemes normally enjoy is not always open to contributions going to pension schemes in other Member States. Another obstacle named by the Pensions Forum is compulsory membership, as those who fall under such a scheme are not free to leave it.[732]

However, current EU law offers only very limited possibilities for portability. The Safeguard Directive does not address the Commission's objective of guaranteeing cross-border membership, except for posted workers.[733] That directive exempts posted workers and their employer from the obligation of paying contributions in another Member State for the duration of the posting.[734] The Supplementary Pension Rights Directive contains no provisions on cross-border membership at all, and in fact even its first proposal of

---

729 Commission of the European Communities, 'Towards a Single Market for supplementary pensions' COM (1999) 134 final 15. In various places, COM(1999) 134 final touts the advantages of cross-border membership, but also the difficulties surrounding it implementation. For instance, it notes that "Cross-border membership, at least for some categories of migrant workers moving for a short period to another member State, could be useful in order to avoid changes from one scheme to another and losses of pension rights. However, cross-border membership of workers will be very difficult to realise in practice. Apart from the harmonisation of prudential rules presented in the previous chapter, it will require mutual recognition of the relevant fiscal provisions in Member States and a series of amendments to existing national regulations governing labour conditions. However, cross-border membership would strongly facilitate labour mobility in the Union and is asked for by representatives of the industry. It should thus be seen as a medium to long-term objective for the European Union." See 27-28.

730 European Commission, 'Commission Decision of 9 July 2001 on the setting-up of a committee in the area of supplementary pensions' 2001/548/EC. See, for more information, K. Kalogeropoulou, 'European Governance after Lisbon and Portability of Supplementary Pensions Rights' (2006) Vol 2 (1) Journal of Contemporary European Research 75, footnote 15 therein.

731 European Commission, 'Pensions Forum - Draft Reports of the Three Working groups' (2001), 7 et seq., available at https://ine.otoe.gr/uploads/files/ine_EC_Working_groups.doc accessed 3 January 2020.

732 ibid.

733 C Bittner, 'Occupational Pensions: a Matter of European Concern' (2001) Vol 2 (2) European Business Organization Law Review 401, 408.

734 F. Pennings, European Social Security Law (Intersentia 2015) 232.

2005[735] has omitted any reference to it.[736] However, the Supplementary Pension Rights Directive does facilitate the cross-border payment of pension benefits once a worker retires, "net of any taxes and transaction charges which may be applicable, of all benefits due under such schemes"[737]

The first IORP Directive was meant to become the first step towards enabling cross-border membership to an IORP, an important step to improve cross-border mobility of workers but also a way for multinationals to manage their pension affairs from one Member State.[738] But the IORP II Directive, like its predecessor IORP I, also does not offer the portability of pension schemes, as cross-border membership was deemed too difficult to achieve by the Commission.[739]

As noted in the introduction, the IORP directive has made cross-border mobility easier in that, for some groups of European workers, it avoids the need for transfers to a new pension provider as a new pension scheme can be opened within the same IORP when relocating to a different Member State and/or employer. This is true in particular for employees of a multinational corporation or for European researchers whose employer are affiliated with RESAVER. RESAVER was set up in the context of the European Partnership for Researchers, and the Commission pledged to help set up this fund by providing technical support to the Consortium of the Retirement Savings Vehicle for European Research Institutions.[740] That Consortium was set up in October 2014 to create a single pension arrangement for research institutions with a view to stop pension issues "being a barrier to researchers' mobility" and thereby facilitate their mobility across the EU.[741] It has been in place since 2015, and fully operational since 2017[742] and has a Belgian *Organisme de Financement des Pensions* (OFP), a Belgian IORP, as its pension

---

735 Commission of the European Communities, 'Proposal for a Directive on improving the portability of supplementary pension rights' COM(2005) 507 final.

736 I. Guardiancich, 'The cross-border portability of supplementary pensions: Lessons from the European Union' (2012) Vol 12 (3) Global Social Policy 300, 305; M Del Sol & M Rocca, 'Free movement of workers in the EU and occupational pensions: conflicting priorities? Between case law and legislative interventions' (2017) Vol 19 (2) European Journal of Social Security 141, 146.

737 Council Directive 98/49/EC of 29 June 1998 on safeguarding the supplementary pension rights of employed and self-employed persons moving within the Community [1998] OJ L 209/46 (Safeguard Directive), Article 4.

738 European Commission, 'Towards a Single Market for Supplementary Pensions: Results of the Consultations on the Green Paper on supplementary pensions in the Single Market' COM(1999) 134 final 25.

739 See Chapter 3, section 2.3.

740 European Commission, 'Horizon 2020 Work Programme 2016-2017: 16. Science with and for Society', European Commission Decision C(2017)2468 of 24 April 2017.

741 European Commission, 'Directorate-General for Research and Innovation: Annual Activity Report 2014' 35, available at https://ec.europa.eu/info/sites/info/files/activity-report-2014-dg-rtd_august2015_en.pdf accessed 3 January 2020.

742 'RESAVER Pension Fund fully operational' (*RESAVER.eu*, 31 May 2017) available at: https://www.resaver.eu/news/index.html accessed 3 January 2020.

vehicle.[743] In order to enable mobile researchers to remain with RESAVER as they move across the EU, RESAVER has been set up to have local sections for each Member State, complying with local legislation.[744] RESAVER enables the cross-border pooling of pension plans, making it possible for a scheme member to accumulate pension benefits without interruption, irrespective of the country or institution of employment.[745] Besides improving mobility and the continuity of pension benefits accumulation, the program is expected to decrease overhead costs, give access to "high-quality investment regardless of the country where the employee is based", provide a pan-European risk pooling solution as well as a centralised portal for tracking and administering pension contribution."[746] This provides many advantages for a mobile researcher, not in the last place because that individual's pension will be accrued with the same provider. Nonetheless, the fund cannot overcome the national legislative requirements discussed in Part 1 as well as the mobility-related legislation to be discussed in this Part, apparently adding some complexity and therefore extra cost. On the other hand, such obligation ensure compliance with all local requirements of the Member State(s) in which the researcher works. RESAVER therefore does not seem to be able to provide one *uniform* pension scheme throughout the EU, but rather a collection of separate schemes, each adapted to local laws and requirements, which are operated by the same provider.

The same principle behind RESAVER can be used also for multinational corporations. For organisations such as these, the possibility of having a "one-stop-shop"[747] for mobile workers could enhance their mobility since they can avoid complex series of transfers from one pension arrangement to another and have the possibility of centralising their benefits within a single European fund also means dealing with one payout institution.[748] Additionally, workers would have the benefit of consistent and comparable benefit structures, as the pension schemes for the several Member States in which the employer is active can mimic these.[749]

However, the development of such cross-border membership was evidently hamstrung: save for posted workers, cross-border membership remains an impossibility.

---

743 B. Ottawa, 'Resaver to receive first payments in March', (*Investments & Pensions Europe*, 6 February 2017) available at https://www.ipe.com/resaver-to-receive-first-payments-in-march-amended/10017443.article accessed 3 January 2020.

744 'The RESAVER Pension Fund in Detail', available at https://www.resaver.eu/resaver/pension-fund/how-it-works/ accessed 3 January 2020.

745 European Commission, *State of the Innovation Union 2015* (Publications Office of the European Union 2015) 27.

746 European Commission, 'Horizon 2020 Work Programme 2016-2017: 13. Europe in a changing world – inclusive, innovative and reflective Societies', European Commission Decision C (2015)6776 of 13 October 2015.

747 Impact Assessment Part 2/2 (see footnote 575) 16.

748 Ernst & Young, Pan-European pension funds in a future world (Ernst & Young 2009) 17.

749 European Federation for Retirement Provision, European institutions for occupational retirement provision: the EFRP model for Pan-European pensions (European Federation for Retirement Provision 2003) 19.

3   ACQUISITION AND PRESERVATION OF PENSION RIGHTS: THE SUPPLEMENTARY PENSION RIGHTS DIRECTIVE

A major hurdle identified by the Commission in its 1999 Green Paper on Pensions standing in the way of worker mobility were burdensome requirements for the acquisition of pension rights, such as waiting and vesting periods.[750] The Supplementary Pension Rights Directive regulates matters regarding the acquisition and preservation of pension rights, as well as information requirements.[751]

The initial proposal was the subject of fierce political debate and its contents were watered before its final adoption.[752] It has also been limited in scope.[753] Nonetheless, the Supplementary Pension Rights Directive contains provisions helping a mobile European worker.

As noted in Chapter 3,[754] the Supplementary Pension Rights Directive, which initially went by the name of Portability Directive,[755] is the outcome of a long and troubled legislative process.[756] Reiner[757] notes a number of reasons for the difficult negotiations surrounding the directive, including the diversity of European occupational pension systems, the high number of stakeholders involved in the implementation of the directive and the financial consequences of the initial proposal's provisions for employers and/or employees.[758]

---

750 E Oliver, 'From portability to acquisition and preservation: the challenge of legislating in the area of supplementary pensions' (2009) Vol 32 (4) Journal of Social Welfare & Family Law, 173, 174.

751 'Supplementary Pensions (*European Commission*) available at https://ec.europa.eu/social/main.jsp?catId=468&langId=en accessed 3 January 2020.

752 On the history of the directive's inception, see W Baugniet, The protection of occupational pensions under European Union law on the freedom of movement for workers, dissertation European University Institute Florence (2014), Guardiancich (see footnote 720), I Guardiancich & D Natali, 'The Changing EU 'Pension Programme': Policy Tools and Ideas in the Shadow of the Crisis' in D Natali (ed), *The New Pension Mix in Europe: Recent Reforms, Their Distributional Effects and Political Dynamics* (PIE Peter Lang 2017), Kalogeropoulou 2006 (see footnote 730), K Kalogeropoulou, 'Addressing the Pension Challenge: Can the EU respond? Towards facilitating the portability of supplementary (occupational) pension rights' (2014) Vol 16 (4) European Journal of Law Reform 747, Del Sol & Rocca (see footnote 736); M Reiner, 'Entwicklung und Probleme des europäischen Betriebspensionsrechts am Beispiel der Mobilitätsrichtlinie' (2017) Vol 1 (2) Journal für Arbeitsrecht und Sozialrecht 168.

753 For instance, the Supplementary Pension Rights Directive does not apply to occupational pension schemes that have been closed to new entrants (Article 2(2)(a)), does not apply retroactively (Article 2(4)) and applies only to cross-border situations (Article 2(5)).

754 See sections 3.

755 COM(2005) 507 final.

756 See on this process Kalogeropoulou 2014 (see footnote 752); Kalogeropoulou 2006 (see footnote 752); Reiner 2017 (see footnote 752); Baugniet 2014 (see footnote 752);

757 Reiner 2017 (see footnote 752) 173. See also Baugniet 2014 (see footnote 752).

758 Regarding these financial consequences, Reiner notes that the provisions regarding acquisition could cause cost increases for employers and/or a reduction of benefits for employees, stemming from stricter vesting requirements. These vesting requirements would lead to fewer situations in which the pension contributions can be forfeited to the benefit of the employer or the remaining employees. See Reiner 2017 (see footnote 752) 173.

A. Acquisition of Pension Rights

Waiting and Vesting Periods

A waiting period is the period of time an employee must work for an employer before they become eligible to participate in the pension scheme. A vesting period is a period during which benefits are being accrued, but not yet vested, i.e. scheme members are not entitled to their benefits before the vesting period has elapsed. Vesting periods were the "bone of contention" during the legislative process of the Supplementary Pension Rights Directive,[759] an issue that arose over different viewpoints of the purpose of occupational pensions and vesting periods.[760] The question of vesting periods "raised practical issues of cost, as well as moral and philosophical arguments as to the very nature of occupational pensions"[761] – in particular in Germany where some employers regard occupational pensions as a reward for employee loyalty.[762] The Commission regards long vesting periods as an obstacle to labour mobility.[763]

The initial proposal for the Supplementary Pension Rights Directive contained a maximum waiting period of one year, as well as a vesting period that may not exceed two years.[764] The final directive prescribes that pension rights are irrevocably acquired ("vested") no later than three years of employment[765] – capping any applicable waiting and/or vesting period to a maximum of three years – and that the contributions paid by the employee or on their behalf are to be reimbursed in accordance with national law if the worker's pension rights have not yet become vested.[766]

With this cap on waiting and vesting periods, the directive has made an end to long waiting and vesting periods. For mobile workers in Member States featuring particularly long vesting periods, this is a development that should be welcomed. Though, of course, waiting and/or vesting periods shorter than three years remain an obstacle.

---

759 Guardiancich & Natali 2017 (see footnote 752) 10.

760 See Baugniet 2014 (see footnote 752) for an extensive discussion of conditions of acquisition under the Supplementary Pension Rights Directive 245 et seq.

761 Baugniet 2014 (see footnote 752) 250. See also Oliver (see footnote 750).

762 I Guardiancich & Natali 2017 (see footnote 752) 10; Reiner 2017 (see footnote 752) 173.

763 Commission of the European Communities, 'Supplementary Pensions in the Single Market: A Green Paper' COM(97) 283 final 15 (1997 Green Paper).

764 COM(2005) 507 final, Article 4.

765 Article 4(1)(a) of the Supplementary Pension Rights Directive notes that "where a vesting period or a waiting period, or both, is applied, the total combined period shall under no circumstances exceed three years for outgoing worker". In accordance with Article 4(1)(b) of the directive, the minimum age for the vesting of pension rights, if applicable, shall not exceed 21 years for outgoing workers.

766 Article 4(1)(c) Supplementary Pension Rights Directive.

Minimum Age Requirements

Regarding minimum age requirements, two types can be distinguished: a minimum age to join a pension scheme and the age at which the employee, member of the scheme, has acquired rights.[767] In both cases, a worker leaving his or her employer before either requirement is met will lead to the worker not vesting any pension rights.[768] In order to help the mobility of younger workers, the directive limits the maximum age for the vesting of pension rights at 21.

B. Preservation of Vested Pension Rights

The Safeguard Directive was the first step at regulating occupational pensions at the EU level, and the first step towards the removal of the obstacles experienced by mobile workers in relation to occupational pensions.[769] It does this mainly ensuring the safeguarding of occupational pension rights through equal treatment. Such equal treatment entails non-discrimination between scheme members who leave a pension scheme and join a new scheme within the same Member State and those who leave a scheme to join another scheme in another EU Member State.[770] The Directive also ensures that benefits can be paid on a cross-border basis.[771] Importantly, however, the Safeguard Directive does not contain requirements on waiting and vesting periods, and therefore any accumulated pension rights that are not yet vested are lost.[772]

The Supplementary Pension Rights Directive therefore introduced potentially important benefits for the position of mobile workers within the EU. Besides its previously described provisions on the vesting and waiting periods, it also contains stipulations on the preservation of occupational pension rights.

The directive ensures that a worker's vested pension rights can remain in the scheme (preserved), but reserves the right for Member States to allow pension schemes (with "the worker's informed consent") to instead pay the outgoing worker "a capital sum equivalent to the value of the vested pension rights to the outgoing worker, as long as the value of the vested pension rights does not exceed a threshold established by the Member State concerned."[773]

---

767 European Commission, 'Commission Staff Working Document. Annex to the: 'Proposal for a Directive of the European Parliament and the Council on the Improvement of Portability of Supplementary Pension Rights', SEC(2005) 1293.
768 ibid.
769 Kalogeropoulou 2014 (see footnote 752) 764; Guardiancich 2012 (see footnote 736).
770 Article 4 Safeguard Directive (see footnote 737).
771 Article 5 Safeguard Directive.
772 Guardiancich & Natali 2012, p. 305.
773 Article 5(3) Supplementary Pension Rights Directive.

The Supplementary Pension Rights Directive requires that the vested pension rights of an outgoing worker either be treated in the same manner as the pension rights of active scheme members or, alternatively, in other ways that are "fair".[774] It provides two examples of "fair" treatment: for entitlements to nominal sums, the nominal value of the dormant rights must be safeguarded and for adjustable pension rights, those rights may be adjusted in accordance with interest rates built into the scheme, investment returns or inflation rates and salary levels. The Member States are, however, given a significant margin of discretion in determining how to preserve the pension rights of pension scheme members.[775]

Such provisions on the preservation of pension rights are important, as workers who leave their employer usually are also no longer entitled to continue to be members of the pension scheme, i.e. they may no longer contribute to it and continue to accumulate pension rights. This is because most occupational pension schemes are set up by (groups of) employers or social partners. Once the worker leaves the (group of) workers the scheme is intended for, they become a deferred member.

4   TRANSFERABILITY OF PENSION RIGHTS

Job leavers have two choices when deciding what to do with accrued pension rights: the rights can be preserved in the pension scheme in which they were acquired, or they can be transferred if the scheme allows this. In the latter case, a capital sum is paid out equal to the accrued rights which can then be transferred into a new pension scheme, again if the new pension scheme allows this.[776]

As to why an individual should wish to opt for a transfer of pension rights, the Pensions Forum notes that "While good preservation of vested rights can be seen as a substitute for transferability, it should be noted that a transfer of pension rights might often be the more practical solution."[777] Both the employee as well as the employer can benefit, as there would be fewer small pension entitlements to manage. The first proposal of the Supplementary Pension Rights Directive explained that the goal of transferability would be to "avoid excessive administrative costs stemming from the management of a high number of low-value dormant rights."[778]

The transferability of pension rights is frequently made more difficult by national legislation or the conditions of the pension scheme, and EIOPA notes that the applicable

---

774 See article 5 Supplementary Pension Rights Directive.
775 Guardiancich 2012 (see footnote 736) 305.
776 1997 Green Paper (see footnote 763) 24.
777 European Commission, 'Pensions Forum - Draft Reports of the Three Working groups' (2001), 5, available at https://ine.otoe.gr/uploads/files/ine_EC_Working_groups.doc accessed 3 January 2020.
778 Commission of the European Communities, 'Proposal for a Directive on improving the portability of supplementary pension rights' COM(2005) 507 final 7.

regimes on pension transfers vary widely between the Member States.[779] It also notes that
"It is generally not allowed to transfer occupational pension rights upon ending active
membership to any pension scheme the member wishes to, as almost all Member States
provide for conditions/restrictions regarding the receiving scheme where a member has
the statutory right to transfer. As a consequence of the requirements for transferring and
receiving schemes, many transfers cannot be carried out."[780] To the extent that transfers
are allowed, there are restrictive conditions in many Member States or limitations in the
timeframe in which transfers are permitted with strict deadlines.[781] In addition, the value
of the acquired rights can be calculated in a manner that penalises scheme leavers or the
host Member State may not grant tax relief, constituting "severe impediments to labor
mobility."[782]

Transferability in EU Pension Law

The initial proposal for the Supplementary Pension Rights Directive, then still called the
Portability Directive, contained provisions guaranteeing the possibility of transferring
pension rights – hence the proposal's name portability directive.[783] As noted, the goal
was to avoid the costs associated with the management of a high number of low-value
dormant rights. To that end, "the proposal provides for the option not to preserve these
pension rights but to use a transfer or a payment of a capital sum representing the acquired rights when these do not exceed a threshold established by the Member State
concerned."[784]

Another significant advantage to mobile workers under the Supplementary Pension
Rights Directive's first proposal would have been that transferred pension rights would
not be subject to new acquisition conditions – waiting and vesting periods – in the new
scheme: the proposal guaranteed in its Article 6 that "[u]nder the supplementary pension
scheme to which the rights are transferred, the rights shall not be subject to conditions

---

779 EIOPA, 'Final Report on Good Practices on individual transfers of occupational pension rights' (2015) BoS-
    15/104 13, available at eiopa.europa.eu/Publications/Reports/EIOPA-BoS-15-
    104_Final_Report_on_Pensions_Transferabity.pdf accessed 3 January 2020. See also European Commis-
    sion, 'Commission Staff Working Document. Annex to the: 'Proposal for a Directive of the European
    Parliament and the Council on the Improvement of Portability of Supplementary Pension Rights', SEC
    (2005) 1293.
780 EIOPA 2015 (see footnote 779) 15.
781 ibid 19.
782 ibid 45.
783 See Article 6 of COM(2005) 507 final. Article 6(1) of COM(2005) 507 final stipulates that "Unless a capital
    payment is made in accordance with Article 5(2), the Member States shall take the necessary action to
    ensure that if an outgoing worker is not covered by the same supplementary pension scheme in his new
    job, he may obtain on request and within 18 months after the termination of his employment the transfer
    within the same Member State or to another Member State of all his acquired pension rights."
784 COM(2005) 507 final 7.

governing acquisition and shall be preserved at least to the same extent as dormant rights [...]"[785] The goal was to remove barriers to acquisition and ensure its continuity, but this provision was also "seen as the most controversial provision of the proposed Portability Directive."[786]

It appears that this provision was intended – to the extent possible – to mimic the rules on aggregation as applicable in the Coordination Regulations on Social Security. Those rules ensure that mobile Europeans have a theoretically unified career by using the partial pensions method.[787] This method works by basing the total pension a person receives on the sum of the pensions accrued in the Member States where he or she was employed.[788] It does this by using the principle of aggregation, which is designed to ensure that all periods of work are taken into account for the waiting period and thereby preventing any eligibility problems, such as those posed by a minimum requirement on the years of social insurance.

Although the rules on aggregation were deemed unsuitable for application to occupational pensions by the European legislator[789] as well as the European Court of Justice[790] – the financial and administrative burden on employers would be considerable – this proposed provision would have increased the protection of mobile workers by preventing the application of new vesting and waiting periods upon entering a new pension scheme. The Safeguard Directive reduces these to a combined maximum of three years – bringing down sometimes exceptionally long vesting periods to a more reasonable term – but the proposed Article 6 would have done away with these entirely once the worker completed the acquisition requirements in the first Member State. Regardless, the provision was not adopted into the final Supplementary Pension Rights Directive.

In light of the complexity involved in enshrining a transfer option in law, the final version of the Supplementary Pension Rights Directive contains no provisions on transferability,[791] which it makes explicit in its recitals.[792] In the end, the Commission ac-

---

785 ibid Article 6(3).

786 Baugniet 2014 (see footnote 752) 270.

787 Pennings 2015 (see footnote 734) 216.

788 For a more detailed explanation on the coordination of statutory old-age pensions, see Pennings 2015 (see footnote 734) 216 et seq.

789 See recital 4 of the Safeguard Directive, recital 3 of the Supplementary Pension Rights Directive, 1991 Communication (see footnote 718) 18.

790 Case C-379/09 Casteels [2011] ECLI:EU:C:2011:131 para 22.

791 See European Commission, 'Amended proposal for a Directive of the European Parliament and of the Council on minimum requirements for enhancing worker mobility by improving the acquisition and preservation of supplementary pension rights' COM(2007) 603 final 3: "The European Parliament considers that the introduction of a compulsory transfer option at this time would place too great a burden on some supplementary pension schemes and would, furthermore, cause considerable technical difficulties."

792 Recital 24 of the Supplementary Pension Rights Directive notes that: "This Directive does not provide for the transfer of vested pension rights. However, in order to facilitate worker mobility between Member States, Member States should endeavour, as far as possible, and in particular when introducing new supplementary pension schemes, to improve the transferability of vested pension rights."

knowledged in its revised proposal the European Parliament's concerns over the burden
on occupational pension schemes and of other "considerable technical difficulties."[793]
The Commission therefore agreed to the removal of the proposal's provision on transferability, taking into account the EP's concerns and the views of the experts within the
Council working group. This was also the moment the title of the directive was changed,
removing any references to portability and instead naming it the "Proposal for a directive
on the minimum requirements for enhancing worker mobility by improving the acquisition and preservation of supplementary pension rights."[794]

The Safeguard Directive does not deal with the transferability of pension rights at all,
and therefore misses an important opportunity to boost the mobility of workers.[795] The
fact that the Safeguard Directive provides for the previously mentioned reimbursement of
any contributions towards a scheme of which the rights have not become vested, should
not be seen as an adequate alternative to transferability for the obvious reason of the
obstacles to the transfer of pension rights noted above. The refunded contributions can,
however, be used towards a private, third-pillar pension product.[796]

Consequently, neither the Safeguard Directive nor the Supplementary Pension Rights
Directive contain provisions on transferability. The IORP II Directive contains only provisions on collective transfers[797] but not on individual transfers,[798] therefore providing
no help to an individual changing jobs and moving to another Member State.

Nonetheless, the issue of transferability remained on the agenda, and the Commission
asked EIOPA for further input and advice on the topic of transfers of supplementary
occupational pension rights.[799] EIOPA published a non-legally binding set of Good Practices on the transferability of occupational pension rights.[800]

5   ROLE OF THE EUROPEAN COURT OF JUSTICE

The previous discussion has revealed a number of problematic aspects in current EU
pension legislation for mobile workers. The problems relate in particular to an absence
of the regulation at EU level of individual transfers of accrued pension rights, an absence

---

793 COM(2007) 603, p. 3.
794 ibid.
795 K Borg, A Minto & H van Meerten, 'The EU's regulatory commitment to a European Harmonised Pension
    Product (PEPP): The Portability of Pension Rights vis-à-vis the Free Movement of Capital' (2019) 5 *Journal
    of Financial Regulation* 2019 1, 24.
796 ibid.
797 Article 12 IORP II.
798 L van der Vaart & H van Meerten, 'De pensioen opPEPPer?' (2018) 1 Tijdschrift voor Pensioenvraagstukken
    38.
799 EIOPA, 'Final Report on Good Practices on individual transfers of occupational pension rights' (2015) BoS-
    15/104 7, available at eiopa.europa.eu/Publications/Reports/EIOPA-BoS-15-104_Final_Report_
    on_Pensions_Transferabity.pdf accessed 3 January 2020.
800 ibid.

of a possibility of cross-border membership and vesting and waiting periods shorter than three years. Despite this, EU primary law seems to provide solace to workers who find themselves in a situation not covered by current EU occupational pension legislation.

Chapter 2 described Articles 45 and 48 TFEU as legal bases upon which the EU legislator can adopt acts guaranteeing the mobility of workers by removing obstacles formed *inter alia* by occupational pensions. Those provisions can, under the circumstances outlined below, also be invoked by individuals in legal proceedings as a consequence of the direct effect[801] of those provisions. Chapter 2 also briefly noted the ECJ's influence on pension law. Its role in protecting the mobility of workers in the context of occupational pensions will be considered in some more detail below.

The Court has accepted the direct effect, i.e. the possibility for individuals to invoke a provision of EU law before a national court, of Articles 45 and 48 TFEU. The direct effect of Article 45 TFEU is horizontal[802] as well as vertical,[803] meaning it can be invoked by individuals against a Member State or another individual, such as an employer,[804] before a national court. Article 48 TFEU appears to possess only vertical direct effect.[805]

Vertical Direct Effect of Article 48 TFEU

The Article was denied horizontal direct effect in *Casteels*, in which the Court decided that Article 48 TFEU "does not have the objective of laying down a legal rule which is operative as such", but rather is a legal basis upon which the European Parliament and the Council can adopt legislation in the field of social security.[806] It therefore, according to the Court, "cannot confer rights on individuals which those individuals might be able to rely on before their national courts." Whether the Court's intention was to also deny vertical direct effect seems unclear. Based on the wording it used in the aforementioned quote, that seems to be the case. However, it then concludes by noting that "48 TFEU does not have any direct effect capable of being relied on by an individual against his private-sector employer in a dispute before national courts", apparently limiting its conclusions to horizontal relations. This seems to mean that individuals could invoke this

---

801 P Craig & G de Búrca, *EU Law: Text, Cases and Materials* (6th edn, Oxford University Press 2015)184 et seq.

802 See, for instance, Case C-379/09 Casteels [2011] ECLI:EU:C:2011:131.

803 The Court first accepted Article 45 TFEU's vertical direct effect in Case 41/74 *Van Duyn v. Home Office* [1974] ECLI:EU:C:1974:133.

804 Case C-379/09 *Casteels* [2011] ECLI:EU:C:2011:131 para 19: "It should be noted at the outset that Article 45 TFEU not only applies to the action of public authorities but also extends to rules of any other nature aimed at regulating gainful employment in a collective manner (see Case C-325/08 *Olympique Lyonnais* [2010] ECR I-0000, paragraph 30 and the case-law cited)."

805 The Court has accepted the vertical direct effect of this provision in C-443/93 *Vougioukas* [1995] ECLI:EU: C:1995:394. It has rejected the provision's horizontal direct effect in *Casteels*, paras 13-16.

806 See paras 13-16 *Casteels*, as well as Pennings 2015 (see footnote 734) 232-233; F Pennings, 'Case C-379/09, *Maurits Casteels v. British Airways plc*, Judgment of the Court (Third Chamber) of 10 March 2011, nyr.' (2012) Vol 49 (5) Common Market Law Review 1787, 1792 et seq.

provision against a Member State in the event they are being denied, or hampered in, the exercise of their right to free movement by a Member State's legislation, including that relating to occupational pensions.

Vertical Direct Effect of Article 45 TFEU

As noted in Chapter 2, the Court's interpretation of the free movement of workers from the perspective of occupational pensions entailed that Article 45 TFEU "militate[s] against any national measure which, even though applicable without discrimination on grounds of nationality, is capable of hindering or rendering less attractive the exercise by Community nationals of the fundamental freedoms guaranteed by the Treaty."[807] In that light, "measures which have the effect of causing workers to lose, as a consequence of the exercise of their right to freedom of movement, social security advantages guaranteed them by the legislation of a Member State have in particular been classed as obstacles."[808]

For pension scheme members, it must be borne in mind that the preservation of rights is not always an attractive option, given that deferred benefits are not always well protected against inflation or do not rise with a worker's future earnings, as well as the fact that the administrative costs involved with keeping a number of small pension entitlements can be detrimental to the pension entitlements of a worker.[809] As a consequence, workers may invoke Article 45 TFEU against their own Member State in the event that national provisions prevent or render less attractive the exercise of a worker's right to free movement. The two cases from which the quotes in the previous paragraph have been taken are examples of such instances. Whether the measures hindering worker mobility can be justified will depend on the circumstances of each case.

Horizontal Direct Effect of Article 45 TFEU

Regarding the acquisition of pension rights, the Court has ruled in its *Casteels*[810] judgment that acquisition requirements can pose an obstacle to the free movement of workers. This particular case revolved around a vesting period that prevented a British Airways employee working for the same employer in a number of EU Member States form acquiring pension rights in Germany.[811] British Airways disputed Mr. Casteels' entitlement to occupational pension benefits, contending the he had not completed the requisite term of employment and left his BA workplace in Germany for one in France voluntarily.

---

807 See Case C-212/06, *Gouvernement de la Communauté française and Gouvernement wallon* [2008] ECLI:EU:C:2008:178 para 45 and the case law quoted there; *Casteels*. See also L van der Vaart & H van Meerten, 'De pensioen opPEPPer?' (2018) 1 Tijdschrift voor Pensioenvraagstukken 38.
808 Case C-212/06, para. 46.
809 1991 Communication (see footnote 718) 21.
810 *Casteels*.
811 See paras 6-11 of *Casteels*.

The Court was not swayed by BA's attempts at justification, and arrived at its conclusion by applying Article 45 TFEU and the obstacle/justification test.

Del Sol & Rocca argue[812] – with caveats – that the ECJ's case law provides a greater degree of protection than the Supplementary Pension Rights Directive. They contend that, since the Court arrived at its conclusion in *Casteels* on the basis primary EU law, *any* obstacle occupational posed by occupational pensions hindering or rendering the use by workers of the right to free movement less attractive are in straight violation of EU law. This would bring any measure within the scope of this test against EU primary law, including those not covered by the Supplementary Pension Rights Directive (or indeed any other source of EU pension law), such as excessively burdensome transferability of accrued pension entitlements.

Pennings argues along the same lines,[813] though cautions that it is unclear what exact consequences this judgment would have for other instances in which workers who, unlike Mr. Casteels, are *not* employed by the same employer are faced with long waiting periods.[814] In the case of waiting and vesting periods, arguments such as staff loyalty could still persuade the Court[815] if it does not find such periods disproportionate and inappropriate for attaining that objective.[816]

6   CONCLUSION TO PART 2

While cross-border IORPs help the mobility of just a part of mobile European workers, the IORP II Directive as well as other sources of European pension law have made important contributions to the position of mobile European workers. Those contributions were made in particular with respect to the conditions for the acquisition and preservation of pension rights. The individual transferability of accrued pension rights and cross-border membership have not yet been meaningfully addressed.

First, cross-border membership remains an impossibility to this day, save for posted workers. This was a major contribution by the 1998 Safeguard Directive. Otherwise, it has had a fairly limited effect on this mobility,[817] however it was the first step in regulating occupational pensions at the EU level, and the first step towards the removal of the

---

812 Del Sol & Rocca (see footnote 736).

813 F Pennings, 'Case C-379/09, *Maurits Casteels v. British Airways plc*, Judgment of the Court (Third Chamber) of 10 March 2011, nyr.' (2012) Vol 49 (5) Common Market Law Review 1787, 1792.

814 Pennings 2015 (see footnote 734) 234.

815 See, on this, paras. 62-72 of the Case C-379/09 *Casteels* [2011] opinion of A-G Kokott ECLI:EU:C:2010:675 and the case law cited there.

816 Pennings 2015 (see footnote 734) 234.

817 See, for example, Bittner (see footnote 733) 408; D Mabbett, 'Supplementary pensions between social policy and social regulation' (2009) Vol 32 (4) West European Politics 774, 780-781; Guardiancich & Natali 2017 (see footnote 752); I Guardiancich, 'Portability of Supplementary Pension Rights in Europe: A Lowest Common Denominator Solution' (2015) Vol 1 (1) European Policy Analysis 74, 82-83

obstacles experienced by mobile workers in relation to the occupational pensions. Through the principle of equal treatment, it ensures non-discrimination between scheme members who leave a pension scheme to join a new scheme within the same Member State and those who leave a scheme to join another scheme in another EU Member State. The Directive also ensures that benefits can be paid on a cross-border basis. The IORP II Directive and the Supplementary Pension Rights Directive do not address cross-border membership directly, although the IORP II Directive has made mobility less burdensome for some categories of workers, such as employees of multinationals or mobile research-ers.

Regarding the conditions for the acquisition and preservation of pension rights, the Supplementary Pension Rights Directive fills a "profound gap" in EU legislation.[818] It has introduced caps on waiting and vesting periods, one of the most important pensions-related obstacles to worker mobility identified by the Commission. Studies prior to the adoption of the directive noted that as much as 15% of all defined benefit schemes in Europe required vesting periods of five years or more.[819] Exceptional cases, such as a French final salary schemes, precluded vesting before retirement altogether, "meaning that early leavers lose all their rights".[820] Germany was known for notoriously long vest-ing periods, allowing periods of up to ten years up until 2002.[821] In addition, dormant rights were not always protected against inflation, causing a loss of their value over time.

Although the Supplementary Pension Rights Directive has not been able to do away with vesting and waiting periods shorter than three years, and is limited in scope *inter alia* because of the pension schemes it excludes and the fact that it does not apply retro-actively, it should nevertheless be regarded as a boon for mobile European workers. The Supplementary Pension Rights Directive has also made an important addition to the preservation of vested pension rights vis-à-vis the Safeguard Directive. Whereas the latter relies on non-discrimination – not helping those in Member States where departing scheme members are poorly protected as it is[822] – the Supplementary Pension Rights Directive sets new minimum requirements. In combination with the cap on waiting and vesting periods, these provisions seem to make a profound difference in the position of mobile European workers.

However, despite its decade-long involvement in this area, current EU pension law seems to have missed a number of important targets.

First, there is the matter of individual transferability of pension rights, the regulation of which is still conspicuous by its absence. Although the provisions on preservation enshrined in the Supplementary Pension Rights Directive provide an alternative for the

---

818 I Guardiancich 2015 (see footnote 817) 75.
819 ibid 78-79.
820 ibid.
821 Baugniet 2014 (see footnote 752) 249-250.
822 Mabbett 2009 (see footnote 817) 780-781.

protection of accrued pension rights, the lack of a transferability option still means that the growing group of mobile European workers can still be left with a number of small pension entitlements in a number of different Member States. This situation is ideal neither for the workers themselves nor for the provider of the pension schemes, who is left with the cumbersome and costly task of dealing with these small pension entitlements.

Despite initial proposals of the Supplementary Pension Rights Directive containing provisions regulating this point, it was left out of the final directive.

Further EU action advancing the mobility of European workers would therefore seem desirable. One solution to resolve the issue of worker mobility as well as the problems caused by differing legislation of the Member States could be the introduction of a so-called second regime. A second regime exists in parallel to national legislation, and is an overarching system setting its own rules at EU level. That second regime could be introduced as a general system, designed in principle for all European workers and the self-employed, or for specific sectors of industry. By standardising many of the relevant features of a pan-European pension scheme, such as options for portability and transferability of occupational pension rights, it would be possible to give uniform definitions to such features. This would not only solve conflicts between home and host state legislation, but could also enable cross-border membership. A number of suggestions for such a system have been made. Recently, EIOPA initiated a survey on the idea of a pan-European Occupational Defined Contribution Framework.[823] That framework would constitute a second regime and "usable at the discretion of employers, pension providers and members who would otherwise maintain their national workplace pension's frameworks."[824]

Such a solution had already been suggested by a respondent in 2011 to an EIOPA consultation on the review of the IORP I Directive.[825] Before that, in 2005, the European Financial Services Roundtable (EFR) also suggested the idea of a "Pan-European Pension Plan", offering the "advantages of being able to continue with a single pension arrange-

---

823 'Engagement Survey on the idea of a pan-European Occupational Defined Contribution Framework (*EIOPA*) available at https://eiopa.europa.eu/Pages/Surveys/Engagement-Survey-on-the-idea-of-a-pan-Europea n-Occupational-Defined-Contribution-Framework.aspx accessed 4 January 2020.

824 F Briganti, 'Guest viewpoint: Francesco Briganti, EBWI Employee Benefits and Welfare Institute' (*IPE Magazine,* May 2017) available at https://www.ipe.com/analysis/guest-viewpoint/guest-viewpoint-francesc o-briganti-ebwi-employee-benefits-and-welfare-institute/10018610.article accessed 4 January 2020.

825 EIOPA, 'Summary of Comments on Consultation Paper Draft Response to *Call for Advice on the review of Directive 2003/41/EC* - EIOPA-CP-11/001' EIOPA-CP-11/001, J.P. Morgan Worldwide Services responded that "The pensions market has changed significantly in the past few years, and a key change has been the advent of Defined Contribution arrangements that will in time eclipse Defined Benefit schemes. Our view is that the Commission should consider leaving the current IORP directive unchanged and address a framework for the development of a pan European defined contribution arrangement."

ment irrespective of where one happens to be working at any particular time."[826] Similar solutions have also been proposed in academic literature.[827] Both in the interest of pension scheme members, as well as the practical potential for providers to become active on a significant basis throughout the EU, it is to be hoped that such a solution can be implemented.

The question is, however, whether the EU could ever achieve the establishment of such systems. The second pillar seemingly requires the application of social and labour legislation, including pension security mechanisms, waiting periods, vesting periods and legislation governing the pension contributions and benefits. Certainly in Member States that rely to a great extent on occupational pensions, such rules ensure not only adequate protection of pension entitlements, but also that at the end of a worker's career, the pension result is sufficient to provide adequate pension benefits. Additionally, Chapter 2 explained that while the EU possesses the legal powers to influence Member States' pension systems, the political will – both on the part of the EU legislator as well as on the part of the Member States – means that introducing such a second-pillar system at EU level is challenging.

Chapter 6 will discuss another potential option for mobile Europeans in the third pillar, which has recently become available.

CONCLUSION TO CHAPTER 4

A. Cross-Border IORPs' Use of the Internal Market

Retirement income security is a primary concern of pension scheme members. In this respect, the IORP II Directive appears to give cross-border schemes extra security by requiring full funding. However, on the other hand, its minimum harmonisation character affords the Member States a great deal of discretion in the definition of their social and labour laws and prudential standards. It seems that this can lead to conflicts and legal uncertainty, which is not in the interest of a pension scheme member. Bearing this in mind, it seems that this distinction – however understandable in its current from the perspective of the EU's limited competences in the field of occupational pensions – should have been made with a clearer demarcation of both concepts. It does seem possible to bring some more clarity by taking inspiration from the solution adopted in the Posted Workers Directive. Without defining the substance of the categories, a provision could be added to the IORP II Directive outlining which groups of legislation are to be

---

826 European Financial Services Roundtable, 'Pan European Pension Plans: deepening the concept' (2005), available at http://www.efr.be/documents/publication/26.2005.12.%20EFR%20Report%20-%20Follow-up% 20on%20Pan%20European%20Pensions%20plans%2020Dec2005.pdf accessed 12 January 2020.

827 M. Wienk, 'Europese coördinatie van aanvullende pensioenen' (Doctoral dissertation, Koninklijke Universiteit Brabant 1999).

social and labour law provisions. Other alternatives seem possible as well, to be discussed in the next two chapters.

In the face of the privatisation and marketisation of occupational pensions, European workers are finding themselves in a situation in which they are responsible for shoulder-ing the risks associated with occupational retirement provision – such as investment and biometric risk – as the role of occupational pension provision is on the rise. The latter trend is due to the retrenchment of the public pension pillar in a number of Member States. Cross-border IORPs aim to bring to the table heightened efficiency and higher yields for pension scheme members through economies of scale. Such economies of scale are achieved through the cross-border consolidation of a multitude of schemes operated for a multitude of Member States from one IORP.

This chapter studied to what extent a cross-border IORP can support the social func-tion of occupational pensions. It concluded that the IORP Directive appears to favour cross-border DC schemes over DB schemes. Its requirement of full funding and the application of the national social and labour law of any of the EU's Member States in which the schemes are offered makes the cross-border provision of DB schemes relatively more onerous. This is not to say, however, that the Directive leads to cross-border IORPs failing to fulfil this social function because of this. Although there is a risk that employers will seek to move their pension schemes to Member States with lower prudential stand-ards, the IORP II Directive contains a number of mechanisms protecting scheme mem-bers from cross-border relocations of schemes.

Regarding prudential supervision in cross-border pension provision, pension scheme members of foreign cross-border IORPs are subject to another Member State's prudential requirements, including funding requirements, investment rules, pension fund govern-ance provisions. This can lead to disadvantages for pension scheme members if the leg-islation in the IORP's home member state is of a lower protective standard than the Member State of the pension scheme members. However, the IORP II Directive provides a number of provisions protecting the position of prospective members and active mem-bers. Not only does the directive foresee that the same social and labour law requirements remain applicable, it also prescribes rigorous information requirements both for prospec-tive scheme members as well as active scheme members facing a cross-border transfer of their scheme. The IORP II Directive has also shored up governance standards, raising the requirements for proper management of an IORP. Finally, a cross-border transfer of pension schemes requires the consent of pension scheme members, the employer as well as the home and host state supervisory authorities who are to consider *inter alia* the long term interests of pension scheme members and whether entitlements of the members and beneficiaries of the scheme to be transferred are at least the same after the transfer.

B. Scheme Member Mobility

With respect to cross-border mobility for European workers, this chapter has shown that
– despite the many tangible advances EU legislation has brought in this area – there are
still a few areas in which current EU legislation is lacking. Specifically, the absence of a
regulated process for the transferability of accrued pension rights means that European
workers still find themselves at the mercy of national legislation and pension scheme
rules penalizing (international) pension transfers. There is also the matter of lacking
portability/cross-border membership.

This is a situation that needs correcting, and solutions seem available. Whether these
are attainable will depend, as ever, on the political will both at EU and the national level.
Chapter 6 will consider a possible solution to the problem of scheme member mobility.
Before that, Chapter 5 will study to what extent cross-border IORPs run into obstacles as
they pursue cross-border activity. It will also draw a final conclusion on the EU's initiatives regulating the second pillar, based on the findings of Chapters 4 and 5.

Chapter 5: Cross-Border IORPs in the Single Market – The Perspective of Pension Providers

1 Introduction

Cross-border IORPs offer, in theory, substantial benefits to pension scheme members. Such benefits include scale economies, which can lead to a better pension result for workers.[828] IORPs achieve such benefits by taking advantage of the Single Market, and the previous chapter concluded that the manner in which cross-border IORPs do this offers mixed results for pension scheme members: the IORP II Directive contains a number of features that benefit pension scheme members, such as the requirement of full funding and they seem to offer advantages to (some groups of) mobile workers, such as in the case of RESAVER. In addition, the social and labour law provisions of the host Member State protecting pension scheme members remain applicable, and rigorous powers of intervention ensure that these are complied with. In conclusion, cross-border IORPs appear to be quite adept at protecting pension scheme members' interests, with the caveat that some improvements must be made.

Now that cross-border IORPs have been discussed from the perspective of a pension scheme member, it is time to examine the IORP II Directive from the perspective of a (prospective) cross-border IORP to find out how well IORPs can take advantage of their freedom to provide services. Cross-border IORPs face a number of challenges in their venture across European borders, and as noted in the introduction, a relatively small number of IORPs is active on a cross-border basis: Chapter 1 noted that so far just 73 IORPs out of a total of 155,481 were active on a cross-border basis at the end of 2016.[829] The potential reasons for this seem manifold and are both legal as well as non-legal.

---

828 See Chapter 1, section 5.3.
829 EIOPA, '2017 Market development report on occupational pensions and cross-border IORPs' (2018) EIO-PA-BOS-18/013, 26, available at eiopa.europa.eu/publications/reports accessed 3 January 2020 19.

Respondents to an EIOPA Call for Advice on the review of the IORP I Directive, consisting of a diverse group of *inter alia* governments and ministries, social partners, pension providers, associations of pension providers and academics, provided their input to EIOPA on the revision of the Directive on two occasions.[830] Respondents were asked, among other questions, about their view on the (definition of) cross-border activity of IORPs as well as the scope and definition of social and labour law. The respondents presented a number of reasons as to why in their opinion the number of cross-border IORPs is low. Among these reasons was that employers seem already satisfied with the arrangements that they currently have, that the process of setting up such schemes is too burdensome, that there are practical difficulties in the cooperation between prudential supervisors and that there are cultural barriers.[831]

A significant number of respondents, however, also pointed to legal reasons as the main obstacles to cross-border activities of IORPs. In their view, the lack of take-up has to do with the differences in Member States' overall legal and taxation systems, rather than an outright lack of ambition to look across borders.[832] UK grocery chain Tesco, for example, reported that in its opinion a lack of demand may be primarily due to "differences in member states' social and labor laws (including taxation)", and even though it operates in six countries it has "no intention to set up a cross-border scheme for exactly those reasons."[833] According to the European Federation for Retirement Provision, demand is

---

830 EIOPA consulted between 8 July and 15 August 2011 on the scope, cross-border activity, prudential regulation and several governance aspects of the call for advice. 49 responses to this consultation were received. See EIOPA, 'Draft response to Call for Advice on the review of Directive 2003/41/EC: Scope, cross-border activity, prudential regulation and governance' (2011) EIOPA-CP-11/001, available at https://eiopa.euro-pa.eu/Pages/Consultations/Consultation-38.aspx accessed 7 January 2020.
EIOPA's second consultation was on the entire advice and was between 25 October 2011 and 2 January 2012. 170 responses were received by the deadline. See EIOPA, 'Response to Call for Advice on the review of Directive 2003/41/EC: second consultation' (2011) EIOPA-CP-11/006, available at https://eiopa.europa.eu/Pages/Consultations/Consultation-32.aspx accessed 7 January 2020.
831 EIOPA, 'Summary of Comments on Consultation Paper: Response to the Call for Advice on the review of the IORP Directive 2003/41/EC: second consultation' (2012) EIOPA-BoS-12/016, 2012, available at: https://eiopa.europa.eu/Publications/Consultations/2.EIOPA_s_Resolutions_on_comments_received.pdf accessed 7 January 2020.
832 EIOPA, 'Summary of Comments on Consultation Paper: Response to the Call for Advice on the review of the IORP Directive 2003/41/EC: second consultation - EIOPA-CP-11/006' (2012) EIOPA-BoS-12/016, available at https://eiopa.europa.eu/Publications/Consultations/1.EIOPA_s_Resolutions_on_comments_re-ceived.pdf accessed 7 January 2020. See, for example, the responses by AEIP (p. 12), Assoprevidenza (p. 49), BT Group plc (p. 93), Deutsche Post (p. 142), Dutch Ministry of Social Affairs and Employment (pp. 157-158), Federation of Dutch Pension Funds (p. 199), FNV Bondgenoten (p. 207), PMT-PME-MnServices (p. 230), IMA Investment Management Association (p. 238), Siemens AG (p. 315), Trades Union Congress (p. 353). See also EIOPA, 'Summary of Comments on Consultation Paper: Response to the Call for Advice on the review of the IORP Directive 2003/41/EC: second consultation - EIOPA-CP-11/006 - Q 1-11' (2012) EIOPA-BoS-12/016, available at https://eiopa.europa.eu/Publications/Consultations/2.EIOPA_s_Resolu-tions_on_comments_received.pdf accessed 8 January 2020.
833 See page 5 of TESCO's response to the Call for Advice on the review of the IORP Directive 2003/41/EC: second consultation, available at https://eiopa.europa.eu/Publications/Comments/IORP-Cfa-2nd-Respon-se_TESCO.pdf accessed 7 January 2020.

limited to those companies that bear the initial costs of setting up a cross-border scheme. At the same time, some pension industry professionals signal that they are receiving signs of 'pent-up demand' from multinational corporations.[834] EIOPA's most recent Market Development Report[835] has also found that although the number of active cross-border IORPs has stagnated over the last years, there was an increase in multi-employer IORPs, operating schemes for more than one employer, as well as an expansion of multi-country cross-border IORPs.

Following a brief discussion of the non-legal obstacles, a discussion of the legal obstacles will take place. The main legal obstacles that are mentioned recurrently both in academic literature[836] as well as Commission[837] and EIOPA[838] documents are the result of uncertainty over the scope of application those of differing tax and other legislative requirements, in particular the social and labour laws of the Member States – complicating the activity of cross-border IORPs – as well as the added prudential requirements.

---

834 C Thomas, 'A New Dawn for Cross-Border Pensions?' (*Chief Investment Officer* 4 March 2014) available at https://www.ai-cio.com/news/a-new-dawn-for-cross-border-pensions/ accessed 7 January 2020. See also M Dowsey, 'Review of the IORP Directive' (2012) Vol 17 (3) Pensions 158; L Kok & H Geboers, Grensoverschrijdende Pensioenuitvoering (SEO Economisch Onderzoek 2016); J Lommen, 'De API is een no-brainer' (2009) No 25 Netspar NEA Papers; O Boschman, 'Nog weinig animo voor pensioenuitvoering over de grens' (*PensioenPro* 5 January 2017); and C Senior, 'Stumbling block' (*European Pensions* April 2012), available at https://www.europeanpensions.net/ep/april-stumbling-block.php accessed 7 January 2020.

835 EIOPA, '2017 Market development report on occupational pensions and cross-border IORPs' (2018) EIOPA-BOS-18/013, 26, available at eiopa.europa.eu/publications/reports accessed 3 January 2020 19.

836 See, for example, H. van Meerten, *EU Pension Law* (Amsterdam University Press 2019); T van den Brink, H van Meerten & S de Vries, 'Regulating Pensions: Why the European Union Matters' (2011) Netspar Discussion Paper, 4, available at ssrn.com/abstract=1950765 accessed 7 January 2020; B Starink & H van Meerten, 'Cross-border obstacles and solutions for pan-European pensions' (2011) Vol 20 (1) EC Tax Review 30; H van Meerten, 'The Scope of the EU 'Pensions'-Directive: Some Background and Solutions for Policymakers' in U Neergaard and others (eds), *Social Services of General Interest in the EU* (TMC Asser Press 2013); P Borsjé & H van Meerten, 'A European pensions union: Towards a strengthening of the European pension systems' in F Pennings & G Vonk (eds), *Research Handbook on European Social Security Law* (Edward Elgar Publishing 2015); I Guardiancich & D Natali, 'The EU and Supplementary Pensions: Instruments for Integration and the Market for Occupational Pensions in Europe' (2009) 2009.11 ETUI Working Paper 19; I Guardiancich, 'Pan-European pension funds: Current situation and future prospects' (2011) Vol 64 (1) *International Social Security Review* 15; M Haverland, 'When the welfare state meets the regulatory state: EU occupational pension policy' (2007) Vol 14 (6) Journal of European Public Policy 886; P Dejmek, 'No Flying Start but a Bright Future for EU Directive 2003/41/EC on Occupational Pension Institutions' (2006) Vol 17 (5) European Business Law Review 1381.

837 See, for instance, European Commission, 'Green Paper towards adequate, sustainable and safe European pension systems' COM(2010) 365 final (Green Paper) 11-12; European Commission, 'An Agenda for Adequate, Safe and Sustainable Pensions' COM(2012) 55 final (White Paper) 21; European Commission, 'Proposal for a directive of the European Parliament and of the Council on the activities and supervision of institutions for occupational retirement provision' COM(2014) 167 final.

838 See the previously discussed consultations by EIOPA.

2 THE OBSTACLES FACED BY CROSS-BORDER IORPs

As noted, cross-border IORPs face legal as well as non-legal obstacles. Both these categories of obstacles will be discussed below. An important legal obstacle that – in spite of the EU's and ECJ's efforts[839] – has not been entirely resolved is caused by differences in taxation between the Member States of occupational pension contributions and benefits. Mismatches between the Member States could result in double taxation or non-taxation. However, as tax law is beyond the scope of this dissertation, this chapter will not focus on this obstacle.

2.1 Non-Legal Obstacles to the Cross-Border Activity of IORPs

On the non-legal side, a supposed lack of demand for cross-border occupational pension solutions is cited by various sources. This lack of demand is ascribed by some as stemming from the divergences in applicable legislation, such as social and labour law as well as tax impediments.[840] Other respondents attribute this lack of demand to the availability of other methods to achieve scale economies, high costs of implementing cross-border solutions,[841] as well as the outright absence of cross-border ambitions by pension funds.[842] In addition, an underdeveloped market could be part of the reason. However, pension industry professionals do point out that there is indeed interest from employers in cross-border pension solutions.[843] EIOPA provides as reasons a lack of awareness of the existence and the possibilities regarding cross-border pension solutions, a lack of critical mass of employees in other Member States that could justify the expense of setting up a cross-border solution, lengthy and onerous administrative processes as well as a simple lack of capable providers.[844]

Another practical problem could stem from anxiety felt by employers and (prospective) pension scheme members, sparked by the idea that a foreign pension provider will

---

839 See footnotes 465 and 466.
840 EIOPA, EIOPA's Advice to the European Commission on the review of the IORP Directive 2003/41/EC (2012) EIOPA-BOS-12/015, 29; In addition, a fair number of respondents to the EIOPA's Call for Advice on the review of the IORP Directive 2003/41/EC expressed their opinion that the relatively limited cross-border activity is due to lack of demand (see footnote 831).
841 See page 4 of BusinessEurope's response to the Call for Advice to Call for Advice on the review of the IORP Directive 2003/41/EC: second consultation, available at https://eiopa.europa.eu/Publications/Comments/IORP-Cfa-2nd-Response_BUSINESSEUROPE.pdf accessed 7 January 2020. IBM, Gesamtmetall, BAVC, Bayer share that view.
842 See page 12 of the National Association of Pension Funds' (NAPF) response to the Call for Advice to Call for Advice on the review of the IORP Directive 2003/41/EC: second consultation, available at https://eiopa.europa.eu/Publications/Comments/IORP-Cfa-2nd-Response_NAPF.pdf accessed 7 January 2020
843 Senior 2012 (see footnote 834).
844 EIOPA, '2017 Market development report on occupational pensions and cross-border IORPs' (2018) EIOPA-BOS-18/013, 22-24.

manage their hard-earned pension assets. The possibility for pension scheme members or their representatives to block pension transfers to another Member State could therefore also be a contributing factor to the relatively few cross-border IORPs. As will be explained below, the system of the IORP II Directive requires that IORPs respect the local legislation applicable to occupational pension of the country in which they operate a given scheme. However, the legislation regulating the IORP *as an institution* – for instance solvency requirements, investment rules and governance requirements – are those of the Member State in which the IORP is located. It is conceivable that the notion that a foreign institution manages the pension assets under foreign legislation causes unease among prospective clients.

2.2 *Legal Obstacles to the Cross-Border Activity of IORPs*

The original IORP Directive was revised for five main reasons,[845] that were translated into four specific problems.[846] Three of these specific problems, namely the insufficiency of governance and risk management requirements, the inefficiency of the information provided to scheme members and the supervisory powers of the national competent authorities were discussed in Part 1, Section b of Chapter 4. The other problem that was mentioned in the Commission's Impact Assessment to the IORP II proposal was that "cross-border activity is still expensive and complex for employers, which prevents IORPs from fully benefiting from the Single Market."[847] The document describes the long and complicated process of setting up a cross-border IORP:

> "The experience of employers, IORPs and supervisors over the past years has clearly shown that important prudential barriers restricting cross-border operations of IORPs remain. The mere preparations, i.e. feasibility studies by sponsoring employers, may take two years or even more. Setting-up a cross-border IORP takes nine months to a year, while adding an additional host MS takes about six months on average (Hewitt Associates, 2010). There is evidence

---

845 European Commission, 'Impact Assessment Accompanying the document Proposal for a Directive of the European Parliament and of the Council on the activities and supervision of institutions for occupational retirement provision' SWD(2014) 103 final Part 1/2, 1. These reasons are the following: First, prudential barriers remain which make it more expensive for employers to join an IORP in another MS. Second, market developments require a regulatory response since the number of Europeans relying on defined-contribution (DC) schemes, which shifts risks from IORPs and employers to individuals, has increased significantly. Third, recent financial and economic crises have shown that current minimum levels of protection for scheme members and beneficiaries need to be improved. Fourth, citizens do not receive essential information in a comprehensible manner, which prevents them from making informed decisions about their retirement financing. Fifth, supervisory powers are insufficient in several areas.
846 ibid 10.
847 ibid.

that establishing cross-border IORPs can be a burdensome task and projects
are therefore often abandoned (Annex E). Feedback from stakeholders suggests
that there are two categories of problem drivers."[848]

The particular problems named in respect of setting up a cross-border IORP were the A)
additional prudential requirements for cross-border IORPs as well as B) the lack of clarity
of several of the definitions and procedures for cross-border activity.

A) Prudential Requirements

Regarding the additional prudential requirements, the Commission's Impact Assessment
to the then-proposed IORP II Directive noted, first, the IORP I Directive's possibility for
competent authorities of host Member States to impose specific investment rules for the
assets involved in cross-border activity.[849] The Commission said that "[t]his leads to a
situation where either sponsoring employers or the IORP are faced with a number of
different national investment rules, thereby imposing additional investment rules on
IORPs wishing to operate in other [Member States]."[850]

The provision allowing national competent authorities to impose such extra requirements was abolished in the IORP II Directive,[851] with the recitals of the directive noting
explicitly that "IORPs should be allowed to invest in other Member States in accordance
with the rules of their home Member States in order to reduce the cost of cross-border
activity" and that "the host Member States should not be allowed to impose additional
investment requirements on IORPs located in other Member States."[852]

Secondly, the Commission expressed the wish to abolish the fully-funded-at-all-times
requirement for cross-border IORPs. This is because, while "domestic IORPs are allowed
to have considerable recovery periods (up to 10 years or more)", cross-border IORPs face
the more stringent and more costly requirement to always be fully funded. As noted in
Section c of Part 1 of Chapter 4, that requirement was ultimately kept, albeit slightly
weakened.

---

848 ibid 13.
849 ibid 13. This possibility was enshrined in Article 18(7) IORP I. See also that Directive's 34th recital.
850 ibid.
851 Article 19(8) IORP II.
852 Recital 50 IORP II. See also European Commission, 'Proposal for a directive of the European Parliament and
    of the Council on the activities and supervision of institutions for occupational retirement provision' COM
    (2014) 167 final, 7-8.

B) Definitions and Procedures for Cross-Border Activity

In the Commission's view, there were three specific problems regarding the definitions and procedures for cross-border activity.[853]

The first was that the IORP I Directive provided no clear definition of what constitutes cross-border activity. EIOPA found that national supervisors used the definition of cross-border activity differently to determine whether there was cross-border activity.[854] This issue is important, as it defines, for instance, which Member State's tax, contract, social and labor and prudential law is applicable.[855] Another problem identified by EIOPA was that the use of different definitions that "has led to a number of cases where two (or more) Member States potentially involved in a cross-border activity have come to different conclusions on whether the proposed activity is cross border or not. This has created considerable difficulties in both the operation of cross border IORPs and the notification, authorisation and approval processes."[856]

The problem of the definition of cross-border activity has been rectified by including a definition of what it entails.[857] That new definition determines that cross-border activity means operating a pension scheme where the relationship between the sponsoring undertaking, and the members and beneficiaries concerned, is governed by the social and labour law relevant to the field of occupational pension schemes of a Member State other than the home Member State of the IORP.[858] The new definition, together with the clarified article on cross-border activities and procedures, should put an end to the previous confusion.

The second problem identified by EIOPA in respect of the definitions and procedures for cross-border activity was that the IORP I Directive did not contain any provisions on the transfer of occupational retirement schemes. The IORP II Directive now contains a provision on the collective transfer of a pension scheme. The (lack of options for) transferability of individual pension rights was discussed Part 2 of Chapter 4.

Third and finally, the Commission pointed out that the scope of and – therefore the interaction between – prudential regulations and social and labour law is unclear. EIOPA calls the "lack of clarity about the different scope of the member states social and labour law and the prudential law" a "significant hurdle to cross border IORPs."[859] As a consequence, it is not always clear which Member State's legislation must be complied with.

---

853 Impact Assessment Part 1/2 (see footnote 845) 13.

854 EIOPA, EIOPA's Advice to the European Commission on the review of the IORP Directive 2003/41/EC (2012) EIOPA-BOS-12/015, 28

855 Starink & van Meerten (see footnote 836) 33.

856 EIOPA, 'Response to Call for Advice on the review of Directive 2003/41/EC: second consultation' (2011) EIOPA-CP-11/006, 29, available at https://eiopa.europa.eu/Pages/Consultations/Consultation-32.aspx accessed 7 January 2020.

857 See Article 6(19) IORP II.

858 ibid.

859 EIOPA 2011 (see footnote 856) 29.

The Commission notes that "[a] sponsoring employer that intends to set-up a cross-border IORP needs to know whether it has to comply with the laws of the home or host MS. The different scope of prudential regulations in MSs causes legal uncertainty for sponsoring employers, IORPs and supervisors, involving legal costs for the sponsoring employer, which might increase overall transaction costs and, consequently, discourage such transactions."[860] The 16th recital of the IORP II Directive notes that "Despite the entry into force of Directive 2003/41/EC, cross-border activity has been limited due to the differences in national social and labour law." The IORP II Directive was meant to correct this by adding a provision, the current Article 46 IORP II, which lists a number of items belonging to prudential supervision, but it seems questionable whether this provision has succeeded in quelling the uncertainty about the scope of prudential and social and labour law.

While the issue of additional prudential requirements and the first two of the problems regarding the definitions and procedures for cross-border activity seem to have been dealt with to some extent by the IORP II Directive, the last issue arguably has not been. For this reason, the section below will consider the relationship between social and labour law and prudential law in greater detail. Since respondents to EIOPA's consultations indicated that there are still social and labour law barriers hampering IORPs' cross-border activity, the next section will examine these from the perspective of the freedom to provide services.

3   SOCIAL AND LABOUR LAW

3.1   Introduction

IORPs may carry out cross-border services in accordance with Article 11 IORP II:

> Without prejudice to national social and labour law on the organisation of pension systems, including compulsory membership and the outcomes of collective bargaining agreements, Member States shall allow an IORP registered or authorised in their territories to carry out cross-border activity. Member States shall also allow undertakings located in their territories to sponsor IORPs which propose to or carry out cross-border activity.

Article 11 of the IORP II Directive "reflects the aprioristic impossibility of reaching unanimity at supranational level on social security issues," in that IORPs' freedom to provide services throughout the EU is in principle "unqualified and unrestricted," save

---

860 Impact Assessment Part 1/2 (see footnote 845) 14.

for the requirement that cross-border IORPs must abide by the national social and labour law in which they operate a pension scheme.[861]

As noted in the introduction to this chapter, the requirement to abide by local social and labour legislation is said to be a (significant) obstacle to the cross-border activity of IORPs. This is because it can be costly and time-consuming for IORPs to familiarise themselves with the local requirements. After the necessary information has been gathered, however, cross-border activity can go ahead in accordance with all applicable requirements.

3.2 What is the Origin of the Directive's Deference to National Social and Labour Law?

As described in Chapter 2, the EU's internal market competence stemming from Article 114 TFEU is its most commonly used legal basis. This was also one of the IORP II Directive's legal bases.[862] As a consequence of the principle of conferral,[863] the EU may only act within the limits of the powers conferred to it: the competences "not conferred upon the Union in the Treaties remain with the Member States."

When legislating, the EU legislator must take into account the principle of subsidiarity as well. According to this principle, the EU may act only where it is better placed than the Member States to take action in respect of a certain matter. In summary, in the event that new legislation is considered by the EU legislator, the first step is to determine whether the EU has the *competence* to act on the basis of an appropriate legal basis. The second step is then to determine whether the EU should *exercise* its competence to legislate.[864] Finally, the principle of proportionality must be taken into account: EU legislative initiatives may not "exceed what is necessary to achieve the objectives of the Treaties."[865]

---

861 Guardiancich 2011 (see footnote 836) 24.
862 The IORP II Directive, as well as its predecessor IORP I, were adopted on the basis of internal market provisions, in particular articles 53, 62 and 114 TFEU. Article 62 TFEU is the legal basis for acts on the exercise of the freedom to provide services.
863 Articles 4 and 5 TEU.
864 van den Brink, van Meerten & de Vries 2011 (see footnote 836) 3.
865 Article 5(4) TEU.

The Directive's deference to national social and labour law appears to be a matter of competence:[866] the arrangement of national pension systems is primarily a matter for the Member States.

The Commission stated in the very first version of the proposal to the original IORP Directive that the cross-border management of pension schemes must comply with social and labour legislation of the scheme in which the scheme is established: "Schemes must be run in conformity with national provisions, regardless of where the IORP is located."[867] In addition, the proposal stated that the "competence of the Member States" to arrange pension provision in accordance with national circumstances and requirements "e.g. existing local regulations in the fields of labour, social and taxation" is to be respected.[868] The explanatory memorandum of the revised IORP II Directive largely retains this formulation.[869]

It is worth noting that the statement that the Member States have full responsibility over their pension systems is, at the very least, inaccurate. That prerogative of the Member States is on the one hand subject to the requirements of European law – among which is the freedom to provide services – and the other, the EU's own initiatives pursued on the basis of *its* prerogatives. Those Union prerogatives include not just those serving the creation of a Single Market – in the present context a single market for occupational pensions and the freedom of movement of workers – but also those of Article 153(1) TFEU, the same article that in its fourth paragraph notes that measures adopted pursuant to it are not to prejudice the right of Member States to define the fundamental principles of their social security systems or the financial equilibrium thereof. Article 153(1) TFEU,

---

866 The IORP II Directive's 19th recital proclaims that "*In accordance with the principle of subsidiarity* [emphasis added], Member States should retain full responsibility for the organisation of their pension systems as well as for the decision on the role of each of the three pillars of the retirement system in individual Member States. In the context of the second pillar, they should also retain full responsibility for the role and functions of the various institutions providing occupational retirement benefits, such as industry-wide pension funds, company pension funds and life insurance undertakings. This Directive is not intended to call this prerogative of Member States into question, but rather encourage them to build up adequate, safe and sustainable occupational retirement provision and facilitate cross-border activity."
It seems that this recital should have read: "In accordance with the principle of attribution." The EU has no express general competence to regulate fundamental aspects of Member States' pension systems and therefore, it seems, the national social and labour laws of the Member States, save where these conflict with EU law. See, on this, van den Brink, van Meerten & de Vries 2011 (see footnote 836) 9; van Meerten 2019 (see footnote 836) 36-37.

867 Commission of the European Communities, 'Proposal for a directive of the European Parliament and of the Council on the activities of institutions for occupational retirement provision' COM(2000) 507 final. See on this also Haverland 2007 (see footnote 836) 898 and Y Stevens, 'The meaning of "national social and labour legislation" in directive 2003/41/EC on the activities and supervision of institutions for occupational retirement provision' (2004) Research report commissioned by the European Association of Paritarian Institutions (AEIP) 11.

868 COM(2000) 507 final.

869 COM(2014) 167 final 6; "Under the proposed action, Member States retain full responsibility for the organisation of their pension systems. The revision does not call this prerogative into question. Neither does the revision cover issues of national social and labour, fiscal or contract legislation."

serving to achieve social policy objectives, proclaims that the EU shall support and complement the activities of the Member States in, *inter alia*, social security and social protection of workers. Although the practical value of Article 153 TFEU remains questionable as a legislative basis,[870] the EU's Single Market powers have yielded several legislative acts on occupational pensions that are of direct influence on Member States' pension systems.

During the negotiations on the first IORP Directive, the Netherlands was particularly concerned about the fate of its pension system that consists in large part of compulsory sectoral funds, and pressed for the addition of the phrase "including compulsory membership and the outcomes of collective bargaining" in the Council.[871] The country had concerns about the system of compulsory membership in face of this Directive. It expressed concern over what is now article 11 IORP II on cross-border activity in particular, when it mused over what consequences the possibility to freely choose for a provider (from another Member State) could have for the system of mandatory participation in the Netherlands.[872] The State Secretary also voiced apprehension over the proposed Directive's system of supervision on IORPs – on which the first proposal left some doubts[873] – in particular, as the State Secretary viewed matters, that Dutch social and labour law would come under the supervision of the authorities of an IORP's home Member State rather than Dutch authorities.[874] Haverland notes that "[a]lthough autonomy with regard to national and social labour law was already part of the European Commission's proposal, the Dutch government feared that it might not be sufficient to shelter the Dutch system when it was challenged in the ECJ."[875]

This fear reflects the important social value that social and labor legislation has in the protection of pension scheme members. In the Netherlands, compulsory membership is justified by the social goals that the pension funds operating these schemes pursue: the

---

870 Measures in the field of social security and social protection of workers requires hard-to-achieve unanimity in the Council, in accordance with a special legislative procedure, after consulting the European Parliament and the said Committees. See Article 153(2) TFEU; W Baugniet, The protection of occupational pensions under European Union law on the freedom of movement for workers, dissertation European University Institute Florence (2014).

871 Haverland 2007 (see footnote 836) 898.

872 Kamerstukken II 2000/01, 25 694, nr. 9, p. 6.

873 European Parliament, *Report on the proposal for a European Parliament and Council directive on the activities of institutions for occupational retirement provision* (Session document 21 June 2001) A5-0220/2001 final, 39 (The Karas Report).

874 Kamerstukken II 2000/01, 25 694, nr. 9, p. 6: "Daarnaast houdt de ontwerp-richtlijn in dat bij de uitvoering van een Nederlandse pensioenregeling door een buitenlandse instelling op de naleving van de sociaalarbeidsrechtelijke bepalingen die op die pensioenregeling van toepassing is, toezicht plaatsvindt door de bevoegde autoriteiten van het land waar die instelling is gevestigd. Het zal niet eenvoudig zijn om een buitenlandse autoriteit toezicht te laten uitoefenen op de eerder reeds genoemde specifiek Nederlandse materieel beschermende bepalingen."

875 Haverland 2007 (see footnote 836) 898.

schemes feature a high degree of solidarity between various cohorts of scheme members.[876] It also serves the social goal of ensuring the coverage of all workers in a given sector by occupational pension schemes.[877]

Although it is in principle up to the Member States to define their own requirements of social and labour law, that power of the Member States is limited by the requirements under EU law. The same caveat must be made in the context of Member States' powers to organise their own social security systems. The power of the Member States to define national social and labour law is therefore not absolute.

3.3   The Scope of Social and Labour Law and Prudential Law

In the face of the absence of a definition of social and labour law in the directive, and the Member States' prerogative to define what is part of the social and labour legislation that IORPs from other Member States must comply with, the concept of social and labour law as it is used in the IORP II Directive is practically impossible to define given the diversity of the Member States' legal systems. The previous chapter has already shown how challenging it can be to distinguish between social and labour law and prudential law in respect of pension security mechanisms. In addition, social and labour standards are dynamic and change with economic and political conditions as well as their place on not just on national agendas, but also that of the EU.[878] Nevertheless, it is possible to gain a closer understanding of the topic.[879]

The relevant[880] social and labour law for the purposes of the IORP II Directive is the legislation of the Member States applicable to the operation of occupational pension schemes.[881] Article 11 IORP II makes clear that compulsory membership and the out-

---

876 H van Meerten & E Schmidt, 'Compulsory Membership of Pension Schemes and the Free Movement of Services in the EU' (2017) 19 (2) European Journal of Social Security 118.

877 ibid.

878 B. Bercusson, 'Introduction: Interpreting the EU Charter in the context of the social dimension of European integration' in B. Bercusson (ed), *European labour law and the EU Charter of Fundamental Rights – Summary Version* (ETUI 2002) 9.

879 See, on this, the contributions by Stevens and Reiner: Stevens 2004 (see footnote 867); Y Stevens, 'The development of a legal matrix on the meaning of "national social and labour legislation" in directive 2003/41/EC with regard to five member states: Belgium – France – Germany – Italy – Netherlands' (2006) Research report by the European Association of Paritarian Institutions (AEIP); M Reiner, 'Strukturfragen zum Zusammenspiel von Aufsichts- und Arbeitsrecht im europäischen Pensionsfondsgeschäft gemäß IORP II' in D Krömer and others (eds), *Arbeitsrecht und Arbeitswelt im Europäischen Wandel* (Nomos 2016) 193.

880 Recital 36 IORP II requires that "[t]he exercise of the right of an IORP established in one Member State to manage an occupational pension scheme contracted in another Member State should fully respect the provisions of the social and labour law in force in the host Member State insofar as it is relevant to occupational pension schemes, for example the definition and payment of retirement benefits and the conditions for transferability of pension rights."

881 Dejmek 2006 (see footnote 836) 1391.

comes of collective bargaining – both of which are named as examples by this provision –
are part of social and labour law. What else can be said to be part of social and labour law?
EIOPA's registry of national social and labour law requirements shows that matters such
as vesting and waiting periods, provisions regarding pension contributions and benefits,
contract law, legislation on guarantees and risk sharing and pension transfers are to be
considered part of social and labor law.[882] However, the lists provided by the Member
States of the social and labour applicable to pension schemes offered within their borders
are often non-exhaustive and sometimes outdated, which again makes it difficult to gain
an overview.

Delineating Social and Labour Law and Prudential Law

The operation of IORPs *as institutions* is covered by prudential legislation. The aforementioned Article 46 IORP II gives an indication of what is to be considered part of
prudential regulation. But as explained before, neither IORP II nor its predecessor
IORP I regulate matters of social and labour law, or indeed matters of fiscal or contract
law.[883] The Member States are left with a wide margin of discretion in determining what,
according to them, constitutes their own national social and labour law, and are competent to do so within the boundaries set by EU law.[884] More on that in the following
sections.

As noted, the IORP II Directive was meant to create greater clarity with respect to the
distinction between social and labour law and prudential law by including a list of items
belonging to prudential supervision.[885] In other words, the Directive has – so it would
seem at first glance – placed the items on this list outside of the scope of social and labour
law, potentially making it easier to infer what social and labour law entails. In this respect,
Reiner argues that the regulation of one aspect automatically also leads to the regulation
of another: "the more belongs to the scope of prudential law (of the home Member State),
the less remains for the labor law (of the host Member State)."[886]

At the same time, the definition of prudential supervision does not automatically
result in a definition of social and labour law given the great diversity of such legislation
in the Member States. However, Reiner surmises that the enumeration of what constitutes prudential supervision also has an effect on what can be social and labour law and that
therefore, the Directive's proclamation that it does not affect social and labour law is at

---

882 EIOPA 'Social and Labour Law', available at https://eiopa.europa.eu/regulation-supervision/pensions/occu-
    pational-pensions/social-and-labour-law accessed 3 January 2020.
883 COM(2014) 167 final; recital 3 of the IORP II Directive.
884 Stevens 2004 (see footnote 867).
885 See the last sentence of recital 70 of IORP II; Article 46 IORP II. See also COM(2014) 167 final 11.
886 Reiner 2016 (see footnote 879) 210.

the very least imprecise. He arrives at this conclusion as, according to him, the enumerated prudential law can no longer form part of social and labour law.[887]

The Directive's list of prudential supervision in Article 46 includes ten items.[888] It could be argued that this list defines the full spectrum of prudential supervision, in other words, that this list is exhaustive. Reiner argues that prudential law for the purposes of the Directive concerns only the aspects enumerated in that article. He supports this argument with the observation that the fields of supervision enumerated in Article 46 – save for "conditions of operations"[889] – correspond to the titles with the legal provisions in the Directive itself. He therefore posits that "Prudential supervision" is not some abstract notion from which the remit of prudential supervision for the purposes of Article 46 must be deduced, but rather that the scope of prudential supervision is defined by the list of Article 46 itself. As a supporting argument, he notes that the country of origin principle applicable to prudential supervision is made acceptable by the minimum harmonisation of prudential standards enumerated in the directive.

This approach seems contestable on two fronts. First, there is the wording of Article 46 IORP II. The provision is worded as follows: "Member States shall ensure that IORPs are subject to prudential supervision *including* the supervision of the following where applicable" (italics added ES). The word "including" suggests that the items listed in this provision are not exhaustive.

Second, there appears to be nothing in the Directive to suggest that matters of prudential supervision are automatically excluded from the remit of social and labour law and vice versa. It was shown in Chapter 4 that the line between the two is, at times, vague and that there are conceivably situations where a provision could simultaneously fall under both social and labour law as well as prudential law.

Although the enumeration of prudential supervision helps in defining the limits of the concept, and perhaps also serves to indicate somewhat more clearly the demarcation of social and labour law, the omission of a definition of what constitutes social and labour law still seems to be a problem. The IORP II Directive helps somewhat by providing examples of what constitutes social and labour law, such as compulsory membership and the outcomes of collective bargaining,[890] or "the definition and payment of retirement benefits and the conditions for transferability of pension rights."[891] But the great diversity of national social and labour laws, and the Directive's deference to it, means that

---

887 ibid.

888 Article 46 IORP II lists the following items: (a) conditions of operation, (b) technical provisions, (c) funding of technical provisions, (d) regulatory own funds, (e) available solvency margin, (f) required solvency margin, (g) investment rules, (h) investment management, (i) system of governance and (j) information to be provided to members and beneficiaries.

889 There is no article in the directive with the heading "conditions of operation". Reiner 2016 (see footnote 879) points out that this could be an error in redaction, as the IORP I Directive did contain such a heading in the old Article 9, which is now article 10 in IORP II and headed "Operating requirements".

890 Recital 35 IORP II.

891 Recital 36 IORP II.

the Directive contains no autonomous definition of the concept, but is defined nationally instead.[892]

3.4   Conclusion

The concept of social and labour law is difficult to define: there is no EU-level definition.[893] Additionally, the Member States themselves are competent to define what they consider social and labour law.[894] Therefore, "[w]hat is social and labour law in one [Member State] is [...] not necessarily social and labour law in another".[895] In some cases, it may be unclear what falls under social and labour law and what falls under prudential law, and it seems that the same is true with respect to prudential law, as was shown in Chapter 4.

The obligation to comply with host State social and labour law is named as an obstacle to the cross-border activity of IORPs and is often named as one of the major reasons for the fairly low number of cross-border IORPs. At the same time, it appears to be consistently named as a surmountable hurdle by employers who have actually set up cross-border IORPs.[896] This would seem to suggest that differences in social and labour law represent more of a speed bump than an outright barrier. In addition, there is the obvious importance of provisions of social and labour legislation in the protection of pension scheme members. These provisions should therefore not be sacrificed too easily in the pursuit of the achievement of an internal market for occupational pensions.

However, there appear to be some provisions in Member States' social and labor law that could make it impossible for a cross-border IORP to operate a pension scheme from another Member State. These will be discussed below. This discussion is a non-exhaustive representation of the hurdles cross-border IORPs may encounter in their cross-border activity.

---

892 Reiner 2016 (see footnote 879) 210.
893 Stevens 2004 (see footnote 867) 27.
894 ibid 56.
895 Impact Assessment Part 1/2 (see footnote 845) 13.
896 B Nürk & J Macco, 'Cross-Border – von Frankfurt nach Wien: Nicht so einfach nach Österreich' (LEITERbAV.de, 08 December 2015) www.lbav.de/nicht-einfach-so-nach-oesterreich/ accessed 13 November 2019; N Trappenburg, 'Pensioenverhuizing naar België bijna een feit' *Financieel Dagblad* (2 June 2016); B Ottawa, 'HINTERGRUND: Erster deutsch-österreichischer pensionfonds am Start" *IPE Institutional Investment* (23 November 2015); L Kok & H Geboers, *Grensoverschrijdende Pensioenuitvoering* (SEO Economisch Onderzoek 2016); Ernst & Young, *Pan-European pension funds in a future world* (Ernst & Young 2009) 17.

4   The IORP II Directive and the Freedom to Provide Services

As noted, Article 11(1) of the IORP II Directive gives specific expression to the freedom to provide services in respect of IORPs and qualifies this freedom by subjecting it to host State social and labour law.[897]

Since the Directive does not give any further explanation of the circumstances under which Member States may curtail the freedom to provide services, and because the Directive itself is subordinated to the Lisbon Treaty, it is important to consider, first, the obligations of the Member States under the freedom to provide services in general and, second, whether the Member States – which are free to determine their own national social and labour law under the directive – may uphold any restriction of the freedom to provide services by invoking the social and labour law exception.

4.1   The Freedom to Provide Services

IORPs are typically service providers and are in principle free to provide their services free of restrictions within the territory of the EU.[898] The freedom to provide services is enshrined in Article 56 TFEU and applies to providers of services, such as IORPs.[899] In accordance with Article 56 TFEU, "restrictions on the freedom to provide services within the Union shall be prohibited in respect of nationals of Member States who are established in a Member State other than that of the person for whom the services are intended."

The direct effect of article 56 TFEU was established by the Court in *van Binsbergen*,[900] and the provision may therefore be invoked by individuals as well as legal persons, such as pension providers who find that their freedom to provide services was unduly hindered.

The Treaties are the most important legal framework that govern cross-border economic activity between the Member States of the Union, and the IORP II Directive is subordinated to the Treaties. Important EU objectives with respect to the realisation of a European market for pensions are the establishment of an internal market, the promotion of a high level of social protection, improvement of the standard of living and economic and social cohesion and solidarity between the Member States.[901] With respect to

---

897 Recitals 13, 21 35, 36; Article 11 of IORP II.
898 See, for example, COM(2000) 507 Final; Case C-678/11, *Commission v. Spain* [2014] ECLI:EU:C:2014:2324, para. 37; Case C-422/01 *Skandia and Ramstedt* [2003] ECLI:EU:C:2003:380, paras 22-24; Case C-136/00, *Danner*, [2002], ECR I-8147, paras 25-27.
899 ibid.
900 Case 33/74 *van Binsbergen* [1974] ECLI:EU:C:1974:131.
901 L. Roos, *Pensioen en werknemersmobiliteit in de EU – Fiscale en juridische aspecten* (Universiteit van Tilburg 2006) 32.

the provision of cross-border pension services, it is especially the freedom to provide services that is of importance; the IORP Directive was to be the first step in the achievement of an internal market for occupational retirement provision organised on a European scale.[902] The ECJ gives further guidance on the application of those freedoms to social mechanisms in general and pension services in particular. See Section 4.2.

4.2 Restrictions of the Freedom to Provide Services: General

In accordance with Article 56 TFEU, restrictions on the freedom to provide services are, in principle, prohibited. The ECJ's case law identifies three main types of restrictions: measures that are directly discriminatory, indirectly discriminatory or by means of restrictions that do not apply with either direct or indirect distinction to nationality.

Direct discrimination concerns cases in which persons are being treated differently explicitly on account of their nationality. The concept of direct discrimination was described in the *Gouda*[903] case: "In this respect, the Court has consistently held [...] that Article 59 [now Article 56 TFEU] of the Treaty entails, in the first place, the abolition of any discrimination against a person providing services on account of his nationality or the fact that he is established in a Member State other than the one in which the service is provided."

Indirect discrimination concerns cases in which persons are being treated differently on what appears not to be based on nationality, but which has the effect of disadvantaging persons from other Member States.

The concept of *restrictions* is broader than discrimination. In paragraph 12 of its *Säger*[904] judgment, the Court ruled that what is now Article 56 TFEU requires not just the elimination of any discriminatory measures, but the abolition "of any restriction, even if it applies without distinction to national providers of services and to those of other Member States, when it is liable to prohibit or otherwise impede the activities of a provider of services established in another Member State where he lawfully provides similar services."

It therefore follows that any obstacle that "is liable to prohibit, impede or render less advantageous the activities of a provider of services established in another Member State where he lawfully provides similar services"[905] is prohibited, even if that restriction is minor.[906] The formula extracted by the Court in *Säger* is similar to that in the seminal

---

902 Recital 6 IORP I and Recital 6 IORP II.
903 Case C-288/89 *Stichting Collectieve Antennevoorziening Gouda v. Commissariaat de Media* [1991] ECLI:EU:C:1991:323, para 10.
904 Case C-76/90 *Säger* [1991] ECLI:EU:C:1991:331.
905 Joined Cases C-369/96 *Arblade* and C-376/96 *Leloup* [1999] ECLI:EU:C:1999:575.
906 Case C-49/89, *Corsica Ferries France v. Direction générale des douanes françaises* ECLI:EU:C:1995:411.

Dassonville[907] case, which was decided in the area of the free movement of goods. In
Dassonville, the Court ruled that all trading rules enacted by Member States that are
capable of "hindering, directly or indirectly, actually or potentially, intra-Community
trade" are unlawful. Over time, the ECJ's case law has shown that market access is the
main criterion for adjudicating free movement cases, "which entails that national rules
preventing or hindering market access are unlawful, irrespective of whether they discriminate against other persons, services or capital."[908]

For cross-border IORPs, the social and labour legislation that must be complied with
by IORPs operating pension schemes across borders can be an obstacle. Not only can it
be cumbersome and costly to comply with local legislation, some Member State legislation can present an outright barrier to market access for IORPs. That is the case for
Member State legislation that does not recognizs the type of IORP (Section 6) or the
pension scheme (to be) operated by (Section 7). Alternatively, it could be the case that
neither the type of IORP nor the scheme are the problem, but the fact that national
legislation or the outcomes of collective bargaining prohibit a cross-border IORP from
operating the pension scheme(s) for a particular sector of industry in a given Member
State (Section 5). Finally, the rules on scheme transfers can be so disadvantageous that a
transfer is factually impossible (Section 8).

Although the Court's interpretation of what constitutes an obstacle to the freedom to
provide services is seemingly broad, it is not unlimited. In a judgment similar to the
Keck[909] case on selling arrangements in the context of the free movement of goods, the
Court ruled that measures that merely have the effect of raising the costs of services and
that have the same effect within the Member State as they do between Member States do
not constitute restrictions. In the words of the Court: "By contrast, measures, the only
effect of which is to create additional costs in respect of the service in question and which
affect in the same way the provision of services between Member States and that within
one Member State, do not fall within the scope of Article 59 [Article 56 TFEU] of the
Treaty."[910]

This is an important consideration in the context of cross-border IORPs, as the widely
divergent legislative standards across EU Member States are often said to be an obstacle
to the proliferation of such IORPs, as well as raising costs for providers.

In order to discover the clause's limits, this exception must be tested against the provisions of the Lisbon Treaty – a function of a directive's subordination to it – as well as
the case law of the ECJ. The Treaties and the Court's case law mandate unrestricted
freedom to provide services *in principle*. Exceptions to the freedom to provide services

---

907 Case C-8/74 *Dassonville* [1974] ECLI:EU:C:1974:82.
908 S. Prechal & S. de Vries, 'Seamless web of judicial protection in the internal market?' (2009) Vol 31 (1)
European Law Review 5, 8.
909 Joined Cases C-267/91 and C-268/91 *Keck* [1993] ECLI:EU:C:1993:905.
910 Joined Cases C-544/03 and 545/03 *Mobistar and Belgacom Mobile* [2005] ECLI:EU:C:2005:518.

are allowed only under strict circumstances. The matter of justification will be discussed
in Section 9.

5 OBSTACLE NO. 1 TO THE FREEDOM TO PROVIDE SERVICES: COMPULSORY MEMBERSHIP

5.1 Introduction

Compulsory membership and the outcomes of collective bargaining can have the effect of
excluding providers from a particular market.[911] Therefore, compulsory membership and
the outcomes of collective bargaining can constitute far-reaching limitations on the freedom to provide services.[912] Collective bargaining is not only essential to the organisation
of occupational pension systems in a number of EU Member States, but is also a fundamental right recognised in the EU Charter of Fundamental Rights.[913]

There are a number of reasons why membership of pension funds can be made mandatory. In the Netherlands, for example, there is a twofold rationale for making participation in a sectoral pension fund mandatory is twofold. The first aim of compulsory membership is to prevent a race to the bottom in respect of employment conditions, caused by
competing employers.[914] Second, compulsory membership serves a social goal by ensuring that all employees within a certain sector have identical pension arrangements so as to
protect weaker workers,[915] adding a solidarity element.[916] The latter element was also
under consideration in the *Albany* case law, to be discussed below, and was given expression by such features as the absence of risk selection, the use of a uniform contribution
rate, (conditional) indexation and other risk sharing features.[917]

Compulsory membership can take a number of different forms. First, there can be a
general statutory obligation for all employees and/or employers within the scope of a
collective labour agreement to contribute to a pension *account* while the choice for a
provider and a pension plan is free for either the employers or employees. In such a

---

911 See, on this, Case C-67/96, Albany [1999] ECLI:EU:C:1999:430 paras 47-50 in which Albany contends that
the collective agreement restricts access to the market; Case C-437/09 AG2 R Prévoyance v. Beaudout Père et
Fils SARL [2011] ECLI:EU:C:2011:112.

912 M van der Poel, *De houdbaarheid van verplichtgestelde bedrijfstakpensioenfondsen en beroepspensioenregelingen: Toetsing aan het mededingingsrecht en het vrij verkeer van diensten en vestiging* (Expertisecentrum
Pensioenrecht Vrije Universiteit Amsterdam 2013) 57.

913 Article 28 Charter of Fundamental Rights of the European Union.

914 M Heemskerk, *Pensioenrecht* (Boom Juridische Uitgevers 2015) 92.

915 ibid.

916 E. Schols-van Oppen, *Inleiding pensioenrecht* (Wolters Kluwer 2015), 149.

917 D Chen & R Beetsma, 'Mandatory Participation in Occupational Pension Schemes in the Netherlands and
Other Countries: An Update' (2015) No 10/2015-032 Netspar Academic Series, 19-20, available at ssrn.com/
abstract=2670476 accessed 7 January 2020.

system, employees who are outside the scope of a collective agreement may choose their own fund while being under a general obligation to contribute to a pension scheme.[918] Such a system does not appear to exist in the EU. Australia and Chile feature such system.[919]

Second, membership to a specific *pension scheme* can be made mandatory – either by collective agreement or law – while the choice of provider remains (to a certain extent) free for employees. Sweden's occupational pension system, for example, is an example of such a system, which features four main schemes agreed by collective agreements.[920]

Third, membership to a particular pension *provider* can be made mandatory, such as is the case in the Netherlands.[921] The percentage of workers covered by collectively negotiated sectoral pension schemes is roughly the same in the Netherlands and Sweden. In the Netherlands, some collective agreements also dictate the pension provider the employees and employers within a given sector must be affiliated to.[922]

5.2 The Design of Occupational Pension Systems: A Member State Prerogative within the Limits of EU Law

5.2.1 The Organization of National Pension Systems is Subject to the Freedom to Provide Services ...

The European Court of Justice ruled that although it is for the Member States to determine the setup of their occupational pension systems,[923] the Member States must still comply with provisions of Union law in exercising that prerogative. In *Kattner*[924] – a case about mandatory social insurance schemes with mandatory affiliation to one provider –

---

918 ibid 2015.

919 H van Boven, 'Keuzevrijheid van pensioenuitvoerder: een Nederlands model', *Netspar Academic Series Paper* 2017, available at https://www.netspar.nl/assets/uploads/P20170611_Tias-Netspar010_Boven.pdf accessed 7 January 2020.

920 N Barr, *The pension system in Sweden*, Report to the Expert Group on Public Economics of the Swedish Ministry of Finance 2013:7 (Elanders Sverige 2013) 40; L Bovenberg, R Cox & S Lundbergh, 'Lessons from the Swedish Occupational Pension System: Are Mutual Life Insurance Companies a Relevant Model for Occupation Pensions in the Netherlands' (2015) Netspar Industry Paper Series no 45, 19, available at https://pure.uvt.nl/ws/portalfiles/portal/9092186/netspar_design_paper_45.pdf accessed 7 January 2020; K Anderson, *Occupational Pensions in Sweden* (Friedrich Ebert Stiftung 2015), available at http://library.fes.de/pdf-files/id/12113.pdf accessed 3 January 2020. There is the SAF-LO scheme for blue-collar workers, the ITP scheme for white-collar workers, the PA 03 scheme for central government employees and the KAP-KL scheme for county council and municipal employees – and a number of smaller schemes. Within those schemes, employees may freely choose from a number of a limited number of providers pre-selected by the social partners. Around 90 per cent of Swedish employees are covered by an occupational pension scheme, and the majority is covered by one of the four main schemes.

921 H van Meerten & E Schmidt, 'Compulsory Membership of Pension Schemes and the Free Movement of Services in the EU' (2017) 19 (2) European Journal of Social Security 118.

922 Chen & Beetsma 2015 (see footnote 917).

923 Case C-103/06 *Derouin* [2008] ECLI:EU:C:2008:185, para 23.

924 Case C-350/07 *Kattner Stahlbau* [2009] ECLI:EU:C:2009:127.

the Commission and the German government contended that the legislation contested in that case, concerning a system of *statutory* mandatory participation, did not fall within the scope of articles 56 and 57 TFEU, but rather within the power of the Member States alone.[925] The Court quickly disposed of that view and reminded that the Member States must exercise their prerogatives in accordance with freedom to provide services.

For this reason, the notion that the Member States alone are empowered to organise their social security systems, a principle that – according to the Court – stems from "consistent case-law",[926] is a notion that is certainly contestable. Not least because of the caveat made by the Court itself, namely that the Member States are to exercise that prerogative only within the limits to EU law, but also because the EU lawmaker has already passed a multitude of legislative documents directly affecting Member States' pension systems.[927]

5.2.2   ... And so Are the Collective Agreements Prescribing Compulsory Membership

What is more, collective agreements within those national pension systems are also subject to the provisions on the freedom to provide services. Such agreements – in some EU Member States – play a significant role in the organisation of occupational pensions as well as compulsory membership to pension funds or schemes. Collective agreements are among the reasons why in Member States such as The Netherlands, Sweden and Denmark, between 80% and 90% of the working population is covered by an occupational pension scheme.[928]

The collective agreements demanding compulsory membership to a pension scheme or fund have been exempt from the purview of *competition law* by the European Court of

---

925 See also Case C-271/08 *Commission v. Germany* [2010] ECLI:EU:C:2010:426, a case on mandatory occupational pensions, in which the Court came to a similar conclusion. That case is a qualification of Case C-222/98 *van der Woude* [2000] ECLI:EU:C:2000:475, in which the Court decided that the social partners may freely decide on the desired sickness insurance scheme and the managing institution. A few years later, in *Commission v. Germany*, the Court cautioned that other provisions of Union law must be taken into account when exercising national prerogatives, such as public procurement law. In particular, the Court noted that Germany had violated the provisions of Directive 92/50 relating to the coordination of procedures for the award of public service contracts and Directive 2004/18 on the coordination of procedures for the award of public works contracts, public supply contracts and public service contracts. These directives implement the freedom of establishment and the freedom to provide services; See, to this effect, D Seikel & N Absenger, 'Die Auswirkungen der EuGH-Rechtsprechung auf das Tarifvertragssystem in Deutschland' (2014) Vol 22 (1) Industrielle Beziehungen 51, 60; See also P Syrpis, 'Reconciling Economic Freedoms and Social Rights—The Potential of *Commission v. Germany* (Case C-271/08, Judgment of 15 July 2010)' (2011) Vol 40 (2) Industrial Law Journal 222.
926 *Kattner* (see footnote 924). In paragraph 71 of that judgment, the Court cites Case C-158/96 *Kohll* [1998] ECLI:EU:C:1998:171, Case C-157/99 *Smits and Peerbooms* [2001] ECLI:EU:C:2001:404 and Case C-372/04 *Watts* [2006] ECLI:EU:C:2006:325.
927 For instance, the IORP I and II Directives, the Supplementary Pension Rights Directive and the Safeguard Directive.
928 van Meerten & Schmidt 2017 (see footnote 921).

Justice. The same goes for mechanisms for extending the application of a collective agreement to all employers and employees for an entire sector of industry. Such mechanisms exist in some Member States[929] to extend the application to an entire sector, while in others they do not.[930]

Applying competition rules to collective agreements would defy their purpose, said the Court in the *Albany* case, and they should therefore be excluded from those rules "by virtue of their nature and purpose."[931] The Court finds that the collective agreement in question fulfils those requirements. With respect to the agreement's nature, the Court concludes that the agreement at issue in the main proceedings was the product of social dialogue, was concluded in the form of a collective agreement and is the outcome of collective negotiations between organisations representing employers and workers." Second, the purpose of the agreement was to establish a mandatory occupational pensions scheme, which guaranteed a certain level of pension "and therefore contributes directly to improving one if their working conditions, namely their remuneration."

By virtue of the same arguments, the Court ruled that the Dutch government's decision to extend the application of the collective agreement to the entire sector was also legitimate. It decided that, while granting an exclusive right to the pension fund at issue constituted a violation of the competition rules, such a violation could be justified because of the task of general economic interest that the fund performed.

It has, however, been erroneously assumed before the ECJ that this exemption from competition law – as was established, *inter alia*, *Albany* – also means that collective agreements are exempt from the fundamental freedoms, such as the freedom to provide services.[932]

Whereas in *Albany*, the Court exempted the collective agreement in question from the purview of the competition rules, it held in *Viking*[933] that the fact that an agreement or an activity are excluded from the scope of competition law does not mean that that agreement or activity also falls outside the scope of the Treaty provisions on the free movement of persons or services since those two sets of provisions are to be applied in different circumstances.[934] With respect to collective agreements, it held that "the terms of collective agreements are not excluded from the scope of the Treaty provisions on freedom of movement for persons."[935]

---

929 Such as The Netherlands, France, Belgium and Germany.
930 Such as Denmark and Sweden.
931 *Albany* (see footnote 911) paras 59-60.
932 See, for instance, C-341/05 *Laval* [2007] ECLI:EU:C:2007:809, para. 86; Case C-438/05 *Viking* [2007] ECLI:EU:C:2007:772, paras 48-50; Case C-271/08 *Commission v. Germany* [2010] ECLI:EU:C:2010:426, paras 36-45.
933 *Viking* (see footnote 911).
934 *Ibid.*, para. 53.
935 *Ibid.*, para. 54.

The Court followed that line of reasoning in *Commission v. Germany*,[936] a case on compulsory occupational pensions. It embarked on a balancing act similar to the one in *Laval*.[937] In assessing whether EU law had been breached, the Court began by referring to *Laval* and *Viking*, where it recalled that "the terms of collective agreements are not excluded from the scope of the provisions on freedom of movement for persons,"[938] and that the fundamental right to bargain collectively must be exercised in accordance with EU law. The Court held that such a right must be reconciled with the freedoms stemming from the freedoms protected by the Lisbon Treaty,[939] among which is the freedom to provide services.

To conclude, a system of compulsory membership in occupational pensions must comply with the provisions of the Treaty, in particular those on the freedom to provide services.[940] Both the prohibition of discrimination as well as the prohibition of other restrictions are basic tenets of market access. But although the freedom to provide services should be unimpeded in principle, this freedom is not absolute: obstacles to free movement may be justified.

5.2.3 Compulsory Membership: An Obstacle to the Freedom to Provide Services?

Compulsory membership can be an obstacle to the freedom to provide services. Such agreements can restrict or hinder the two components of the freedom to provide services – the freedom to provide services and that to receive services[941] – by obstructing or preventing market access for pension providers from other Member States.[942] In the Netherlands, for instance, non-Dutch pension funds are statutorily barred[943] from operating compulsory sectoral pension schemes.[944] Affiliation to a particular fund or scheme can be made mandatory as a result of a statutory obligation, or as a result of collective agreements that may or may not have been made generally applicable by ministerial decision. In Sweden, collective bargaining agreements can prevent market access by appointing a set number of eligible providers from which pension scheme members can choose.[945] Germany has recently passed a new law[946] increasing the role of social partners in occupational pension provision with a view to increasing the coverage of such pension

---

936 *Commission v. Germany* (see footnote 932).
937 *Laval* (see footnote 932).
938 *Commission v. Germany* (see footnote 932) para. 42
939 ibid para. 44.
940 *Kattner* (see footnote 924) para 76.
941 Cases 286/82 and 26/83, *Luisi & Carbone*, [1984] ECLI:EU:C:1984:35.
942 See, for instance Kattner (see footnote 924).
943 Kamerstukken II 2006/07, 28 294, 29.
944 Van Meerten & Schmidt 2017 (see footnote 915).
945 Bovenberg, Cox & Lundbergh 2015 (see footnote 920) 16.
946 Gesetz zur Stärkung der betrieblichen Altersversorgung und zur Änderung anderer Gesetze (Betriebsrentenstärkungsgesetz) Vom 17. August 2017

in Germany; the so-called *Sozialpartnermodell*,[947] potentially also limiting the freedom to provide services for pension providers by enabling social partners to (pre-)select a (number of) providers. As a consequence of the wording in the IORP II Directive, such arrangements fall under national social and labour legislation.

In order to find out whether a system of compulsory membership is an obstacle to the freedom to provide services, it is necessary to gauge whether the system 1) is likely to restrict the ability of providers established in other Member States to offer their services relating to some or all of the risks in question on the market of the first Member State and, 2) whether it discourages undertakings established in that first Member State, in their capacity as recipients of services, from taking out pension services with a provider in another Member State.[948]

If a restriction to the freedom to provide services is found, such restrictions may be justified where that restriction reflects overriding requirements relating to the public interest, is suitable for securing the attainment of the objective which it pursues and does not go beyond what is necessary in order to attain it.[949]

6   OBSTACLE NO. 2 TO THE FREEDOM TO PROVIDE SERVICES: NON-RECOGNITION
     OF THE IORP BY HOST STATE LEGISLATION

The IORP II Directive defines an IORP as "an institution, irrespective of its legal form, operating on a funded basis, established separately from any sponsoring undertaking or trade for the purpose of providing retirement benefits in the context of an occupational activity on the basis of an agreement or a contract agreed [individually or collectively] and which carries out activities directly arising therefrom."[950] As a consequence, institutions that are to be considered IORPs within the meaning of the Directive must be allowed to carry out cross-border activities.[951]

On the other hand, the Member States ought to "retain full[952] responsibility for the organisation of their pension systems" and in the context of the second pillar "they should also retain full responsibility for the role and functions of the various institutions providing occupational retirement benefits, such as industry-wide pension funds, company pension funds and life insurance undertakings"[953] Accordingly, Member States have set requirements that regulate which types of pension providers may operate occu-

---

947 J. Zülch, 'Das Sozialpartnermodell nach dem Betriebsrentenstärkungsgesetz' (*Heldt, Zülch & Partner*) available at http://www.heldt-zuelch.de/das-sozialpartnermodell-nach-dem-betriebsrentenstaerkungsgesetz/ accessed 7 January 2020.
948 *Kattner* (see footnote 924) para 77.
949 *Kattner* (see footnote 924) para 84.
950 Article 6(1) IORP II.
951 Article 11 IORP II.
952 Chapters 2 and 3 have qualified that prerogative.
953 Recital 19 IORP II.

pational pension schemes within their territory, for instance with regard to their legal personality.

The question then arises whether pension providers from other Member States may operate pension schemes even if they do not comply with the requirements set by the legislation of a given Member State. Bittner, who appears to be the only one to have dealt with this question, calls providers who do not fall within the ambit of recognized providers "atypical providers."[954]

With its five so-called *Durchführungswege* or implementation paths for occupational pensions,[955] it seems that Germany is particularly strict in its definition of eligible providers for the provision of occupational pension schemes. The five implementation paths are *Direktzusage* (direct pension commitment),[956] *Unterstützungskasse* (support funds),[957] *Direktversicherung* (direct insurance),[958] *Pensionskasse*[959] and *Pensionsfonds*.[960] Consequently, there are five possible pension providers that can operate occupational pension schemes in Germany, which Bittner qualifies as a *numerus clausus*.[961]

This *numerus clausus*, according to Bittner, presents a non-discriminatory obstacle to the freedom to provide services, as it excludes atypical providers regardless of where they are established.[962] As a consequence, all IORPs, including those from other Member States, that do not fall within the scope of one of the five *Durchführungswege* are barred from operating occupational pension schemes in Germany, and German employers are unable to choose an "atypical" pension provider.

In principle, all requirements that hinder market access to cross-border IORPs from other Member States by not recognising them as an eligible provider are an obstacle to the freedom to provide services. The justification for an exclusion of categories of IORPs will be discussed below in Section 9.

---

954 C Bittner, *Europäisches und internationales Betriebsrentenrecht* (Mohr Siebeck 2000) 186.

955 Article 1(1) BetrAVG

956 This is a direct commitment by the employer to an employee or a group of employees to pay a promised level of occupational retirement benefits. The funding of the direct commitment is internal within the company. See §1(1) BetrAVG.

957 A separate institution with legal capacity established to provide occupational retirement benefits, without any legal claim to benefits. See §1b(4) BetrAVG.

958 The employer takes out a life insurance policy for the benefit of employee(s). See §1b(2) BetrAVG.

959 Artt. 232-235a Insurance Supervision Act (VAG). A *Pensionskasse* is a life insurance undertaking whose purpose is the protection against a loss of income due to old age, invalidity or death. *Pensionskassen* are subject to the provisions that apply to small insurance undertakings to the extent that these provisions refer to life insurance and no special regulations exist. See https://www.bafin.de/EN/Aufsicht/VersichererPensi onsfonds/Einrichtungen_bAV/System/system_bav_node_en.html accessed 7 January 2020.

960 Artt. 236-243 Insurance Supervision Act (VAG). A *Pensionsfonds* is a pension institution that offers occupational retirement provision in the form of funded pension schemes for one or several employers. The greatest difference between a *Pensionsfonds* and a *Pensionskasse* is that a *Pensionsfonds* may

961 Bittner 2000 (see footnote 954) 187 et seq; see also A Schlewing et al, *Arbeitsrecht der betrieblichen Altersversorgung* (Verlag Dr. Otto Schmidt 2019) 101.

962 Bittner 2000 (see footnote 954) 189 et seq.

7   OBSTACLE NO. 3 TO THE FREEDOM TO PROVIDE SERVICES: NON-RECOGNITION
     OF THE PENSION SCHEME

This section will study again the security mechanisms in host State legislation, as studied
in Part 1, Section a of Chapter 4, but this time from the perspective of an IORP pursuing
cross-border activity. The introduction of this chapter noted that the differences in national legislation – in particular national social and labour law – are named as one of the
primary reasons why so few cross-border IORPs have been set up so far. It is said that, for
cross-border IORPs, complying with local legislation is complicated and costly, and that
the necessity to set up a local scheme in each jurisdiction is cumbersome.[963] The obligation for schemes operated by cross-border IORPs to respect host State social and labour
legislation requires thorough knowledge of the legislation of other Member States. Even if
that profound knowledge is present, disagreement could still potentially arise between a
cross-border IORP and a host State's supervisory authorities in case the latter is not
convinced of the scheme's compliance with local legislation.

Applicable social and labour legislation, while in most cases undoubtedly a boon to
scheme members, may pose an obstacle to cross-border IORPs' operation of a pension
scheme. This would be the case if the pension scheme does not comply with the requirements set by national law, such as in respect of the security mechanisms discussed in
Chapter 4.

For instance, Dutch pension legislation[964] requires old age occupational pension
schemes to provide for fixed or variable benefits.[965] Suppose an IORP from a Member
State outside the Netherlands would like to operate a pension scheme that it wishes to
market as one providing *fixed benefits*. The Dutch supervisory authority determines
whether the scheme may be marketed as one providing fixed benefits. However, the
Dutch Pension Act does not provide a definition of "fixed benefits." The Act's Explanatory Memorandum notes that the term "fixed benefit" was included in the Pensions Act
in order to underscore that the benefits may not fluctuate after retirement on the basis of
uncertain factors.[966] It therefore seems that, logically, the onus to provide such fixed
benefits is on the employer and/or the IORP. The hypothetical IORP's scheme does not
feature a sponsor support obligation that could make up for any shortfalls, and clearly
states that there is a possibility that benefits will be reduced under adverse conditions. In

---

963 F Brigant, 'Guest viewpoint: Francesco Briganti, EBWI Employee Benefits and Welfare Institute' (*IPE Magazine*, May 2017) available at https://www.ipe.com/analysis/guest-viewpoint/guest-viewpoint-francesco-bri
ganti-ebwi-employee-benefits-and-welfare-institute/10018610.article accessed 4 January 2020.
964 Article 1 Dutch Pension Act (Pw).
965 Variable pension benefits are dependent on investment results. The amount of the benefits is redetermined
each year as a function of investment results. In either case (fixed or variable benefits), the benefits must be
lifetime benefits. See the explanatory memorandum to the *Wet variabele pensioenuitkering*, Kamerstukken II
2014/15, 34 344, nr. 3.
966 Kamerstukken II 2005/06, 30 413, nr. 3 (Memorie van Toelichting Pensioenwet).

addition, Dutch pension legislation features the option of cutting pension benefits under certain circumstances in the event of a funding shortfall.[967]

Given this possibility for Dutch pension funds to reduce benefits under certain circumstances, the notion of a "fixed benefit" under Dutch law seems illusory. Whether the scheme qualifies as one providing "fixed benefits" seems debatable. The scheme does not have a sponsor support obligation, and includes the possibility of reducing benefits. However, Dutch pension providers also have the possibility to reduce benefits.

In the example provided above, the result is that the cross-border IORP cannot become active in the Netherlands if the supervisory authority refuses to authorise the scheme as one providing a fixed benefit. Given the Court of Justice's broad understanding of what constitutes an obstacle to the freedom to provide services, even though the IORP II Directive is explicitly deferent to national social and labour law, it seems clear that national requirements for occupational pension schemes that are to be observed by pension providers from other Member States may constitute an obstacle to market access for cross-border IORPs.[968] It seems, however, that since social and labour law provisions are primarily meant to protect pension scheme members and retirees, they can be justified. Section 9 will consider justifications for these obstacles.

This example could be extended to any of the security mechanisms discussed in Part 1, Section a of Chapter 4 if an IORP does not or cannot comply with it. In most cases, however, it seems that social and labour law obligations that set requirements for the pension scheme do not seem to be in most cases outright barriers to market entry, but rather requirements that could merely increase the costs of service provision.[969] The argument that social and labour legislation should not be sacrificed at the altar of the freedom to provide services seems right, given its importance for the protection of pension scheme members.

8   OBSTACLE NO. 4 TO THE FREEDOM TO PROVIDE SERVICES: CONDITIONS APPLICABLE TO THE TRANSFER OF PENSION RIGHTS TO AN IORP FROM ANOTHER MEMBER STATE

Part 2 of Chapter 4 discussed the (lack of) an option for individual transfer options for occupational pension rights in EU law. It found that the transferability of pension rights for individuals is frequently made more difficult by national legislation or the conditions of the pension scheme. EIOPA noted that not only do rules between EU Member States vary widely, but also that that it is generally very difficult or even impossible for individuals to transfer their accrued rights from one scheme to another. If transfers are allowed,

---

967 Article 134 of the Pension Act. This possibility is a measure of last resort.
968 See Section 4 above.
969 *Keck* (see footnote 909). See section 4.2.

the rules are generally very restrictive. That chapter also discussed the position of pension scheme members vis-à-vis their right to free movement.

From the perspective of the freedom to provide services for IORPs, restrictive transfer rules can also form an obstacle to the freedom to provide services. In the case of individual transfers, neither the pension scheme member intending to transfer his or her accrued pension rights, nor the IORP that is intended to receive the accrued rights can benefit from the freedom to provide services. In the case of collective scheme transfers, by which the rights of all members and beneficiaries of a pension scheme are to be transferred, legislation barring or encumbering such transfers form, by analogy to the previous case of individual transfers, an obstacle to the freedom to provide services.

As noted in the previous chapter, the IORP II Directive has introduced a new procedure for *collective* cross-border transfers of pension schemes. Article 12 IORP II specifies that Member States must allow IORPs registered or authorized in their territories to be able to "transfer all or a part of a pension scheme's liabilities, technical provisions, and other obligations and rights, as well as corresponding assets or cash equivalent thereof, to a receiving IORP." This provision seems to give effect to the principle of mutual recognition, the operation of which has seemingly been made less problematic by the reinforcement of the prudential requirements in IORP II.

The Directive requires that collective cross-border transfers are subject to prior approval by a majority of members and a majority of the beneficiaries concerned or, where applicable, by a majority of their representatives.[970] What constitutes a majority is to be defined by national law. The information on the conditions of the transfer shall be made available to the members and beneficiaries concerned and, where applicable, to their representatives before the application for a transfer is submitted. The sponsoring undertaking, if there is one, must also give its approval to the transfer.[971]

Where legislation governing the transfer of accrued pension rights differentiates between domestic and cross-border transfers, a breach of the free movement provisions seems evident.[972] Van Meerten & Slagmaat[973] and Van Meerten & Geerling[974] argue that even the IORP II Directive itself is in contravention with primary EU law on account of the fact that it sets requirements for cross-border transfers that it does not apply equally to domestic transfers.

But even if legislation governing transfers makes no distinction between domestic and cross-border transfers, the free movement provisions – including the free movement of workers and services – can still be breached if the effect is to hinder or render less attrac-

---

[970] Article 12(3)(a) IORP II.
[971] Article 12(3)(b) IORP II.
[972] H van Meerten & L Geerling, 'Build that wall? Het onderscheid tussen binnenlandse en grensoverschrijdende waardeoverdrachten van pensioenregelingen' (2019) No 2 Tijdschrift voor Recht en Arbeid 11.
[973] H van Meerten & M van Slagmaat, 'Implementatie IORP II roept vragen op' (2017) Pensioen & Praktijk 5.
[974] Van Meerten & Geerling 2019 (see footnote 972).

tive "the exercise by Community nationals of the fundamental freedoms guaranteed by the Treaty."[975]

9 JUSTIFYING RESTRICTIONS ON THE FREEDOM TO PROVIDE SERVICES: GENERAL

9.1 Introduction

Now that the obstacles to the free movement of services for IORPs have been discussed, the next step is to explore under which circumstances such a restriction may be justified. The justification for obstacles to the freedom to provide services in general will be discussed before a discussion of the four specific obstacles studied in the previous sections.

Justification of breaches of the fundamental freedoms – the free movement of goods, services, workers and capital – serves as "a necessary safety valve" to safeguard sensitive matters of national concern.[976] Such justifications may, under certain circumstances to be discussed below, also be used to protect national pension systems. The grounds for justification differ depending on whether the obstacles in question discriminate indirectly or is non-discriminatory. These grounds will be discussed below.

The exceptions to the freedom to provide services can be found in the Treaty itself in the explicit grounds for derogations found in a number of Treaty provisions. First, article 51 *juncto* 62 TFEU disapplies the provisions on the freedom to provide services for activities that are connected with the exercise of official authority. Second, article 52 TFEU provides grounds for justification in three specific instances, namely for "special treatment of foreign nationals on the grounds of public policy, public security or public health."

In addition to the Treaty exceptions, the ECJ has developed in its case law a number of criteria that may justify restrictions on the free movement clauses in the Treaty.[977]

It must be noted at this point that the first Treaty exception, that of the exception ground for the exercise of official authority, is interpreted narrowly by the Court; the mere circumstance that some tasks in a Member State are provided by public authorities cannot be used to successfully invoke Article 51 TFEU.[978] Rather, the activity must be connected directly and specifically with the exercise of official authority. The exercise of official authority "is that which arises from the sovereignty and majesty of the State; for

---

975 See See Case C-212/06, *Gouvernement de la Communauté française and Gouvernement wallon* [2008] ECLI: EU:C:2008:178 para 45 and the case law quoted there; Case C-379/09 Casteels [2011] ECLI:EU:C:2011:131. See also L van der Vaart & H van Meerten, 'De pensioen opPEPPer?' (2018) 1 Tijdschrift voor Pensioenvraagstukken 38.

976 S Weatherill, '*Viking and Laval*: The EU Internal Market Perspective' in M Freedland & J Prassl (eds), *EU Law in the Member States*: Viking, Laval and Beyond (Hart Publishing 2014) 34.

977 D Cahill et al, *European Law* (Oxford University Press 2011) 36.

978 F Weiss & C Kaupa, *European Union Internal Market Law* (Cambridge University Press 2014) 210.

him who exercises it, it implies the power of enjoying the prerogatives outside the general
law, privileges of official power and powers of coercion over citizens."[979] Pension services
do not fall under such activities.

9.2   Justifying Discriminatory Measures

Discriminatory measures may be justified in principle *only* by the derogations mentioned
explicitly in Article 52 TFEU *juncto* 62 TFEU, however the Court has over the years also
used the rule of reason for directly discriminatory obstacles, as will be explained below.[980]
The derogations in Article 52 TFEU are public policy, public security and public health.

The Court interprets the exceptions narrowly. On the other hand, the Court generally
allows Member States "considerable discretion" to define their own requirements in respect of public policy, public security and public health.[981] For instance, in the *Alpine
Investments* case, the Court accepted that a measure that was implemented out of concern
for the protection of the reputation of the Dutch financial sector can be an acceptable
justification for a restriction on the freedom to provide financial services.[982]

As public security and public health are not at issue in the context of occupational
pensions, only the public policy exception will be discussed here.

The public policy exception, in its application to companies, is "governed by the
Treaty and by the general principles of EU law, and more recently by the relevant provisions of the Services Directive."[983] That directive gives an explanation of what the public
policy exception entails. Although the Services Directive[984] does not appear to apply to
occupational pensions[985] its interpretation of the public policy exception is nonetheless
instructive.

---

979 Case 2/74 *Reyners* [1974] opinion of AG Mayras ECLI:EU:C:1974:59.
980 C Barnard, *The Substantive Law Law of the EU: The Four Freedoms* (6ᵗʰ edn Oxford University Press, 2019)
214.
981 Weiss & Kaupa 2014 (see footnote 978) 209.
982 H van Meerten & JC van Haersolte, 'Zelfrijzend Europees Bakmeel: de Voorstellen Voor Een Nieuw Toezicht Op de Financiële Sector' (2010) No 2 Nederlands Tijdschrift voor Europees Recht 33, 34.
983 P Craig & G de Búrca, *EU Law: Text, Cases and Materials* (5th edn, Oxford University Press 2011) 770.
984 Directive 2006/123/EC of the European Parliament and of the Council of 12 December 2006 on services in
the internal market [2006] OJ L 376/36 (Services Directive).
985 ibid, Recital 18: "Financial services should be excluded from the scope of this Directive since these activities
are the subject of specific Community legislation aimed, as is this Directive, at achieving a genuine internal
market for services. Consequently, this exclusion should cover all financial services such as banking, credit,
insurance, including reinsurance, occupational or personal pensions, securities, investment funds, payments
and investment advice, including the services listed in Annex I to Directive 2006/48/EC of the European
Parliament and of the Council of 14 June 2006 relating to the taking up and pursuit of the business of credit
institutions." This broad-brush exclusion should perhaps be taken with a grain of salt. Arguably, particular
aspects of the excluded financial services that are not governed by their own directives still fall within the
remit of the Services Directive. See to that effect H van Meerten, 'Vrij verkeer van diensten voor verzekeraars
en pensioeninstellingen: Solvency II basic en de verplichtstelling' (2012) No 7/8 Tijdschrift voor Financieel
Recht 291-292.

The Services Directive describes that exception as follows: "The concept of 'public policy', as interpreted by the Court of Justice, covers the protection against a genuine and sufficiently serious threat affecting one of the fundamental interests of society and may include, in particular, issues relating to human dignity, the protection of minors and vulnerable adults and animal welfare."[986] This definition originates from the *Bouchereau* case.[987]

It is also possible to derogate from EU law, such as the freedom to provide services, by invoking fundamental rights on public policy grounds.[988] The Court has accepted this possibility explicitly in *Omega*.[989] The public policy exception can be invoked in the context of occupational pensions, for instance in order to protect the rights of the elderly to lead a life of dignity and independence and to participate in social and cultural life, as enshrined in Article 25 of the Charter of Fundamental Rights of the European Union, or the right to bargain collectively.

The Member States may not take unlimited advantage of the possibility to use public policy exceptions, but must take account of the purpose of the Directive and the fundamental freedoms of the Directive.[990] The fact that the public policy exception is to be interpreted narrowly has been stated repeatedly by the Court.[991] In addition, "measures which restrict the freedom to provide services may be justified on public policy grounds only if they are necessary for the protection of the interests which they are intended to guarantee and only in so far as those objectives cannot be attained by less restrictive measures."[992] Moreover, the particular circumstances justifying recourse to the concept of public policy may vary from one country to another and from one period to another, and it is therefore necessary in this matter to "allow the competent national authorities an area of discretion within the limits imposed by the Treaty."[993]

---

986 Services Directive (see footnote 984) Recital 41.

987 Case C-30/77 *Bouchereau* [1977] ECLI:EU:C:1977:172.

988 O Cherednychenko, 'Fundamental Rights, European Private Law, and Financial Services' in H Micklitz (ed), *Constitutionalization of European Private Law (Vol. XXII/2)* (Oxford University Press 2014) 173.

989 Case C-36/02 *Omega* [2004] ECLI:EU:C:2004:614.

990 Case C-319/06 *Commission v. Luxembourg* [2007] opinion of AG Trstenjak ECLI:EU:C:2007:516.

991 See, to this effect, footnote 18 of the Opinion of AG Trstenjak in *Commission v. Luxembourg* (see footnote 990) "In that regard the Court has always emphasised that the public policy exception constitutes a derogation from the fundamental principle of freedom of movement, which, as is the case with all exceptions from fundamental Treaty principles, must be interpreted strictly and the scope of which cannot be determined unilaterally by the Member States. See Case 67/74 *Bonsignore* [1975] ECR 297, paragraph 6; Case 36/75 *Rutili* [1975] ECR 1219, paragraph 27; Case 30/77 *Bouchereau* [1977] ECR 1999, paragraph 33; Case C-348/96 *Calfa* [1999] ECR I-11, paragraph 23; Joined Cases C-482/01 and C-493/01 *Orfanopoulos and Oliveri* [2004] ECR I-5257, paragraphs 64 and 65; Case C-503/03 *Commission v. Spain* [2006] ECR I-1097, paragraph 45; Case C-441/02 *Commission v. Germany* [2006] ECR I-3449, paragraph 34; and Case C-50/06 *Commission v. Netherlands* [2007] ECR I-4383, paragraph 42."

992 *Omega* (see footnote 989) para 36.

993 *Commission v. Luxembourg* (see footnote 990) para. 42.

9.3   Justifying Indirectly Discriminatory and Non-Discriminatory Measures

In addition to the explicit Treaty derogations, the Court has developed an open category of justificatory grounds – so-called public interest requirements[994] or rule of reason – that can be used by Member States for the justification of indirectly discriminatory *as well as* non-discriminatory national rules. In addition, Article 52 TFEU can also be used to justify indirectly-, as well as non-discriminatory measures.[995] The Court has, however, granted the use of the public interest requirements also in the case of directly discriminatory measures in a few instances.[996]

Public interest justifications may concern the protection of certain national interests which are "worthy of protection (such as consumer protection, worker protection and cultural policy) which are compatible with the objectives of the EU, and which should take precedence over the free movement provisions".[997] It is an open-ended category, and examples of interests accepted as grounds for justification include consumer protection,[998] the cohesion of the tax system,[999] the financial equilibrium of social security systems[1000] and the protection of employees and the labour market.[1001]

In its case law, specifically in its *Gebhard*[1002] judgment, the Court formulated the criteria that a restriction of the freedom to provide services must meet. It ruled that "national measures liable to hinder or make less attractive the exercise of fundamental freedoms guaranteed by the Treaty must fulfil four conditions: they must be applied in a non-discriminatory manner; they must be justified by imperative requirements in the general interest; they must be suitable for securing the attainment of the objective which they pursue; and they must not go beyond what is necessary in order to attain it."[1003]

Justifying Directly Discriminatory, Indirectly Discriminatory and Non-Discriminatory Measures: Proportionality

All justifications for measures curtailing the freedom to provide services are to be subject to a proportionality test, regardless of whether the measure is directly, indirectly or non-

---

994 Also known as "rule of reason" in the context of the free movement of goods. See Case 120/78 *Cassis de Dijon* [1979] ECLI:EU:C:1979:42, para 8.
995 Weiss & Kaupa 2014 (see footnote 978) 209.
996 See, to that effect, for instance *Smits and Peerbooms* (see footnote 926); Case C-385/99 *Müller-Fauré* [2003] ECLI:EU:C:2003:270; Case C-379/98 *PreussenElektra* [2000] ECLI:EU:C:2001:160.
997 Barnard 2019 (see footnote 980) 217.
998 Case C-393/05 *Commission v. Austria* [2007] ECLI:EU:C:2007:722; Case C-404/05 *Commission v. Germany* [2007] ECLI:EU:C:2007:723.
999 Case C-204/90 *Bachmann* [1992] ECLI:EU:C:1992:35.
1000 Case C-158/96 *Kohll* [1998] ECLI:EU:C:1998:171.
1001 Joined Cases 62/81 and 63/81 *Seco* [1982] ECLI:EU:C:1982:34.
1002 Case C-55/94, *Gebhard* [1995] ECLI:EU:C:1995:411.
1003 ibid para 37.

discriminatory. These are the final two requirements of the *Gebhard* case: suitability and necessity. These entail an assessment of a measure on its aptness to achieve the stated goal, as well as the question whether it goes beyond what is necessary to attain the stated goal.

In order for a measure to be proportionate, a measure must be both appropriate for securing the attainment of the objective pursued and may not go beyond what is necessary for attaining that objective.[1004]

9.4   *Justifying Obstacle No. 1: Compulsory Membership*

It was noted above that compulsory membership to a single pension provider constitutes an obstacle to the freedom to provide services. The question is now under which conditions such an obstacle can be justified.

In order to answer that question, it is useful to first consider the ECJ's relevant case law. In *Albany*, the Court acquiesced fully to the Dutch system of compulsory participation to sectoral pension funds at issue in that case. This compulsory membership is the result of collective bargaining, a process by which one sectoral pension fund as the sole provider for the sectoral pension scheme is appointed, the application of which is then extended to all undertakings and employees of the sector by ministerial decision.

That case, however, was decided in relation to *competition law*. The Court exempted the collective agreement from the competition rules on the grounds that its nature, namely the outcome of a social dialogue, and its goal, to advance worker rights, warranted such a decision. In addition, the Court found that the exclusive right that the pension fund at issue in that case received by ministerial decision was a necessary condition for it to carry out its essential social function.

Had that case been decided under the *freedom to provide services*, it is not unreasonable to assume that the Court would have taken issue with that system: the Dutch system directly excludes non-Dutch providers, a case of direct discrimination. The ECJ decided in its *Viking*[1005] and *Laval*[1006] judgment that, although the protection of social objectives is a recognised goal of the EU, the strategies designed and implemented by the Member States to advance those social objectives should not be so rigorous that they breach EU law provisions, such as the freedom to provide services.[1007] Those cases showed that,

---

1004 See, for instance, Joined Cases C-171/07 and C-172/07 *Apothekerkammer des Saarlandes* [2009] ECLI: EU:2009:316; Case C-169/07 *Hartlauer* [2009] ECLI:EU:C:2009:141.
1005 *Viking* (see footnote 932).
1006 *Laval* (see footnote 932).
1007 *Viking* para 88 et seq; *Laval* para 108 et seq.

although collective agreements are exempt from the competition rules, they are still within the remit of the freedom of movement provisions. That finding was echoed in later case law by the Court in *Commission v. Germany*[1008] and *UNIS*,[1009] where the Court explicitly noted that the social partners as well as the public authorities in the Member States must observe the requirements stemming from *inter alia* the freedom to provide services.

For the freedom to provide services for IORPs, any type of compulsory membership that can limit market access for IORPs can be seen as an obstacle to the freedom to provide services. It seems that this is in particular the case for the third type of compulsory membership discussed in Section 5: the membership to a particular pension *provider*. But also compulsory membership to a pension scheme can limit market access for IORPs if there is a pre-selection for providers, to the exclusion of all providers who have not been selected to be eligible to operate the scheme in question.

When it comes to justifying this obstacle to the freedom to provide services, there can be a number of avenues to take.

Directly Discriminatory Forms of Compulsory Membership

As noted previously, under the freedom to provide services, directly discriminatory measures may be justified in principle only on grounds of public policy, public health or public security. Of those three, it seems that only public policy would lend itself as a possible ground for exception in the context of compulsory affiliation. The Member States may not take unlimited advantage of the possibility to use public policy exceptions, but must take account of the purpose of the Directive and the fundamental freedoms of the Directive.[1010]

IORP II specifically aims to further the Single Market for occupational pensions, and for that reason gives specific expression to the freedom to provide services in the area of

---

1008 *Commission v. Germany* (see footnote 932). On this judgment, see among others Y Stevens, 'Het Europees recht en het sociaal recht nogmaals onder hoogspanning: de Albany voorwaarde getest op de openbare aanbesteding', (2011) (2) *Chroniques de droit social/Sociaalrechtelijke kronieken*, 61; Syrpis 2011 (see footnote 925) 222-229.
1009 Joined Cases C-25/14 and C-26/14, *UNIS*, [2015], ECLI:EU:C:2015:821.
1010 Case C-319/06 *Commission v. Luxembourg* [2007] opinion of AG Trstenjak ECLI:EU:C:2007:516.

occupational pensions. It is consistent case law of the Court that the public policy exception is to be interpreted narrowly.[1011] In addition, "measures which restrict the freedom to provide services may be justified on public policy grounds only if they are necessary for the protection of the interests which they are intended to guarantee and only in so far as those objectives cannot be attained by less restrictive measures."[1012]

As noted above, the Dutch system of compulsory membership for sectoral pension schemes discriminates directly against non-Dutch providers. The Dutch Act on Compulsory Membership of a Sectoral Pension Fund 2000 empowers the Dutch Minister of Social Affairs and Employment to make participation in a sectoral pension fund (known in the Netherlands as a *bedrijfstakpensioenfonds*, or 'Bpf') of a particular sector of industry mandatory at the request of a 'significant majority' of social partners in that sector. As a consequence of such a ministerial decision, in principle all those who fall within its scope must participate in the sectoral pension fund. This mechanism can also be found in Belgium, France and Germany. However, the Dutch system seems unique in the sense that it explicitly disallows non-Dutch pension providers from operating sectoral pension schemes.[1013]

It is not easy to see how this outright exclusion of non-Dutch providers could fall under the public policy exception. Additionally, even if one accepts that this type of compulsory membership could theoretically lend itself to the rule of reason exception, as the Court has accepted in a number of occasions involving directly discriminatory measures, one is presented with the question as to which justification could be invoked. Could the Court's findings in the *Albany* judgment, for instance, in the field of competition law be applied by analogy to the freedom to provide services?[1014] In that case, the Court found that the pension scheme's features of solidarity protecting the interests of pension scheme members justified a restriction of the competition rules. Whether or not Article 106(2) TFEU, which allows Member States to derogate from certain provisions of European law for the organisation of services of general economic interest, applies also to

---

1011 See, to this effect, footnote 18 of the Opinion of AG Trstenjak in Case C-319/06 (see footnote 1010): "In that regard the Court has always emphasised that the public policy exception constitutes a derogation from the fundamental principle of freedom of movement, which, as is the case with all exceptions from fundamental Treaty principles, must be interpreted strictly and the scope of which cannot be determined unilaterally by the Member States. See Case 67/74 *Bonsignore* [1975] ECR 297, paragraph 6; Case 36/75 *Rutili* [1975] ECR 1219, paragraph 27; Case 30/77 *Bouchereau* [1977] ECR 1999, paragraph 33; Case C-348/96 *Calfa* [1999] ECR I-11, paragraph 23; Joined Cases C-482/01 and C-493/01 *Orfanopoulos and Oliveri* [2004] ECR I-5257, paragraphs 64 and 65; Case C-503/03 *Commission v. Spain* [2006] ECR I-1097, paragraph 45; Case C-441/02 *Commission v. Germany* [2006] ECR I-3449, paragraph 34; and Case C-50/06 *Commission v. Netherlands* [2007] ECR I-4383, paragraph 42."

1012 *Omega* (see footnote 989) para 36.

1013 Van Meerten & Schmidt 2017 (see footnote 921).

1014 Q Detienne & E Schmidt, 'Social Pensions and Market Values: A Conflict?' (2019) Vol 15 (2) Utrecht Law Review 81.

the freedom to provide services seems immaterial to this question as the application of the rule of reason would likely yield the same outcome.[1015]

It seems that solidarity within pension schemes could be used as a valid reason to restrict the free movement of services, given its important function for the social protection of workers. The Court found in several of its judgments that the risk of seriously undermining the financial equilibrium of a social security system may constitute an overriding reason in the public interest capable of justifying an obstacle to the principle of freedom to provide services.[1016] The compulsory affiliation in that scheme ensured the financial equilibrium of the system and, moreover, enabled the scheme at issue "to operate in a way that applies the principle of solidarity."[1017] It was for national courts to determine whether that is the case. In this instance, then, the Court was convinced that solidarity requirements *can* be a reason to restrict the freedom to provide services. However, *Commission v. Germany*[1018] illustrates that the argument of solidarity cannot justify *any* restriction. In this judgment, the Court builds on its *Viking* and *Laval* case law, where it balances "the elusive balance between the economic and the social in the internal market context"[1019] by assessing the arguments brought forward by the German government supporting why the collective agreement at issue should be exempt from the public procurement rules (and, on a more basic level, the freedom to provide services).[1020]

The Court concluded that the arguments that Germany presented in a bid to justify the complete and indefinite disapplication of the procurement rules, propagated by the directives at issue[1021] and giving expression to the freedom to provide services, were inadequate. Among the arguments put forward was the argument of solidarity.[1022] On this point, the Court found that the elements of solidarity brought forward are "not inherently irreconcilable" with the application of a procurement procedure. The Court reached the same conclusion for the three other arguments.

1015 ibid.

1016 See among others Case C-158/96 *Kohll* [1998] CLI:EU:C:1998:171 para 41; Case C-385/99 *Müller-Fauré* [2003] ECLI:EU:C:2003:270, para 73; Case C-372/04 *Watts* [2006] ECLI:EU:C:2006:325, para 103; Case C-173/09 *Elchinov* [2010] ECLI:EU:C:2010:581, para 42; Case C-490/09, *Commission v. Luxembourg*, [2011] ECLI:EU:C:2011:34, para 43; *Kattner* (see footnote 918) para 85-86.

1017 *Kattner* (see footnote 924) para 87.

1018 *Commission v. Germany* (see footnote 932).

1019 P Syrpis 2011 (see footnote 925) 223.

1020 *Commission v. Germany* (see footnote 932) paras 51-67.

1021 Council Directive 92/50/EEC of 18 June 1992 relating to the coordination of procedures for the award of public service contracts [1992] OJ L 209/1 and Directive 2004/18/EC of the European Parliament and of the Council of 31 March 2004 on the coordination of procedures for the award of public works contracts, public supply contracts and public service contracts [2004] OJ L 134/114.

1022 *Commission v. Germany* (see footnote 932), para 57: Germany points out that solidarity is achieved by risk pooling by, *inter alia*, the payment of lifelong annuities as well as the absence of medical examinations as selection criteria.

Although the abovementioned caselaw concerns statutory social security schemes, the considerations within them regarding solidarity could apply by analogy to occupational pensions.

Regardless, it seems that the exclusion of pension providers from other Member States would fail the proportionality test, as it is not apparent that any legitimate interests would be protected by such a rule.

Indirectly or Non-Directly Discriminatory Forms of Compulsory Membership

Indirectly discriminatory or non-discriminatory forms of compulsory membership include compulsory membership to a pension *scheme*, in which case the selection of a pension provider remains free, as well as compulsory membership to a pension *provider*, without a nationality requirement.

There can be very good reasons to make affiliation to a pension *scheme* mandatory, as it allows for scale economies and enhanced risk-sharing, which could improve the pension benefits of workers. The same could be said of compulsory membership to a pension provider. National social policies can be important to protect or improve the working conditions, and are therefore deserving of protection from unbridled free market policies. On the other hand, "[p]rotectionist rules and doctrines can be easily presented as public interest, consumer protection or labour protection measures."[1023]

It seems that systems of compulsory affiliation without a nationality requirement for the provider can be justified. Fundamental rights, such as the right to bargain collectively[1024] or the right for the elderly to lead a life of dignity and independence and to participate in social and cultural life[1025] can be a legitimate interest which, in principle, seems to justify a restriction of the obligations imposed by Community law, even under a fundamental freedom guaranteed by the Treaty, such as the free movement of goods or the freedom to provide services.[1026] And as discussed above, the goal of solidarity within a pension scheme, in which risks are shared, also appears to be a legitimate reason to curtail this freedom.

As the freedom to provide services is one of the fundamental pillars of the EU, "a restriction on that freedom is warranted only if it pursues a legitimate objective compatible with the Treaty and is justified by overriding reasons of public interest; if that is the case, it must be suitable for securing the attainment of the objective which it pursues and not go beyond what is necessary in order to attain it."[1027]

1023 D Leczykiewicz, 'Conceptualising Conflict between the Economic and the Social in EU Law in EU Law after *Viking* and *Laval*' in M Freedland & J Prassl (eds), *EU Law in the Member States*: Viking, Laval *and Beyond* (Hart Publishing 2014) 308.
1024 Its fundamental rights status was accepted in, *inter alia*, Laval in paragraph 90.
1025 Article 25 of the Charter of Fundamental Rights of the European Union.
1026 *Laval* (see footnote 932) para 93.
1027 *Laval* (see footnote 932) para 101.

Finally, when public authorities exercise an exclusive right – such as a ministerial decision to extend the application of a collective agreement to appoint a single body for the administration of an insurance or pension scheme – they must comply with the principle of transparency,[1028] a principle that stems from the principles of equal treatment and non-discrimination. According to the ECJ in *UNIS*, the principle does not necessarily require a public call for tenders, but it does require "a degree of publicity sufficient to enable, on the one hand, competition to be opened up and, on the other, the impartiality of the award procedure to be reviewed."[1029] So, while Member States may create exclusive rights for certain service providers, the principle of transparency must be complied with. This obligation applies also to the social partners.[1030]

Provided that indirectly and non-discriminatory systems of compulsory membership do not violate the proportionality test, we can conclude that there can be legitimate reasons to justify their restrictive effects on the freedom to provide services.

9.5   Justifying Obstacle No. 2: Non-Recognition of the IORP

It was established in Section 6 that national legislation setting requirements as to the legal form of pension providers can be an obstacle to the freedom to provide services.

Discriminatory measures leading to non-recognition of the IORP

An outright ban against IORPs from another Member State seems, in analogy to the previous paragraph on the justification for discriminatory forms of compulsory membership, difficult to uphold.

Non-Discriminatory and Indirectly Discriminatory Measures Leading to Non-Recognition of the IORP

Bittner[1031] argues that the *numerus clausus* imposed by German pension law, which seemingly affects German and non-German providers equally, can be justified with a view to ensuring legal certainty and the protection of workers. She explains that German legislation regulating the financial supervision and/or insolvency of German providers serves to protect German workers and that it is, moreover, not possible to gauge sufficiently the adequacy of the level of protection offered by atypical pension providers.[1032]

1028 *UNIS* (see footnote 1009) para 37.
1029 ibid para 39.
1030 Van Meerten & Schmidt 2017 (see footnote 921) 127-128.
1031 Bittner 2000 (see footnote 954) 190 et seq.
1032 ibid 192.

Since this publication by Bittner,[1033] the IORP I and IORP II Directives have been adopted. The IORP I Directive has introduced a system of prudential requirements to be mutually recognised, such as the requirement that cross-border IORPs be fully funded at all times in principle. In addition, all IORPs are to be established separately from any sponsoring undertaking. Moreover, the IORP II Directive has reinforced those requirements and has also introduced extensive governance requirements aimed at ensuring the stability of the IORP and, by extension, the protection of pension scheme members.

In the case of new cross-border activity, which in the case of the present example would entail a non-German IORP accepting scheme sponsorship from a German scheme sponsor/employer for a new pension scheme, the German competent authorities would seemingly not be allowed to block this activity on the basis of apparently insufficient prudential requirements to which the IORP is subject. However, the reinforced prudential requirements in IORP II as well as the German authorities' task of monitoring the IORP's compliance with German social and labour law,[1034] the IORP II Directive seems to offer sufficient safeguards for German pension scheme members whose pension schemes are being operated by an IORP in another Member State.

As noted in Part 2 of Chapter 4, in the case of a transfer of existing pension schemes the competent authorities of the transferring IORP's home Member State, so it appears, also cannot block a transfer on the basis of prudential concerns. However, these authorities must, in accordance with Article 12 IORP II, ensure that the individual entitlements of the members and beneficiaries are at least the same after the transfer. Moreover, those authorities must also assess whether the assets corresponding to the pension scheme to be transferred are sufficient to cover the liabilities in accordance with the requirements of the transferring IORP's home Member State. That should mean that at the time of the transfer, sufficient cash is present to cover the outstanding liabilities at the time of transfer. After the transfer, the requirement of full funding for cross-border IORPs in the IORP II Directive[1035] should ensure that pension scheme members' pension entitlements are backed with sufficient assets. If the aforementioned requirements are not met, the competent authorities of the transferring IORP may refuse the authorisation to transfer.

Considering these measures, it therefore seems that, while the protection of the interests of pension scheme members would be an important ground for justification of an obstacle to the freedom to provide services, an *a priori* exclusion of IORPs that do not match the prescribed requirements cannot pass a proportionality test.

1033 See also C Bittner, 'Occupational Pensions: a Matter of European Concern' (2001) Vol 2 (2) European
Business Organization Law Review 401.
1034 Article 11(10) IORP II.
1035 Article 14(3) IORP II.

10   JUSTIFYING OBSTACLE NO. 3: NON-RECOGNITION OF THE PENSION SCHEME

National requirements for pension schemes can be an obstacle to the freedom to provide services for IORPs in the event that the scheme they intend to operate in another Member State does not comply with said requirements. The IORP II Directive does not regulate the requirements of the pension schemes themselves, and the rules governing these are accordingly set by national legislation.

To the extent that these do not discriminate directly, it appears that such requirements can be justified. The primary goal of social and labour legislation is to protect the interests of the pension scheme members. In the case of the example in Section 7, the requirement that pension schemes in the Netherlands must provide lifetime fixed or variable benefits is of essential importance to the financial position of Dutch scheme members, and therefore worthy of protection against pension schemes that do not offer such protection. In the Netherlands, occupational pensions are, together with the first pillar, the most important source of retirement income.[1036] Income derived from the second pillar therefore functions as an essential, lifetime supplement to pensioners' income from the first pillar.[1037] Because of their role in income provision of retirees, the Dutch government found it undesirable that the income from occupational pensions fluctuates.[1038] Provided that the measure is proportional, the desire to maintain the reliability of this income source by requiring to keep it at a constant level seems to be a necessary measure to ensure the retirement income of Dutch retirees.

Therefore, to the extent that the legislative requirements are not disproportionate, it seems that requirements set by national legislation for pension schemes can be justified in respect of the freedom to provide services.

11   JUSTIFYING OBSTACLE NO. 4: CONDITIONS APPLICABLE TO THE TRANSFER OF
      PENSION RIGHTS TO AN IORP FROM ANOTHER MEMBER STATE

It was discussed in Section 8 that the measures encumbering or barring a cross-border transfer of accrued individual pension rights and indeed entire schemes with all their assets and liabilities can be a breach of the free movement provisions. As noted, some authors opine that the IORP II Directive itself is in contravention with primary EU law on account of the fact that it sets requirements for cross-border transfers that it does not apply equally to domestic transfers.

1036 Kamerstukken II 2014/15, 34 344, nr. 3, p. 2.
1037 ibid 10.
1038 ibid 2.

Discriminatory Measures

To the extent that national legislation governing the transfer of individual pension rights or pension schemes differentiates between domestic and cross-border transfers, it seems evident that those measures represent an obstacle to the freedom to provide services that must be justified.

A cross-border transfer can have far-reaching consequences for pension scheme members, as it leads to the transfer of their acquired rights and future rights to an IORP in another Member State to which another Member States' prudential requirements apply.[1039] Legislation aiming to protect the interests of pension scheme members therefore serves an important sociopolitical goal.

The transfer of whole, or parts of, pension schemes is regulated by Article 12 of the IORP II Directive. The conditions under which such a transfer can be refused are defined in that provision. As discussed previously,[1040] the pension scheme members, their representatives, the scheme sponsor as well as the supervisory authorities all have a say in the transfer process. Based on the specificity wording of that provision, it seems that Member States or, for instance, social partners, may not impose stricter conditions in respect to the aspects covered in Article 12. Aspects of pension scheme transfers not covered by that provision can be regulated at national level. Legislation regulating those aspects not covered by IORP II and that makes a direct distinction between domestic and cross-border transfers, as well as discriminatory legislation covering individual pension transfers, can be justified if those measures pursue a legitimate and proportional objective. Given the involvement, in the case of collective transfers, of multiple parties who can block a transfer, as well as the prudential floor in the IORP II Directive, it seems that the bar is set quite high for Member State legislation that poses an obstacle to such transfers. On the other hand, if such measures are based on a legitimate concern, such as for instance concerns over the prudential standards of IORPs in a particular Member State, it appears that these measures could be justified.

Non-Discriminatory or Indirectly Discriminatory Measures

Non-discriminatory or indirectly discriminatory measures that are obstacles to cross-border transfers seem less burdensome to justify than discriminatory measures. As stated, pension scheme transfers can have far-reaching effects for pension scheme members, whether they occur within a Member State or across borders. In that respect, legislation that ensures that the long-term interests of scheme members and beneficiaries are taken into account and that they are well-informed of the consequences of the transfer are

---

1039 See Chapter 4. See also Kamerstukken I 2018/19, 34934, E, p. 6; Van Meerten & Geerling 2019 (see footnote 972) 12.
1040 See Part 2 of Chapter 4.

necessary, even if they can lead to indirect or non-discriminatory obstacles to cross-border transfers. Provided that the measures are proportional and suitable to serve their aim, it seems that such legislation can be justified.

CONCLUSION TO CHAPTER 5

The discussion in this chapter found that the four categories of obstacles to the freedom to provide services, if they are directly discriminatory, seem difficult to justify. However, if the obstacles are non-discriminatory in nature, it seems that these can in many cases be justified. That conclusion seems to fit in well with the IORP II Directive's intention that "cross-border activity of IORPs should be without prejudice to national social and labour law" of the host Member State.

These provisions of social and labour law, such as the four categories discussed in the previous section, can make it more difficult for cross-border IORPs to become active on a cross-border basis. While the differences in national social and labour legislation are far from the only reasons for the low number of cross-border IORPs (see Section 2), these differences have been identified by a number of respondents to EIOPA's consultations as a (major) contributing factor.

The question is then, from the perspective of the freedom to provide services for cross-border IORP, whether some of these legislative obstacles can be removed where appropriate in order to facilitate cross-border activity for IORPs. The further proliferation of cross-border IORPs seems beneficial to pension scheme members in that cross-border IORPs can provide pension scheme members with advantages in areas such as scale efficiencies and a facilitation of mobility for some groups of workers. While the categories of social and labour law discussed in this chapter can hamper cross-border activity of IORPs, the same provisions of social and labour legislation are important for the protection of pension scheme members. Each of these categories of social and labour legislation serves important goals. For instance, compulsory membership, while it can block market access to IORPs from other Member States, ensures in some EU Member States the enrolment of workers in occupational pension schemes, which is particularly important in States where statutory systems provide only a minimal income. The security mechanisms described in Part 1, Section a of Chapter 4 can make it more difficult for an IORP from another Member State to familiarize itself with the required legislation, but at the same time it can ensure that the promised level of pension benefits to a pension scheme member is kept, and/or that the financial stability of the scheme is ensured. Conditions regarding scheme transfers can hinder cross-border IORPs from taking up business from other Member States, but there can be good reasons to block transfers in the interest of pension scheme members.

A solution that could be introduced to overcome this problem, as well as the legal
uncertainty potentially caused by the IORP II Directive as discussed in the Part 1, Section
a of Chapter 4 and the obstacles to worker mobility discussed in Part 2 of Chapter 4, is the
introduction of a dedicated second regime, organized at EU-level for occupational pensions (2nd pillar) existing alongside the national pension systems of the Member States as
described in Chapter 4.[1041]

CONCLUSION ON CROSS-BORDER IORPs (CHAPTERS 4 AND 5)

The EU's success at regulating the second pillar has, from the perspective of pension
scheme members seen modest success. While some important contributions have been
made to scheme member mobility, a true European market for occupational pensions, in
which pension scheme members can fully reap the advantages of scale economies without
a risk of losing the protection of important security mechanisms, has not yet materialised.
In addition, despite the aforementioned contributions to worker mobility, the current
system of EU occupational pension law still features important shortcomings for mobile
workers.

From a market perspective, the IORP II Directive has been a success in the sense that a
number of European companies have set up cross-border IORPs that appear to satisfy
these employers' needs. The fact that these cross-border IORPs have materialised, despite
remaining obstacles to their cross-border activity, shows that IORPs can be an attractive
solution to employers. However, not only has the number of cross-border IORPs remained fairly low, European occupational pension systems remain fragmented to this
day. From a legal point of view, this fragmentation manifests itself primarily in the areas
of taxation – which is beyond the scope of this dissertation – as well as social and labour
legislation and prudential law. Chapters 4 and 5 have shown that both pension scheme
members as well as cross-border IORPs are affected by this legal fragmentation.

Chapters 4 and 5 have shown that IORPs face different social and labour law challenges than do pension scheme members. While pension scheme members face legal
uncertainty in particular with respect to pension security mechanisms – caused by lacking clarity on the scope of both prudential law and social and labour law – IORPs face
barriers to market entry caused by differences in national legislation. It seems that the
problems identified for pension scheme members can be resolved with reasonable effort
by amending the IORP II Directive, but the obstacles faced by cross-border IORPs could
be more challenging to resolve. This is because the problems for pension scheme members identified in Part 1 of Chapter 4 can seemingly be rectified without defining the
substance of the applicable legislation. On the other hand, the social and labour legislation that IORPs must comply with, which makes their cross-border activity more com-

---

[1041] Conclusion to Part 2 of Chapter 4.

plex and costly, seems to require significant changes to the substance of Member States' occupational pension systems. For this reason, the solution proposed in Section 3.3 of Section a, Part 1, Chapter 4 regarding the adoption of a list of categories of applicable social and labour legislation would not be a solution for IORPs facing barriers to market access in other Member States. For such barriers to be removed, first, the legislation applicable to pension schemes would need to be harmonized to some extent to facilitate less complex cross-border activity. This is a proposition that was clearly rejected during the legislative process of the IORP I Directive.[1042] Such harmonisation could prevent (some of) the differences in national social and labour law discussed in this chapter if the rules applicable to compulsory membership and pension schemes, the types of IORPs that are allowed access to host Member State Markets and rules on transfers were harmonized across the EU. In addition, aspects such as the role and influence of social partners and systems of compulsory membership – equally highly sensitive topics during the directive's genesis – would require changing. Although the EU appears to have the legislative prerogatives to make such changes, it seems unwilling to do so. In addition, an attempt at making such changes in the interest of the freedom to provide services for IORPs would very likely be fiercely opposed by the Member States, and it can be easily imagined that sacrificing the measures enshrined in national pension law that are valuable in protecting the interests of pension scheme members would undermine confidence in the concept of cross-border IORPs. Though it is true that previous EU occupational pension legislation has effectuated changes in national second-pillar systems already – the Safeguard Directive, Supplementary Pension Rights Directive and the IORP Directives have each had significant effects on national systems – it has also become apparent in Chapter 3 with what difficulty these directives have been adopted. All have been watered down to various extents.

Compounding these problematic aspects for pension scheme members and IORPs are a host of other reasons for lacking cross-border activity of IORPs: absent demand, the time and cost associated with setting up a cross-border IORP (due in part to differences in Member States' legislation), differences in tax law and so forth. The discussion in Chapters 2 and 3 has shown that the EU's competences and political latitude for regulating the second pillar were slim. Because of this, it is not to expected that a cross-border IORP revolution solving these problems will take place any time in the foreseeable future.

Given these difficulties, Chapter 6 will study an EU initiative in the third pillar. That chapter will discuss, based on the prerogatives it has to regulate pensions and role of those pillars, whether the EU is perhaps better able to regulate third-pillar pensions and to see whether its initiative in the third pillar can offer a (partial) solution to the problems found for pension scheme members in its regulation of the second pillar.

1042 See Chapter 3.

Chapter 6: PEPP – A Third-Pillar Complement to Second-Pillar EU Pension Law?

1   Introduction

The previous chapters have focused on cross-border IORPs and concluded that the EU legislator's regulation of occupational pensions at the EU level has seen only modest success. Although cross-border IORPs can have considerable advantages to pension scheme members, there are some drawbacks to the current IORP II framework. Those drawbacks seem to affect pension scheme members of cross-border IORPs as well as IORPs wanting to take up business in other Member States than their own home state. The latter are faced with legal as well as non-legal factors complicating their cross-border activity. Pension scheme members face drawbacks with respect to mobility: the current options to transfer individual accrued pension rights seem insufficient and cross-border membership is currently impossible. Cross-border IORPs seem to be able to facilitate some groups of mobile workers, but the full extent of the EU's plans on worker mobility were neither reached by the IORP (II) Directive or the Safeguard and Supplementary Pension Rights Directives. In addition, the current lack of guidance on the concept of social and labour law in relation to cross-border IORPs can be problematic for pension scheme members.

All these problems can be traced back to differences in the legislation between the Member States and the lack of competence of the EU legislature, but also political barriers to take these away. Chapter 3 described that the EU legislator faced active resistance from the Member States and other stakeholders when it attempted to harmonise the above-mentioned aspects of Member States' pension law. This sensitivity surrounding second-pillar pension systems, together with the seemingly limited prerogatives the EU has to interfere directly with Member States' pension systems, appears to be the culprit for these remaining shortcomings of EU occupational pension law. Although the Member States certainly appear to have good reasons for their caution, it appears that European workers, especially mobile workers, pay the price for the lacking coordination of Member States' pension systems.

Could the EU be better placed, then, to provide solutions for (mobile) Europeans in the third pillar, the market for personal pension products? To find out, this chapter will study a recent EU effort in the third pillar: the so-called Pan-European Personal Pension Product (PEPP). PEPPs are private, voluntary retirement products complementary to any statutory or occupational pension product: PEPPs are "available to all individuals who are keen to save for retirement, be they employed, unemployed, in work or in education."[1043] The main apparent advantages of PEPPs in comparison to other third pillar products and occupational pension schemes are the options for portability (i.e. remaining with the same provider and scheme regardless of where one lives and works) and transferability throughout the whole of the EU's territory. The PEPP represents a new initiative taken by the EU in the field of pensions, and its governing Regulation[1044] was recently adopted. It is expected that the first PEPPs will be offered at the end of 2021.[1045] The PEPP initiative is meant to serve in particular mobile Europeans by enabling the portability and transferability of their retirement savings: the proposed Regulation provides the guarantee that PEPP savers can remain with their provider irrespective of where in the EU they work or reside, and also guarantees the possibility for them to change provider. It is also meant as an additional manner for Europeans who do not have (sufficient) access to other means of retirement savings to bolster their old-age provisions.

Although at first glance a comparison of apples and oranges – as opposed to the IORP II Directive, the focus of PEPP Regulation is not on the providers but rather on the product; a Pan-European Pension Product (PEPP) – this chapter will consider the product features of the PEPP, as well as whether the PEPP could provide a solution for mobile European workers who are not (yet) helped by EU pension law.

2   What Is a PEPP?

A PEPP is a personal retirement savings product that is – in principle – in the third pillar. That means that the product can be concluded individually without the involvement of an employer – unlike occupational schemes. The PEPP Regulation standardises several features of the product so as to make cross-border marketability, transferability and portability easier. Article 2(2) PEPP Regulation defines the PEPP as "a long-term savings personal pension product, which is offered by a PEPP provider or PEPP distributor and subscribed to voluntarily by an individual PEPP saver in view of retirement, with no or strictly limited redeemability and which is registered in accordance with this regulation".

1043 European Commission, 'Pan-European Personal Pension Product (PEPP) – Frequently asked questions' Fact Sheet 29 June 2017, available at https://ec.europa.eu/commission/presscorner/detail/en/MEMO_17_1798 accessed 8 January 2020.

1044 Regulation 2019/1238 of the European Parliament and of the Council of 20 June 2019 on a Pan-European Pension Product (PEPP) [2019] OJ L 198/1 (PEPP Regulation).

1045 D Newman, F Webster & S Rousseau, 'EU Advances Pan-European Personal Pension Product (PEPP) Proposal' (Mercer 11 April 2019) available at https://www.mercer.com/content/dam/mercer/attachments/global/gl-2019-eu-advances-pan-european-personal-pension-product-proposal.pdf accessed 8 January 2020.

The PEPP can be described as a "European brand of personal pension product to be distributed on a cross-border basis" or a "wrapper".[1046] This "wrapper" description stems from the fact that the regulation does not seek to harmonise national legislation on personal pension products, but rather defines and standardises a framework within which existing personal pension products can be registered with national competent authorities as PEPPs to be marketed across borders in the EU. The forms of pension payouts are an example: the Regulation does not prescribe a single form of payout but rather obliges PEPP providers to offer PEPP savers four options: annuities, lump sums, drawdown payments or a combination of the previous options.[1047]

The simplicity and safety of PEPPs were key considerations during the legislative process: the Commission, in its Action Plan on Capital Markets Union of September 2015, announced that it "will assess the case for a policy framework to establish a successful European market for simple, efficient and competitive personal pensions, and determine whether EU legislation is required to underpin this market."[1048] In early 2016, the European Parliament expressed its concerns "about the lack of available and attractive risk-appropriate (long-term) investments and cost-efficient and suitable savings products for consumers", and stressed that innovation in financial products is important for the delivery of "adequate, safe and sustainable pensions, such as, for example, the development of a Pan European Pension Product (PEPP), with a simple transparent design."[1049] The Commission announced in the fall of 2016 that it would "consider proposals for a simple, efficient and competitive EU personal pension product."[1050]

One of the ways in which the simplicity and safety are expressed is the PEPP Regulation's provision that allows PEPP providers to offer "PEPP savers",[1051] as it calls PEPP scheme members, a maximum of six investment options that PEPP savers can choose

---

1046 H van Meerten & S Hooghiemstra, 'PEPP—Towards a Harmonized European Legislative Framework for Personal Pensions' (2017) Working paper June 2017, 23 et seq, available at https://ssrn.com/abstract=2993991 accessed 8 January 2020.

1047 Article 58(1) PEPP Regulation (see footnote 1044).

1048 European Commission, 'Communication from the Commission to the European Parliament, the Council, the European Economic and Social Committee and the Committee of the Regions: Action Plan on Building a Capital Markets Union' COM(2015) 468 final, 19.

1049 European Parliament, Resolution of 19 January 2016 on stocktaking and challenges of the EU Financial Services Regulation: impact and the way forward towards a more efficient and effective EU framework for Financial Regulation and a Capital Markets Union, 2015/2106(INI), point 20, available at http://www.europarl.europa.eu/doceo/document/TA-8-2016-0006_EN.html accessed 8 January 2020.

1050 European Commission, 'Communication from the Commission to the European Parliament, the Council, the European Central Bank, the European Economic and Social Committee and the Committee of the Regions: Capital Markets Union – Accelerating Reform' COM(2016) 601 final, 4.

1051 A "PEPP saver" is defined as a natural person who subscribes to a PEPP with a PEPP provider. It should be noted that a PEPP provider need not be 'worker', but can also be a self-employed individual or someone with no occupation at all. See H van Meerten & A Wouters, 'Can A Dutch IORP offer A PEPP' (CBBA-Europe Review 2018) 8-32, available at https://www.cbba-europe.eu/wp-content/uploads/2018/07/CBBA-Europe- review_July-2018.pdf accessed 8 January 2020.

from, including a so-called "Basic PEPP."[1052] This Basic PEPP – apparently aimed at the less adventurous or financially savvy – is a type of default PEPP that should be a "safe product", that is on the basis of a so-called risk-mitigation technique or on the basis of guarantees providing guarantees that "at least cover the contributions during the accumulation phase after deduction of all fees and charges."[1053] The risk-mitigation technique should be "consistent with the objective of allowing the PEPP saver to recoup the capital."[1054] The basic PEPP also provides a cap on costs and charges with a maximum of 1% of the accumulated capital per year.[1055]

3 THE PEPP REGULATION

The regulation is based on Article 114 TFEU. This provision allows for the approximation of laws with a view to advancing the functioning of the EU's internal market. Therefore, the use of Article 114 TFEU has as a consequence that the PEPP Regulation must in the first place focus on the alleviation of any obstacles to the functioning of the internal market,[1056] in this case the ability of providers of personal pension products to offer their products across borders and the ability of European citizens to move to another Member State without being faced with any risks to their personal pension plan.[1057]

In line with the Commission's vision on the benefits of the use of the single market for IORPs, the EU's efforts in buttressing the development of personal retirement savings alongside statutory and occupational pensions was to take advantage of the same principle of realising "further efficiency gains through scale economies, risk diversification and innovation."[1058] The creation of the PEPP was in line with the Commission's 2011 White

---

1052 Article 42(1) and (2) PEPP Regulation.
1053 54th Recital PEPP Regulation.
1054 Article 45(1) PEPP Regulation as well as the 54th recital.
1055 Article 45(2) PEPP Regulation.
1056 M. Reiner & R. Horvath, 'Das neue europäische private Altersvorsorgeprodukt PEPP (Pan European Personal Pension Product) und seine Marktgängigkeut im Binnenmarkt: Eine kritische Intervention' (2018) Working Paper 98/2018 by the University of Applied Sciences BFI Vienna, 8.
1057 9th Recital PEPP Regulation.
1058 EIOPA, 'Towards an EU-single market for personal pensions – An EIOPA Preliminary Report to COM' (2014) EIOPA-BoS-14/029, 4, available at https://eiopa.europa.eu/Publications/Reports/EIOPA-BoS-14-029_Towards_an_EU_single_market_for_Personal_Pensions-_An_EIOPA_Preliminary_Report_to_COM.pdf accessed 8 January 2020. See also van Meerten & Hooghiemstra 2017 (see footnote 1046) 14 et seq.

Paper "An Agenda for Adequate, Safe and Sustainable Pensions",[1059] in which the Commission expressed the goal of developing complimentary retirement savings – which includes occupational and personal pension savings – in accordance with that principle.

From a "Patchwork of Rules" …

The access for personal pension products to the aforementioned benefits of the Single Market was hitherto obstructed by a "patchwork of rules" at EU and national levels, preventing a single market for personal pension products from materialising.[1060] The Commission wished to address the various challenges in the area of personal pension products. In the Commission's view, market fragmentation is an impediment to the exploitation of scale economies, risk diversification and innovation,[1061] driving up costs for consumers and providers alike.[1062] The European Parliament shared these concerns.[1063] The absence of consistent rules and regulations throughout the EU may be a barrier to market entry of providers, while at the same time consumers may suffer from a lack of portability and transferability. "Thus, the fragmented nature of the EU PPP market can

---

1059 European Commission, 'Proposal for a Regulation of the European Parliament and the Council on a Pan-European Personal Pension Product (PEPP)' COM(2017) 343 final, 4. See also European Commission, 'An Agenda for Adequate, Safe and Sustainable Pensions' (White Paper) COM(2012) 55 final, 6: The Commission concludes that complementary retirement savings, which include occupational and personal pensions, life insurance and other forms of asset accumulation that can be used to maintain living standards after retirement, "can also help secure adequate replacement rates in the future. Some countries have introduced measures to complement their public pay-as-you-go pension schemes with private funded schemes, but there is much scope for further development of complementary pension savings opportunities in many Member States. This would require, though, that funded private pension schemes become safer and more cost-effective, as well as more compatible with flexible labour markets and mobility."

1060 European Commission, 'Commission Staff Working Document – Impact Assessment Accompanying the document Proposal for a Regulation of the European Parliament and the Council on a Pan-European Personal Pension Product (PEPP) and Commission Recommendation on the tax treatment of personal pension products, including the pan-European Personal Pension Product' SWD(2017) 243 final, 4.

1061 COM(2017) 343 final, 2.

1062 The Commission notes that "Second, regarding the effectiveness test, action at EU level can help remedy the consequences of market fragmentation, particularly in terms of costs. If no EU action is taken, asset pools are likely to remain small and limited to national borders, without economies of scale, and competition would remain limited to domestic providers. Individual savers are therefore unlikely to benefit from the lower prices and better product ranges that would result from efficiency gains and returns on large asset pools. Fragmentation is expensive also for providers: divergence in national regulation means extra compliance costs. There are limited incentives for providers to offer products cross-border, mainly due to high costs. By contrast, a standardised EU personal pension product is expected to cut providers' costs by creating larger asset pools. For example, a study has shown that spreading fixed costs over a larger pool of members could reduce administration costs by 25 %". See COM(2017) 343 final, 6.

1063 Resolution 2015/2106(INI) (see footnote 1049) point 20.

be clearly reflected in the maze of national rules and approaches applied, rendering any prospects of portability or cross-border supply, improbable."[1064]

… To a "Largely Standardised" Product?

According to the Regulation, its harmonisation of PEPPs' features will lead to the creation "of a largely standardised pan-European product, available in all Member States", allowing consumers to take advantage of the internal market by receiving access to providers throughout the EU and the creation of more competition between providers.[1065] According to the European Commission, that standardisation represents the added value of the PEPP Regulation relative to personal pension products currently in existence, since standardisation "could contribute to making PEPPs less expensive than the already existing personal pension products. [...] Thus, the supply of this partially standardised PEPP would be easier and bring about economies of scale; its take-up would potentially be higher, prompted by better recognition and confidence on the part of customers."[1066]

The PEPP Regulation aims to resolve the problems caused by diverging legislation by bringing about a single market for PEPPs, for the purposes of which the PEPP Regulation harmonizes some product features through a so-called second regime. That regime exists alongside the various national systems in lieu of an initiative that is to alter, replace or harmonise existing national personal pension schemes. The second regime was seen as a necessity to facilitate cross-border activity for the PEPP, since the current rules covering personal pension products differ widely.[1067] This second regime, as will be seen below, also facilitates the PEPP's portability and transferability. The Commission sees the standardisation of the product features as the key to cross-border activity and lower costs.[1068]

Although the PEPP Regulation does standardise a number of product features, it leaves some aspects unregulated, as will be discussed in Section 4.9.[1069] On the one hand, that enables the adaptability of the product to suit the needs of the markets in which it is offered. This flexibility means that technically it should be possible to create a PEPP that in terms of its features does not differ from a traditional DB pension scheme, while at the same time providing the flexibility – for example in terms of portability (see Part 2) – of third-pillar pension product. In that respect, "[a]rguably, 2nd pillar schemes

---

1064 K Borg, A Minto & H van Meerten, 'The EU's regulatory commitment to a European Harmonised Pension Product (PEPP): The Portability of Pension Rights vis-à-vis the Free Movement of Capital' (2019) 5 *Journal of Financial Regulation* 2019 1, 7.
1065 Recital 21 of the PEPP Regulation.
1066 SWD(2017) 243 final, 48.
1067 EIOPA, 'Consultation Paper on the creation of a standardised Pan-European Personal Pension Product (PEPP)' (2015) EIOPA-CP-15/006, 13, available at https://eiopa.europa.eu/Publications/Consultations/ EIOPA-CP-15-006-Consultation-paper-Standardised-Pan-European-Personal-Pension-product.pdf accessed 8 January 2020.
1068 SWD(2017) 243 final, 33 et seq.
1069 See also Reiner & Horvath 2018 (see footnote 1056).

could also be transformed into a PEPP."[1070] On the other hand, matters unregulated by the PEPP Regulation could have as a consequence that the PEPP faces some of the same challenges as occupational pension schemes that are being operated across borders: differences in national legislation.[1071] For that reason PEPPS in the third pillar may have better prospects. The next section will take a closer look at the product features and governance requirements regulated by the PEPP Regulation in order to find out to what extent the PEPP is harmonised.

Part 1: The PEPP on the Single Market

4   PEPP Features

4.1   PEPP Product Features & Governance

The PEPP is an integral part of the Commission's strategy to achieve safe, adequate and sustainable pensions. This section will examine the way PEPPs can be offered in the internal market. The PEPP Regulation's standardisation of a number of the product's features should make the cross-border distribution of PEPPs relatively easier than is the case for cross-border operation of occupational pension schemes, as the Regulation has harmonised a number of product features. This goes in particular for the Basic PEPP. As a consequence of the (partial) harmonisation of product features, all Member States must allow PEPPs to be offered in accordance with the Regulation.

4.2   PEPP Security Mechanisms

This section will consider the security mechanisms[1072] that a PEPP can be equipped with. These security mechanisms are put in place to secure the outcome of the scheme. As will be explained, the security mechanisms available to secure the accrued benefits applicable to the particular PEPP depend not only on the PEPP at issue, but also on the provider of the PEPP. With respect to the latter, the sectoral directives that govern the providers dictate the applicable security mechanisms, except those prescribed in the PEPP Regulation itself which apply to all providers. To that effect, Article 11 of the Regulation stipulates that "PEPP providers and PEPP distributors shall comply at all times with the pro-

---

1070 Borg, Minto & van Meerten 2019 (see footnote 1064) 22.
1071 Reiner & Horvath 2018 (see footnote 1056) list matters such as the contribution design, the details of benefit structures, the basis for the calculation of benefits, risk sharing etc.
1072 Pension security mechanisms serve to protect the scheme against potential dangers, such as low interest rates and disappointing investment returns.

visions of this Regulation, as well as with the relevant prudential regime applicable to
them in accordance with the legislative acts [applicable to them]."

According to Article 6(1) of the proposed PEPP Regulation, there are six different
types of PEPP providers: credit institutions (banks), insurance undertakings, IORPs (to
the extent authorized and supervised under national law to provide personal pension
products), investment firms, investment companies or management companies or alternative investment funds (AIFs). These providers are each bound to comply with their
own sectoral legislation. This means that credit institutions are to comply with the Fourth
Capital Requirements Directive (CRD IV),[1073] insurance undertakings with the Solvency
II Directive,[1074] IORPs with the IORP II Directive,[1075] investment firms with MiFID
II,[1076] investment companies or management companies with UCITS Directive[1077] and,
finally, alternative investment funds with the AIFMD.[1078] The practical consequence of
this regime is that, for instance, pension funds (IORPs) must comply with the IORP II
Directive, whereas insurance companies must comply with the Solvency II Directive, and
that the applicable prudential regime defines the possibilities and limits of a PEPP.[1079]

4.3   PEPP Funding

During the EIOPA consultations, "views were evenly split" among respondents whether
identical solvency standards should apply to all types of PEPP provider offering guaran-

---

1073 Regulated in accordance with Directive 2013/36/EU of the European Parliament and of the Council of
   26 June 2013 on access to the activity of credit institutions and the prudential supervision of credit institutions and investment firms, amending Directive 2002/87/EC and repealing Directives 2006/48/EC and
   2006/49/EC [2013] OJ L 176/338.
1074 Regulated in accordance with Directive 2009/138/EC of the European Parliament and of the Council of
   25 November 2009 on the taking-up and pursuit of the business of Insurance and Reinsurance (Solvency
   II) [2009] OJ L 335/1.
1075 Regulated in accordance with Directive 2016/2341/EU of the European Parliament and of the Council of
   14 December 2016 on the activities and supervision of institutions for occupational retirement provision
   (IORPs) (recast) [2016] OJ L 354/37.
1076 Regulated in accordance with Directive 2014/65/EU of the European Parliament and of the Council of
   15 May 2014 on markets in financial instruments and amending Directive 2002/92/EC and Directive
   2011/61/EU (MiFID II) [2014] OJ L 173/349.
1077 Regulated in accordance with Directive 2009/65/EC of the European Parliament and of the Council of
   13 July 2009 on the coordination of laws, regulations and administrative provisions relating to undertakings for collective investment in transferable securities (UCITS) (recast) [2009] OJ L 302/32.
1078 Regulated in accordance with Directive 2011/61/EU of the European Parliament and of the Council of
   8 June 2011 on Alternative Investment Fund Managers and amending Directives 2003/41/EC and 2009/65/
   EC and Regulations (EC) No 1060/2009 and (EU) No 1095/2010 [2011] OJ L 174/1.
1079 O Boschman, 'Apart toezichtsregime voor pan-Europees persoonlijk pensioenproduct overbodig' (Pensioenpro 20 June 2017).

tees and coverage of biometrical risk – such as the Solvency II regime – or whether sectoral legislation should apply.[1080]

Ultimately, the solvency requirements for the providers of PEPPs are defined in the relevant sectoral legislation. The PEPP Regulation itself is mum on the funding requirements for the product itself, however, which seems to mean that the EU sectoral legislation applicable to the provider – as well as the prudential requirements of the provider's home Member State – indirectly define the funding position of the PEPP. The requirement for full funding, as required for cross-border IORPs, does not appear to exist for PEPPs. Therefore, it seems possible for a PEPP other than a pure DC-type PEPP to be underfunded.

4.4 Guarantees and Biometric Risks

Guarantees

PEPP providers may offer up to six investment options to PEPP savers,[1081] including a Basic PEPP.[1082] Each of the six investment options must be designed on the basis of a guarantee or risk-mitigation technique "which shall ensure sufficient protection for PEPP savers."[1083] In accordance with Article 42 of the PEPP Regulation, only insurance undertakings and credit institutions may provide offer guarantees. It notes that IORPs, UCITS management companies, AIF managers and investment firms may only provide guarantees in cooperation with insurance undertakings or credit institutions, provided that these can "provide such guarantees according to the sectorial law applicable to them. Those institutions or undertakings shall be solely liable for the guarantee."[1084]

The Basic PEPP is to be offered on the basis of a risk-mitigation technique or a guarantee on the capital invested. The risk mitigation technique must be designed to "recoup the capital" invested in the PEPP.[1085] If a guarantee is offered, that guarantee should cover "at least" the contributions during the accumulation phase after deduction of all fees and charges.[1086] "Guarantees could also cover the fees and charges and could provide for full or partial coverage of inflation. A guarantee on the capital invested should be due

---

1080 EIOPA, 'Final Report on Public Consultation No. CP-15/006 on the creation of a standardised Pan-European Personal Pension product (PEPP)' (2016) EIOPA-16-341, 6, available at https://eiopa.europa.eu/Publications/Reports/EIOPA-16-341-Final-Report-PEPP-fin.pdf accessed 8 January 2020.
1081 Article 42(1) PEPP Regulation.
1082 Article 42(2) PEPP Regulation.
1083 Article 42(3) PEPP Regulation.
1084 Article 42(5) PEPP Regulation.
1085 Article 45(1) PEPP Regulation.
1086 54th recital PEPP Regulation. See also Article 45 PEPP Regulation

at the start of the decumulation phase and during the decumulation phase, where applicable."[1087]

Biometric Risks

Only insurance undertakings that can cover those risks according to the sectorial law applicable to them may offer coverage against biometric risks.[1088] Coverage against biometric risks may be provided by credit institutions, IORPs, UCITS management companies, AIF managers and investment firms only "by cooperating with insurance undertakings that can cover those risks according to the sectorial law applicable to them. The insurance undertaking shall be fully liable for the coverage of biometric risks."[1089]

4.5   *Costs and Charges*

In order to achieve the PEPP Regulation's goal of EU-wide portability for PEPPs, the Regulation aims to make it possible to switch providers once every five years after a minimum of five years from the conclusion of the PEPP contract, and, in case of subsequent switching, after five years from the most recent switching.[1090] During the decumulation phase,[1091] however, PEPP providers are not obliged to offer an option to switch providers where PEPP savers are receiving out-payments in the form of lifetime annuities.[1092] The costs for switching providers are capped by the Regulation; the total fees and charges billed to the PEPP saver for the closure of an account by the transferring PEPP provider may amount to no more than 0.5% of the corresponding amounts or monetary value of the assets-in-kind to be transferred to the receiving PEPP provider.[1093] In addition, the Regulation shields PEPP savers from financial loss caused by the PEPP provider during switching process by stipulating that "[a]ny financial loss, including fees, charges and interest, incurred by the PEPP saver and resulting directly from the non-compliance of a PEPP provider involved in the switching process with its obligations under Article 53 shall be refunded by that PEPP provider without delay."[1094] For the purposes of the

---

1087 54th recital PEPP Regulation. See also Article 45 PEPP Regulation.
1088 Article 49(3) PEPP Regulation. Article 2(29) of the Regulation defines biometric risks as the risks linked to death, disability and/or longevity.
1089 ibid.
1090 Article 52(3) PEPP Regulation.
1091 This is the period during which assets accumulated in a PEPP account may be drawn upon to fund retirement or other income requirements.
1092 Article 52(2) PEPP Regulation.
1093 Article 54(3) PEPP Regulation.
1094 Article 55(1) PEPP Regulation. See also recital 67.

switching services, PEPP savers are to have free access to their personal information held by either the transferring or receiving PEPP provider.[1095]

With regard to other costs, the Regulation largely follows the EIOPA technical advice in that it foregoes any other caps on costs while aiming for transparency,[1096] except in the case of the basic PEPP. The Commission explained that taking no action in the area of costs could result in overcharging of consumers, which would allow a fundamental problem in the field of personal pensions to persist, "undermining the attractiveness of these products and limiting returns and outcomes at retirement."[1097] Instead, transparency on costs as achieved by current sectoral legislation (such as PRIIPS, IDD or IORP II) would "establish a level playing field while ensuring consumer protection."[1098] EIOPA, advising the Commission on PEPP, considered that consumers would be sufficiently protected under this solution, although in its Report on the Public Consultation it did leave room for the Member States to set their own limits.[1099] The final Regulation requires that the costs and fees for the Basic PEPP shall not exceed 1% of the accumulated capital per year.[1100]

4.6   *Increasing Premiums*

Providers can under certain circumstances increase the premiums to secure the benefits of DB-type PEPPs or DC-type PEPPs with guarantees. The Regulation does not seem to regulate a possible increase in pension contributions. Sectoral legislation also contains scant references to the possibility to increase contributions. The IORP II, CRD IV, MiFID II, UCITS and AIFMD Directives contain no direct provisions regulating such an increase. The Solvency II Directive notes that "Mutual and mutual-type associations with variable contributions may call for supplementary contributions from their members (supplementary members' calls) in order to increase the amount of financial resources that they hold to absorb losses."[1101] PEPP providers qualifying as mutual and mutual-type associations under Solvency II may count such additional contributions towards their so-called ancillary own funds, which are funds other than basic own funds which can be called up to absorb losses.[1102]

1095 Article 54(1) and (2) PEPP Regulation.
1096 EIOPA, 'EIOPA's advice on the development of an EU Single Market for personal pension products (PPP)' (EIOPA-16/457, 2016) see for instance 53, available at eiopa.europa.eu/Publications/Consultations/EIOPA's%20advice%20on%20the%20development%20of%20an%20EU%20single%20market%20for%20personal%20pension%20products.pdf accessed 8 January 2020.
1097 SWD(2017) 243 final.
1098 ibid.
1099 EIOPA 2015 (see footnote 1067) 8.
1100 Article 45(2) PEPP Regulation.
1101 Solvency II (see footnote 1074) Recital 52.
1102 Solvency II (see footnote 1074) Article 89.

4.7   Benefit Adjustment Mechanisms

The final PEPP Regulation contains few references to benefit adjustment mechanisms. The initial proposal noted that "PEPP beneficiaries should also be informed of any reduction in the level of benefits due, prior to the application of any such reduction, after a decision which will result in a reduction has been taken. As a matter of best practice, PEPP providers are recommended to consult PEPP beneficiaries in advance of any such decision."[1103] Although the proposed regulation contained no specific reference to the relationship between the possibility to cut benefits and any guarantees, it is likely that any such guarantees would not have precluded the possibility to cut benefits. As noted, the final Regulation contains no references to benefit cuts, and it seems that this matter has been left to national legislation and/or the contractual freedom of the PEPP provider and saver.

Another benefit adjustment mechanism is the (suspension) of indexation. The initial PEPP proposal contained two scant references to indexation, noting in the preamble that "PEPP providers could in addition include an inflation indexation mechanism to at least partly cover inflation"[1104] in the Basic PEPP, and that "capital protection, allowing the PEPP saver to recoup the capital invested and providing an inflation indexation mechanism, shall be consumed at the moment of switching providers."[1105] Both these references to the possibility of indexation have been stricken from the proposal by the time it was presented, on 15 May 2018. The omission of any reference to indexation means that this matter is left to national law and/or the contractual freedom of the PEPP providers and consumers.

The final Regulation states that the guarantees offered under the basic PEPP, "could also cover the fees and charges and could provide for full or partial coverage of inflation."[1106]

4.8   PEPP Governance

Under the IORP II framework, pension scheme members may find themselves faced with a situation in which they see their pension savings being administered by a pension provider from another Member State. That can potentially lead to outcomes that are not possible had the pension savings been kept in the scheme member's own Member State. An example are the solvency standards that differ from Member State to Member State. Such differing standards can have different consequences for the scheme member's

---

1103 COM(2017) 343 final, Recital 31.
1104 COM(2017) 343 final, Recital 39.
1105 COM(2017) 343 final, Article 49.
1106 PEPP Regulation, Recital 45.

exposure to the economic climate in the sense that indexation or cutting of pension benefits can be more or less likely with higher or lower solvency standards. In the case of a PEPP, the PEPP savers themselves choose the provider and are therefore more in control of the supervisory framework they choose. That framework remains the same until the PEPP saver chooses another PEPP to which another supervisory framework is applicable, regardless of the employer or Member State the PEPP saver resides in.

As explained, PEPP is a "wrapper" product, the providers of which are already regulated under their own respective sectoral regimes.[1107] This system makes it possible to forgo the regulation of detailed prudential or governance requirements. As the products that could qualify as PEPPs are "already based upon intermediary regulation adopted under the AIFMD, UCITSD V, MiFID II, IORPD II, CRD IV and Solvency II", additional regulation would not only be superfluous but also too cumbersome to put into practice.[1108] The PEPP Regulation subjects these providers to additional requirements for the purposes of the PEPP as a product, including governance standards. These are minimal rules on governance. This is because the Regulation was intended to keep the regulatory burden for PEPP providers at a minimum.[1109] The sectoral legislation already contains provisions on governance and, what is more, "financial intermediaries regulated on the EEA level show remarkable cross-sectoral consistencies in the way how they are regulated."[1110] For instance, the general organizational requirements impose similar requirements on the management structures of providers and their personnel. Such requirements include fit & proper senior management; minimum capital requirements that vary upon the type of financial service/product provided; a business plan; adequate risk organization etc.[1111]

The different categories of providers do offer different kinds of products and have, accordingly, different risk profiles. Consequently, some parts of the operating conditions are similar while many are sector-specific, such as the applicable solvency rules.[1112]

The governance requirements included in the PEPP Regulation can be found in Chapter IV of the Regulation on distribution and information requirements. It contains general requirements, such as the requirements that PEPP providers and distributors "shall always act honestly, fairly and professionally"[1113] in the best interests of their customers, and more specific requirements pertaining to the information to be provided to the consumer in the pre-contractual phase as well as during the term of the contract. In order to ensure the safety of a PEPP, the Regulation sets product oversight and governance standards that require PEPP providers maintain, operate and review a process for the approval

---

1107 Van Meerten & Hooghiemstra 2017 (see footnote 1046) 52.
1108 ibid.
1109 ibid 46.
1110 ibid.
1111 ibid 46-47.
1112 ibid 56.
1113 PEPP Regulation, Article 22.

of each PEPP, or significant adaptations of an existing PEPP, before it is distributed to PEPP customers.[1114]

In addition, rigorous information requirements ensure that (potential) PEPP savers are given the information they need to make informed choices. This information is key in overcoming the so-called "information asymmetry gap", by virtue of which one party – namely the provider – possesses all the relevant information and the other – the consumer – does not. EIOPA believes that this gap reduces trust in personal pension products and could also result in suboptimal decisions.[1115] For this reason, the PEPP Regulation foresees the provision of such information before the conclusion of a contract in a so-called PEPP Key Information Document.[1116] This document is the "cornerstone of providing pre-contractual information" and the proposed Regulation describes the requirements in detail.[1117] The provider is to draw up this document before the offering the PEPP on the market and must contain key information on the product, such as a description of the retirement benefits, the retirement age, general information on portability etc. Complementing the Key Information Document is the PEPP Benefit Statement, which provides the consumer with "key personal and generic data" about the PEPP scheme, "contain relevant and appropriate information to facilitate the understanding of pension entitlements over time and across schemes and serve labour mobility."[1118] In addition to these information documents, a PEPP provider or distributor is to give advice to a prospective customer prior to the conclusion of a contract.[1119] These information requirements help to keep a PEPP saver informed about all the relevant details of a PEPP product before and during the term of the contract. However, like pension scheme members of a cross-border IORP find themselves subject to the prudential requirements of another Member State, PEPP savers appear to find themselves in the same position.

Although the PEPP Regulation itself contains some general governance standards, the specific sectoral legislation of each of the eligible PEPP providers sets more detailed rules. In addition, the national legislation of the Member States sets more detailed rules regarding governance standards. On the one hand, because the PEPP is a third pillar product, consumers can shop around for the type of provider in the Member State with the governance standards to suit their needs. On the other, all these different sources of legislation containing governance requirements can make it difficult for consumers to choose a provider that meets their needs. In this respect, the product safety of even the

---

1114 PEPP Regulation, Article 25. This process is to be proportionate to the nature of the PEPP provided and the product itself must be revised regularly. The providers of the product must make any appropriate information available to distributors, so that they are properly informed about the product's features and its target market.
1115 EIOPA 2015 (see footnote 1067) 25 et seq.
1116 PEPP Regulation, Article 26.
1117 COM(2017) 343 final 13.
1118 PEPP Regulation, Recital 43; Articles 35 and 36.
1119 PEPP Regulation, Article 34.

basic PEPP – with its guarantees – is dependent on appropriate legislation that ensures that the promises made under the PEPP can be kept.

4.9   Analysis and Conclusion

The previous sections have discussed the concept of the PEPP, the PEPP Regulation as well as the product features and governance requirements of the PEPP. Although the PEPP Regulation does standardise a number of the product's features, a number of items have not been standardised by the Regulation. That partial standardisation leads to two questions surrounding the PEPP: to what extent the degree of standardization of the PEPP 1) influences the marketability of the PEPP and 2) the potential attractiveness to consumers of the PEPP.

Marketability of the PEPP: Different Member States, Different PEPPs?

Article 5(2) of the Regulation dictates that the registration of a PEPP shall be valid in all Member States, and that the successful registration into the register of EIOPA entitles the PEPP Provider to distribute the PEPP throughout the EU in accordance with Chapter II of the Regulation. But what is the scope of this EU-wide passport? The previous section showed that a number of the PEPP's features have not been harmonised, such as some of the security mechanisms, funding requirements as well as the substantive governance standards. Can a PEPP truly be marketed in any Member State? The extent to which Member States may apply their own legislation to PEPPs from other Member States is essential to answer that question.

Chapter III, Section 1 of the Regulation gives expression to the freedom to provide services and the freedom of establishment for PEPP providers. The provisions in Chapter II of the Regulation define the relevant notification procedures. The aforementioned Article 5(2) of the Regulation proclaims that the PEPP registration is valid throughout the EU. This would suggest at first glance that the PEPP products authorised by EIOPA need only comply with the aspects regulated in the Regulation and the relevant sectoral legislation applicable to the providers, and not with other aspects not regulated by it, such as socio-political aspects.[1120] However, Article 3(b) requires that the registration, manufacturing, distribution and supervision of PEPPs shall be subject to, *inter alia*, "the laws adopted by Member States in implementation of relevant sectoral Union law and implementation of measures relating specifically to PEPPs" as well as "other national laws which apply to PEPPs."[1121] In addition, the Regulation makes clear that it does not aim

---

1120 Reiner & Horvath 2018 (see footnote 1056) 13 et seq.
1121 Article 3(b)(ii) and (iii) PEPP Regulation.

to regulate national contractual, social, labour and tax law.[1122] That is an essential consideration, as the matters not regulated by the PEPP Regulation itself or the relevant EU sectoral legislation of eligible PEPP providers remain defined by national legislation.

What is more, the portability service enshrined in the Regulation – to be discussed in Part 2 – requires a so-called sub-account[1123] within each PEPP account. In accordance with Article 19(1), PEPP providers must ensure that when a new sub-account is opened within each individual PEPP account, it shall correspond to the legal requirements and conditions "determined at national level as referred to in Article 47 and 57 for the PEPP by the Member State to which the PEPP saver moves." Articles 47 and 57 call for the adaptation of the sub-accounts to national legislation for the accumulation[1124] and decumulation[1125] phases, respectively. These national requirements for the accumulation phase include "age limits for starting the accumulation phase, minimum duration of the accumulation phase, maximum and minimum amount of in-payments and their continuity."[1126] For the decumulation phase, such conditions "may include in particular the setting of the minimum age for decumulation, of a maximum period before reaching the retirement age for joining a PEPP, as well as conditions for redemption before the minimum age for decumulation, notably in case of particular hardship."[1127] These obstacles cannot be removed by the PEPP product passport.

Indeed, Article 16 of the Regulation the Regulation requires the competent authorities to enforce the requirements contained within it (see recitals 31, 32 and 71). In particular, Article 16 PEPP Regulation provides that where the competent authorities of the host Member State have reason to consider that a PEPP or sub-account is distributed within its territory that infringes any obligations resulting from the applicable rules as referred to in Article 3, they shall refer their findings to the competent authorities of the home Member State of the PEPP provider or the PEPP distributor. Article 16 of the Regulation requires the home and host state authorities to cooperate and to take "appropriate measures without delay to remedy the situation". In addition, the Regulation grants the com-

---

1122 Recital 23 of the PEPP Regulation.

1123 According to Article 2(23) PEPP Regulation, a "'sub-account' means a national section which is opened within each PEPP account and which corresponds to the legal requirements and conditions for using possible incentives fixed at national level for investing in a PEPP by the Member State of the PEPP saver's residence; accordingly, an individual may be a PEPP saver or a PEPP beneficiary in each sub-account, depending on the respective legal requirements for the accumulation phase and decumulation phase."

1124 Article 2(11) PEPP Regulation: "'accumulation phase' means the period during which assets are accumulated in a PEPP account and ordinarily runs until the decumulation phase starts."

1125 Article 2(12) PEPP Regulation: "'decumulation phase' means the period during which assets accumulated in a PEPP account may be drawn upon to fund retirement or other income requirements."

1126 Council of the European Union, 'Proposal for a Regulation of the European Parliament and of the Council on a pan-European Personal Pension Product (PEPP) (first reading) - Confirmation of the final compromise text with a view to agreement', 5919/19 (PEPP Proposal of 8 Feb 2019), Article 47(2), available at https://eur-lex.europa.eu/legal-content/EN/TXT/PDF/?uri=CONSIL:ST_5915_2019_INIT&from=EN accessed 8 January 2020.

1127 ibid, Article 57(2).

petent authorities product intervention powers if the PEPP offered in their territory is not in compliance with the PEPP Regulation.[1128] As the Regulation includes references to Member State legislation, those intervention powers will likely also be applicable to PEPP violations of national legislation. These intervention powers – which are the prohibition or restriction of the marketing or distribution of a PEPP in or from a Member State – can be used if a PEPP places the protection of PEPP savers at risk or if the PEPP poses a risk to the orderly functioning and integrity of financial markets or the stability of whole or part of the financial system within at least one Member State.[1129]

Finally, regarding the tax requirements, the PEPP Regulation does not oblige Member States to apply to PEPPs the same tax rules as they would to similar national personal pension products, but are merely encouraged to so in a Commission Recommendation to extend the benefits of the tax advantages they grant to national personal pension products to PEPPs, "even when it does not fulfil all the national criteria for tax relief."[1130] As a result, the regulation dictates that a PEPP must be adapted to the specificities of (tax) legislation in each Member State in which it is offered.[1131] This has consequences both for the marketability as well as the portability of the product. As will be explained in more detail below, the portability of the PEPP hinges on the opening of new sub-accounts (or "compartments" as previous iterations of the proposal named them) per Member State jurisdiction to comply with local laws and regulations in order to benefit from favourable tax treatment.[1132] To the PEPP saver, the scheme and the provider stay the same, but the provider must adapt the scheme in each of the sub-compartments so as to remain compliant with local laws and regulations. On the other hand, the Regulation also stipulates that, in the event the PEPP provider is not able to ensure the opening of a new sub-account corresponding to the applicable laws and regulations of the PEPP saver's new Member State of residence, the PEPP saver must be given the option to either switch providers or to continue contributing to the last sub-account opened.[1133]

1128 Article 61 et seq PEPP Regulation.
1129 Article 63 PEPP Regulation.
1130 European Commission, 'Commission Recommendation of 29.6.2017 on the tax treatment of personal pension products, including the pan-European Personal Pension Product' C(2017) 4393 final 3.
1131 Articles 19 and 20 of the PEPP Regulation.
1132 See Article 2(23) PEPP Regulation. See also H van Meerten & A Wouters, 'The PEPP Regulation (PEPPR): Pepper for the Capital Markets Union?' (2019) Zeitschrift für Versicherungsrecht 1.
1133 Article 20(5) PEPP Regulation.

This would suggest that Member States may refuse a PEPP from being offered within their territory on the basis that it does not comply with its national legislation, but that the Member States cannot ban the payment of contributions to a PEPP authorised within another Member State. They can, so it seems, discourage the take-up of such a product within another Member State by denying them favourable tax treatment, as long as that denial of favourable tax treatment is a justifiable obstacle to the free movement of capital.[1134] To some extent, then, the PEPP's pan-European character is still defined by the national laws of the Member States in respect of matters left unregulated by the PEPP Regulation. That appears to afflict the PEPP Regulation with a seemingly similar situation as cross-border IORPs: the pension schemes offered by cross-border IORPs must also be in conformity with the requirements of Member States' national law. It was noted in Chapter 5 that the differences in national legislation, burdening cross-border IORPs, was a reason for the relatively low prevalence of cross-border IORPs. The 1% limit for costs and fees for the Basic PEPP and the cost cap for switching providers will certainly provide (prospective) PEPP providers with an additional challenge. Since the PEPP is very new, practical experience will have to show to what extent differences in national legislation can cause problems for PEPP providers as they (can) do in the case of cross-border IORPs. Some industry professionals expect PEPP to become a (commercial) success,[1135] while others remark that the basic PEPP, the provision of which, as a "default investment option"[1136] is mandatory, offers too little perspective for profit[1137] and that the portability service can be financially and administratively burdensome to both the consumer as well as the provider.[1138]

The Commission addressed the issue of differences in Member States' legislation during the Regulation's genesis, where it noted that maximum harmonisation of national

---

1134 EIOPA noted in its Preliminary Report to the Commission (see footnote 1058) that "The extent of social law aspect differs among MS. In most cases they comprise eligibility criteria for membership, means of entry into the system (mandatory, voluntary), possibility to pay additional contributions to the pension fund, etc." This is because personal pension plans "usually reflect" the existence of their national social security system, and are interlinked with the aspects of national social security systems. "Firstly, it is the national social legislation that recognises and defines a financial product as PPP and distinguishes it from other similar long term investment products. Secondly, national social legislation also identifies the main characteristics of personal pension plans, with reference for example to the participation requirements. Thirdly, the benefit structure of a PPP is modelled by social law requirements regarding retirement age."

1135 H van Meerten & S Hooghiemstra, 'The PEPP: A Pension Solution for the Future' (2017) Fall Issue, Pension & Longevity Risk Transfer for Institutional Investors, 44; H van Meerten & J van Zanden, 'Pensions and the PEPP: The Necessity of an EU Approach' (2018) 15 No 3 European Company Law Journal 66.

1136 Article 45(1) PEPP Regulation.

1137 W Mulder & J Barnard, 'PEPP: More questions than answers' (November 2019) Investments & Pensions Europe, available at https://www.ipe.com/pepp-more-questions-than-answers/10034193.article accessed 8 January 2020.

1138 PensionsEurope, 'PensionsEurope Position paper on the pan-European Personal Pension Product (PEPP)' (2018) 12-13, available at https://www.pensionseurope.eu/system/files/PensionsEurope%20position%20paper%20on%20PEPP%2020180308.pdf accessed 8 January 2020.

regimes would have contributed to the establishment of a real single market for personal pension products as well as genuine pan-European products. It also concluded that "the differences between Member States' personal pensions regimes, both in terms of tax and labour law, and Member States' insufficient willingness to change their personal pension taxation rules."[1139] Although the EU legislator has succeeded in harmonising some product features, something that was explicitly rejected by the Member States and other stakeholders during the legislative history of the IORP I Directive, the creation of a fully harmonised 2nd regime was seemingly also not possible on the basis of current EU prerogatives and willingness of the Member States. In spite of that, the next part on mobility will discuss an apparent major advantage for PEPP savers vis-à-vis current EU law regulating occupational pensions that *has* been achieved through harmonisation.

The Potential Attractiveness to Consumers of the PEPP

Although entering the PEPP market appears to have some challenges for providers, PEPP savers should find the product attractive. Based on a review of its features, it should be a safe and transparent product. That certainly goes for the basic PEPP with its risk mitigation and/or guarantee. What is potentially the greatest advantage to mobile Europeans are the PEPP's options for mobility.

Whether PEPP savers will face the same type of (potential) challenges regarding the applicability of security mechanisms as discussed in respect of IORPs in Chapter 4 seems difficult to assess on the basis of the Regulation. At the outset it must be said that the discussion of the security mechanisms in Chapter 4 does not seem to apply to PEPP. The legislation discussed in that chapter focused on the social and labour law applicable to occupational pension schemes, which does not apply to personal pension products like the PEPP. Rather, the rules applicable to personal pension products are referred to by EIOPA as *general good* rules.[1140] These rules have been set up in accordance with national social and labour law – the different pension pillars are coordinated legislatively in the Member States – to cover matters such as investment restrictions, rules pertaining to cashing out retirement savings before retirement, as well as legislation on caps on costs and charges, minimum return guarantees, retirement age, mandatory advice and decumulation (e.g. pay-out) of retirement benefits.[1141] Compliance with general good rules is important for the pension product to be eligible for beneficial tax treatment[1142] and for a PEPP to be legally offered in a Member State.[1143] These have been partially harmonised by the Regulation to allow for cross-border marketability and portability.

1139 SWD(2017) 243 final 37.
1140 EIOPA 2015 (see footnote 1067) 13.
1141 ibid 14.
1142 ibid 13.
1143 See the aforementioned Article 3 of the PEPP Regulation.

As noted above in relation to the scope of a product passport of a PEPP, not all legislative requirements have been harmonised by the Regulation, and it was noted that the aspects not harmonised by the Regulation are regulated by national law and the sectoral legislation of the PEPP providers. One of those matters not regulated by the Regulation are the prudential regimes applicable to the providers. Article 11 requires PEPP providers and distributors to comply with the prudential regime applicable to them in accordance with the respective sector legislation applicable to them. For IORPs in particular, the PEPP Regulation seems confusing: the IORP II Directive defines IORPs as institutions, operating on a funded basis, established for the purpose of providing retirement benefits in the context of an *occupational* activity. However, a PEPP can be concluded separately from any employment relationship. That leaves the question whether the prudential requirements enshrined in the IORP II Directive apply to PEPPs offered by IORPs, especially since the PEPP Regulation requires "all assets and liabilities corresponding to PEPP provision business [to] be ring-fenced, without any possibility to transfer them to the other retirement provision business of the institution."[1144] IORPs' PEPP business therefore appears to be separate from their occupational pension business, to which the IORP II Directive applies. The question is therefore which prudential requirements apply to PEPPs offered by IORPs. The PEPP Regulation seems unclear on this matter.

Finally, the obligation for a PEPP to be compliant with national law appears to have no direct consequences for the pension-related mobility of mobile Europeans. Even if a PEPP provider has no local PEPP sub-account, a saver can continue to contribute to sub-account last opened, albeit with the possible loss of favourable tax treatment. That will be explained below.

PART 2: WORKER MOBILITY

It seems that the PEPP Regulation's greatest advantage vis-à-vis EU legislation covering occupational pensions are the options for portability and transferability. Chapter 4 explained that EU law thus far provides no real facilities for pension scheme members to take their second pillar pension savings to other Member States without the threat of putting a (sometimes severe) dent in pension rights as a consequence of diverging legislative frameworks and fiscal arrangements.[1145] In that sense, EU legislation regulating the second pension pillar have consistently fallen short of their initial objectives.[1146] Under the PEPP Regulation, on the other hand, mobile Europeans moving between Member

---

1144 Article 6(1)(c) PEPP Regulation.
1145 See Part 2 of Chapter 4.
1146 This concerns the Safeguard Directive (98/49/EC) and the Supplementary Pesnsion Rights Directive (2014/50/EU). See L van der Vaart & H van Meerten, 'De pensioen opPEPPer?' (2018) 1 Tijdschrift voor Pensioenvraagstukken 38.

States are guaranteed the mobility of their PEPP: they may choose to remain with their PEPP provider, regardless of the Member State in which they live, or, alternatively, transfer the assets accrued under the PEPP to another PEPP provider. These options are referred to in the PEPP Regulation as the portability service[1147] and the switching service[1148] respectively, and will be discussed in the subsequent sections. The portability service in the PEPP Regulation is a feature that, according to the Regualtion, has added value also vis-à-vis other third pillar pension products currently available owing to the hitherto highly fragmented EU market for such products.[1149] Mobile workers and self-employed persons should benefit from the provisions regulating portability in the PEPP Regulation. The explanatory memorandum to the PEPP Regulation's legislative proposal noted with respect to portability:

"The portability of personal pension products is a concern for people moving to another EU country while trying to maintain the same product and provider. Currently, when moving to another Member State, people have no choice but to search for a new product offered by a provider in the new Member State with substantially different rules, instead of continuing to save in their former Member State. National tax incentives encourage people to save for retirement and are key to promoting the take-up of personal pensions. Losing such tax benefits when moving to another Member State is a major barrier to the cross-border portability of personal pension products. Member States acting alone cannot remedy such portability issues."[1150]

In comparison to the EU directives governing occupational pensions discussed in the previous chapters, the options for mobility offered by the PEPP are strikingly different from what is possible under the second pillar. The following sections will address, first, the PEPP Regulation's provisions enabling mobility. Second, Section 7 will reflect on the barriers to mobility found in Chapter 4 regarding second-pillar pension schemes, and examine whether perhaps the PEPP Regulation could provide any solutions for second-pillar pension scheme members facing pension-related obstacles to their mobility.

1147 See Article 17 et seq PEPP Regulation.
1148 See Article 52 et seq PEPP Regulation.
1149 Recital 9 PEPP Regulation: "Currently, the internal market for personal pension products does not function smoothly. In some Member States there is not yet a market for pension products. In others, personal pension products are available, but there is a high degree of fragmentation between national markets. As a result, personal pension products have only a limited degree of portability. This can result in difficulties for individuals to make use of their basic freedoms. For instance, they may be prevented from taking up a job or retiring in another Member State. In addition, the possibility for providers to use the freedom of establishment and the freedom to provide services is hampered by the lack of standardisation of existing personal pension products."
1150 COM(2017)343, 6.

5 PORTABILITY

The portability of the PEPP is one of the central features of the product, and is regulated in Section II of Chapter III of the Regulation. Article 17 of the Regulation explains that the portability service allows PEPP savers to continue contributing to their PEPP even if they have changed their domicile by moving to another Member State. It contributes to the safeguarding of pension rights of Europeans who exercise their right to free movement under Articles 21 and 45 TFEU.[1151] The regulation explains that "Portability involves the PEPP saver changing residence to another Member State without changing PEPP providers, whereas the switching of PEPP providers does not necessarily involve a change of residence."[1152]

Despite the fact that cross-border membership for occupational pension schemes has been a goal since the beginning of the EU's involvement in regulating the second pillar, this kind of portability has as yet not been achieved under the EU's legislation covering occupational pensions, save for posted workers.[1153] The PEPP Regulation has made cross-border membership possible. The portability system works with so-called sub-accounts: a new sub-account is opened within the PEPP savers' main account that is in compliance with the legal requirements and conditions applicable to the accumulation and decumulation phase in the Member State to which the saver moves.[1154] The Regulation notes specifically that the contributions to and withdrawals made from the sub-account(s) may be subject to separate terms and conditions. This is important for a PEPP saver to keep in mind, as a move to another Member State may not only have fiscal consequences, but could also have adverse consequences originating from other local legislation that applies to the PEPP, for instance in terms of taxation.[1155] In this respect, a new sub-account seems to be, legally speaking, an entirely new PEPP, although from the perspective of the PEPP saver that need not be noticeable.

An apparent shortcoming in the PEPP portability service is that the Regulation only requires providers to provide sub-accounts in at least two Member States.[1156] Although PEPP savers may, if the provider offers no local sub-account in the saver's new Member State of residence, switch PEPP provider (see next section), the usefulness of the possibility to switch provider is entirely dependent on how successful PEPPs will be throughout the EU: there is nothing to choose from if a saver moves to a Member State where no PEPP providers are active. Alternatively, the PEPP Regulation gives PEPP savers the opportunity to simply continue contributing to the last-opened sub-account, but it seems that this could have potentially costly (to the saver) consequences if the sub-account is

---

1151 Recital 33 PEPP Regulation.
1152 ibid.
1153 See chapter 3, section 2.3, Part 2 of Chapter 4.
1154 Article 19 PEPP Regulation.
1155 ibid.
1156 Article 18(3) PEPP Regulation.

not in conformity with the fiscal requirements of the PEPP saver's new Member State of residence. Borg, Minto and van Meerten note that the taxation involved in switching providers remains a problem.[1157] The opening of a new sub-account could potentially be an onerous process for both the provider as well as the consumer. The process involves "amending the PEPP contract between the PEPP saver and the PEPP provider and signing an annex to it, in compliance with the applicable contract law."[1158] The applicable contract law indicated in the cited provision is presumably the contract law of the new Member State into which the PEPP saver moves.[1159] The result is that PEPP savers must be aware of the applicable legal provisions of the Member State in which they move. In addition, the compartments must be updated to comply with any changes in legislation.[1160]

Nevertheless, the fact that this type of mobility, namely cross-border membership, has been made possible by the PEPP Regulation, seems like a boon for mobile Europeans. In particular, mobile workers could benefit from being able to retain the same pension pot, regardless of where in the EU they live and work. Section 7 will study whether workers who are in principle obliged to contribute to a second-pillar scheme, could be exempt from such an obligation and contribute to a PEPP instead.

6 TRANSFERABILITY: THE SWITCHING SERVICE

Chapter VII of the PEPP Regulation deals with the switching of PEPP providers. This concerns another harmonised procedure that the Regulation standardises across all PEPPs. The possibility of switching provider is essential for consumers to find their preferred provider as their expectations or needs change – for instance because they want more control over their investments – and should afford consumers more flexibility.[1161]

In order to do that, the PEPP Regulation makes it possible for consumers to switch both during the accumulation as well as the decumulation phase through – as the Regulation puts it – "a clear, quick and safe procedure."[1162] Under the system of the proposed Regulation, provision of the switching service by the provider is mandatory. However, the consumers' opportunity to switch may occur no sooner than after a minimum of five years from the conclusion of the PEPP contract, and, in case of subsequent switching, after five years from the most recent switching.[1163] In addition, PEPP providers are not

---

1157 Borg, Minto & van Meerten 2019 (see footnote 1064) 19.
1158 Article 20(6) PEPP Regulation
1159 M. Baroch Castellevi & G. Bähr, 'Europäische Altersversorgung mit PEPP' (*DLA Piper*, 13 March 2018) available at https://www.dlapiper.com/de/germany/insights/publications/2018/03/europaische-altersversor gung-mit-pepp/ accessed 8 January 2020.
1160 ibid.
1161 Van Meerten & Hooghiemstra 2017 (see footnote 1135) 35.
1162 Recital 62 PEPP Regulation.
1163 Article 52(3) PEPP Regulation.

obliged by the Regulation to provide a switching service for PEPPs where PEPP savers are receiving out-payments in the form of lifetime annuities.[1164] The fees and charges involving the switching service are capped by the Regulation.[1165]

As noted, a PEPP saver may also switch PEPP provider at any time, free of charge, in case the PEPP provider is not able to ensure the opening of a sub-account.[1166] Alternatively, in this situation the PEPP Regulation also gives the saver the option of continuing to contribute to the last sub-account opened.[1167] The Regulation limits the possibility to switch between PEPP providers. Whether or not the Regulation allows switching from a PEPP to an "ordinary" personal pension product is not made clear by the document, however there is nothing in it that suggests that that should be impossible.

7   COULD THE PEPP BE AN ALTERNATIVE TO SECOND PILLAR SCHEMES FOR
      MOBILE EU CITIZENS?

The previous sections have described the various product features that the PEPP Regulation demands of all PEPPs. These product features appear to have advantages for, in particular, mobile workers. The fact that portability (cross-border membership to the same PEPP) and transferability are guaranteed by the PEPP Regulation seems to be a major advantage vis-à-vis second-pillar pension arrangements as well as non-PEPP third-pillar pension products. Chapter 4 explained that cross-border membership is not possible under current EU occupational pension law (owing, in particular to differences in national social, labour and tax legislation), and that the individual transferability of accrued pension rights is unregulated by EU law and can be problematic due to national legislation on pension transfers. Another apparent advantage under PEPP is that the social and labour law provisions of Member States that seemingly make the transferability and cross-border membership of an occupational scheme impossible, do not appear to apply to the third pillar. It is true, however, that the PEPP sub-accounts must still comply with national tax law in order to benefit from beneficial tax treatment, and must also be in conformity with local general good requirements. Regarding transferability, potential uncertainty may arise as the PEPP Regulation provides no guidance as to the calculation of the value of the assets to be transferred. This should not be a problem for a pure DC-type PEPP – as the assets are simply equal to the balance in the account – but determining the present value of the pension assets could be problematic for a DB-type PEPP that provides, for instance, a guaranteed pension result. It appears that the latter considera-

---

1164 Article 52(2) PEPP Regulation.
1165 See section 4.5.
1166 See Article 20(5) PEPP Regulation.
1167 ibid.

tions, but in particular PEPPs' eligibility for beneficial tax treatment, will be significant factors in determining the popularity of PEPPs.

While cross-border IORPs can, to some extent, help the mobility of some categories of workers who remain with the same IORP, it appears that the PEPP Regulation provides a greater degree of mobility to workers because the PEPP regulation itself guarantees such mobility (i.e. portability and transferability). The opening of sub-accounts itself seems in principle not much different from a cross-border IORP providing a local pension scheme, compliant with local social and labour legislation, for workers in another Member State. But the possibility for workers to remain with the same IORP is determined by the employer they work for, as well as the availability of a pension scheme for the Member State the worker moves to. For this reason, the system of sub-accounts cannot be simply transferred to occupational pensions, because the membership to an occupational pension system is dependent on the employer. Of course, a problematic aspect of PEPP sub-accounts is that PEPP providers are obliged by the PEPP Regulation to offer the possibility of opening sub-accounts (i.e. enable PEPP portability) for just two Member States.[1168] But alternatives are available. First, there is the guaranteed possibility to transfer the accrued rights to another PEPP provider at no cost if the current provider can provide no local account for the new Member State.[1169] Second, where the PEPP provider is not able to ensure the opening of a new sub-account corresponding to the PEPP saver's new Member State of residence, the PEPP saver may simply continue contributing to the sub-account where contributions were made before changing residence.[1170] However, the practicality of the alternative of switching PEPP providers depends on the availability PEPP providers in the Member State to which the PEPP saver relocates. The prevalence of PEPP providers will depend on whether offering a PEPP will be profitable for providers. The attractiveness for PEPP savers continuing to contribute to their last-opened sub-account if no Member State-specific sub-account is available depends on the availability of favourable tax treatment. Such favourable tax treatment could make a significant difference in the amount of savings available to a PEPP saver, and would therefore seem to be a significant factor in the popularity of PEPPs.

The PEPP-Exemption?

In spite of the concerns discussed in the previous section, a PEPP can still be a welcome opportunity for many self-employed and/or mobile Europeans. Especially in light of the mobility concerns surrounding second-pillar pension arrangements and the EU's hitherto limited success at regulating pension-related mobility issues in the second pillar, the PEPP Regulation could present a third-pillar option for some groups of workers to but-

---

1168 Article 18(3) PEPP Regulation.
1169 See section 5; Article 20(5)(a) PEPP Regulation.
1170 Article 20(5)(b) PEPP Regulation.

tress their retirement savings, especially if such groups could be exempt from national obligations to contribute to a second-pillar scheme in favor of a PEPP (the PEPP exemption). These groups of workers could consist of workers who would otherwise be at risk of either losing pension entitlements entirely (as a result of not satisfying waiting and vesting periods) or would run a serious risk of being negatively affected by having multiple small pension entitlements in various Member States. It was noted in Section 4, Part 2 of Chapter 4 that the costs charged to such small pension entitlements could put a major dent in pension savings. The following groups could be considered.

Posted Workers

Posted workers may, under Article 6 of the Safeguard Directive, continue to be a member of their original pension scheme for the duration of their posting.[1171] As a consequence, the posted worker and/or their employer are exempted from any obligation to make contributions to a supplementary pension scheme in another Member State for the duration of the posting.[1172] For the maximum duration of such an arrangement, the Safeguard Directive refers to the definition in Regulation 1408/71,[1173] which has been succeeded by Regulation 883/2004.[1174] The latter Regulation specifies that the provisions on posting apply if the posting does not exceed 24 months, though the Member States may derogate from that provision.[1175] Where a posting exceeds the duration covered by Article 6 Safeguard Directive, the posted worker is no longer able to remain covered by his or her original pension scheme and would also no longer be exempted from any obligation to make contributions to a supplementary pension scheme in another Member State. A situation could arise in which the posted worker has not satisfied either the waiting and/or vesting period of the original occupational pension scheme to which they may no longer contribute by virtue of not being covered by Article 6 Safeguard Directive, nor the waiting and/vesting period of any new pension scheme in the Member State to which this worker has been posted. As a result, a loss of pension rights could occur.

For this reason, workers posted to another Member State who are not covered by Article 6 Safeguard Directive could be given the option to contribute to a PEPP for the duration of their posting, and to be exempt from any national obligation to contribute to an occupational pension scheme. Such an obligation could arise from a system of compulsory membership or because workers are obliged by law to participate in the occupa-

---

1171 See Part 2 of Chapter 4.

1172 Article 6(2) Safeguard Directive.

1173 Council Regulation EEC No 1408/71 of 14 June 1971 on the application of social security schemes to employed persons and their families moving within the Community [1971] OJ L 149/2.

1174 Regulation (EC) No 883/2004 of the European Parliament and the Council of 29 April 2004 on the coordination of social security systems [2004] OJ L 166/1.

1175 ibid 883/2004; G Essers & K Distler, *Guide for Mobile European Workers* (European Trade Union Confederation 2017) 57 et seq.

tional pension scheme of their employer. In the event that the waiting and/or vesting periods of the original pension scheme were not satisfied, the contributions made to that scheme should be transferable to the PEPP if there is no option to resume the membership to the original scheme after the posting. Workers in this situation could be allowed to take advantage of the PEPP-exception if their employer has no local occupational pension scheme available in the country to which they have been posted, or if such a scheme is not appropriate, for instance because of the duration of the posting would not satisfy the applicable waiting and vesting periods.

Other Workers

There are also groups of workers other than posted workers who could seemingly benefit from being exempted from an obligation to contribute to an occupational scheme in favour of an obligation to save for retirement in a PEPP. In Member States with well-developed second-pillar systems, many workers are already covered by occupational pension schemes, either because there is a system of compulsory membership in place or in the event that workers or obliged by law to participate in the pension scheme of their employer.[1176] In these Member States, the necessity for additional pension savings seems limited in most cases, however there seem to be situations in which a convincing argument could be made that some individuals who are compelled by law to contribute to an occupational should under certain circumstances be exempted from such an obligation. While saving for retirement in an occupational scheme is certainly a good thing for workers who contribute to such a scheme for long enough to satisfy requirements such as waiting and vesting periods, and do not change workplace so often as to acquire pension benefits with a number of pension providers in different Member States – and are therefore not confronted with potentially burdensome transfer conditions (see Part 2 of Chapter 4) – other types of more mobile workers could lose their pension rights when changing employer and Member State of residence. For the same reasons as for posted workers described above, namely the potential loss of pension rights, these workers, who are mobile between Member States and frequently change employer, could benefit from being exempted of any obligations to contribute to an occupational scheme in lieu of a PEPP. Groups of workers that come to mind are employees of multinational corporations, academics and migrant workers such as construction workers and seasonal workers.

The eligibility of such workers for the PEPP-exemption could be determined as follows. Mobile workers could be exempted from an obligation to contribute to an occupational pension scheme if consecutive employment contracts are in different Member States, with the contract(s) in each new Member State being shorter than a certain period

---

1176 See Chapter 1, section 2.

(the exemption period). That exemption period could be three years, in analogy with the maximum waiting and vesting periods set by the Supplementary Pension Rights Directive.[1177] If the worker leaves the Member State to which he or she most recently relocated for a new Member State within the exemption period, the worker can continue contributing to the same PEPP during his stay in the new Member State – again within a new exemption period of three years. This system would avoid a situation in which a worker racks up a number of small pension entitlements in a number of different Member States, each with their own financial and administrative burden.[1178] Should the worker end up remaining with one or more employers in a new Member State for longer than three years, the funds accrued under the PEPP during the stay in that particular Member State could be retained within that PEPP, or could be transferred to an occupational pension scheme that is in accordance with the legislation of that Member State. In either case, from the date of the expiration of the exemption period, the worker will become subject to the full legislative requirements of that Member State (including compulsory membership) applicable to the 2nd pillar pension system. The pension benefits accrued in a previous Member State in which the worker has been a member of an occupational pension scheme, either by virtue of the expiration of an exemption period or because this was the original Member State from where the worker began a mobile career, are to be treated in conformity with the Safeguard Directive and the Supplementary Pension Rights Directive, but could be transferred to the PEPP optionally should the conditions for vesting not have been met.

How to Implement Such a System

In the introduction to Part 2, it was noted that it was striking that the EU legislator was able to harmonise aspects of the PEPP that it was not able to harmonise in the second pillar. These aspects concern some core features of the PEPP (see Section 4.9) as well as the PEPP Regulations' provisions on mobility. This seems striking especially because the EU legislator appears to have been able to take away major obstacles to the mobility of European citizens – by enabling transferability and cross-border membership – caused by pensions. It has done that on the basis of Article 114 TFEU, which is the legal basis of the PEPP Regulation. That is the same legal basis upon which the IORP II Directive is based (the IORP II Directive is based additionally on Articles 53 and 62 TFEU). It seems that, because of the degree to which some Member States rely on second-pillar pension provision, (partial) EU harmonisation of the second pillar is less palatable to the Member States than (partial) harmonisation in the third pillar. It seems regrettable that EU legislation has not given mobile workers the same options regarding portability and transfer-

---

1177 See Part 2 of Chapter 4.
1178 See Part 2 Chapter 4, Section 4.

ability in the second pillar as it has in the third. Nevertheless, as the previous section discussed, it could be possible to allow mobile workers an exemption from an obligation to contribute to an occupational scheme in favour of a PEPP. This would, so it seems, give some groups of mobile Europeans access to a form of pension that gives them room for mobility.

However, the previous chapters have shown how long and difficult the process of the EU's regulating of occupational pension systems has been. It seems apparent that any proposed EU initiative in the field of occupational pensions has been met with varying degrees of resistance form the Member States, and that that resistance to proposed EU legislative initiatives has resulted in a sometimes substantial watering-down of initial proposals. At the same time, the possible loss of pension rights for mobile Europeans face should be addressed. Mindful of this reality, by limiting the option of an exemption from any obligation to make contributions to an occupational pension scheme in a Member State to a limited group of workers, the proposed PEPP-exemption should not interfere more than necessary with national pension systems.

Therefore, an EU-mandated possibility for an exemption from any obligation to make contributions to an occupational pension scheme in a Member State should only be given if exempt persons are obliged to contribute to a PEPP, so that these individuals continue to save for their retirement. Additionally, in order not to burden national occupational pension systems too greatly, for instance in terms of administrative and cost burdens, vested pension entitlements under compulsory occupational systems should not be transferable to a PEPP.

The next question is how to enshrine such a system in European legislation. In the case of posted workers, this could be done via an amendment to Article 6 of the Safeguard Directive. That amendment could specify that posted workers who find themselves outside the scope of subsections 1 and 2 of that provision, can be exempted from any obligation to make contributions to a supplementary pension scheme in both the Member State they were posted from as well as the Member State they were posted to. That directive would seem like a logical place to enshrine the PEPP-exemption for posted workers, as it already contains a reference to this group in the context of the second pillar, and is already based on Article 48 TFEU. That provision is the legal basis for the EU to adopt measures in the field of social security that are necessary to provide freedom of movement for workers. For groups of workers, a new provision could be added to the Supplementary Pension Rights Directive allowing those proposed groups an exemption from an obligation to contribute to a national occupational pension system. That Directive is based on Article 46 TFEU, which is the legal basis for the adoption of measures to achieve the free movement of workers as enshrined in Article 45 TFEU. In addition, for the option to transfer accrued PEPP capital to an occupational scheme, a change to Article 6 of the PEPP Regulation would be required. That provision currently forbids IORPs from transferring assets and liabilities accrued under a PEPP to the "other retirement business of the institution."[1179] That provision seems to target only capital transfers from a PEPP to an occupational scheme within the same IORP and not from a PEPP provider to – IORP or not – to another IORP, but should nonetheless be changed for PEPP-to-occupational-scheme within the same IORP.

Regarding the legal basis for the amendments to the Safeguard Directive and the Supplementary Pension Rights Directive pursuing the implementation of the PEPP-exception, the directives appear to be based already on the suitable provisions. As the PEPP-exemption pursues the same objective as the two directives, namely the free movement of workers, this is unsurprising. Therefore, the provisions on free movement are the correct source of EU legislative competence to protect the pension rights of migrant workers.[1180] The differences between Article 46 and 48 TFEU are subtle, with Article 48 TFEU referring specifically to the worker mobility in the context of social security, but either article seems to be appropriate.[1181] With respect to subsidiarity, the PEPP-exception appears to match the justification for the choice of a directive: both directives indicate in their recitals that directives were chosen in view of the diverse nature of occupational pension schemes.[1182] The amendment of the current directives would allow the Member States to implement the PEPP-exemption in accordance with the intricacies of their pension systems. Also, in both instances, it is clear that if the mobility of workers throughout the EU is to be facilitated, legislation should be made at EU-level rather than the national level.

The proportionality of the measure may encounter more resistance, as the Netherlands in particular has been keen to protect the operation of its system of compulsory membership,[1183] and the pensions industry could oppose the additional administrative efforts involved in putting this exception into operation. Finally, the social partners will likely be reluctant to grant exceptions to participation in pension arrangements set up by them. Nevertheless, the mobility of EU workers is on a steady rise,[1184] which means that the problems relating to pension-related obstacles to worker mobility are become more urgent. This means that some form of action must be taken. Given the fact that the PEPP-exception would apply to just a relatively small group of mobile workers, the effects on national pension systems would seem limited, and therefore proportional.

If the Member States and social partners were to accept the possibility of an exemption from national obligations to contribute to a second-pillar systems, mobile European citizens could benefit from having an extra option regarding their retirement savings. Where an obligation to contribute to a national occupational pension system becomes

---

1179 Article 6(1)(c) PEPP Regulation.

1180 W Baugniet, The protection of occupational pensions under European Union law on the freedom of movement for workers, dissertation European University Institute Florence (2014) 194.

1181 ibid 209-210.

1182 Recital 16 of the Safeguard Directive; Recital 26 of the Supplementary Safeguard Directive.

1183 See Chapter 5, section 3.2.

1184 European Commission, *2018 Annual Report on intra-EU Labour Mobility* (Publications Office of the European Union 2019) 48 et seq.

an impediment to a workers' freedom of movement throughout the EU, it could be argued that the Member States are obliged under EU law to provide an exemption such an obligation. Chapter 4, Part 2, Section 5 discussed the *Casteels*[1185] case. In that case, the Court found that Article 45 TFEU "militates against any measure which, even though applicable without discrimination on grounds of nationality, is capable of hindering or rendering less attractive the exercise by European Union nationals of the fundamental freedoms guaranteed by the Treaty."[1186]

While cautioning against too broad an interpretation of *Casteels*, Del Sol and Rocca identify several reasons that suggest a broader applicability of *Casteels* than the mere facts of this case, among which is the fact that the Court arrived at its conclusions on the basis of primary Union law – "so that a contested measure just needed to be liable to hinder free movement of workers (even in a non-discriminatory way) to be scrutinised."[1187] They also contend that a breach of the free movement of workers may be difficult to justify.[1188] Van der Vaart and van Meerten take this to mean that the free movement of workers prohibits any measure that is liable to hinder or render less attractive the accrual of pension rights and thus, indirectly, the portability of such pension rights.[1189] Borg, Minto and van Meerten posit, regarding the *Casteels* case, that "despite the fact that in the Casteels case the recognition of the accrual of pension rights was concerned, it can be argued that this recognition should not be made illusory by national rules on portability."[1190]

It seems that the findings in *Casteels* could be expanded also to national obligations to contribute to a second-pillar pension scheme. This is because the Court found that "[i]t is [...] settled case-law that all of the provisions of the FEU Treaty relating to the freedom of movement for persons are intended to facilitate the pursuit by European Union nationals of occupational activities of all kinds throughout the European Union, and preclude measures which might place such nationals at a disadvantage when they wish to pursue an economic activity in the territory of another Member State [...]" Consequently, Article 45 TFEU militates against any measure which, even though applicable without discrimination on grounds of nationality, is capable of hindering or rendering less attractive the exercise by European Union nationals of the fundamental freedoms guaranteed by the Treaty.[1191] Mobile Europeans who could face a loss of pension rights upon exercising their right to free movement would certainly be placed at a disadvantage vis-à-vis non-

---

1185 Case C-379/09 *Casteels* [2011] ECLI:EU:C:2011:131.
1186 ibid, para 22 and the case law cited there.
1187 M Del Sol & M Rocca, 'Free movement of workers in the EU and occupational pensions: conflicting priorities? Between case law and legislative interventions' (2017) Vol 19 (2) European Journal of Social Security 141.
1188 ibid.
1189 Van der Vaart & van Meerten (see footnote 1146).
1190 Borg, Minto & van Meerten (see footnote 1064).
1191 *Casteels*, paras 21-22.

mobile citizens. Although the Safeguard Directive and the Supplementary Pension Rights Directive provide protection to some extent, matters such as waiting and vesting periods shorter than three years and the avoidance of a number of small pension pots in different Member States, are beyond the scope of those directives. Europeans could be deterred from exercising their right to free movement because of this, which would constitute an obstacle to their free movement.

Since this PEPP-exemption would, certainly in its initial stages, apply to just a limited group of workers who would be at risk of losing (a portion) of their pension entitlements, the Member States may find it difficult to justify obstacles to this exemption. It was noted in Chapter 1[1192] that the group of mobile workers is limited in relative terms, and so the financial stability of (compulsory) occupational pension systems would almost certainly not be placed at risk. On the other hand, in absolute numbers, there were still 12 million Europeans of working age living in an EU Member State other than their country of citizenship in 2016. For these 12 million people, an adequate EU system of pension law must be in place so as not to hinder their free movement.

CONCLUSION TO PART 2

Chapter 2 discussed the EU's powers in the field of occupational pensions. It seems that *inter alia* these limited powers the EU has upon which it can regulate occupational pensions, together with the political discussions during the legislative processes of the EU's occupational pension legislation have left their marks on these provisions. Differences in national legislation present a variety of hurdles, ranging from cost increases to outright barriers and conflicts that could have repercussions for pension scheme members. The previous chapters, for instance, discussed a failure to make occupational pensions portable in a manner that was imagined in the 1990s. In addition, the individual transferability of pension rights is neither possible under the IORP II Directive nor the Safeguard or Supplementary Pension Rights Directives. For this reason, Part 2 examined the options for portability (cross-border membership) as well as transferability under the PEPP. It argued for a possibility for some groups of mobile workers to be exempted from obligations under national law to contribute to an occupational pension scheme – an obligation which could arise out of collective labour agreements making such contributions compulsory for sectors of industry (compulsory membership) or because of a statutory obligation for workers to participate in their employers' pension scheme – in favour of a PEPP.

Such a PEPP-exemption could help groups of mobile workers who would otherwise face a loss of pension rights upon exercising their right to free movement. Although it could be difficult for the Member States to agree to such an exemption, the fact that it

---

1192 See Section 3.3 of Chapter 1.

applies to a limited group of workers could assuage Member States' concerns. Finally, on the basis of the *Casteels* case, it could be argued that the Member States must refrain from erecting any barrier which is capable of hindering or rendering less attractive the exercise by European Union nationals of the fundamental freedoms guaranteed by the Treaty. This seems to include an obligation to contribute to an occupational pension scheme that could result in a (partial) loss of pension rights. Where that could happen, the Member States could arguable be obliged to grant an exemption in favour of a PEPP.

9   ANALYSIS AND CONCLUSION TO CHAPTER 6

In the particular context of this dissertation, the initial reason why the PEPP was explored was because the previous chapters found that the EU's legislation covering the second pillar has shortcomings that can affect European workers, in particular mobile workers. IORPs wishing to be active on a cross-border basis are also affected by differing legislation between the Member States, in that this fragmented pension law landscape could hinder their freedom to provide services. With respect to the IORPs' freedom to provide services, however, Chapter 5 concluded that many of these obstacles emanating from social and labour law appear justifiable. The latter fact likely means that, going forward, the proliferation of cross-border IORPs will remain modest, depriving pension scheme members of their advantages in terms of scale economies and, for some groups of workers, of cross-border mobility. The impression with regard to the EU legislation covering the second pillar is one of partial success. The remaining differences in national legislation causing difficulties for pension scheme members appear difficult to remove, as evidenced by this legislation's difficult legislative history.

The question for this chapter was, whether the EU legislator is more adept at adopting legislation in the third pillar. Based on an analysis of the PEPP Regulation, it appears that it is. While the marketability of the PEPP could prove challenging, owing again to differences in national legislation and caps on costs and charges, the opportunities for mobility the PEPP provides mobile workers are a remarkable breakthrough in EU pension law. Not only has the Regulation achieved an important degree of harmonisation for third-pillar personal pension products which, in the wording of the first proposal for the PEPP Regulation was made up of a patchwork of rules, it appears that this advantage vis-à-vis current EU occupational pension law could be opened up to some groups of mobile Europeans who are in principle under an obligation to contribute to the second pillar. The fact that PEPPs must conform to host State legislation could be a challenge to PEPP providers, who must familiarise themselves with the legislation of another jurisdiction, but this fact appears to pose no obstacle for mobile PEPP savers. If anything, it increases their protection, as the requirements of the host Member State applicable to a PEPP is tailored to the specific conditions of that Member State. Where no local sub-account is

available, the Regulation provides seemingly adequate alternatives: the mobile PEPP saver
may either choose to switch to a provider which has a sub-account for that Member State
available, or remain with the same provider and continue contributing to the last-opened
PEPP sub-account. The latter option could, however, come at the cost of favourable tax
treatment.

Despite these concerns, the provision of these institutionalised and legally enforceable
options for mobility provided by the PEPP Regulation is all the more remarkable because
it was achieved on the basis of Article 114 TFEU, the same legal basis as the IORP II
Directive. Neither the IORP II Directive nor other EU occupational pension law provides
such options. During the negotiations on the first IORP Directive, portability has been
abandoned in the early stages of Directive's germination in the 1990s.[1193] EU law thus far
provides no real facilities for pension scheme members to take their second pillar pension
savings to another Member States without the threat of putting a (sometimes severe) dent
in pension rights as a consequence of diverging legislative frameworks and fiscal arrangements. In that sense, EU legislation attempting to provide such facilities have consistently
fallen short of their initial objectives. Although IORP II now contains provisions on
collective value transfers between Member States[1194] by which entire pension schemes
may be moved from one IORP to another across EU borders, *individual* value transfers,
by which one scheme member would change pension funds, remains unaddressed and
would potentially destabilise collectively organised national occupational pension systems.

As to why the EU legislator was able to achieve portability and transferability in the
third pillar and not for the second, it seems plausible that the different roles these pension
pillars play could be the explanation. Whereas in some Member States the second pillar
plays a major role in the pension mix, it appears that the third pillar does not play such a
big role. It therefore seems likely that the Member States, and other stakeholders to the
EU's legislative process such as the social partners, could be more easily swayed for harmonisation in the third pillar.

Nevertheless, in some respects, the differences between the Member States' legislation
proved too great for the Member States to be open to maximum harmonisation. The
Commission noted that maximum harmonisation, even for a second regime in the third
pillar such as the PEPP, would go beyond what the Member States were ready to accept.
In that respect, the PEPP appears to suffer some of the same shortcomings as the cross-
border operation second-pillar pension schemes. For the PEPP, national standards still
apply where they are not harmonised by the PEPP Regulation. These aspects concern, for
instance, age limits for starting the accumulation phase, minimum duration of the accumulation phase, maximum and minimum amount of contributions and their duration in

---

1193 See Chapter 3.
1194 See, on this, R Veugelers, A van Damme & B Buggy, 'Waardeoverdracht op de schop door Europese
richtlijn' (2017) Pensioen Magazine 11.

accumulation phase, as well as related conditions pertaining to the decumulation phase are not regulated by the Regulation. As in the case of cross-border IORPs currently active, however, the potential obstacles posed by such differences in national legislation will likely be overcome. The extent to which such fragmentation will play a role in practice remains to be seen as prospective PEPP providers get ready to enter the market.

Nevertheless, the PEPP Regulation is to be recognised for its achievement of finally regulating the portability and transferability of pensions, even that is currently reserved for PEPPs.

Chapter 7: Conclusion

Review of the Research Results and the State of Affairs

The regulation of occupational pensions began three decades ago. In a 1991 Communication, the Commission explored the role of occupational pension schemes in the social protection of workers, and what the implications of such schemes are for workers' freedom of movement. In the years that followed, several measures were tabled, beginning with a proposal for a directive regulating the activity of pension funds as financial institutions in the Internal Market. This proposed directive placed the pension institutions, instead of the scheme member, at the centre of attention and focused on the freedom of management and investment of the funds held by IORPs. That proposal was subsequently withdrawn, after being amended, and culminated in a row between France and the Commission. By the late 1990s, a more holistic approach of occupational pension appeared to surface with attention both for the position of pension scheme members as well as for the role of IORPs in the internal market. In 1997, the Commission published a Green Paper which focused on the role of occupational pensions for the maintenance of retirement income levels and how the Single Market could help in facilitating their growth. The Commission predicted that the role of occupational pensions would grow, and apparently felt pressed to adopt legislation in this field.

Over the course of the 1990s and early 2000s, these efforts resulted in two concrete directives, the first being the Safeguard Directive, and the other the IORP I Directive. The Safeguard Directive was important in that it was the EU's first legislative measure to regulate occupational pensions. It has made an important contribution by making cross-border membership for posted workers possible, but its effects on the position of mobile workers are said to have been fairly limited: it applies the principle of non-discrimination to scheme members who leave a pension scheme to join a new scheme within the same Member State and those who leave a scheme to join another scheme in another EU Member State. The Directive also ensures that benefits can be paid on a cross-border basis. Later, the 2014 Supplementary Pension Rights Directive further improved the position of mobile Europeans, adding limits on waiting and vesting periods.

The IORP I Directive was the first step towards the creation of a European single market for occupational pensions. In the face of the EU's demographic developments, the Commission recognised a growing role for supplementary (2nd and 3rd pillar) pension provision. Cross-border IORPs were seen as one of the contributing solutions to ensuring the adequacy and safety of national pension systems. They would do that *inter alia* through achieving scale economies, with the added benefit that employees of multinational corporations could also benefit from remaining with the same IORP: this would ensure a lower administrative burden for workers as well as a more uniform benefit structure.

The EU's wish to realise its objectives to ensure better use of the common market for occupational pensions as well as the promotion of worker mobility has resulted in a body of EU legislation regulating occupational pension systems that has brought mixed results. Substantial contributions to worker mobility have been made through, for example, the limitation of waiting and vesting periods and the non-discriminatory treatment of accrued pension rights of workers leaving their Member State to pursue employment opportunities in other Member States (posted workers). In addition, occupational pension scheme members have been given the chance to benefit from the Single Market: not only have IORPs' investments been liberalised, giving them access to a greater pool of investment opportunities, these IORPs now also have the opportunity to pool assets and liabilities. According to the Commission and in the apparent practical experience of the employers who have set up cross-border IORPs, this Single Market gives them access to scale economies, at least theoretically benefiting pension scheme members.

Despite the Adoption of These Directives, Some Problems Remain.

With respect to IORPs' use of the internal market, Chapter 4 found that the IORP II Directive's minimum harmonisation character affords the Member States a great deal of discretion in the definition of what belongs to their social and labour laws and prudential standards respectively. The lack of a more precise definition of what constitutes social and labour law and what constitutes prudential law for the purposes of IORPs' cross-border activity may lead to conflicts that could negatively influence the position of pension scheme members. That lack of clarity could be used by IORPs and/or employers arguing that certain security mechanisms protecting the interests of pension scheme members do not apply. It could also make the supervision of cross-border IORPs' compliance with social and labour legislation more strenuous. Since it appears unlikely that social and labour law could – or should, considering the diversity of legislation in the Member States, the integrity of pension systems and the protection it provides to the workers – be harmonised for the purpose of the IORPs, this problem is hard to overcome unless the Directive provides stricter guidance on the distinction between labour law and prudential law. For this purpose I proposed to include into the IORP II Directive a limitative list of categories of social and labour legislation (without defining the substance of these categories). That proposed amendment to the IORP II Directive would solve the lack of clarity regarding the scope of the concepts of social and labour law and prudential law, benefiting the legal certainty of pension scheme members of cross-border IORPs. However, that proposed amendment will not be a solution to the barriers to market access IORPs face when seeking to offer their services in other Member States. Regarding their actual possibility to become active on a cross-border basis, Chapter 5 found that there is a myriad of legal as well as non-legal reasons why cross-border IORPs have not become more popular. The legal reasons encompass mainly differences in applicable social and labour legislation as well as fiscal obstacles preventing cross-border IORPs from proliferating. As fiscal legislation is beyond the scope of this dissertation, Chapter 5 studied a number of obstacles emanating from national social and labour legislation. It found that, provided they are not provided in a discriminatory manner, these obstacles to IORPs' freedom to provide services will likely be justifiable. Although that seems to be in the interest of pension scheme members – the legislation of their Member State that applies to occupational pension schemes is not thrown overboard in the interest of the freedom to provide services – the barriers to cross-border activity that IORPs face will remain in place. In summary, the problems regarding the security mechanisms are essential for the legal certainty of pension scheme members and can be resolved. On the other hand, the barriers to market access for IORPs resulting from differing legislation between the Member States can make their cross-border activity more complex, but not to such an extent that such activity is made impossible. The IORPs currently active on a cross-border basis attest to that.

With respect to worker mobility, occupational pension scheme members can face constraints on their mobility, although arguably less so when they are in a position to remain with the same IORP – for example as an employee of a multinational company. The absence of a regulated process for the transferability of accrued pension rights means that European workers still find themselves at the mercy of national legislation and pension scheme rules penalising (international) pension transfers. The possibility of preserving accrued pension rights cannot be seen as a full alternative to transferability of pension benefits: highly mobile workers will be confronted with a multitude of small entitlements, each incurring costs for both provide as well as scheme member, while at the same time being an administrative burden. The absence of a possibility for cross-border membership of a pension scheme, or portability, certainly has not made the situation of mobile workers any easier. In this regard, all three EU occupational pension directives have fallen short of their aims.

To some extent, the IORP II Directive's shortcomings in terms of worker mobility and scheme member protection can be explained by the fact that its focus is primarily on IORPs as financial institutions in the internal market, and not in the first place on the interests of pension scheme members. During the legislative history of the first IORP Directive, the closer integration of the rules that apply to occupational pension schemes was explicitly rejected, while differences in such rules seem to be the reason for many of the problems found in this dissertation. The result is that the IORP II Directive has fallen short of its objectives. There number of cross-border IORPs has remained low, and as a consequence, relatively few European workers have access to the benefits that the EU's Single Market could bring for pension scheme members. In addition, the Safeguard Directive and the Supplementary Pension Rights Directives have also fallen short of their initial aims, despite their greater focus on the interests of (mobile) pension scheme members. So there are several structural problems for realising the EU pension objectives.

A major structural problem, for both the IORP and the other two directives mentioned in the preceding paragraph, is the impact of the differences between Member States' social and labour law on the second pillar. Occupational pensions and "IORPs are wholesale products that by the nature of their activity are deeply integrated into national social protection systems and therefore regulated by national social and labour laws."[1195] The Member States have therefore tailored their occupational pension systems to their national policy objectives and national systems. Given the level of complexity of national pension systems and the diversity of these,[1196] it is difficult to have a system of IORPs that does not take account of social and labour law. The responses of stakeholders to a consultation on the review of the IORP Directive[1197] make clear how delicate the matter of social and labour legislation is. Several respondents noted that, while the lacking clarity on the scope of social and labour law and prudential in the IORP I Directive presented some difficulties, they believed that care should be taken that the EU legislator should overstep its boundaries, pointing to the subsidiarity principle. The amendment to the IORP II Directive clarifying what constitutes social and labour law presented in Chapter 4 would not likely run into subsidiarity problems, as it would not define the content of the categories listed in the provision.

Prospects for Future Regulation of Occupational Pensions by the EU

The EU's attempts to realise its objectives for occupational pension systems have always been a controversial topic. The legislative histories of the current EU directives regulating occupational pensions seem to attest to that. Regardless of the (political) sensitivity of the topic, the EU seems to have at its disposal an array of legal bases that give it the possibility to regulate extensively the pension systems of the Member States. Such powers include in particular the legal bases to regulate the Single Market, in particular those pertaining to the freedom to provide services and the free movement of workers, as well as Article 114 TFEU. These legal bases give it the power to remove obstacles to the free movement of workers caused by possible losses of occupational pension rights, obstacles to the freedom to provide services of IORPs and obstacles to the free movement of capital, such as those standing in the way of the cross-border payment of pension benefits to scheme retirees or

---

1195 See the Confederation of British Industry's response to the Call for Advice on the review of the IORP Directive 2003/41/EC (second consultation), available at https://eiopa.europa.eu/Publications/Comments/IORP-Cfa-2nd-Response_CBI.pdf accessed 8 January 2020.

1196 See Chapter 1.

1197 EIOPA, 'Summary of Comments on Consultation Paper: Response to the Call for Advice on the review of the IORP Directive 2003/41/EC: second consultation - EIOPA-CP-11/006 - Q 1-11' (2012) EIOPA-BoS-12/016, available at https://eiopa.europa.eu/Publications/Consultations/2.EIOPA_s_Resolutions_on_comments_received.pdf accessed 8 January 2020.

of the freedom of IORPs to invest in other Member States. Finally, Articles 48 TFEU and 153 TFEU even give the EU specific powers to regulate the social security and social protection of workers. In fact, Article 48 TFEU even obliges the EU to adopt measures in the field of social security which are necessary to provide freedom of movement for workers.

However, the Member States have defended their own prerogatives for the organisation of their pension systems. It is difficult to say where exactly the dividing line between the Member States' powers and those of the EU can be found in the field of occupational pensions. Although there seems to be an agreement[1198] that the Member States are responsible for the fundamental principles of their pension systems, there seems to be no guidance as to what these fundamental principles entail. The IORP II Directive names as an example "the decision on the role of each of the three pillars of the retirement system in individual Member States".[1199] One could deduce, on the basis of the legislative histories of the EU occupational pension directives, that matters such as the basic level of protection of workers under occupational pension schemes – see the debate on the inclusion of social elements during the legislative discussions on the IORP I Directive in Chapter 3 – and the transferability and portability of occupational pension rights also belong to those basic principles of which the Member States are in charge, since these could not be harmonised at EU level despite repeated efforts. However, the EU occupational pensions directives do arguably already regulate fundamental matters such as consumer protection, pension fund governance, waiting and vesting periods, the treatment of dormant pension rights and the cross-border membership of posted workers. All these aspects can be used to determine, for example, the control of an employer over a worker's pension rights (waiting and vesting periods), the level of protection a scheme member enjoys (consumer protection and governance standards) and the mobility of workers (treatment of dormant pension rights and cross-border membership of posted workers). Another apparent basic principle of occupational pension systems appears to be tax policy, which can stimulate or penalise specific forms of pension savings. Primary EU law – in particular the free movement of capital – and the Commission's tax communication[1200] dictate that discriminatory tax treatment of occupational pension contributions and benefits is not allowed.

Certainly in light of the broad formulation of the EU's prerogatives to regulate occupational pensions in order to realise free movement, the EU possesses the required powers in order to ensure the free movement of capital, services and persons in the field of pensions. These powers have also led to it regulating even what are arguably more

---

1198 See, for instance, Recital 19 of the IORP II Directive and Recital 9 of the Supplementary Pension Rights Directive.

1199 Recital 19 IORP II Directive.

1200 European Commission, 'The elimination of tax obstacles to the cross-border provision of occupational pensions' COM(2001) 214 final.

fundamental aspects of Member States' pension systems as well. Whether or not the EU legislator chooses to use these powers, and whether the Member States allow it to use these, is another matter. Ultimately, it seems a matter of political will to regulate any aspect of occupational pensions at EU level, both on the part of the Member States as well as the EU.

More Concrete: Solutions to the Problems Identified

In order to address the remaining obstacles to worker mobility and the difficulty created by differences in national social and labour legislation, EIOPA, industry professionals as well as academics have proposed the introduction a dedicated 2nd regime for occupational pensions. Such a regime, organised at EU level alongside the pension systems of the Member States, would have as an advantage a (partially) harmonised system, allowing for relatively less complicated transfers of pension rights and perhaps even cross-border membership. The issue of differing national social and labour legislation would also seemingly be resolved to some extent due to this harmonisation. EIOPA appears to be drawing inspiration for such an EU-level DC scheme from the PEPP Regulation. The PEPP Regulation has introduced a new personal pension product in the third pillar, which is available throughout the EU, with guaranteed transferability and the possibility of cross-border membership. This means that mobile employees can keep contributing to the same pension pot, regardless of where they live and work in the EU.

Since the implementation of an EU-wide second regime for occupational pensions is doubtlessly difficult and time-consuming to implement – it would require the start of an entirely new legislative procedure – I suggest that mobile workers could be exempted from national obligations to contribute to an occupational pension system in favour a solution that already exists: the PEPP. In order for this system to work, these individuals should be exempt from any applicable systems of compulsory membership under national law. Such a system could be introduced on the basis of Articles 45 and 48 TFEU. This exception would make use of existing EU legislation and, in the initial phase, access to this exemption would be for limited groups of individuals only, such as mobile construction workers, employees of multinational corporations or academics. Because the introduction of this exemption would (initially) be limited in scope and would not require the design of an entirely new system, but rather a coordination between the PEPP Regulation and occupational pension systems, it could be implemented quite quickly. With its introduction, the possible loss of occupational pension rights and the accumulation of small pension entitlements with a number of providers in different Member States – both of which are still problems in the EU for mobile workers – would be addressed.

The recent adoption of the PEPP Regulation seems to show that the regulation of pension scheme features as well as their transferability and portability can be regulated in respect of the third pillar, indicating that the Member States would be more open to

EU legislation in the third pillar rather than the second. This can be explained by the generally smaller role played by third-pillar systems in the retirement provision of Europeans, making Member States more likely to be open to EU-level legislation. If occupational pensions are to provide the same degree of flexibility and mobility as a PEPP, major changes to Member States' pension systems would be needed. In order for a system of national sub-accounts, such as that in the PEPP Regulation allowing cross-border membership, to be implemented in the second pillar, it appears that occupational pension schemes must also be uncoupled from the employer. This is because second-pillar pension schemes are tied to the employer who offers the scheme. Because the Member States are – rightfully – cautious about major changes to their pension systems, and because changing the occupational pension systems of all Member States so that an EU-wide system of occupational pensions can be implemented hardly seems proportional, it is unlikely that this can be achieved. For this reason, the coordination between the second and the third pillar for mobile workers, by allowing some groups of mobile workers to be exempt from national obligations to contribute to an occupational pension scheme in favour of a PEPP, seems to be a feasible and – for mobile workers – useful option.

Bibliography

Books and Contribution to Books

Arnot S, *Directive 2003/41/EC on the Activities and Supervision of Institutions for Occupational Retirement Provision* (European Federation for Retirement Provision 2004.

Anderson K, *Occupational Pensions in Sweden* (Friedrich Ebert Stiftung 2015), available at http://library.fes.de/pdf-files/id/12113.pdf accessed 3 January 2020.

Anderson K, 'Pension Reform in Europe: Context Drivers, Impact' in S Scherger (ed), *Paid Work Beyond Pension Age. Comparative Perspectives* (Palgrave Macmillan 2015).

Barr N & Diamond P, *Reforming Pensions: Principles and Policy Choices* (Oxford University Press 2008).

Barr N, *The pension system in Finland: Adequacy, sustainability and system design* (Finnish Centre for Pensions 2013).

Barnard C, *The Substantive Law Law of the EU: The Four Freedoms* (6th edn Oxford University Press, 2019).

Baugniet W, *The protection of occupational pensions under European Union law on the freedom of movement for workers*, dissertation European University Institute Florence (2014).

Bittner C, *Europäisches und internationales Betriebsrentenrecht* (Mohr Siebeck 2000).

Bodie Z & Mitchell O, 'Pension Security in an Aging World' in Z Bodie, O Mitchell & J Turner (eds), *Securing Employer-Based Pensions: An International Perspective* (University of Pennsylvania Press 1996).

Borsjé P & van Meerten H, 'A European Pensions Union: Towards a Strengthening of the European Pension Systems' in F Pennings & G Vonk (eds), *Research Handbook on European Social Security Law* (Edward Elgar Publishing 2015).

Cahill D and others, *European Law* (Oxford University Press 2011).

Cherednychenko O, 'Fundamental Rights, European Private Law, and Financial Services' in H Micklitz (ed), *Constitutionalization of European Private Law (Vol. XXII/2)* (Oxford University Press 2014).

Copeland P & ter Haar B, 'The Coordinated governance of EU social security policy: Will there ever be enough?' in F Pennings & G Vonk (eds), *Research Handbook on European Social Security Law* (Edward Elgar Publishing 2015).

Craig P & de Búrca G, *EU Law: Text, Cases and Materials* (5th edn, Oxford University Press 2011).

Craig P & de Búrca G, *EU Law: Text, Cases and Materials* (6th edn, Oxford University Press 2015).

Davis E P, *Portfolio Regulation of Life Insurance Companies and Pension Funds (OECD Insurance and Private Pensions Compendium for Emerging Economies, Book 2 Part 1:3)a* (OECD 2001) 30-31. Available at: http://www.oecd.org/daf/fin/private-pensions/1815732.pdf .

Dijkhoff A, *International social security standards in the European Union: The Cases of the Czech Republic and Estonia* (Intersentia 2011).

Ebbinghaus B & Gronwald M, 'The Changing Public-Private Pension Mix in Europe: From Path Dependence to Path Departure' in B Ebbinghaus (ed), *The Varieties of Pension Governance: Pension Privatization in Europe* (Oxford University Press 2011).

Ernst & Young, *Pan-European pension funds in a future world* (Ernst & Young 2009).

Essers G & Distler K, *Guide for Mobile European Workers* (European Trade Union Confederation 2017).

European Federation for Retirement Provision, *European institutions for occupational retirement provision: the EFRP model for Pan-European pensions* (European Federation for Retirement Provision 2003).

Goudswaard K, 'Blijft het Nederlandse pensioenstelsel bijzonder?' in R Bijl et al (eds) *Opvallend gewoon. Het bijzondere van Nederland* (Sociaal en Cultureel Planbureau 2013).

Guardiancich I & Natali D, 'The Changing EU 'Pension Programme': Policy Tools and Ideas in the Shadow of the Crisis' in D Natali (ed), *The New Pension Mix in Europe: Recent Reforms, Their Distributional Effects and Political Dynamics* (PIE Peter Lang 2017).

Hartlapp M, 'Intra-Kommissionsdynamik im Policy-Making: EU-Politiken angesichts des demographischen Wandels' in I Tömmel (ed), *Die Europäische Union: Governance und Policy-Making* (VS Verlag für Sozialwissenschaften 2007).

Heemskerk M, *Pensioenrecht* (Boom Juridische Uitgevers 2015).

Hennessy A, *The Europeanization of Workplace Pensions: Economic Interests, Social Protection, and Credible Signaling* (Cambridge University Press 2013).

Hinrichs K & Lynch J, 'Old-Age Pensions' in F Castles and others (eds), *The Oxford Handbook of the Welfare State* (Oxford University Press 2010).

Hooghiemstra S, *Depositaries in European Investment Law: Towards Harmonization in Europe*, dissertation Utrecht University (Eleven International Publishing 2018).

Hopfner S & Erdmann KU, *Praxishandbuch Arbeitsrecht: Beginn, Durchführung und Beendigung des Arbeitsverhältnisses* (VVW 2017).

Houwerzijl M & Verschuren H 'Free Movement of (Posted) Workers and Applicable Labour and Social Security Law' in T Jaspers, F Pennings & S Peters (eds), *European Labouw Law* (Intersentia 2019).

International Labour Organization, *Coordination of Social Security Systems in the European Union: An explanatory report on EC Regulation No. 883/2004 and its Implementing Regulation No. 987/2009* (ILO 2010).

Kok L, van der Lecq F, Lutjens E, *Verplichtgestelde bedrijfstakpensioenfondsen en het algemeen pensioenfonds* (SEO Economisch Onderzoek 2015).

Kok L & Geboers H, *Grensoverschrijdende Pensioenuitvoering* (SEO Economisch Onderzoek 2016).

Leczykiewicz D, 'Conceptualising Conflict between the Economic and the Social in EU Law in EU Law after *Viking* and *Laval*' in M Freedland & J Prassl (eds), *EU Law in the Member States: Viking, Laval and Beyond* (Hart Publishing 2014) 308.

Leino P, 'The Institutional Politics of Objective Choice: Competence as a Framework for Argumentation' in S Gerben & I Govaere (eds), *The Division of Competences Between the EU and the Member States: Reflections on the Past, Present and the Future* (Hart Publishing 2017).

Mackenzie B et al, *Wiley Interpretation and Application of International Financial Reporting Standards* (Wiley 2014).

Maletić I, *The Law and Policy of Harmonisation in Europe's Internal Market* (Edward Elgar Publishing 2013).

van Meerten H, 'The Scope of the EU 'Pensions'-Directive: Some Background and Solutions for Policymakers' in U Neergaard and others (eds), *Social Services of General Interest in the EU* (TMC Asser Press 2013).

van Meerten H & Borsjé P, 'Pension Rights and Entitlement Conversion ('invaren'): Lessons from a Dutch Perspective with Regard to the Implications of the EU Charter' (2016) 18 (1) European Journal of Social Security 46.

van Meerten H, *EU Pension Law* (Amsterdam University Press 2019).

Natali D, *Pensions in Europe, European Pensions* (PIE Peter Lang 2008).

OECD, *Private Pensions: OECD Classification and Glossary* (OECD Publishing 2005) 14.

OECD, 'Pension Country Profile: Denmark' in: *OECD Private Pensions Outlook 2008* (OECD Publishing 2009).

OECD, *Ageing and Employment Policies: The Netherlands 2014: Working Better with Age* (OECD Publishing 2014).

Orenstein M, *Privatizing Pensions: The Transnational Campaign for Social Security Reform*, (Princeton University Press 2008).

Palier B (ed), *A Long Goodbye to Bismarck?: The Politics of Welfare Reform in Continental Europe*, (Amsterdam University Press 2010.

Pennings F, *European Social Security Law* (Intersentia 2015).

Pieters D & Vansteenkiste S, *The Thirteenth State: Towards a European Community Social Insurance Scheme for Intra-Community Migrants* (Acco Uitgeverij 1993).

Pochet P, 'Pensions: the European debate' in G L Clark and N Witheside (eds), *Pension security in the 21st century* (Oxford University Press 2003.

van der Poel M, *De houdbaarheid van verplichtgestelde bedrijfstakpensioenfondsen en beroepspensioenregelingen: Toetsing aan het mededingingsrecht en het vrij verkeer van* *diensten en vestiging* (Expertisecentrum Pensioenrecht Vrije Universiteit Amsterdam 2013).

Reiner M, 'Strukturfragen zum Zusammenspiel von Aufsichts- und Arbeitsrecht im europäischen Pensionsfondsgeschäft gemäß IORP II' in D Krömer and others (eds), *Arbeitsrecht und Arbeitswelt im Europäischen Wandel* (Nomos 2016) .

Roos L, *Pensioen en werknemersmobiliteit in de EU – Fiscale en juridische aspecten* (Universiteit van Tilburg 2006).

Schlewing A et al, *Arbeitsrecht der betrieblichen Altersversorgung* (Verlag Dr. Otto Schmidt 2019).

Schols-Van Oppen E, 'De collectieve beschikbarepremieregeling' in *De CDC-Regeling: stand van zaken anno 2008* (Sdu Fiscale & Financiële Uitgevers 2008).

Schols-van Oppen E, *Inleiding pensioenrecht* (Wolters Kluwer 2015).

Schütze R, 'EU Competences: Existence and Exercise' in A Arnull & D Chalmers (eds), *The Oxford Handbook of European Law* (Oxford University Press 2015).

Sjåfjell B, 'Quo vadis, Europe? The significance of sustainable development as objective, principle and rule of EU law' in C Bailliet (ed), *Non-State Actors, Soft Law and Protective Regimes: From the Margins* (Cambridge University Press 2012).

Uebelhack B, *Betriebliche Altersversorgung – Grundlagen und Praxis* (C.F. Müller 2011).

Vielle P, 'How the Horizontal Social Clause can be made to Work: The lessons of Gender Mainstreaming' in N Bruun, K Lörcher & I Schömann (eds), *The Lisbon Treaty and Social Europe* (Hart Publishing 2012).

Weatherill S, '*Viking* and *Laval*: The EU Internal Market Perspective' in M Freedland & J Prassl (eds), *EU Law in the Member States:* Viking, Laval *and Beyond* (Hart Publishing 2014).

Weiss F and Kaupa C, *European Union Internal Market Law* (Cambridge University Press 2014).

Wienk M, 'Europese coördinatie van aanvullende pensioenen' (Doctoral dissertation, Koninklijke Universiteit Brabant 1999).

World Bank, *Averting the Old Age Crisis* (Oxford University Press 1994).

Zeckhauser, R 'Investing in the Unknown and the Unknowable' in F Diebold, N Doherty & R Herring (eds), *The Known, the Unknown, and the Unknowable in Financial Risk Management: Measurement and Theory Advancing Practice* (Princeton University Press 2010).

Journal Articles, Working Papers, Discussion Papers

Adascalitei D & Domonkos S, 'Reforming against all odds: Multi-pillar pension systems in the Czech Republic and Romania' (2015) Vol 68 (2) International Social Security Review 85.

Atchley R, 'Retirement Income Security: Past, Present and Future' (1997) Vol 21 (2) Generations.

Beechinor G & Hoekstra C, 'CDC Focus: Has CDC already had its day?' (2014) UK Plansponsor.

Bercusson B, 'Introduction: Interpreting the EU Charter in the context of the social dimension of European integration' in B. Bercusson (ed), *European labour law and the EU Charter of Fundamental Rights – Summary Version* (ETUI 2002) 9.

Betson, 'Member states are blocking "prudent man" directive' (Investment & Pensions Europe, 24 October 2001) available at https://www.ipe.com/member-states-are-blocking-prudent-man-directive/4578.article accessed 2 January 2020.

Bikker J, 'De kostenefficiëntie van pensioenfondsen' (2013) Vol 4 Tijdschrift voor pensioenvraagstukken 15.

Bikker J, 'De optimale schaal van pensioenfondsen' (2013) 98(4662) Economisch Statistische Berichten 378.

Bittner C, 'Occupational Pensions: a Matter of European Concern' (2001) Vol 2 (2) European Business Organization Law Review 401.

Blake D, 'Two Decades of Pension Reform in the UK: What Are the Implications for Occupational Pension Schemes?' (2000) Vol 22 (3) Employee Relations 223.

Bodie Z, 'Pensions as retirement income insurance' (1989) National Bureau of Economic Research Working Paper No. 2917.

Bodie Z, 'Pension funds and financial innovation' (1989) National Bureau of Economic Research Working Paper No. 3103.

Boon L-N et al, 'Pension Regulation and Investment Performance: Rule-Based vs. Risk-Based' (2014) Netspar Discussion Paper, available at https://ssrn.com/abstract=2414477 accessed 2 January 2020.

Borg K, Minto A & van Meerten H, 'The EU's regulatory commitment to a European Harmonised Pension Product (PEPP): The Portability of Pension Rights vis-à-vis the Free Movement of Capital' (2019) 5 *Journal of Financial Regulation* 2019 1.

van Boven H, 'Keuzevrijheid van pensioenuitvoerder: een Nederlands model', *Netspar Academic Series Paper* 2017, available at https://www.netspar.nl/assets/uploads/P20170611_Tias-Netspar010_Boven.pdf accessed 7 January 2020.

Bovenberg L, 'European pension reform: A way forward' (2010) Vol 16 (2) Pensions 76.

Bovenberg L, Cox R & Lundbergh S, 'Lessons from the Swedish Occupational Pension System: Are Mutual Life Insurance Companies a Relevant Model for Occupation Pensions in the Netherlands' (2015) Netspar Industry Paper Series no 45, 19, available at https://pure.uvt.nl/ws/portalfiles/portal/9092186/netspar_design_paper_45.pdf accessed 7 January 2020.

Bovenberg L & Gradus R, 'Reforming occupational pension schemes: the case of the Netherlands' (2015) Vol 18 (3) Journal of Economic Policy Review 244.

van den Brink T, van Meerten H & de Vries S, 'Regulating Pensions: Why the European Union Matters' (2011) Netspar Discussion Paper, available at ssrn.com/abstract=1950765 accessed 20 November 2019.

Broadbent J, Palumbo M & Woodman E, 'The Shift from Defined Benefit to Defined Contribution Pension Plans – Implications for Asset Allocation and Risk Management' (2006) Paper prepared for a Working Group on Institutional Investors, Global Savings and Asset Allocation established by the Committee on the Global Financial System.

Broeders D & Chen A, 'Pension Benefit Security: A Comparison of Solvency Requirements, a Pension Guarantee Fund and Sponsor Support' (2013) Vol 80 (2) The Journal of Risk and Insurance 239, 240.

Brooks S, 'Interdependent and domestic foundations of policy change: The diffusion of pension privatization around the world' (2005) Vol 49 (2) International Studies Quarterly 273.

Carone G and others, 'Pension Reforms in the EU since the Early 2000's: Achievements and Challenges Ahead' (2016) European Commission Discussion Paper 042, available at ec.europa.eu/info/sites/info/files/dp042_en.pdf accessed 27 November 2019.

CESifo, 'Bismarck versus Beveridge: A Comparison of Social Insurance Systems in Europe' (2008) 4/2008 DICE Report available at www.ifo.de/DocDL/dicereport408-db6.pdf accessed 18 September 2019.

Chen D & Beetsma R, 'Mandatory Participation in Occupational Pension Schemes in the Netherlands and Other Countries: An Update' (2015) No. 10/2015-032 Netspar Academic Series, available at ssrn.com/abstract=2670476 accessed 25 September 2019.

Chybalski F & Gumola M, 'The similarity of European pension systems in terms of OMC objectives: A cross country study' (2018) Vol 52 Social Policy & Administration 1425, available at onlinelibrary.wiley.com/doi/epdf/10.1111/spol.12406 accessed 4 December 2019.

Clemens J & Förstemann T, 'Das System der betrieblichen Altersversorgung in Deutschland' (2015) Vol 95 (9) Analysen und Berichte Rentenpolitik 628.

Cui J, de Jong F & Ponds E, 'Intergenerational risk sharing within funded pension schemes' (2011) Vol 10 (1) Journal of Pension Economics and Finance 1.

Davis E P, 'Prudent person rules or quantitative restrictions? The regulation of long-term institutional investors' portfolios' (2001) Vol 1 (2) Journal of Pension Economics and Finance 157.

Davis E P & Hu Y-W, 'Should Pension Investing be Regulated' (2009) Vol 2 (1) Rotman International Journal of Pension Management 34.

Dejmek P, 'No Flying Start but a Bright Future for EU Directive 2003/41/EC on Occupational Pension Institutions' (2006) Vol 17 (5) European Business Law Review 1381.

Del Sol M & Rocca M, 'Free movement of workers in the EU and occupational pensions: conflicting priorities? Between case law and legislative interventions' (2017) Vol 19 (2) European Journal of Social Security 141.

Detienne Q & Schmidt E, 'Social Pensions and Market Values: A Conflict?' (2019) Vol 15 (2) Utrecht Law Review 81.

Dowsey M, 'Review of the IORP Directive' (2012) Vol 17 (3) Pensions 158.

Draghi & R Pozen, 'US-EU Regulatory Convergence: Capital Markets Issues' (2003) Harvard Law School Discussion Paper No. 444, 10, available at https://ssrn.com/abstract=460560 accessed 2 January 2020.

Draper N, Nibbelink A & Uhde J, 'An Assessment of Alternatives for the Dutch First Pension Pillar the Design of Pension Schemes' (2013) CPB Discussion Paper 259.

Eckardt M, 'The open method of coordination on pensions: an economic analysis of its effects on pension reforms' (2005) Vol 15 (3) Journal of European Social Policy 247.

Ebbinghaus B & Wiß T, 'Taming Pension Fund Capitalism in Europe: Collective and State Regulation in Times of Crisis' (2011) Vol 17 (1) Transfer 15.

Ebbinghaus B & Whiteside N, 'Shifting responsibilities in Western European pension systems: What future for social models?' (2012) Vol 12 (3) Global Social Policy 266.

Ebbinghaus B, 'The Privatization and Marketization of Pensions in Europe: A Double Transformation Facing the Crisis' (2015) Vol 1 (1) European Policy Analysis 56.

Franzen D, 'Managing Investment Risk in Defined Benefit Pension Funds' (2010) OECD Working Papers on Insurance and Private Pensions No 38.

Fultz E, 'The retrenchment of second-tier pensions in Hungary and Poland: A precautionary tale' (2012) Vol 65 (3) International Social Security Review.

Goode R, 'Occupational Pensions: Securing the Pension Promise' (1994) Vol 9 (1) The Denning Law Journal 15.

Gradus R, 'Bouwstenen voor een toekomstbestendig pensioenstelsel' (2014) Vol 19 (4) PensioenMagazine 30.

Guardiancich I & Natali D, 'The EU and Supplementary Pensions: Instruments for Integration and the Market for Occupational Pensions in Europe' (2009) 2009.11 ETUI Working Paper.

Guardiancich I, 'Denmark: Current pension system: first assessment of reform outcomes and output'(2010) European Social Observatory, available at www.ose.be/files/publication/2010/country_reports_pension/OSE_2010_CRpension_Denmark.pdf accessed 27 November 2019.

Guardiancich I, 'Pan-European pension funds: Current situation and future prospects' (2011) Vol 64 (1) International Social Security Review 15.

Guardiancich I & Natali D, 'The cross-border portability of supplementary pensions: Lessons from the European Union'(2012) Vol 12 (3) Global Social Policy 300.

Guardiancich I, 'Portability of Supplementary Pension Rights in Europe: A Lowest Common Denominator Solution' (2015), Vol 1 (1) European Policy Analysis 74.

Guardiancich I, 'The "Leap" from Coordination to Harmonization in Social Policy: Labour Mobility and Occupational Pensions in Europe' (2016) Vol 54 (6) Journal of Common Market Studies 2016 1313.

Hartlapp M, 'Deconstructing EU old age policy: Assessing the potential of soft OMCs and hard EU law' (2012) European Integration Online Papers (EIoP), Special Mini-Issue 1, Vol 16, Article 3, available at eiop.or.at/eiop/texte/2012-003a.htm accessed 4 December 2019.

Haverland M, 'When the welfare state meets the regulatory state: EU occupational pension policy' (2007) Vol 14 (6) Journal of European Public Policy 886.

Hinrichs K, 'Elephants on the move. Patterns of public pension reform in OECD countries' (2000) European Review 353.

Hinrichs K, 'Active Citizens and Retirement Planning: Enlarging Freedom of Choice in the Course of Pension Reforms in Nordic Countries and Germany' (2004) ZeS-Arbeitspapiere/Universität Bremen No 11/2004.

Holzmann R, 'Global pension systems and their reform: Worldwide drivers, trends and challenges' (2013) Vol 66 (2) International Social Security Review 1.

Jacqueson C & Pennings F, 'Equal Treatment of Mobile Persons in the Context of a Social Market Economy' (2019) Vol 15 (2) Utrecht Law Review 64.

Kalogeropoulou K, 'European Governance after Lisbon and Portability of Supplementary Pensions Rights' (2006) Vol 2 (1) Journal of Contemporary European Research 75.

Kalogeropoulou K, 'Addressing the Pension Challenge: Can the EU respond? Towards facilitating the portability of supplementary (occupational) pension rights' (2014) Vol 16 (4) European Journal of Law Reform, 747.

Khort J, 'Regulation of Pension Fund Investment Allocations in Private Equity; Analysis of the IORP Directive of 2003/41/EC Reform' (2015) Uppsala Faculty of Law Working Paper 2015:1, available at https://www.jur.uu.se/digitalAssets/585/c_585476-l_3-k_wps2015-1.pdf accessed 2 January 2020.

Kiveron P & van Meerten H, '"DBization", a continuing story' (2014) Pensioen Magazine 30.

Knoef M et al, 'Nederlandse pensioenopbouw in internationaal perspectief' (2015) Netspar Industry Series Paper, 18, available at https://www.netspar.nl/assets/uploads/Netspar_design_41-WEB-1.pdf accessed 3 January 2020.

Krzyzak K, 'Czech second-pillar pension system to close by January 2016' (Investment and Pensions Europe, 13 November 2014) available at www.ipe.com/news/regulation/czech-second-pillar-pension-system-to-close-by-january-2016/10004774.fullarticle accessed 25 September 2019.

Krzyzak K, 'Czech second-pillar pension closure moves ahead' (Investment and Pensions Europe, 23 June 2015) available at www.ipe.com/countries/cee/czech-second-pillar-pension-closure-moves-ahead/10008615.fullarticle accessed 25 September 2019.

Lannoo K, 'The Draft Pension Funds Directive and the Financing of Pensions in the EU' (1996) 21 The Geneva Papers on Risk and Insurance 114.

Lodge M, 'Comparing Non-Hierarchical Governance in Action: the Open Method of Co-ordination in Pensions and Information Society' (2007) Vol 45 No 2 Journal of Common Market Studies 343.

Lommen J, 'De API is een no-brainer' (2009) No 25 Netspar NEA Papers, available at www.netspar.nl/assets/uploads/NEA_25_WEB.pdf accessed 20 November 2019.

Luijken C, 'Fiscaal kader voor indexatie van pensioenen' (2015) *NTFR Beschouwingen.*

Mabbett D, 'Supplementary pensions between social policy and social regulation' (2009) Vol 32 (4) West European Politics 774.

Marshall J & Butterworth S, 'Pensions Reform in the EU: The Unexploded Time Bomb in the Single Market' (2000) Vol 37 (3) Common Market Law Review 739.

van Meerten H & van Haersolte JC, 'Zelfrijzend Europees Bakmeel: de Voorstellen Voor Een Nieuw Toezicht Op de Financiële Sector' (2010) No 2 Nederlands Tijdschrift voor Europees Recht 33.

van Meerten H, 'Vrij verkeer van diensten voor verzekeraars en pensioeninstellingen: Solvency II basic en de verplichtstelling' (2012) No 7/8 Tijdschrift voor Financieel Recht 290.

van Meerten H & Borsjé P, 'Pension Rights and Entitlement Conversion ('invaren'): Lessons from a Dutch Perspective with Regard to the Implications of the EU Charter'(2016) 18 (1) European Journal of Social Security 46.

van Meerten H & Schmidt E, 'Compulsory Membership of Pension Schemes and the Free Movement of Services in the EU' (2017) Vol 19 (2) European Journal of Social Security 118.

van Meerten H & van Slagmaat M, 'Implementatie IORP II roept vragen op' (2017) Pensioen & Praktijk 5.

van Meerten H & Wouters A, 'Can A Dutch IORP offer A PEPP' (CBBA-Europe Review 2018) 8-32, available at https://www.cbba-europe.eu/wp-content/uploads/2018/07/CBBA-Europe- review_July-2018.pdf accessed 8 January 2020.

van Meerten H & Wouters A, 'The PEPP Regulation (PEPPR): Pepper for the Capital Markets Union?' (2019) Zeitschrift für Versicherungsrecht 1.

van Meerten H & van Zanden J, 'Pensions and the PEPP: The Necessity of an EU Approach' (2018) 15 No 3 European Company Law Journal 66.

van Meerten H & Geerling L, 'Build that wall? Het onderscheid tussen binnenlandse en grensoverschrijdende waardeoverdrachten van pensioenregelingen' (2019) No 2 Tijdschrift voor Recht en Arbeid.

van Meerten H & Hooghiemstra S, 'PEPP—Towards a Harmonized European Legislative Framework for Personal Pensions' (2017) Working paper June 2017, 23 et seq, available at https://ssrn.com/abstract=2993991 accessed 8 January 2020.

van Meerten H & Hooghiemstra S, 'The PEPP: A Pension Solution for the Future' (2017) Fall Issue, Pension & Longevity Risk Transfer for Institutional Investors, 44.

Minnaard M, 'Bijstorting: wettelijke of contractuele plicht?' (2013) PensioenMagazine.

Natali D, 'The Open Method of Coordination on Pensions: Does it De-politicise Pensions Policy?' (2009) Vol 32 (4) West European Politics 810.

Natali D, 'Reforming Pensions in the EU: National Policy Changes and EU Coordination' (2011) European Social Observatory, available at www.ose.be/files/publication/dnatali/Natali_2011_-FLCaballero_251011.pdf accessed 27 November 2019.

Natali D, *Pensions after the financial and economic crisis: a comparative analysis of recent reforms in Europe* (2011) Etui Working Paper 2011.07.

Oliver E, 'From portability to acquisition and preservation: the challenge of legislating in the area of supplementary pensions' (2009) Vol 32 (4) Journal of Social Welfare & Family Law, 173.

Orenstein M, 'Pension privatization in crisis: Death or rebirth of a global policy trend?' (2011) Vol 11 (3) International Social Security Review 65.

Ottawa B, 'Resaver to receive first payments in March', (Investment and Pensions Europe, 6 February 2017) available at https://www.ipe.com/resaver-to-receive-first-payments-in-march-amended/10017443.article accessed 3 January 2020.

Pennings F, 'Case C-379/09, *Maurits Casteels v. British Airways plc*, Judgment of the Court (Third Chamber) of 10 March 2011, nyr.' (2012) Vol 49 (5) Common Market Law Review 1787.

Reiner M, 'Entwicklung und Probleme des europäischen Betriebspensionsrechts am Beispiel der Mobilitätsrichtlinie' (2017) Vol 1 (2) Journal für Arbeitsrecht und Sozialrecht 168.

Reiner M & Horvath R, 'Das neue europäische private Altersvorsorgeprodukt PEPP (Pan European Personal Pension Product) und seine Marktgängigkeut im Binnenmarkt: Eine kritische Intervention' (2018) Working Paper 98/2018 by the University of Applied Sciences BFI Vienna.

Rohwer A, 'Bismarck versus Beveridge: Ein Vergleich von Sozialversicherungssystemen in Europa' (2008) Vol 61 (21) ifo Schnelldienst, ifo Institut für Wirtschaftsforschung an der Universität München 26.

Prechal S & de Vries S, 'Seamless web of judicial protection in the internal market?' (2009) Vol 31 (1) European Law Review 5.

Schop E, 'België-route niet omstreden, wel lastig' (2015) *PensioenAdvies*.

Seikel D & Absenger N, 'Die Auswirkungen der EuGH-Rechtsprechung auf das Tarifvertragssystem in Deutschland' (2014) Vol 22 (1) Industrielle Beziehungen 51.

Starink B & van Meerten H, 'Cross-border obstacles and solutions for pan-European pensions' (2011) Vol 20 (1) EC Tax Review 30.

Stevens Y, 'Het Europees recht en het sociaal recht nogmaals onder hoogspanning: de Albany voorwaarde getest op de openbare aanbesteding', (2011) (2) *Chroniques de droit social/Sociaalrechtelijke kronieken*, 61.

Stevens Y, 'The silent pension pillar implosion' (2017) Vol 19 (2) European Journal of Social Security 98.

Stewart F, 'Benefit Security Pension Fund Guarantee Schemes' (2007) OECD Working Papers on Insurance and Private Pensions No 5.

Syrpis P, 'Reconciling Economic Freedoms and Social Rights—The Potential of *Commission v. Germany* (Case C-271/08, Judgment of 15 July 2010)' (2011) Vol 40 (2) Industrial Law Journal 222.

Url T, 'Occupational Pension Schemes in Austria' (2003) 2/2003 Austrian Economic Quarterly 64.

van der Vaart L & van Meerten H, 'De pensioen opPEPPer?' (2018) 1 Tijdschrift voor Pensioenvraagstukken 38.

Zaidi A, Grech A & Fuchs M, Pension policy in EU25 and its possible impact on elderly poverty (2006) Centre for Analysis of Social Exclusion paper 116.

Zavvos G, 'Pension Fund Liberalization and the Future of Retirement Financing in Europe' (1994) Vol 31 (3) Common Market Law Review 609.

EU Legislation

Council regulation EEC No 1408/71 of 14 June 1971 on the application of social security schemes to employed persons and their families moving within the Community, OJ L 149/2.

Council Regulation 574/72 of 21 March 1972 fixing the procedure for implementing Regulation (EEC) No 1408/71 on the application of social security schemes to employed persons and their families moving within the Community, OJ L 74/1.

Council Directive 77/187/EEC of 14 February 1977 on the approximation of the laws of the Member States relating to the safeguarding of employees' rights in the event of transfers of undertakings, businesses or parts of businesses [1977] OJ L 61/26.

Council Directive 80/987/EEC of 20 October 1980 on the approximation of the laws of the Member States relating to the protection of employees in the event of the insolvency of their employer [1980] OJ L 283/23.

Council Directive 86/378/EEC of 24 July 1986 on the implementation of the principle of equal treatment for men and women in occupational social security schemes [1986] OJ L 225/40.

Council Directive 92/50/EEC of 18 June 1992 relating to the coordination of procedures for the award of public service contracts [1992] OJ L 209/1 and Directive 2004/18/EC of the European Parliament and of the Council of 31 March 2004 on the coordination of procedures for the award of public works contracts, public supply contracts and public service contracts [2004] OJ L 134/114.

Directive 96/71/EC of the European Parliament and of the Council of 16 December 1996 concerning the posting of workers in the framework of the provision of services, [1997] OJ L 18/1.

Council Directive 98/49/EC of 29 June 1998 on safeguarding the supplementary pension rights of employed and self-employed persons moving within the Community [1998] OJ L 209/46.

Council Directive 2000/78/EC of 27 November 2000 establishing a general framework for equal treatment in employment and occupation [2000] OJ L 303/16.

Council Directive 2001/23/EC of 12 March 2001 on the approximation of the laws of the Member States relating to the safeguarding of employees' rights in the event of transfers of undertakings, businesses or parts of undertakings or businesses [2001] OJ L 82/16.

Directive 2003/41/EC of the European Parliament and of the Council of 3 June 2003 on the activities and supervision of institutions for occupational retirement provision [2003] OJ L 235/10.

Directive 2006/54/EC of the European Parliament and of the Council of 5 July 2006 on the implementation of the principle of equal opportunities and equal treatment of men and women in matters of employment and occupation (recast) [2006] OJ L 204/23.

Regulation 988/2009 of the European Parliament and the Council of 16 September 2009 amending Regulation (EC) No 883/2004 on the coordination of social security systems [2009] OJ L 284/43.

Directive 2009/65/EC of the European Parliament and of the Council of 13 July 2009 on the coordination of laws, regulations and administrative provisions relating to undertakings for collective investment in transferable securities (UCITS) (recast) [2009] OJ L 302/32.

Directive 2009/138/EC of the European Parliament and of the Council of 25 November 2009 on the taking-up and pursuit of the business of Insurance and Reinsurance (Solvency II) [2009] OJ L 335/1.

Directive 2011/61/EU of the European Parliament and of the Council of 8 June 2011 on Alternative Investment Fund Managers and amending Directives 2003/41/EC and 2009/65/EC and Regulations (EC) No 1060/2009 and (EU) No 1095/2010 [2011] OJ L 174/1.

Directive 2014/50/EU of the European Parliament and of the Council of 16 April 2014 on minimum requirements for enhancing worker mobility between Member States by improving the acquisition and preservation of supplementary pension rights [2014] OJ L 128/1.

Directive 2014/65/EU of the European Parliament and of the Council of 15 May 2014 on markets in financial instruments and amending Directive 2002/92/EC and Directive 2011/61/EU (MiFID II) [2014] OJ L 173/349.

Regulation (EC) No 883/2004 of the European Parliament and the Council of 29 April 2004 on the coordination of social security systems [2004] OJ L 166/1.

Directive 2008/94/EC of the European Parliament and of the Council of 22 October 2008 on the protection of employees in the event of the insolvency of their employer [2008] OJ L 283/36.

Directive 2013/36/EU of the European Parliament and of the Council of 26 June 2013 on access to the activity of credit institutions and the prudential supervision of credit institutions and investment firms, amending Directive 2002/87/EC and repealing Directives 2006/48/EC and 2006/49/EC [2013] OJ L 176/338.

Directive 2014/50/EU of the European Parliament and of the Council of 16 April 2014 on minimum requirements for enhancing worker mobility between Member States by improving the acquisition and preservation of supplementary pension rights [2014] OJ L 128/1.

Directive 2016/2341/EU of the European Parliament and of the Council of 14 December 2016 on the activities and supervision of institutions for occupational retirement provision (IORPs) [2016] OJ L 354/37.

Directive 2018/957/EU of the European Parliament and of the Council of 28 June 2018 amending Directive 96/71/EC concerning the posting of workers in the framework of the provision of services [2018] OJ L 173/16.

Regulation 2019/1238 of the European Parliament and of the Council of 20 June 2019 on a Pan-European Pension Product (PEPP) [2019] OJ L 198/1 (PEPP Regulation).

EU Case Law

Case 2/74 *Reyners* [1974] ECLI:EU:C:1974:68.

Case C-8/74 *Dassonville* [1974] ECLI:EU:C:1974:82.

Case 33/74 *van Binsbergen* [1974] ECLI:EU:C:1974:131.

Case 41/74 *Van Duyn v. Home Office* [1974] ECLI:EU:C:1974:133.

Case C-30/77 *Bouchereau* [1977] ECLI:EU:C:1977:172.

Case C-149/77 *Defrenne* [1978] ECLI:EU:C:1978:130.

Case 120/78 *Cassis de Dijon* [1979] ECLI:EU:C:1979:42.

Joined Cases 62/81 and 63/81 *Seco* [1982] ECLI:EU:C:1982:34.

Cases 286/82 and 26/83, *Luisi & Carbone*, [1984] ECLI:EU:C:1984:35.

Case C-152/84 *Marshall* [1986] ECLI:EU:C:1986:84.

Case C-262/88 *Barber* [1990] ECLI:EU:C:1990:209.

Case C-49/89, *Corsica Ferries France v. Direction générale des douanes françaises* ECLI:EU:C:1995:411.

Case C-288/89 *Stichting Collectieve Antennevoorziening Gouda v. Commissariaat voor de Media* [1991] ECLI:EU:C:1991:323.

Case C-76/90 *Säger* [1991] ECLI:EU:C:1991:331.

Case C-204/90 *Bachmann* [1992] ECLI:EU:C:1992:35.

Joined Cases C-159/91 and C-160/91, *Poucet & Pistre* [1993] ECLI:EU:C:1993:63.

Joined Cases C-267/91 and C-268/91 *Keck* [1993] ECLI:EU:C:1993:905.

C-443/93 *Vougioukas* [1995] ECLI:EU:C:1995:394.

Case C-55/94 *Gebhard* [1995] ECLI:EU:C:1995:411.

Case C-244/94 *Fédération Française des Sociétés d'Assurance (FFSA)* [1995] ECLI:EU:C:1995:392.

Joined Cases C-430/93 and C-431/93, *Van Schijndel* [1995] opinion of AG Jacobs ECLI:EU:C:1995:185.

Case C-57/95 *France v. Commission* [1997] ECLI:EU:C:1997:164.

Case C-67/96, *Albany* [1999] ECLI:EU:C:1999:430.

Case C-158/96 *Kohll* [1998] ECLI:EU:C:1998:171.

Joined Cases C-369/96 *Arblade* and C-376/96 *Leloup* [1999] ECLI:EU:C:1999:575.

Joined cases C-115/97, C-116/97 and C-117/97, *Brentjens'* [1999] ECLI:EU:C:1999:434.

Case C-219/97, *Drijvende Bokken* [1999] ECLI:EU:C:1999:437.

Joined Cases C-180/98 to C-184/98, *Pavlov and others* [2000], ECLI:EU:C:2000:428.

Case C-222/98 *van der Woude* [2000] ECLI:EU:C:2000:475.

Case C-376/98 *Germany v. European Parliament and Council (Tobacco Advertising I)* [2000] ECLI:EU:C:2000:544.

Case C-379/98 *PreussenElektra* [2000] ECLI:EU:C:2001:160.

Case C-385/99 *Müller-Fauré* [2003] ECLI:EU:C:2003:270.

Case C-136/00 *Danner* [2002] ECLI:EU:C:2002:558.

Case C-422/01 *Skandia and Ramstedt* [2003] ECLI:EU:C:2003:380.

Case C-36/02 *Omega* [2004] ECLI:EU:C:2004:614.

Case C-442/02 *Caixa Bank France* [2004] ECLI:EU:C:2004:586.

Joined Cases C-544/03 and 545/03 *Mobistar and Belgacom Mobile* [2005] ECLI:EU:C:2005:518.

Case C-372/04 *Watts* [2006] ECLI:EU:C:2006:325.

Case C-520/04 *Turpeinen* [2006] ECLI:EU:C:2006:703.

C-341/05 *Laval* [2007] ECLI:EU:C:2007:809.

Case C-393/05 *Commission v. Austria* [2007] ECLI:EU:C:2007:722.

Case C-404/05 *Commission v. Germany* [2007] ECLI:EU:C:2007:723.

Case C-438/05 *Viking* [2007] ECLI:EU:C:2007:772.

Case C-103/06 *Derouin* [2008] ECLI:EU:C:2008:185.

Case C-212/06 *Gouvernement de la Communauté française and Gouvernement wallon* [2008] ECLI:EU:C:2008:178.

Case C-319/06 *Commission v. Luxembourg* [2007] opinion of AG Trstenjak ECLI:EU:C:2007:516.

Case C-161/07 *Commission v. Austria* [2008] ECLI:EU:C:2008:759.

Case C-169/07 *Hartlauer* [2009] ECLI:EU:C:2009:141.

Joined Cases C-171/07 and C-172/07 *Apothekerkammer des Saarlandes* [2009] ECLI:EU:2009:316.

Case C-350/07 *Kattner Stahlbau* [2009] ECLI:EU:C:2009:127.

Case C-555/07 *Kücükdeveci* [2010] ECLI:EU:C:2010:21.

Case C-271/08, *Commission v. Germany* [2010] ECLI:EU:2010:426.

Case C-343/08 *Commission v. Czech Republic* [2010] ECLI:EU:C:2010:14.

Case C-384/08 *Attanasio* [2010] ECLI:EU:C:2010:133.

Case C-173/09 *Elchinov* [2010] ECLI:EU:C:2010:581.

Case C-379/09 *Casteels* [2011] ECLI:EU:C:2011:131.

Case C-379/09 *Casteels* [2011] opinion of A-G Kokott ECLI:EU:C:2010:675.

Case C-437/09 *AG2 R Prévoyance v. Beaudout Père et Fils SARL* [2011] ECLI:EU:C:2011:112.

Case C-490/09, *Commission v. Luxembourg,* [2011] ECLI:EU:C:2011:34.

Case C-424/11 *Wheels* [2013] ECLI:EU:C:2013:144.

Case C-476/11 *Experian* [2013] ECLI:EU:C:2013:590.

Case C-678/11, *Commission v. Spain* [2014] ECLI:EU:C:2014:2324.

Case C-464/12 *ATP PensionService* [2014] ECLI:EU:C:2014:139.

Case C-51/13 *van Leeuwen* [2015] ECLI:EU:C:2015:286.

Case C-497/13 *Faber* [2015] ECLI:EU:C:2015:357.

Joined Cases C-25/14 and C-26/14, *UNIS,* [2015], ECLI:EU:C:2015:821.

Case C-172/14 *ING Pensii* [2015] ECLI:EU:C:2015:484.

Case C-441/14 *Dansk Industri* [2016] ECLI:EU:C:2016:278.

EU Institutions' Documents and Publications

CEIOPS, 'Survey on fully funded, technical provisions and security mechanisms in the European occupational pension sector' (2008) CEIOPS-OPSSC-01/08 Final.

EIOPA, EIOPA's Advice to the European Commission on the review of the IORP Directive 2003/41/EC (2012) EIOPA-BOS-12/015.

EIOPA, 'Summary of Comments on Consultation Paper: Response to the Call for Advice on the review of the IORP Directive 2003/41/EC: second consultation - EIOPA-CP-11/006' (2012) EIOPA-BoS-12/016, available at https://eiopa.europa.eu/Publications/Consultations/1.EIOPA_s_Resolutions_on_comments_received.pdf accessed 7 January 2020.

EIOPA, 'Summary of Comments on Consultation Paper: Response to the Call for Advice on the review of the IORP Directive 2003/41/EC: second consultation - EIOPA-CP-11/006 - Q 1-11' (2012) EIOPA-BoS-12/016, available at https://eiopa.europa.eu/Publications/Consultations/2.EIOPA_s_Resolutions_on_comments_received.pdf accessed 8 January 2020.

EIOPA, Report on QIS on IORPs (2013) EIOPA-BoS-13/124.

EIOPA, 'Towards an EU-single market for personal pensions – An EIOPA Preliminary Report to COM' (2014) EIOPA-BoS-14/029, 4, available at https://eiopa.europa.eu/

Publications/Reports/EIOPA-BoS-14-029_Towards_an_EU_single_market_for_Personal_Pensions-_An_EIOPA_Preliminary_Report_to_COM.pdf accessed 8 January 2020.

EIOPA, *IORPs Stress Test Report 2015*, available at eiopa.europa.eu/Publications/Surveys/EIOPA%20IORPs%20Stress%20Test%20Report%202015%20bookmarks.pdf accessed 25 September 2019.

EIOPA, 'Consultation Paper on the creation of a standardised Pan-European Personal Pension Product (PEPP)' (2015) EIOPA-CP-15/006, 13, available at https://eiopa.europa.eu/Publications/Consultations/EIOPA-CP-15-006-Consultation-paper-Standardised-Pan-European-Personal-Pension-product.pdf accessed 8 January 2020.

EIOPA, 'Final Report on Public Consultation No. CP-15/006 on the creation of a standardised Pan-European Personal Pension product (PEPP)' (2016) EIOPA-16-341, 6, available at https://eiopa.europa.eu/Publications/Reports/EIOPA-16-341-Final-Report-PEPP-fin.pdf accessed 8 January 2020.

EIOPA, 'Final Report on Good Practices on individual transfers of occupational pension rights' (2015) BoS-15/104, available at eiopa.europa.eu/Publications/Reports/EIOPA-BoS-15-104_Final_Report_on_Pensions_Transferabity.pdf accessed 1 October 2019.

EIOPA, *Financial Stability Report December 2015*, available at eiopa.europa.eu/Publications/Reports/Financial_Stability_Report_December_2015.pdf accessed 25 September 2019.

EIOPA, *Financial Stability Report June 2017*, available at https://eiopa.europa.eu/Publications/Reports/Financial_Stability_Report_June_2017.pdf accessed 3 January 2020.

EIOPA, *Financial Stability Report December 2018*, available at eiopa.europa.eu/Publications/Reports/EIOPA%20FSR%20December%202018.pdf accessed 25 September 2019.

EIOPA, 'EIOPA's advice on the development of an EU Single Market for personal pension products (PPP)' (EIOPA-16/457, 2016) available at eiopa.europa.eu/Publications/Consultations/EIOPA's%20advice%20on%20the%20development%20of%20an%20EU%20single%20market%20for%20personal%20pension%20products.pdf accessed 25 September 2019.

EIOPA, '2017 Market development report on occupational pensions and cross-border IORPs' (2018) EIOPA-BOS-18/013, available at eiopa.europa.eu/publications/reports ac-cessed 18 September 2019.

EIOPA, *Seventh Consumer Trends Report* (Publications Office of the European Union 2018).

Eurofound, *Impact of the crisis on working conditions in Europe* (2013), available at www.eurofound.europa.eu/publications/reports/2013/impact-of-the-crisis-on-working-conditions-in-europe accessed 18 September 2019.

Eurofound, *New types of casualisation still put workers at a disadvantage* (2015), available at www.eurofound.europa.eu/sl/news/news-articles/working-conditions-labour-market/new-types-of-casualisation-still-put-workers-at-a-disadvantage accessed 18 September 2019.

Eurofound, *Quality of life: Social insecurities and resilience* (Publications Office of the European Union 2018).

Eurofound, *Living and working in Europe 2015-2018* (Publications Office of the European Union 2019).

European Economic and Social Committee, Opinion on the 'Proposal for a Directive of the European Parliament and of the Council on the activities of institutions for occupational retirement provision', (2001/C 155/07), 2001. Available at http://eur-lex.europa.eu/legal-content/EN/TXT/?uri=celex:52001AE0403 accessed 12 January 2020.

Eurostat, *People in the EU: who are we and how do we live?* (Publications Office of the European Union 2015).

European Central Bank, 'The 2015 Ageing report: How costly will Ageing in Europe be?' Economic Bulletin 2015 (4) 52, available at www.ecb.europa.eu/pub/pdf/other/eb201504_focus07.en.pdf accessed 25 September 2019.

European Central Bank, 'The Impact of Regulating Occupational Pensions in Europe on Investment and Financial Stability' (2014) No. 154 Occasional Paper Series, available at www.ecb.europa.eu/pub/pdf/scpops/ecbop154.pdf accessed 18 September 2019.

European Commission, 'Communication from the Commission concerning its action programme relating to the implementation of the Community Charter of Basic Social Rights for Workers' COM(89) 568 final.

European Commission, 'Supplementary social security schemes: the role of occupational pension schemes in the social protection of workers and their implications for freedom of movement' (Communication from the Commission to the Council) SEC(91) 1332 final.

European Commission, 'Proposal for a Council Directive relating to the freedom of management and investment of funds held by institutions for retirement provisions' COM (91) 301 final.

European Commission, 'Amended proposal for a Council Directive relating to the freedom of management and investment of funds held by institutions for retirement provision' COM (93) 237 final.

European Commission, 'Report from the Commission concerning social protection in Europe 1993' COM(93) 531 final.

European Commission, 'Supplementary Pensions in the European Union: Development, Trends and Outstanding Issues' (1994) Report by the European Commission's Network of Experts on Supplementary Pensions 116, available at http://aei.pitt.edu/33750/4/A310.pdf accessed 3 January 2020.

European Commission, 'Commission Communication on the Freedom of Management and Investment of Funds held by Institutions for Retirement Provision: Communication on an internal market for pension funds' (94/C 360/08). Available at https://eur-lex.europa.eu/legal-content/EN/TXT/PDF/?uri=OJ:JOC_1994_360_R_0007_01& from=BG accessed 12 January 2020.

European Commission, 'Supplementary Pensions in the Single Market: A Green Paper' COM(97) 283 final.

European Commission, 'Overview of the Responses to the Green Paper on Supplementary Pensions in the Single Market - COM(97) 283' of 6 April 1998.

European Parliament, 'Report on the Commission Green Paper entitled 'Supplementary Pensions in the Single Market' (COM(97)0283 - C4-0392/97)', A4-0400/98, available at http://www.europarl.europa.eu/sides/getDoc.do?pubRef=-//EP//NONSGML+REPORT+A4-1998-0400+0+DOC+PDF+V0//EN accessed 2 January 2020.

European Commission, *Report of the High Level Panel on the free movement of persons chaired by Simone Veil* (Publications Office of the European Union 1998).

European Commission, 'Towards a Single Market for supplementary pensions' COM (1999) 134 final.

European Commission, 'Communication from the Commission implementing the Framework for Financial Markets: Action Plan' COM(1999) 232 final.

European Commission, 'Proposal for a directive of the European Parliament and of the Council on the activities of institutions for occupational retirement provision' COM (2000) 507 final.

European Commission, 'The Future Evolution of Social Protections from a Long-Term Point of view: Safe and Sustainable Pensions' (White Paper) COM(2000) 622 final.

European Commission, 'Pensions Forum - Draft Reports of the Three Working groups' (2001), 5, available at https://ine.otoe.gr/uploads/files/ine_EC_Working_groups.doc accessed 3 January 2020.

European Commission, 'Commission Decision of 9 July 2001 on the setting-up of a committee in the area of supplementary pensions' 2001/548/EC.

European Commission, 'Communication from the Commission to the Council, the European Parliament and the Economic and Social Committee - The elimination of tax obstacles to the cross-border provision of occupational pensions' COM(2001) 214 final.

European Commission, 'Supporting national strategies for safe and sustainable pensions through an integrated approach' COM(2001) 362 final.

European Commission, 'Joint report by the Commission and the Council on Adequate and sustainable pensions' (Draft) COM(2002) 737 final.

European Commission, 'Second Implementation Report of the Internal Market Strategy 2003-2006', COM(2005) 11 final.

European Commission, 'Communication from the Commission on the Social Agenda', COM(2005) 33 final.

European Commission, 'Proposal for a Directive on improving the portability of supplementary pension rights' COM(2005) 507 final.

European Commission, 'Working together, working better: A new framework for the open coordination of social protection and inclusion policies in the European Union' COM(2005) 706 final.

European Commission, 'Commission Staff Working Document. Annex to the: 'Proposal for a Directive of the European Parliament and the Council on the Improvement of Portability of Supplementary Pension Rights', SEC(2005) 1293.

European Commission, 'Amended proposal for a Directive of the European Parliament and of the Council on minimum requirements for enhancing worker mobility by improving the acquisition and preservation of supplementary pension rights' COM (2007) 603 final.

European Commission, 'Dealing with the impact of an ageing population in the EU (2009 Ageing Report)' (Communication from the Commission to the European Parliament, the Council, the European Economic and Social Committee and the Committee of the Regions) COM(2009) 180 final.

European Commission, 'Report from the Commission on some key aspects concerning Directive 2003/41/EC on the activities and supervision of institutions for occupational retirement provision (IORP Directive)', COM(2009) 203 final.

European Commission, 'Green Paper towards adequate, sustainable and safe European pension systems' COM(2010) 356 final.

European Commission, 'The final implementation report of the EU Internal Security Strategy 2010-2014' (Communication from the Commission to the European Parliament and the Council) COM(2010) 365 final.

European Commission, *Annex to the Call for Advice from EIOPA for the review of Directive 2003/41/EC (IORP II)* (2011), available at https://eiopa.europa.eu/Publications/Requests%20for%20advice/20110409-a-389075-Letter-to-Bernardino-Annexe.pdf accessed 3 January 2020.

European Commission, 'An Agenda for Adequate, Safe and Sustainable Pensions' (White Paper) COM(2012) 55 final.

European Commission, 'Impact Assessment Accompanying the document Proposal for a Directive of the European Parliament and of the Council on the activities and supervision of institutions for occupational retirement provision' SWD(2014) 103 final.

European Commission, 'Proposal for a directive of the European Parliament and of the Council on the activities and supervision of institutions for occupational retirement provision' COM(2014) 167 final.

European Commission, 'Communication from the Commission to the European Parliament, the Council, the European Economic and Social Committee and the Committee of the Regions: Action Plan on Building a Capital Markets Union' COM(2015) 468 final.

European Commission, *The 2015 Ageing Report: Economic and budgetary projections for the 28 EU Member States (2013-2060)* (Publications Office of the European Union 2015).

European Commission, 'Communication from the Commission to the European Parliament, the Council, the European Central Bank, the European Economic and Social Committee and the Committee of the Regions: Capital Markets Union – Accelerating Reform' COM(2016) 601 final.

European Parliament, Resolution of 19 January 2016 on stocktaking and challenges of the EU Financial Services Regulation: impact and the way forward towards a more efficient and effective EU framework for Financial Regulation and a Capital Markets Union, 2015/2106(INI), available at http://www.europarl.europa.eu/doceo/document/TA-8-2016-0006_EN.html accessed 8 January 2020.

European Commission, 'Commission Recommendation of 29.6.2017 on the tax treatment of personal pension products, including the pan-European Personal Pension Product' C(2017) 4393 final.

European Commission, 'Commission Staff Working Document – Impact Assessment Accompanying the document Proposal for a Regulation of the European Parliament and the Council on a Pan-European Personal Pension Product (PEPP) and Commission Recommendation on the tax treatment of personal pension products, including the pan-European Personal Pension Product' SWD(2017) 243 final.

European Commission, 'Proposal for a Regulation of the European Parliament and pf the Council on a pan-European Personal Pension Product (PEPP)' COM(2017) 343 final.

European Commission, *Pension Adequacy Report 2018* (Publications Office of the European Union 2018).

European Commission, *The 2018 Ageing Report: Economic & Budgetary Projections for the 28 EU Member States (2016-2070)* (Publications Office of the European Union 2018).

European Commission, *2018 Annual Report on intra-EU Labour Mobility* (Publications Office of the European Union 2019).

European Commission, *Country Report Austria 2019,* SWD(2019) 1019 final.

Council of the European Union, 'Quality and viability of pensions – Joint report on objectives and working methods in the area of pensions' (2001) 10672/01 ECOFIN 198 SOC 272.

European Council, *Common position adopted by the Council on 5 November 2002 with a view to the adoption of a Directive of the European Parliament and of the Council on the activities and supervision of institutions for occupational retirement provision* (2002).

European Parliament, *Report on the proposal for a European Parliament and Council directive on the activities of institutions for occupational retirement provision* (Session document 21 June 2001) A5-0220/2001 final.

European Parliament, 'On the demographic challenge and solidarity between generations' (Report of the Committee on Employment and Social Affairs, 6 October 2010) available at www.europarl.europa.eu/sides/getDoc.do?type=REPORT&reference=A7-2010-0268&language=EN accessed 25 September 2019.

European Parliament, Directorate-General for Internal Policies, *Pension systems in the EU – contingent liabilities and assets in the public and private sector* (2011).

European Parliament, Directorate-General for Internal Policies, *Pension Schemes*, Study for the EMPL Committee (Publications Office of the European Union 2014).

European Commission, *State of the Innovation Union 2015* (Publications Office of the European Union 2015).

European Commission, 'Horizon 2020 Work Programme 2016-2017: 13. Europe in a changing world – inclusive, innovative and reflective Societies', European Commission Decision C (2015)6776 of 13 October 2015.

European Parliament, Directorate-General for Internal Policies, *EU Social and Labour Rights and EU Internal Market Law*, Study for the EMPL Committee (Publications Office of the European Union 2015).

European Parliament, Directorate-General for Internal Affairs, *Demography and family policies from a gender perspective*, Study for the FEMM Committee (2016).

European Commission, 'Horizon 2020 Work Programme 2016-2017: 16. Science with and for Society', European Commission Decision C(2017)2468 of 24 April 2017.

European Parliament, 'Prospects for occupational pensions in the European Union' (Briefing of September 2015) available at www.europarl.europa.eu/EPRS/EPRS-Briefing-568328-Prospects-for-occupational-pensions-EU-FINAL.pdf accessed 25 September 2019.

European Parliament, *Precarious Employment in Europe – Part 1: Patterns, Trends and Policy Strategy*, Study for the EMPL Committee (Publications Office of the European Union 2016).

Newspaper Articles, Websites and Blogs

Baxter S, 'IORP II proposal would "kill" European DB cross-border schemes' (*Professional Pensions*, 13 January 2015) available at https://www.professionalpensions. com/professional-pensions/news/2390004/iorp-ii-proposal-would-kill-european-db-cross-border-schemes accessed 3 January 2020.

Blows L, 'Better together', European Pensions February/March 2014, available at www. europeanpensions.net/ep/feb-mar-better-together accessed 9 September 2016.

Boschman O, 'Apart toezichtsregime voor pan-Europees persoonlijk pensioenproduct overbodig' (*Pensioenpro* 20 June 2017).

Boschman O, 'Nog weinig animo voor pensioenuitvoering over de grens' (*PensioenPro* 5 January 2017).

European Commission, 'Commission proposes a directive on the investment and management of pension fund assets' Press release 16 October 1991, available at europa.eu/ rapid/press-release_IP-91-919_en.htm accessed 11 December 2019.

European Commission, 'Supplementary Pensions: the next steps' Press release 19 May 1998, available at https://ec.europa.eu/commission/presscorner/detail/en/IP_98_447 accessed 2 January 2020.

European Commission, 'Commission to tackle tax obstacles to cross-border provision of occupational pensions' Press release 19 April 2001, available at http://europa.eu/rapid/press-release_IP-01-575_en.htm?locale=en accessed 2 January 2020.

European Commission, 'Occupational pensions: Commission welcomes Council's definitive adoption of the Pension Funds Directive' Press Release 13 May 2003, available at http://europa.eu/rapid/press-release_IP-03-669_en.htm?locale=en accessed 2 January 2020.

European Commission, 'Pensions taxation: Commission decides to refer Denmark to Court over discrimination and to open infringement procedures against the UK and Ireland' Press release 9 July 2003, available at https://ec.europa.eu/commission/press-corner/detail/en/IP_03_965 accessed 2 January 2020.

European Commission, 'Pension taxation: Commission tackles discrimination against foreign pension funds in six Member States' Press release 5 February 2004, available at https://ec.europa.eu/commission/presscorner/detail/en/IP_03_179 accessed 1 January 2020.

European Commission, 'Five ways to defuse the demographic time bomb' Press Release 12 October 2006, available at europa.eu/rapid/press-release_IP-06-1359_en.htm accessed 25 September 2019.

European Commission, 'July infringements package: key decisions' Press release 19 July 2018, available at europa.eu/rapid/press-release_MEMO-18-4486_en.htm accessed 11 December 2019.

Eurostat, 'EU population up to nearly 513 million on 1 January 2018' News Release 115/2018 of 10 July 2018, available at ec.europa.eu/eurostat/documents/2995521/9063738/3-10072018-BP-EN.pdf/ccdfc838-d909-4fd8-b3f9-db0d65ea457f accessed 25 September 2019.

Frühauf M, 'Anlegen wie die Grossen: So machen's die Pensionskassen', *Frankfurter Allgemeine* 14 January 2018.

Mulder W & Barnard J, 'PEPP: More questions than answers' (November 2019) Investments & Pensions Europe, available at https://www.ipe.com/pepp-more-questions-than-answers/10034193.article accessed 8 January 2020.

Nürk B & Macco J, 'Cross-Border – von Frankfurt nach Wien: Nicht so einfach nach Österreich' (LEITERbAV.de, 08 December 2015) www.lbav.de/nicht-einfach-so-nach-oesterreich/ accessed 13 November 2019.

Ottawa B, 'HINTERGRUND: Erster deutsch-österreichischer pensionfonds am Start" *IPE Institutional Investment* (23 November 2015).

Pelgrim C, 'DNB: korting dreigt bij 60 procent van de pensioenen', *NRC* 3 June 2019.

Pollak S, 'Ageing population leading to 'significant annual deficits' in pension fund', *The Irish Times* 29 November 2018.

Senior C, 'Stumbling block' (*European Pensions* April 2012) available at https://www.europeanpensions.net/ep/april-stumbling-block.php accessed 12 January 2020.

The Economist, 'The demographic time-bomb', *The Economist* 27 August 2008, available at www.economist.com/certain-ideas-of-europe/2008/08/27/the-demographic-time-bomb accessed 25 September.

Thomas C, 'A New Dawn for Cross-Border Pensions?' (*Chief Investment Officer* 4 March 2014) available at https://www.ai-cio.com/news/a-new-dawn-for-cross-border-pensions/ accessed 7 January 2020.

Topham G, 'Pension deficit of UK's leading companies equivalent to 70% of their profits', *The Guardian* 29 August 2017.

Trappenburg N, 'Pensioenverhuizing naar België bijna een feit' *Financieel Dagblad* (2 June 2016).

Weston C, 'Deficits in traditional company pension plans rise to €1.6bn', *The Independent* 31 January 2019.

Willis Towers Watson, 'Perspectives: IORP II – what it means for cross-border pensions' (2016). See also 'Is the Future of European Cross-Border Pensions in DC?' (*Chief Investment Officer* 25 July 2013) available at https://www.ai-cio.com/news/is-the-future-of-european-cross-border-pensions-in-dc/ accessed 3 January 2020.

Woolfe J, 'Letter from Brussels: Social and labour issues' (March 2013) Investment & Pensions Europe, available at www.ipe.com/social-and-labour-issues/50264.fullarticle accessed 4 December 2019.

Zülch J, 'Das Sozialpartnermodell nach dem Betriebsrentenstärkungsgesetz' (*Heldt, Zülch & Partner*) available at http://www.heldt-zuelch.de/das-sozialpartnermodell-nach-dem-betriebsrentenstaerkungsgesetz/ accessed 7 January 2020.

Miscellaneous

Arbeitsgemeinschaft für betriebliche Altersversorgung, 'aba Analyse zum Kompromisstext für die EbAV-II-Richtlinie' (2016) available at http://www.aba-online.de/docs/attachments/9b4b65a7-c2f0-4cf0-91b6-3c422d1e426b/20160810-EbAV-II-Trilogkompromiss-aba-Analysepapier.pdf accessed 3 January 2020.

Arts J, *DC Defaults & Heterogeneous Preferences* (MSc Thesis, Tilburg University 2015) Netspar Academic Series, 7, available at https://www.netspar.nl/assets/uploads/017_-_MSc_-_Arts.pdf accessed 3 January 2020.

Austrian Federal Ministry of Finance, *Austrian Country Fiche on Public Pensions* (2018) available at ec.europa.eu/info/sites/info/files/economy-finance/final_country_fiche_at.pdf accessed 25 September 2019.

Baroch Castellevi M & Bähr G, 'Europäische Altersversorgung mit PEPP' (*DLA Piper*, 13 March 2018) available at https://www.dlapiper.com/de/germany/insights/publications/2018/03/europaische-altersversorgung-mit-pepp/ accessed 8 January 2020.

Barr N, *The pension system in Sweden*, Report to the Expert Group on Public Economics of the Swedish Ministry of Finance 2013:7 (Elanders Sverige 2013).

Beveridge W, *Social Insurance and Allied Social Services* (The Beveridge Report, London, HMSO 1942).

Blake, D, 'We Need a National Narrative: Building a Consensus Around Retirement Income' (2016) Report: Independent Review of Retirement Income.

BusinessEurope, 'Proposal for the revision of IORP Directive' (2014) Position Paper available at https://www.businesseurope.eu/sites/buseur/files/media/imported/2014-00629-E.pdf accessed 3 January 2020.

Centraal Planbureau, 'Internationale vergelijking van pensioenstelsels: Denemarken, Zweden, Chili en Australië' (2015) available at www.cpb.nl/publicatie/internationale-vergelijking-van-pensioenstelsels-denemarken-zweden-chili-en-australie accessed 25 September 2019.

Davies R, 'Occupational Pensions: 'Second pillar' provision in the EU policy context', Briefing Library of the European Parliament (Library of the European Parliament 2013) available at www.europarl.europa.eu/RegData/bibliotheque/briefing/2013/130589/LDM_BRI(2013)130589_REV1_EN.pdf accessed 25 September 2019.

European Commission, 'Frits Bolkestein, European Commissioner for the Internal Market Addressing the Challenges for European Pensions Royal Institute of International Affairs Chatham House, London' Speech 29 February 2000, available at http://europa.eu/rapid/press-release_SPEECH-00-60_en.htm accessed 2 January 2020.

European Financial Services Roundtable, 'Pan European Pension Plans: deepening the concept' (2005), available at http://www.efr.be/documents/publication/26.2005.12.% 20EFR%20Report%20-%20Follow-up%20on%20Pan%20European%20Pensions% 20plans%2020Dec2005.pdf accessed 12 January 2020.

Finnish Pension Alliance TELA, 'The Finnish earnings-related pension system is one of a kind in the EU', available at www.tela.fi/en/pension_sector/legislation/ the_eu_and_the_pension_system accessed 25 September 2019.

FSMA, *Jaarverslag 2013* (2013) 72, available at https://www.fsma.be/nl/news/fsma-public eert-jaarverslag-2013 accessed on 3 January 2020.

Lutjens E, 'Vragen over implementatie IORP Richtlijn: grensoverschrijdende uitvoering in discussie' (2018) supplement to parliamentary debate, available at www.eersteka-mer.nl/overig/20181121/vragen_over_implementatie_iorp/document accessed 11 December 2019.

Ministry of Finance of Sweden, *The Swedish pension system and pension projections until 2070* (2017) available at ec.europa.eu/info/sites/info/files/economy-finance/ final_country_fiche_se.pdf accessed 25 September 2019.

Ministry of Finance of the Czech Republic, *Pension Projections of the Czech Republic* (2017) available at ec.europa.eu/info/sites/info/files/economy-finance/ final_country_fiche_cz.pdf accessed 25 September 2019.

Newman D, Webster F & Rousseau S, 'EU Advances Pan-European Personal Pension Product (PEPP) Proposal' (Mercer 11 April 2019) available at https://www.mercer. com/content/dam/mercer/attachments/global/gl-2019-eu-advances-pan-european-personal-pension-product-proposal.pdf accessed 8 January 2020.

Parliament of the Netherlands, Transcript of the Parliamentary hearing on 14 May 2014, available at www.eerstekamer.nl/behandeling/20140514/aansturing_vanuit_euro-pa_op/document3/f=/vjkdh48wnbzb.pdf accessed 20 November 2019.

Parliament of the Netherlands, Letter from Dutch Parliament to the European Commis-sion, 15 May 2014, www.eerstekamer.nl/eu/overig/20140514/brief_tweede_ka-mer_aan_de/f=/vjjsijdsxjzt.pdf accessed 29 August 2016.

Parliament of the United Kingdom, Report on the European Union Committee 2014-2015, Chapter 2, para 24, available at publications.parliament.uk/pa/ld201516/ldse-lect/ldeucom/11/1105.htm accessed 27 November 2019.

PensionsEurope, 'PensionsEurope Position paper on the pan-European Personal Pension Product (PEPP)' (2018), available at https://www.pensionseurope.eu/system/files/ PensionsEurope%20position%20paper%20on%20PEPP%2020180308.pdf accessed 8 January 2020.

Stevens Y, 'The meaning of "national social and labour legislation" in directive 2003/41/ EC on the activities and supervision of institutions for occupational retirement provi-sion' (2004) Research report commissioned by the European Association of Paritarian Institutions (AEIP) 8.

Stevens Y, 'The development of a legal matrix on the meaning of "national social and labour legislation" in directive 2003/41/EC with regard to five member states: Belgium – France – Germany – Italy – Netherlands' (2006) Research report by the European Association of Paritarian Institutions (AEIP).

Thurley D, 'Occupational Pension Increases', Briefing Paper CBP-05656 of 21 June 2017, House of Commons Library.

Weymouth, L 'IORP II will 'kill off' DB cross-border arrangements, ACA says', (*European Pensions* 13 January 2015), available at http://www.europeanpensions.net/ep/IORP-II-will-kill-off-DB-cross-border-arrangements-ACA-says.php accessed 3 January 2020.